Still Running

Still Running

A MEMOIR

To Mary Louise —

who beautified our many homes and enriched our lives —

with warmest regard —

Susie

Susie Wilson

Still Running: A Memoir
Copyright © 2014 by Susie Wilson
All rights reserved. No part of this book may be reproduced
in any matter whatsoever without written permission

ISBN: 978-0-9854452-2-5

Printed and bound in the United States
Design by Catherine D. Havemeyer

Cover photo: The author in a crowd of activists at the March for Women's Equality and Women's Lives on April 9, 1989.

To Don and our family,

now with two memoirs to read,

with all my love.

To my public family,

colleagues, friends and

those unknown,

who helped me

and contributed to my life story,

my gratitude.

Contents

Author's Note   ix

Beginnings

By Dint of Birth 3
Family Secrets 10

Mummy and Daddy

Life with a Remarkable Father 23
An Extraordinary Woman 39
A Complex Personality 49

Growing Up

Celery Soup 61
God Save the Queen and My Governess 66
A Magical Farm and a First Lady 75
My Riding Life 82
Camp Arcadia 89
Dramatic Stirrings 98
Setting the Stage 108
Theater at Vassar 121

Journalism and Love

Life at *Life* 129
Don: Beginnings 143
Love Letters from a Distance 154
Home Again 161

Washington

Lady-in-Waiting 171
A Washington-Plus Wife 179
Travels with the Kennedys 190
A Farewell to Two Leaders 209

Moving About

    The Manhattan-Princeton Axis. 219

    The World of Work 227

    Our Midlife Crisis 236

Sexuality Education

    Too Young: Waiting to Learn About Sex and Babies 249

    Public Efforts to Fight the Good Fight 253

    A Home at the Network for Family Life Education 268

Running

    My Running Life 285

    A Marathoner's Tale 294

    A Road Not Taken 303

Family Ties

    Parenting Times Three 313

    Becoming a World Citizen 323

    A Creative Marriage 334

    Don, The Last Eight Years 341

    Alone Together 352

    Postscript 365

Generations: The Family Tree

    Love and Mystery on Valentine's Day. 371

    My Paternal Grandfather: Benno Neuberger 377

    My Paternal Grandmother: Stella Mayer Neuberger 384

    My Maternal Grandmother: Elsie Frank Wallach Kridel 390

    My Maternal Grandfather: Samuel Kridel 395

    Author's Thanks   399

Author's Note

There is something about my condominium at 40 Constitution Hill West that encourages the writing of memoirs. At 91, the woman who sold it to us in 2007 was writing a memoir about personal growth and change, the same topics that I explore here. Although I didn't think of her while I was writing *Still Running* at 83, she left me surrounded by good vibes as I sat at my Mac in my upstairs study.

It may have been the memoir goddesses who urged me forward, but my husband, Don, and my younger daughter, Penny, also played roles in this book's evolution. Don set me on the path to examining my life when he encouraged me in his memoir, *The First 78 Years*, to write my own for our children, grandchildren, and future generations of family that I will never know. He wrote his memoir at 4574 Province Line Road, but the finished product arrived at this address as the first telltale signs of Alzheimer's disease claimed his fine intellect.

Don's suggestion was the initial inspiration, and Penny's came next: Growing up, her favorite bedtime story that I told her from my life was "Celery Soup."

"Please, Mommy, write it down," she would beg.

It took me awhile, but I finally agreed.

Paying attention to Don's and Penny's suggestions has led to something of an amalgam in the memoir: a loose chronology of my life starting with my birth and interspersed with a few stories. I have omitted much from the book, especially my daily life as a girl and a woman, a daughter, wife, and mother. Instead, I wanted to create a personal record that my heirs might consult to understand what my life and the times when I lived were like, and how I fit into them and then later moved beyond them. One family member has already asked me about an important change in my life: "Am I going to learn how a woman from as protected a background as yours can become a public advocate for a really tough subject like sex education?" My hope is that he will find a satisfactory answer in these pages.

I was born into wealth and privilege, and I never had to worry if I could pay my taxes, buy clothes, fill a refrigerator, access the best medical care, travel the world, rent city apartments, and buy a country home. I never questioned my good fortune, and I rarely wondered how other people lived. I could have continued to live within the parameters of my small, constricted world, but with growing maturity and the help of mentors, I gradually emerged from a cocoon of self-absorption to learn about other people's struggles and how I could make changes to benefit society.

I didn't begin my activist work until I was in my fifties. I was a late bloomer, but a tenacious one. Perhaps this is the reason I'm "still running"—still advocating for quality sexuality education programs never far from my heart, and sometimes, much to my surprise, adding new causes to my list.

In many ways, my life to date has been both ordinary and extraordinary, and I am grateful for both aspects. Not every life is worthy of a memoir: mine qualifies only because of Don's and my tremendous good luck in connecting with the Kennedy family, including his position in President John F. Kennedy's administration, my connection with First Lady Jacqueline Kennedy, who was a college classmate, and our friendship with Bobby and Ethel, which added value and luster to our lives. The issue of sexuality education does draw some lightning as I write in 2014, but it may not in ensuing years as school programs become more accepted and widespread. However, the glow from the Kennedy fire will always light the world.

Despite using the word "I" until I cringe, I have liked the process of writing this memoir, and I recommend it to my children and grandchildren (then memoir writing may become a family tradition).

I hope that you will find enjoyment, laughter, and a touch of inspiration in my story. This is my wish for you.

Beginnings

By Dint of Birth

If every child was as wanted, welcomed, and protected from the world's harm as I was on January 17, 1930, this might be a different world. My parents' first child, I was born, weighing seven pounds, on a Friday at the York House Sanitarium at 119 East 74th Street in New York City at 2:10 a.m. (To prove how small the world can be, York House became the location of the Episcopal Nursery School that our daughter Penny, who was also born in New York City, attended decades later.) The presiding physician was Dr. Warren Hildreth and the nurse was Margaret E. Gallagher ("Gallie"), who accompanied my mother when she brought me home from the hospital.

I know all this and much more about my first days, weeks, and months because my mother meticulously kept two books to document my birth and early life: the Annals of Babyhood, a gold-trimmed, white-leather book with a little brass plate, "Susan Mary Neuberger, January 17, 1930," on the cover, and a gold-trimmed, blue-leather scrapbook with my name imprinted in gold capital letters on the corner. No detail seemed too small to escape my mother's attention about her firstborn's life. She started both books with my birth announcement, which appeared in the *New York Herald Tribune* on Sunday, January 19, 1930; "Daughter for Neubergers" was the headline of my first press notice. Below it, my mother pasted my first formal calling card, engraved "Susan Mary Neuberger." She grew up in an era when women dropped calling cards at their friends' homes; I grew up in an era where women exchanged business cards at meetings, conferences, and luncheons. (My latest card notes that I am a "Sexuality Educator.")

What amazed me about the books' records is the outpouring of love, best wishes, and gifts that accompanied my birth. From their sheer volume, I could have been the first child of the Duke and Duchess of Cambridge (or William and Kate, as they are more familiarly known) or Princess Aurora in Charles Perrault's fairytale *The Sleeping Beauty*, yet unlike poor Aurora, none of my parents' friends cast an evil spell upon me that took 100 years to overcome. By my count of the little calling and gift cards that my mother listed in the blue book, I received 132 gifts.

In the classic sections covering every aspect of a baby's early life, my mother noted the special gifts from the closest family and friends. The list led with gifts from my maternal grandparents, Elsie and Samuel Kridel, who presented me with a cradle, a trousseau, and a bankbook. In the blue book, I found their tiny personal cards detailing their gifts along with loving best wishes for me. My grandmother Elsie wrote, "We hope the trousseau, your first bank account, and your cradle, in which your mother and grandmother have slept before you, will bring you much joy and comfort. A life of happiness, Susy dear, is the wish your grandmother brings you." My grandfather Sam wrote, "To my darling granddaughter, Susan—welcome to this big world. May you go through it happily and contented is the wish of Grandpa."

Although my grandparents referred to me as Susy and Susan, most of the well-wishers called me by my whole name, Susan Mary, to the point where I wondered if that was indeed what I was going to be called. My parents' friends sent loving notes with their gifts or in wire cables: "May she prove a great blessing," "Simply thrilled by arrival," "May she bring you much happiness," "Congratulations upon the arrival of the Little Princess," and "May the baby be a source of pleasure to you all your lives." I'm rather happy I didn't learn of all these best wishes growing up, as the weight of the responsibilities that came with such wishes might have overwhelmed me.

There were cables and cards in German and French, revealing my family's European roots, and references to my father's work as a stockbroker and the recent market crash of 1929; one of his business friends wrote, "Hurrah at last for the first good news from Wall Street." Another trying for humor wrote, "May this be the only 'Bearish' influence in your life," and a third read, "May the coupon which you cut from your matrimonial bond enjoy the full measure of the world's blessings."

The presents that arrived on the doorstep of the first apartment I lived in, 1192 Park Avenue, reflected the generosity and wealth of my parents' close friends and family. Beside the trousseau from my grandparents, which would have been quite enough for any small person, I received a baby carriage, a cap and a coat, a chifferobe (furniture with drawers and space for hanging clothes), a silver napkin ring and porridge dish, a quilt, sheets and a pillow, a silver cup, a comb and brush set, hangers, and a practical gift: a potty chair. Quite a haul for just being born!

My mother kept detailed records of the orders of my pediatrician, Dr. Harold R. Mixsell, and information about my daily life: my meals (I had no food allergies and ate very well), my height and weight (I went from 7 lbs. to 20 lbs., 6 oz., at 35 weeks and from 19 ½ inches at birth to 32 inches at the end of my first year). She noted my first pair of tiny socks (peach wool); my first steps, games, and journeys; the addresses of my winter and summer homes; and the first time I sat at the table with my parents ("In her high chair while her mother and father eat breakfast and she eats toast with them"). Although my first tooth appeared on July 1, the lower-left middle one, the tooth itself is missing. Of course: the tooth fairy removed it from under the pillow.

My greatest surprise was discovering that my mother nursed me. She writes that one of her good friends left "nursing bras" for her, and she records Dr. Mixsell's orders about nursing times: "6, 10, 2, 6, 10, 2." Babies were placed on strict feeding schedules in the early thirties. My mother may have held some contrary views regarding this rigidity, since she included a newspaper clipping of a Bishop Doane poem, "The Modern Baby," which spoofs child-rearing practices.

> *Then we must feed the baby by the schedule that is made,*
> *And the food that he is given must be measured out and weighed.*
> *He may bellow to inform us that he isn't satisfied,*
> *But he couldn't grow to greatness if his wants were all supplied.*
> *Think how foolish nursing stunted those poor weaklings, long ago,*
> *The Shakespeares and the Luthers and the Bonapartes, you know.*

My mother never mentioned that she nursed me, and upon Dr. Mixsell's orders, she switched from breast to bottle after giving it a brief three months. How surprised she would be to know that it is now commonplace for new mothers to nurse their babies. She also tucked some other articles about child rearing into my baby books, including a little pamphlet from the Commissioner of Health in New York City that reported the "best" advice of the times for mothers, including "listen to your doctor and not to your neighbors," "watch the baby's bowel movements carefully," "boil all used diapers," and "don't let relatives and friends pick up the baby, fondle or kiss it." Times certainly have changed.

She made some notations in Annals of Babyhood through my second and third years of life. She tucked locks of my blonde hair into tiny envelopes, and it seems as golden today as it was when she cut it off my head. She listed some of the books I liked as a toddler: *Peggy and Peter*, *Black Sambo*, and *Nursery Rhymes*. She also included a second newspaper article that may have applied to some behaviors of mine: "The Child Most Stubborn at Two, Survey Shows, Contrariness Laid to Lack of Expression." Friends and colleagues have always told me that I possess perseverance or tenacity. Did the roots of this quality appear in me as early as two?

The books also record the different houses in which we lived and the different nannies who took care of me. From the start of my life, I always lived in two different places: New York City in the winter and Long Island or New Jersey in the summer. I hadn't realized that living in two places apparently was built into my DNA; I continued to do so throughout my married life and child-rearing years. My mother documented our trips by automobile back and forth from our residences.

I enjoyed moving on my own and started walking on September 5, eight months after my birth. Two months later, I walked all over the apartment and could "get up in the middle of the room without holding on." It sounds as if I was truly liberated in May 1931, when Mummy and my nurse allowed me out of my baby carriage in Central Park, where most young children of Upper East Side families played. "She adored it," my mother wrote. I guess after that there was no stopping me.

My parents hired nurses and then eventually governesses to be the primary caregivers. During my first few months, they employed both a day nurse (Gallie) and a night nurse (Miss Edith Gromanty). In April, the two nurses departed, and Miss Martha Turner arrived, staying until December 1931 when Miss Suzanne Rennie came to care for me. The only caregiver I remember, however, was Miss Mona Volckman, who came when I was seven and stayed with us for 12 years, until my sister went to college, although in the later years she became more of a housekeeper than a governess.

I was surprised by how few photographs were in the two books, so I don't have a good visual record of my early years. The pictures that do exist please me because I am smiling in most of them. My mother is beautiful, and I look sturdy—not chubby, but solid. As I grew older, my hair became curlier. My favorite is the picture of me at four or so, sitting in a photographer's studio on a maroon velvet bench facing the camera. It looks as if the photographer colored the photo, as no one could have such rosy cheeks. I am wearing a pretty blue dress with a lacy white collar and white trim on the short sleeve. I have a bow on the right side of my head that matches the blue of the dress, which in turn matches my deep-set eyes. I am not smiling, but my face looks friendly and composed, and my hands are clasped on my breast. Daddy used to tease me about the position of my hands in this picture: "You look as if you have a stomachache," he would say with twinkling eyes. "No, I did not. I definitely do not have a stomachache in the picture," I would reply, revealing once again evidence of that stubborn streak.

A Baby Sister

Eighteen months after my birth, on October 22, 1932, my sister was born. My parents named her Joan Kay; the "Kay" was in honor of my mother, since many of her friends called her "Kay." Much to my disappointment, there is only one reference to her arrival in my two baby books. In a description of my first train ride, in May 1937, Mummy notes that my mother, father, sister, and nurse accompanied me to Elberon, New Jersey, for the summer. ("Susie was thrilled and loved looking out of the window," she wrote.)

The books soon trailed off, perhaps because my mother moved on to create a wonderfully detailed set of baby books for Joanie, as she had for me. I wish I had been able to pour over my sister's baby books and she mine. We would have learned a lot about each other's early days. Of course, I know she was as warmly welcomed into the world as I had been. The photographs of the two of us when we are little are quite charming, and we are usually holding hands and smiling. We are always wearing matching coats, leggings, and cloche hats, which came from a store called Tots Toggery. We wore matching coats and hats for most of our childhoods, up until I was almost a teenager. A picture of us taken on Easter Sunday at St. Patrick's Cathedral in New York City shows us wearing elaborate headwear and the same coats with rose corsages. The only difference in our outfits is that my sister is wearing socks and I have graduated to stockings. These matching outfits were so much a part of our childhood, I even alluded to them in a sonnet, "To My Beloved Sister," that I wrote for her on her 70th birthday.

The early pictures show us hand in hand,
In matching leggings, hats, and bathing suits.
Astride our ponies, playing in the sand,
You took my orders, shunning all disputes.
Together all through school, our father urged
You choose a different college, and break free.
Westward you went—and so our lives diverged—
To test your strength, find your philosophy.
Through marriage, children, years of calm and strife,
You have remained a true and constant friend.
Accepting with much grace the flow of life,
Your kindnesses to all, we do commend.
I say it now on birthday seventieth,
You are my sister dear, till my last breath.

My sister framed the sonnet and keeps it in the bedroom of her home in Vero Beach, Florida, which makes me happy. Although she didn't appear in my baby books, she has always been in my heart.

No child could have had a happier start in life than I did. I was born with the proverbial silver spoon in my mouth, maybe a couple of them, and I had a silver porringer and a silver napkin ring, too. But more important, I had what all newborns deserve—hope. Hope for a safe environment, for good health care, for a chance to go to school and get an education, for the chance to find a good job or husband, for a home with loving parents to ease the way, and for the good fortune to live in a free, democratic country like America.

I had hope by dint of birth.

Family Secrets

Most people are baptized as babies or young children, but Joanie and I received the holy sacrament on October 6, 1940, at eight and ten years old, respectively. Holy baptism made each of us "a member of Christ, the Child of God and an Inheritor of the Kingdom of Heaven." At ten, these were only words to me, but as I grew older, their meaning went far beyond what I could have imagined.

Our short baptismal ceremony—in which the rector, Charles P. Johnson, made the sign of the cross in holy water on my sister's and my foreheads—took place in All Saints Memorial Church, an Episcopalian church in the Navesink Highlands, New Jersey. After the ceremony, which didn't include my father, we returned home to Sunnyside Farm, a 127-acre farm in Lincroft, New Jersey, which my father had purchased in 1932 and was our family's principal residency. Yet my mother didn't hold a celebration for what is usually such a special childhood moment. Even my godmother, Geraldine R. Thompson, didn't join us.

I was puzzled by my mother's lack of excitement, and I sensed that she didn't want to call attention to the religious path she'd chosen for Joanie and me. My new religion started as a secret, yet the deeper one behind it wouldn't be revealed to me until later in life.

The first hint of this secret came from my pediatrician when I was six years old, but it was too obscure for me to understand. Mummy and I were in the Park Avenue office of Dr. Alfred Fischer, whose patients were the children of prominent, wealthy Jews. After giving me a routine physical, Dr. Fischer looked at Mummy and asked, "Have you told her? Have you told her yet?"

"No, I haven't," Mummy replied, turning to me. "Let's hurry. Dr. Fischer has more patients to see, so tie your shoes as quickly as you can."

Told me what? I wondered. I was puzzled that she had obviously dismissed his question. Once out of the office, I hoped she would tell me about this secret, but she didn't—and her silence got under my skin. Somehow I knew it was important for me to hear; otherwise, why would she refuse to tell me about it?

Eight years passed, Dr. Fischer's comment faded into memory, and I didn't think about the secret until the day Joanie came home from summer camp bursting with news.

"You think we're Episcopalians," she confided breathlessly. "Well, we aren't. Our cousin says we're Jewish."

Looking at my no doubt blank face, Joanie explained how our cousin—pretty, blonde Mary Kridel, who lived a few blocks from us in New York City—had spilled the secret beans. A camper had asked Joanie about her religion, and Mary overheard her reply, "I'm an Episcopalian."

"Oh, no you're not," Mary said, interrupting. "You're Jewish, like me."

"I'm an Episcopalian. I go to St. James'," Joanie shot back, standing her ground.

"No, you're not," Mary said emphatically. "You're Jewish."

I was shocked. Joanie told me that both sides of our family were Jewish. My head spun: *Why had we been baptized Episcopalian? What if I didn't want to be Jewish? Could I stay an Episcopalian? Did my friends know? What did they think of all this pretending? Would they stop liking me if they knew I was Jewish?* I felt as if someone had transported me to a new planet. Dr. Fischer's question to my mother returned with a vengeance. *Mummy didn't want me to know that I'm Jewish*, I thought. *That is the secret.*

I sensed that my mother would be displeased if I asked her about being Jewish and why she wanted us to become Christian, and I didn't want to disappoint or anger her. The irony of all this secretiveness was that our last name was Neuberger. My mother had wanted to change it before we were baptized, but my father refused to acquiesce, so most people could tell we were Jewish from our name. Yet if friends asked me about its derivation, I always said, "Neuberger is a German name."

Being Jewish seemed like something to be avoided at all costs. I had never heard anyone, including the Jews I knew, talk about the advantages of it. Yet my Episcopalian friends often mentioned their faith, and my governess said many good things about being a Catholic. Most of the Jewish girls at The Brearley School—the private, all-girls school on East 83rd Street in New York City that I attended from second through 12th grade—were Reform Jews from prominent German-Jewish families and secular Jews who didn't participate in any religious practices. With youthful arrogance and ignorance, I assumed that schools with predominately Jewish students—Ethical Culture, Dalton, Fieldston, and Horace Mann—weren't as "academically good" as Brearley and its all-girls archrival, Chapin, since my parents had sent Joanie and me to Brearley. Although we sang from the Protestant hymnal in school assemblies, Brearley kept religious affiliation out of sight, believing that it was an independent school. I encountered whiffs of anti-Semitism and discrimination only outside of school.

My mother wanted me and my sister to enter the Protestant world, starting with dancing classes and dance events when we were young and extending to holiday parties when we were older—and it was in this world that we first understood discrimination against people who were born Jewish. Leaders of these groups thought Joanie and I were trying to hide our Jewish roots by gaining acceptance into their social world, even though we'd been baptized Episcopalian. It was clear we were not wanted.

⁂

After the family secret was revealed to me, I realized that my parents had let almost all of their Jewish friends slip from their lives. Gradually we stopped seeing our Jewish relatives as much either, with the exceptions of my first cousins, Robert and Donald Coons, the sons of Daddy's sister, Florence, who died when I was a small child, and my mother's brother, Bill Kridel, his wife, Carol, and their son, Billy Jr., and daughter, Linda.

My mother's decision to distance us from the Jewish world affected my adolescent social life. She would drop little hints that she was working to get us invited to the Christmastime dancing parties. The Holidays and the Get-Togethers were the most sought-after social gatherings for teens, and my mother applied for invitations for me and later for my sister, but we were rejected because of our family's background. It didn't make any difference that we were Episcopalian by baptism. My sister's friend, the daughter of a prominent Jewish family, had also been rejected, so Joanie didn't take it badly. I faced the rejection alone, and it stung.

As high school ended, my mother arranged for me to apply to a large, fancy, invitation-only debutante ball for young women of socially prominent Protestant families and a smattering of "others." These balls, held during Christmas vacation my freshman year at Vassar, ranged in order of importance from the most prestigious Junior Assemblies to the Grosvenor Ball and the Debutante Cotillion, the least exclusive of the three. At the time my mother initiated her efforts, only the occasional "Jewish girl" received an invitation to these exclusive parties.

For some inexplicable reason, my mother considered entry into these dances important, and the process seemed as difficult as climbing the world's highest peak. It required letters of recommendation, and it didn't matter if you were a good student, class leader, or star athlete. What counted was your family's social standing and religious background—and the path for Jewish families (even ones that had become Christian, like ours) was steep.

Although she never spoke of it, my mother knew that our Jewish background was a roadblock, but she persisted. She believed that gaining entry into these social circles would benefit her daughters' lives and marriage prospects. Her campaign was effective, and in 1947, I received an invitation to the Debutante Cotillion, which was held in the ballroom of the Waldorf Astoria Hotel. By then social barriers against girls like me were beginning to weaken through the persistence of women like my mother.

Perhaps my sister and I gained entry into these dances more readily than other Jewish girls because we looked like good Christian girls. My sister's features—perfect, blonde pageboy, enormous blue eyes, and small pug nose—certainly smoothed her way. My blondish hair and nose that turned down at the end but didn't look too Semitic helped me pass this social test, but not with as high marks as my sister.

During the 1947-48 debutante season and following the Cotillion, my parents gave me a small tea dance at the Plaza Hotel. It was my official debut, but I didn't really know my way around this social world or know many boys to invite, so they kindly let me be "presented to society" with a classmate of mine from Vassar. (What I remember most from that season was not my debutante party, but the huge snowfalls that hit New York City and what fun it was to walk down Park Avenue, which was closed to traffic, with snowbanks that reached higher than my head.)

Two years later, my parents gave my far-more socially adept sister a beautiful coming-out dinner dance at the St. Regis that was attended by at least four times the number of people who came to my tea dance. Joanie was entirely comfortable being deb of the evening and felt no need to share the party with another friend. She was a successful debutante, even appearing in a classic photo in *Town and Country* magazine that showed her from the rear, holding hands with two boys sitting on either side of her. Joanie navigated the culture as if she'd been born into it. She wasn't nearly as troubled as I was about our early rejection in this snobbish world, perhaps because I went into it ahead of her. I don't think she felt the same hypocrisy I felt about having a Jewish background that I hid from everyone.

⁂

Hiding the truth, even from myself, prevented me from talking to my parents about the Holocaust or the systematic persecution of European Jews in Hitler's Germany during World War II. Daddy tried and failed to bring his cousin out of Germany when the war began. (His cousin later married a Frenchwoman who provided sanctuary in her country.) I only learned about these atrocities from seeing the Broadway play *Anne Frank*. Anne became a heroine to me, because she ultimately believed that "people are good," despite her imprisonment in a space above Otto Frank's company—a secret annex—and eventual death in the Bergen-Belsen concentration camp.

Our family secret also affected our lives in the New Jersey community where our farm was located. My parents became Christians and model Episcopalians. They joined Christ Episcopal Church, a local church in Middletown north of our farm, and actively participated in church life. They practiced what was preached from the pulpit and dotted their community with good works reflecting Jesus Christ's teachings.

During my teen years, when I was sensitive about my social life (or lack of one), my parents sought membership in the Rumson Country Club, a prestigious golf and tennis club that was the center of life in a more upscale area than our town. Some friends who were members had urged my parents to apply, yet even though they had become Episcopalian by then, the board rejected their application, telling my father that if it made an exception in their case, other Jewish families would apply, and "the exclusivity of the club might change."

Daddy, who took the rejection in stride, told me that I should not regard it as a slight to our family. He could always put the kindest light on any situation and see an issue from another person's point of view, which was much more difficult for my mother to do. He felt that my sister and I were strong enough to not be upset by the decision. He added that if my mother hadn't insisted on changing our religion, he would have volunteered to work with the National Council of Christians and Jews to help ameliorate anti-Semitism. He felt that by forsaking his Jewish roots, he had lost his credibility with such an organization and thereby his opportunity to influence its decisions.

The country club's decision, even though it primarily affected my parents, reinforced the rejection I felt when I didn't receive an invitation to the most prestigious debutante balls in New York City, and I wasn't satisfied with the opportunity offered at the Debutante Cotillion. It especially affected my ability to know boys. Growing up, I didn't have much of an opportunity to meet them, since I went to a private, all-girls school, an all-girls camp, and an all-women's college. Had my family been able to join the Rumson Country Club, I might have gotten to know more boys and invite them to go as my partners to the later debutante balls. My social insecurity might not have been as great as it was.

Although I came to it by way of a secret, I joined the Episcopalian religion with enthusiasm, and my Christian faith grew to mean a lot to me in young adulthood. When I look back on my religious life, I think of St. James' Episcopal Church in the city. I liked the church because of its ministers, sermons, and hymns. I was confirmed, took my first communion, attended a yearly series of Lenten services, and got married at the church.

In retrospect, I would have called myself a devout Christian. I wholeheartedly accepted Jesus' story and instructions on how to live life as a good person. I never questioned any aspect of it (although some of Jesus' miracles did seem far-fetched). No one ever pointed out to me that I had a deeper connection to Jesus than a lot of other Christians did, as we both started our religious life as Jews and were baptized Christian in later life. If someone had done so, I might have felt more secure about my religious identity.

My faith played a subdued but steady part in my life during college. I joined a group of students who attended a weekly communion service at a nearby Episcopal church, but the conflict between who I was at the start of my life and who I became never quite vanished from my psyche. Most of my closest friends at Vassar were Christian, even though my classmates included many observant Jews.

A college religion course brought me to a synagogue for the first time. The visit bridged the gap between my early Jewish beginnings and the Christian faith that I practiced, but it didn't shake my confidence in my Episcopalian faith.

Although my mother never explicitly said so, I always felt that she wanted me to marry a Christian, and whenever I met a young man, unless it was obvious from his name or features, a tiny voice inside me asked, *Is he a Christian?* The voice never left me, and the pressure only increased after college when Joanie married a Yale graduate and Episcopalian from Grosse Pointe, Michigan, an enclave of white Anglo-Saxon Protestants (WASPs).

After I dated a young man named Don Wilson seriously for some months, I knew I had to tell him about my Jewish heritage. My father had told me that Don's father—who, like him, owned a seat on the New York Stock Exchange—held some strong anti-Semitic views and that Don might hold similar ones. I summoned the courage to introduce the subject, and after I told him, he simply laughed at me.

"With a name like Neuberger, what was I supposed to think?" he said.

I reached over and gave him a kiss as relief swept over me.

To his credit, Mr. Wilson—or Dad, as I called him—never said a derogatory word about my Jewish background in my presence. Perhaps he was happy that his son, at 32, had at long last decided to marry and that I was presentable.

Marriage helped me feel safer about my religious affiliation. I had a new last name, which offered me the comfort of feeling that I was more solidly Christian but also prompted the guilt that, once again, I was running away from my Jewish ancestry. Don helped me come to terms with my confusion about my religious past, which remained hidden away deep inside me.

One year, I was asked to join the Junior League of Washington, D.C., and was told that if accepted, I would be the first Jewish woman in the association. I asked Don for his advice; without missing a beat, he said that I should turn down the invitation.

"You don't want to be known as the first *Jewish* woman in the Junior League," he said. "You can do things on your own merit; you don't have to break this barrier for a group of white women. Find something to do that is more meaningful."

He was right and, of course, if I had accepted, the old internal conflict about whether I was a Jew or a Jew-turned-Christian would play out again in my mind. It was good advice, and I turned my attention to tutoring African-American children in the public schools. (Joanie joined the Junior League of Detroit, eventually rising to become its president.)

To the best of my recollection, I never experienced any form of prejudice during my years in D.C. I attended a small Episcopal church alone, since Don, who began life as a member of the Congregational Church and suffered through Sunday school, preferred to spend his precious Sunday mornings reading the newspapers.

At the time, Don was working in the Kennedy administration, and because of Bobby and Ethel Kennedy's generosity to their friends, we had almost unlimited access to weekend tennis and swimming at their home, Hickory Hill, so there was no need to join a country club. Don was caught up in Bobby's effort to illuminate racism in some of Washington's famous men's clubs. Under Bobby's leadership, he participated in a boycott of the Metropolitan Club, a men's luncheon club, when it refused to grant membership to a prominent African-American.

Once we arrived in Princeton in 1964, Don was eager to join a country club; I hesitated because I knew the one he chose might discriminate on the basis of religion and race. I didn't want to be a hypocrite and support this type of prejudice. The family secret and the past incidents of snobbery, which affected my parents for no sensible reason, had a long reach. Don wanted to join to play golf with good friends on weekends and assured me that he didn't want to participate in the club's social activities or expect me to make the club the center of our family life.

For his sake, I was a silent, non-participating club member for many years, allowing my name to be listed in its directory. But when I became involved in local politics, I felt that being a member of an all-white club sent a contradictory message to the friends I was helping to win elections, especially an African-American friend who was campaigning to become a state senator. Don was a good sport about asking the club secretary to remove my name from the directory, and although I had some pangs of guilt about hurting his feelings and causing some people to raise eyebrows about my unilateral decision, I stayed away. (Over the years, much has changed at the club, and it now has both Jewish and African-American members.) The breezes of prejudice and discrimination at this club and others, although much fainter now than in the past, linger in our society.

Don and I didn't provide our three children with a solid religious education. All three were christened in different Episcopal churches in ceremonies that Don and I attended with pleasure. None were confirmed or took communion, which had meant so much to me, and we had no time for Sunday school because of our back-and-forth life between New York City and Princeton. Our daughters never criticized us for not offering them the opportunity to experience the value of a religious faith, but when he was in college, our son once chastised me for not giving him a proper religious training.

"I don't understand any religious references in the English literature course I'm taking," he said. "I wish you'd given me a chance to learn about religion."

I wasn't sure how to respond without going into my own confused religious background, so I said, "You're at an institution of higher learning. You might consider taking a course in religion or Biblical literature."

One isn't supposed to tell secrets. I held fast to mine for an unnecessarily long period of time, which was essentially self-defeating. The family secret's long tentacles stretched over decades, but because I have written about it, like an ebbing tide, it is receding. Although it is late in life, I have finally learned how to answer the fraught question, "What is your religion?" It probably won't ever be asked again, but if it were, I would say: "My family was Jewish on both sides over many generations. But when I was ten years old, I was baptized a Christian and became an Episcopalian."

Today my faith isn't as strong as it was when I was younger, but I think Jesus' teachings, particularly those about loving one's neighbors as oneself and treating other people as we would like them to treat us, are powerful and profound. The family secret also helped me to comprehend racial discrimination and increased my empathy for those who feel its powerful sting.

I still keep my holy baptism certificate; it remains tucked into my black leather *Book of Common Prayer* with its slim, gold cross and my initials, "SMN," on the cover. My mother gave it to me to mark the day of my christening. A list of all my godchildren takes up a page near the front. Over the years, I've crammed the book with significant notes and prayer cards, such as the ones distributed at the funerals of John F. and Robert F. Kennedy. I've kept it in the top drawer of my bedroom bureau in every home I've lived in for the past 70 years.

When I catch a glimpse of it, I give it a rueful smile.

Mummy and Daddy

Life with a Remarkable Father

On a shelf in my office, I keep a memento of each of my parents that crystalizes for me the essence of their lives. For my father—or Daddy, as I always called him—it is a small, framed copy of the Catholic prayer attributed to Saint Francis of Assisi, which he gave to my sister and me when we were young adults. He also hung a larger copy of it near the entrance to our Falmouth summer residence, which he loved. It begins

> *Lord, make me an instrument of Thy peace*
> *Where there is hatred, let me sow love*
> *Where there is injury, pardon*
> *Where there is doubt, faith*

Where there is despair, hope
Where there is darkness, light
Where there is sadness, joy

My father was not an outwardly religious man. He was born a Jew—or a "Hebrew," as noted beneath his picture in the 1917 Princeton University yearbook. His boarding school yearbook lists him as a Christian Scientist, and I recall his reading pamphlets by its founder, Mary Baker Eddy. (He loved to quote Psalm 46 from one of the pamphlets: "Be still, and know that I am God.") He became an Episcopalian in midlife at my mother's request, but he lived the fundamental tenets of the Judeo-Christian tradition better than anyone I knew, for which I shall always be in his debt. The values he taught me are as clear to me now in my eighties as when he discussed them in my childhood.

Unfortunately, I never asked Daddy to share stories from his childhood, adolescence, or life prior to marrying my mother, and I only heard bits and pieces about his parents, Benno and Stella Neuberger, while growing up. On his bureau, he kept a picture of his father, a serious-looking, middle-aged bald man with dark eyes, a long, bushy mustache, and a stiff, round collar at his neck.

Daddy never told us much about his father, but I sensed that he loved and respected him. What is surprising about the silence is that Daddy, his older sister, Florence, and his parents had lived in a beautiful townhouse on 55 East 74th Street in Manhattan, only eight blocks north of our family's apartment at 40 East 66th Street, where we lived for many years. One would think the proximity would have spurred more stories from him about their lives.

⁂

My father was born on July 4, 1896, in Far Rockaway Village, in Queens, New York. I've always thought the line "a real, live nephew of my Uncle Sam, born on the fourth of July," from "I'm a Yankee Doodle Dandy," which Daddy loved to sing, described him perfectly. He loved his country, always reminding me and my sister how lucky we were to be born in America, especially during World War II, when millions of Jews were murdered in Hitler's gas chambers.

When Daddy was 18, his father died of a sudden heart attack in Germany, and he crossed the ocean with his mother and sister to bring his father back on his last transatlantic voyage. By age 36, Daddy had lost his father and mother, married, and become a father. He wed my mother, Katherine Alma Kridel, a fellow New Yorker, on March 7, 1929, at the Hotel Ambassador in New York City and later welcomed two daughters.

Daddy surmised that his father's early death might presage an early one for him. Whenever he wanted me to listen to especially vital advice, such as "Don't spend your money on jewelry and boats," he would add, "I've been spared so you can learn from me." Believing that my father's life might be a short one, I listened with far more attention than I might have otherwise.

Early Education, Exeter

Daddy received the best education many thought a young man could receive at the time: two years at Phillips Exeter Academy in New Hampshire (class of 1913) and four years at Princeton University (class of 1917).

He never talked too much about his academic experiences. He was a man of action who never sought to impress us with his intellect or comment on someone else's. He always read newspapers rather than books and encouraged me to read the *New York Times* editorial page, so I'd have something interesting to talk about with the young men who asked me on dates. (It's a habit I continue with pleasure, although my dating days are long over.)

He didn't live long enough to see his grandson, Dwight, attend Exeter and compare notes with him about it, but his memories must have been warm ones. (He established at the school the Benno and Stella Neuberger Scholarship in his parents' names following his mother's death.) I have his small leather booklet, "Class Day Exercises of the Senior Class of Phillips Exeter Academy," which lists his name, and his copy of the commencement magazine, the *Phillips Exeter Monthly*, June 1913. My father's classmate wrote in his farewell address: "To you is confided also the sacred and responsible duty of preserving her democracy, the very essence of the Exeter spirit. Exeter is, and let her ever be called, the great American democratic school."

I remember my father's pride when he spoke about the one African-American member of his class, who became a successful doctor. He believed that accepting this student into Exeter was the start of a slow but steady avenue for creating opportunities for minorities. He would have been pleased that by the time his grandson was at Exeter in the mid-seventies, there were many more African-American students, including the sons of Thurgood Marshall, the first African-American appointed to the United States Supreme Court.

Princeton and Military Service

My father served in the military twice: first in the Army and later in the Marines in World War II. After graduating from Princeton, he attended officers' training camp in Leon Spring, Texas, and was appointed first lieutenant in the 10th Field Artillery, 3rd Division. He went directly to the European battlefield, serving on active duty from November 27, 1917, until his formal discharge in 1919.

If I could relive our time together, I would ask him about his months in France during World War I, especially what it was like to be in battle and shoot to kill other men. He listed three battles on his personal résumé, all of which occurred during the summer of 1918: Champagne-Marne, St. Mihiel; Meuse-Argonne; and Château-Thierry. He also wrote of being "gassed" on July 15, 1918. (The Germans used tear, or mustard, gas as a chemical weapon toward the end of World War I. It was disabling and disorienting but not lethal, and most soldiers at the front used gas masks to protect themselves.)

In particular, I would have asked my father about the night his actions led to his Distinguished Service Cross, the second highest military honor given in wartime, surpassed only by the Congressional Medal of Honor. Knowing his humility, I'm sure he would have downplayed the event and given credit to everyone else. The War Department's General Order No. 44 of April 2, 1919, provided the reason for his honor: "Harry H. Neuberger, first lieutenant, 10th Field Artillery. For extraordinary heroism in action at Courbon, France, July 14-15, 1918. He volunteered and assisted another officer in driving an ambulance, making three trips to Greves Farm under the most intense shell fire. He continued to assist in the evacuation of the wounded even after being gassed."

Daddy's hometown newspaper, the *New York Herald Tribune,* carried the story on February 25, 1919, under the headline, "Lieutenant Neuberger Cited for Heroic Aid to Wounded." The article reports that only three men were left in his regiment; all others were "killed, wounded, or detached." His mother, Stella, kept some of the telegrams that my father had sent to his family after this battle. In them, he simply stressed that he was fine and not suffering any ill effects of his night's work: saving his fellow soldiers.

From the Halls of Montezuma

Daddy may have had a premonition in 1939 that the United States was headed once more to war with Germany, because six months before Pearl Harbor, he became chief of civil protection at the New Jersey Defense Council, in Trenton. He served full time without pay, because he had sufficient income to sustain his lifestyle and care for his family. When he left to join the Marines, Governor Charles Edison praised his efforts in an April 9, 1942, letter: "I know that you have worked day and night for the State of New Jersey for many months without compensation, and I would like to take this opportunity of thanking you for your very constructive efforts, and to compliment you for the quality of your citizenship."

Despite his exemplary war record, Daddy had trouble re-enlisting for military service at 46. He suffered from high blood pressure, which couldn't be treated at the time and left him unfit to return to the Army. Undaunted, he tried the Army Air Corps, but his application was rejected because it arrived two days late. The Marine Corps fulfilled my father's hopes of returning to military service, and he loved to sing the opening verses of the famous Marine Corps Hymn at social gatherings for the rest of his life:

From the Halls of Montezuma
To the Shores of Tripoli;
We fight our country's battles
In the air, on land and sea;
First to fight for right and freedom
And to keep our honor clean;
We are proud to claim the title
of United States Marine.

Like every other Marine Corps recruit, he went through basic training, or "boot camp," at Parris Island, South Carolina. It was exceptionally rigorous, especially for older recruits, but I never heard him complain. When he completed boot camp, he was assigned to the Quartermaster Corps, moving service personnel and materials to troops. Other than a brief posting on a naval base in Crane, Indiana, he spent most of his service near home, commuting to and from Naval Ammunition Depot Earle on the shore of Sandy Hook Bay near Bayonne, New Jersey.

My mother, sister, and I shared one month of Daddy's Marine Corps service during the summer of 1943, when we lived as a family on the naval station in Indiana. I kept asking why the Navy had placed a naval station in the middle of the state, where there wasn't a body of water even far away, but I never received a plausible answer. We set up housekeeping for the first time without any help, and it was quite a challenge. My sister conveniently complained of having a stomachache after supper almost every evening, leaving me to wash and dry dishes alone.

I remember how an officer's rank controlled a family's life. My father was a lowly captain until his promotion to major toward the end of the war—and most officers on base held higher ranks than he did. I always felt that most of the families looked down their noses at us, and I didn't like the snobbery. I found the emphasis on rank and dress for women baffling—officers' wives had to wear hats and white gloves outdoors, even in the broiling sun—given that men were dying for their country every day.

I'm not sure how satisfactory my father's second round in the military was for him, but he never complained. I'm sure he would have preferred to serve in far more dangerous surroundings than Bayonne, but his age precluded active combat. His willingness to volunteer again had everything to do with his deep love of country.

There was a flagpole at my parents' summer house on The Moors in Falmouth, Massachusetts. Families would gather beside it every year on Fourth of July morning to watch my father raise the flag and lead everyone in the Pledge of Allegiance. They would salute him by singing "Happy Birthday" and the Marine Corps hymn. He always sang its final lines with gusto: "If the

Army and the Navy/Ever look on Heaven's scenes/They will find the streets are guarded/By United States Marines."

Daddy relished wearing his Marine Corps ring with its brilliant red stone set in gold. We buried it with him.

Becoming a Gentleman Farmer

Daddy enjoyed multiple careers. He worked in the banking and brokerage business and began his passionate, lifelong avocation as a gentleman farmer between rounds of military service. He had a successful career in finance. For six years, he was a bond trader at Ames, Emerich & Company and then became a partner of Hilson and Neuberger, members of the New York Stock Exchange, and purchased a seat on the exchange, which he held until 1932. That year, his career path took a different turn when he bought Sunnyside Farm.

Daddy and Mummy became residents of New Jersey, which was a lucky day for the state. Daddy commuted by train to Wall Street daily from Red Bank, the town nearest the farm. He dressed with style and would always wear a rosebud in the lapel of his suit jacket in the summer. Our gardener would pick three from our rose garden in the morning, and at breakfast, I would see Daddy's three choices spread out by his china coffee cup and wonder whether he was going to choose the yellow, red, or pink one. I found the ritual mesmerizing.

Anything but a dilettante, Daddy immersed himself in every aspect of his new venture and became a serious gentleman farmer for the rest of his life. It brought him great joy, and we all reveled in the joy as well. The apple orchard didn't bear much fruit, but the rest of the property exceeded all of my father's expectations. The meadows provided lush pastures perfect for raising Jersey dairy cows and Aberdeen Angus beef cattle, and Daddy sold his steers to commercial meatpacking firms to be slaughtered. He took some of his finest specimens to compete at cattle shows and won some blue ribbons for his bulls and steers. We ate pounds and pounds of beef every year, all of which was raised on the farm. My mother would always boast about the "snow-white marbling" of the fat in our steaks and roasts, which she served to our family and dinner guests.

Daddy was usually on solo duty at two o'clock in the morning when the cattle broke through the fences and started walking on the road. He would get out of bed, too considerate to call one of our farmers, and round them up and return them to the field. He never asked me to help him with this task, and I wish I had gotten out of bed and lent him a hand, since he was always so supportive of me. But I just lazily slept and let him do the hard work of rounding up the miscreants.

In the fifties, Daddy still kept his hand in the stock market, and I would often hear him talking to his broker, checking the market's ups and downs and buying and selling his stocks and bonds over the telephone rather than commute to the city. He also devoted himself to good works for local nonprofit organizations and was a wonderfully hard worker. In the last decades of his life, he was board president of the YMCA of Red Bank and board vice president of the Riverview Hospital, raising large sums of money on behalf of these institutions. He never hesitated to ask anyone for a donation, always pressing the potential donor to give more. He also served as a vestryman of Christ Episcopal Church in Middletown, where we eventually held his funeral.

Daddy was a loyal Princeton alumnus, and it seemed to me no one could support his beloved alma mater as he did. He was such a successful class agent that, in 1956, he was named chairman of the university's overall Annual Giving Campaign. I'm sure he devoted hours of his time on the phone cajoling Princeton alumni to give and give again. He also chaired his class's major reunions for many years, including the successful 50th reunion in 1967.

His classmates gave him a large, sterling silver cigarette box—everyone except my father smoked in those days—to show their appreciation for his leadership on the 50th reunion. The inscription read: "To Harry Neuberger, Boss Man of the Best Reunion 1917 Ever Had," with 64 class members' signatures engraved below. The box always sat in the center of the butler's table in our library at Sunnyside Farm, and today my sister displays it prominently on a living room table in her Florida home.

Daddy was such a loyal Princeton alumnus that he and my mother would drive to the university every Saturday when its football team played a home game. I started sitting with him through many games at seven years old. He was such an enthusiastic rooter for Princeton that I found it hard to cheer for any other football team, even when I grew up and married a Yale graduate.

On July 4, 1989—93 years after my father's birth—I received a letter from Bill Sword, a fellow Princetonian and neighbor who had worked side by side with Daddy raising money for the university. His letter about my father was so special to me that I framed it. It read:

> He was a real man the like of which I have seldom met. Harry loved you and K. K. and your sister beyond belief. ... He gave his leadership to Princeton in powerful measure. I consider his leadership of Princeton's Annual Giving program the real foundation of what Princeton enjoys today. ... Harry Neuberger-17 was a great man who happened to choose Wall Street as a career. He would have been successful in almost any field. He had exceptional qualities—an agile, original, and keenly analytical mind, a quick wit, an incredibly retentive memory, and a tremendous gift for influencing people.

Daddy enjoyed his many friends. Whenever my mother was wounding or even sharp to others, he always came to provide balm. Toward the end of his life, he began to use his strong (although untrained) baritone voice to sing at parties. He especially liked singing songs from Broadway shows, and I can still hear him belting out the words to "Some Enchanted Evening" and "Oh, What a Beautiful Mornin'." My mother would on occasion accompany Daddy and the pianist on a set of drums. I was always moved watching their little amateur performances because of the love and warmth that radiated between them and extended to the audience. I never saw them demonstrate these emotions in any other situation, and I felt love and warmth for them in return.

Life with Father

No one could have had a father who so genuinely cared for her happiness as my father did for mine. One of the greatest gifts that he gave me was financial independence and the security that came with it. When I was a young adult, I was able to receive income from trusts that he had established, and I have used the money throughout my life, not only for the necessities of life, but for some of its pleasures.

I know some women who have stayed in unhappy or even abusive marriages because they didn't have the financial means and security to leave and live independently. Daddy gave me a real gift by setting up these trusts, and it showed his understanding of a woman's need to be financially secure, although he never directly spoke to me about the subject.

He was not afraid to teach me about building character and developing good values, and his lessons began when I was young. The "Uncle Don" children's radio show was extremely popular for the ten-and-under set, and I was an avid listener. Folksy Uncle Don encouraged children to let him know when their birthdays were approaching and where a present might be hidden for them around the house. He would announce the information and the child's name on the air, which was enormously exciting—at least to this listener.

I wanted to hear my name announced, and one year when I was eight or nine, I took matters into my own hands. I wrote a letter saying, "Dear Uncle Don … a present for Susie is hiding in the back of the family's Rolls Royce." No doubt, I browbeat my unsuspecting governess into sending it to the radio station. I could hardly wait for my birthday, and Uncle Don held up his end of the bargain when he announced, "There is a present for Susie in the back of the family's Rolls Royce automobile."

We didn't own such a car, and my excitement was short lived as I realized that my father had heard Uncle Don say these words. Like a shot, he was out of his room and into mine with a dark scowl on his face. He was furious that I had lied about having something we didn't and never would have.

"Susie," he said, "You were putting on airs. You behaved like a spoiled little rich girl. We don't own a Rolls Royce and never will. Your punishment is that you cannot listen to that radio program for a month, and I want you to write, 'I will not be someone who I am not' 50 times, and show me the results."

His words sank in deeper with every pencil stroke. I learned my lesson that lying and pretending to be someone grander than myself were worthless pursuits.

Another time, when I was in college, Daddy discovered that I had overdrawn my account at the Bank of New York. He was embarrassed for me and for himself. I had gotten home quite late from a debutante party the night he made the discovery, and I woke up groggily at the crack of dawn to see him standing at the end of my bed. His eyes blazed, and he could hardly control his voice:

"You have disgraced our family by overdrawing your bank account. I want you to get up immediately, get dressed, and arrive at the Bank of New York at nine o'clock when it opens and ask to speak to the president. Then I want you to apologize to him for your sloppy and inconsiderate behavior. Do you understand me?"

I understood him—perfectly. I got out of bed and soon arrived at the bank, trembling. I asked to see the president and was ushered into his beautifully furbished office, where a fire burned in the fireplace. I apologized profusely for overdrawing my account and promised to never do it again. In retrospect, I think it was overkill to have me speak to the president, but Daddy wanted to make a point that I had violated his trust and the bank's requirements and needed to make amends at the highest possible level.

The president had likely heard this promise a hundred times, but he said he understood that "accidents happen." I stumbled out of the bank and back to the safety of the apartment, where I was happy to see that my father had left for Sunnyside Farm.

Daddy could also be mellow and surprise me on occasion with his understanding and kindness when I thought I would receive a lecture. In 1950, I was at my "job" as a summer apprentice at the theater in Falmouth while my parents stayed in the house they'd bought to keep an eye on me as I navigated the theater world. I had a driver's license and was driving Daddy's car, for which he had given permission, when I went through a stop sign and hit a town truck. A police officer arrived and called my father, although there wasn't any damage to the truck or my father's car.

I sat in the front seat feeling miserable and afraid of his reaction, but he couldn't have been kinder when he pulled up in his car. First he wanted to know if I was all right, and then he told me that accidents happen, that I was a good, safe driver, and that I would be more careful when approaching a stop sign in the future. Relief swept over me as I burst into tears.

I have hundreds of memories of my father's kindness to me during difficult moments, and one especially stands out. Joanie married at 21 immediately after graduating from college, and Daddy knew that her wedding was going to be hard for me, as I was the older, unmarried sister. She had an elegant, beautiful wedding in New York City at St. James' Episcopal Church and a sumptuous reception at the St. Regis Roof, the same ballroom where she had had her debutante party. She looked regal in a cream-colored satin dress and wore my mother's long lace veil; it perfectly framed her lovely face and huge blue eyes. She had kindly asked me to be her maid of honor—not the matron of honor most guests would have expected me to be had we married in chronological order. She also put me in a pretty turquoise chiffon dress to stand out from the other bridesmaids in daffodil yellow.

Despite all of her thoughtfulness, I found myself quietly crying toward the end of the ceremony, and my father caught sight of my tears as I walked back up the long aisle with the best man. At the reception, he quickly found and consoled me. He had a right to be angry with me for feeling sorry for and thinking only of myself rather than my responsibilities as my sister's maid of honor. He could have told me to stop crying and not spoil her day, but instead he looked at me sympathetically and reached out to touch my arm.

"Susie," he said, "I know you probably think you're a failure because you didn't get married before Joanie, but finding someone to love and marry isn't a race." Then he added something even more comforting: "I know you are going to find someone wonderful to love and marry. These things take time."

His words helped me so much that I began to smile. He never brought up the subject again, and four years later, after my sister had her first child, I did get married. My father had been right, and his kindness to me made my wedding even sweeter.

―※―

I never heard Daddy say that he wished he'd had a son. In the era in which I grew up, boys were often named after and in honor of their fathers and expected to carry on the family name, business, and wealth. Daddy thought that his daughters were the equals of sons, and he was pleased that I was slowly building a career and drawing a respectable salary as a journalist at *Life*. He would often compliment me with the same words whenever I told him about a raise: "I think you will eventually earn $50,000 a year." In the fifties and sixties, this was a large sum of money, and I felt his pride in my accomplishments.

After his experience serving on the Riverview Hospital board, my father suggested that I consider becoming a hospital administrator. I didn't take his advice, but it was high praise, because he couldn't say enough good words about the importance of administrators in the complex operation of hospitals. Sometimes I wish I had followed his suggestion, as he was a good judge of people's abilities.

My father had particular concern for those less fortunate than us. When I was about eight, we were shopping at one of the Woolworth Five & Dime stores in Red Bank when I snapped at the salesperson waiting on us. After we left the store, he took my hand and said, "Susie, you spoke unkindly and impolitely to the saleswoman. You probably hurt her feelings. If this woman could be doing something more interesting, she wouldn't be working in this store. You must understand that she didn't have the same opportunities of a good education as you have—and a choice of where to work. You should respect her for the effort she is making to help you. If I ever hear you speaking rudely to a salesperson again when we are together, I shall have you apologize immediately."

Needless to say, his lesson of so many years ago still rings true, and I catch myself when I feel rude or impolite words rising in my mouth, particularly in situations when I have more power than the other person.

My father applied this advice to himself. Several of his farmers lived in small houses on our farm, and one of them had three small daughters. I don't think we played with the girls, but he didn't want us to feel superior to them. There was some talk of building a swimming pool for us on the farm, and the only possible location was in plain view of the girls' cottage. My father scotched the idea.

"I don't want those children to look out of the window and see the two of you swimming. I don't want them to feel that they can't use the pool without an invitation," he said.

We never had a swimming pool on the farm. I'm sure that it was my father's concern for those less fortunate than himself that led him to be active in our local YMCA, which was used by many white and African-American working-class families in town. During the two years he served as president, he raised funds to build a swimming pool for the Y's Camp Arrowhead. He wanted to give young people the chance to learn how to swim and enjoy it. After his death, the YMCA renamed a renovated building on the property the Neuberger Hilltop House and dedicated it to him. All children could enjoy the swimming pool on the property, and I felt it was an appropriate way of remembering Daddy, who had not wanted the farmer's daughters to need permission to swim in a pool at Sunnyside.

A Call to Say Goodbye

Daddy died in 1970, two months before his 74th birthday, a ripe old age that he never thought he would reach. (I am grateful that he did. He lived to see the birth of all six of his grandchildren, which was mutually advantageous to everyone concerned.) He had a heart attack while on vacation in the Caribbean, and then another one three years later, which led to a fatal pulmonary embolism. He died in the early morning at the Riverview Hospital he had so lovingly nurtured. He had called me the night before, perhaps with a sense of knowing that death was imminent, but I never returned his call. This failure of mine to at least talk to him, send him my love, and promise a visit returns to haunt me from time to time.

I am not sure I ever said "I love you" to my father; expressing these feelings so explicitly wasn't as customary as it is now, and I regret never having told him how much I loved, adored, and appreciated him. But I am sure he would have forgiven me, because he was a loving, kind, and forgiving person.

Sometime before he died, my father handwrote one of the two verses of Christina Rossetti's poem "When I Am Dead, My Dearest," which he gave to me. He wrote it in pencil on a small piece of his stationery with "From the Desk of Harry H. Neuberger" printed across the top. The verse, in his familiar flowing script, reads:

> *When I am dead, my dearest;*
> *Sing no sad songs for me*
> *Plant thou no roses at my head*
> *Nor shady cypress tree:*
> *Be the green grass above me*
> *With showers and dewdrops wet;*
> *And if thou wilt, remember*
> *And if thou wilt, forget.*

I have kept this little scrap of paper in every wallet I have owned, so it is with me almost every day. I sometimes feel my father's arm around my shoulders when I read it.

My life is still full of my father. Most days, I hope that I live up to his values and that he is proud of what I have tried to do with my life. Since his death, I have often visited the graves in the Fairview Cemetery in Middletown where he and my mother are buried. The cemetery is a few miles from his beloved Sunnyside Farm, which is now a part of the Monmouth County Park System. As I stand beside his gravestone, I sometimes say, "Daddy, I remember what you stood for and what you hoped I would stand for. I have taught my children and try to teach my grandchildren about your lovely character, wonderful values, and zest for life. I am so proud to be your daughter."

After Daddy died, Monmouth County's local newspaper, the *Daily Register*, published an editorial about him. It noted that the mourners at his funeral in Christ Episcopal Church represented all walks of life, and that Daddy's "love and interest in the area knew no bounds; he was a complete gentleman whose concern for others was truly remarkable; and he earned all the fine things that are said about him."

The editorial ended with these words for his family: "Their sorrow at losing him should be softened by the knowledge that his life was so worthwhile."

An Extraordinary Woman

She's Like to Be Governor

It is daunting to write about my mother, Katherine Alma Kridel Neuberger, or K. K. or Kay, as she was more familiarly known. Why wouldn't it be when Thomas H. Kean, then the governor of New Jersey, said this about her shortly after she died on October 15, 1982:

> Mrs. Neuberger spent her lifetime serving the people of the state in political, professional, civic and charitable causes. Her untiring efforts in behalf of her fellow citizens established a standard of service and compassion, which shall remain unsurpassed. All of us who knew her shall miss her charm and her sense of concern for others. The people of New Jersey, whom she served so well, shall miss her.

"Her death is a very deep personal loss to me and to the State of New Jersey," added Governor Kean, who had just reappointed my mother to her third six-year term on the State Board of Higher Education, where she served as chairperson for three years. His comment prompted a series of accolades about Mummy that still warm and impress me more than 30 years later.

Announcements of her death appeared on the front page of the *Star-Ledger*, the leading state newspaper, and in an Associated Press story in the *New York Times*. Editorials about her more than 50 years of accomplishments in higher education, politics, penal reform, and law enforcement appeared in most regional newspapers. Many articles mentioned her honorary degrees for her decades of public service: a Doctor of Humane Letters from Rutgers University and a Doctor of Laws from Fairleigh Dickinson University in 1979, and others from Montclair State College, Monmouth College, and Jersey City State College.

My favorite of all the eulogies and press stories about Mummy's life and work is a column by Bob Braun, the insightful, award-winning education reporter for the *Star-Ledger*. Braun, who covered the State Board of Higher Education and State Board of Education (K-12) on which my mother served, understood what made Mummy different in the world of politics and policymaking. On October 18, 1982, he attended her funeral at Christ Episcopal Church in Middletown, where she faithfully attended services and served on the vestry, and wrote, "A Tribute to Katherine Neuberger, An Extraordinary Woman," which appeared in the *Star-Ledger* four days later. (It now hangs framed on the wall above my computer, so I can see it whenever I raise my eyes from the screen.)

Braun's article captured my mother's clear-headed, honest style of expression, which some might call overly sharp or even insulting. He saw it as unique: "If more people practiced her style—that wonderful, candid, biting, embarrassing, healing style—all government would improve." He recommended renaming the Garden State Scholarships—the only academic awards based on merit—in my mother's honor, because the winners "might learn the lesson of Katherine Neuberger's public life … and might be encouraged to emulate her style." Yet it didn't happen; perhaps that "biting style" had drawn some blood and offended the powers that be. (It wouldn't have surprised me.)

Beginnings of a Public Life

When I was seven years old and safely admitted to second grade at the Brearley School, Mummy embarked on the political and civic life that eventually consumed her. She was prepared for it, since she had majored in political science at Barnard College, graduating in 1927, and completed three years of graduate work in political science and sociology at Columbia University before her wedding. She and Daddy were legal residents of New Jersey, even though my sister and I went to school in New York City, and in 1937, when she was 30, Mummy joined the board of the Monmouth County Organization for Social Services, which provided residents with social, financial, and medical services. She must have found the work worthwhile and satisfying since she remained on the board for 22 years.

Her background in sociology and experience with people in need led Democratic Governor Charles Edison to appoint her vice president of the New Jersey Reformatory for Women in 1940, a post she held for 16 years, chairing its Parole Committee. Our breakfast table conversations changed once she assumed this role; she would talk at great length about biases against imprisoned women, many of whom had committed murder in self-defense against domestic violence and then had to abandon their children by serving a jail sentence. She believed imprisonment didn't help these women and only hurt their children; instead she worked to develop rehabilitation programs for women inmates.

Her experience at the women's reformatory led Republican Governor Alfred E. Driscoll to appoint her to the New Jersey Law Enforcement Council, which investigated organized crime and earned the ire of law enforcement officials who didn't like taking some heat on their questionable activities. She served on the Council from 1952 to 1957 and was its chairman for the last three years.

I often think my mother should have gone to law school before marrying; her younger brother, Billy Kridel, and his two children did, so the profession runs in the family. It was pretty heady stuff to have a mother heading a law enforcement council, especially since New Jersey was notorious for its criminal elements. None of my friends' mothers held such fascinating positions or did the serious type of volunteer work that my mother did. I have kept a little wooden gavel that one of Mummy's friends gave her as a light-hearted Christmas present. It reads "KKN" and the initials "NJLEC," for the New Jersey Law Enforcement Council.

Mummy had always impressed me as a woman with important responsibilities. During World War II, she volunteered with the American Red Cross's Home Service unit to supervise a group of women who informed the families of servicemen killed in action of their loved ones' deaths. She was not a particularly emotional woman on the surface, except for anxious outbursts when she thought we were lost or injured, and this couldn't have been an easy assignment for her. I never heard her complain, and I believe the job made her feel purposeful, which made living with her much easier. She didn't issue as many orders to the household help when she had enough work to channel her tremendous energy.

This energy and her innate organizational skills helped her combine a heavy dose of volunteering with family and household demands. She relished serving on boards of organizations, particularly those related to politics and higher education, and she read the materials carefully and had an amazing capacity for remembering facts and election results. She was also an excellent driver and took herself all over the state to meet her responsibilities without ever getting into an accident, getting lost, or getting a speeding ticket.

Political Adventures

In the late forties, Mummy became involved in party politics through her acquaintance with Geraldine L. Thompson, a prominent, powerful Republican woman who became my mother's mentor and then later my godmother when I was baptized a Christian. She started as a volunteer party worker at the polls. Mrs. Thompson, although considerably older than my mother, lived in a grand mansion on Brookdale Farm, a few miles south of Sunnyside Farm, my parents' home for more than 50 years. She had been an alternate to three Republican nominating conventions and helped my mother get a start in the New Jersey State Federation of Republican Women, a statewide political organization. My mother was elected president of the Federation in 1957 and re-elected two years later to a second term.

Mummy was a moderate Republican, a branch of the party that is nearly extinct in modern politics today. She saw the approach of the conservative right wing way before pundits and others did, and it scared her. When I was a young voter, she used to warn me about the party while we sat at the breakfast table.

"The right wing is going to be the ruination of the Republican Party," she'd say. I can still feel her audacity as she prophesied the future—and she was right. Today she would be horrified at her party's positions and the Tea Party's refusal to make genuine compromises to achieve the goals supported by the American majority.

Mummy was a New Jersey delegate-at-large to the 1960 Republican Convention in Chicago, where she also served on the committee to write the party's platform on a hodgepodge of policies. A highpoint of her political life was when she was chosen to second the nomination of Henry Cabot Lodge as Vice President at the convention. My mother-in-law, Adelaide Wilson, wrote Mummy a note of congratulations afterward, to which she replied, "I got a terrific thrill out of having had the opportunity to play a prominent role in the seconding of Ambassador Lodge." She said the Republicans had chosen a "wonderful ticket," knowing full well that her son-in-law was doing everything in his power to defeat it. (Don and my mother loved to schmooze about politics over vodka and caviar on special occasions like New Year's Day.)

From 1961 to 1976, Mummy was New Jersey's Republican National Committeewoman and served on the National Committee in Washington, which was composed of one male and one female representative from each state. For the last three of those years, she was a member of its Executive Committee. Since Mummy had risen to lead statewide Republican organizations and serve in the prestigious role as Republican National Committeewoman, I always wondered why she hadn't considered a run for public office. One morning in 1963, I put the question to her at the breakfast table as she talked about our longtime Republican congressman, James C. Auchincloss, who was considering retirement.

"Mummy, why don't you run for public office? Why don't you try for the Republican nomination?" I asked. "You'd make a wonderful congresswoman. Washington is where you belong."

She dropped her head and took a long time to answer, which was definitely unlike her. She always had a sharp, quick retort for everything, and I realized that it was a painful question for her to answer. She snapped to.

"Oh, I could never do that," she said. "It wouldn't be fair to your father. He'd be known as the man who's married to the congresswoman from New Jersey. He'd hate to drag about in my shadow. I don't want him to have to do that."

I was amazed at her response and didn't really believe her. My father was always proud of my mother's accomplishments and would have been pleased to follow her to Washington. He never seemed jealous of her appointments, press coverage, or multiple awards. Her answer seemed to reflect more her own insecurities and guilt over leading a political life and leaving her husband and children to rely on the (excellent) household help. She also seemed afraid of suffering a defeat. Sometimes she seemed inscrutable to me.

"I'm sorry, Mummy," I said. "I think you could run and win."

Auchincloss retired and was replaced by James Howard, a Democrat who went on to serve in Congress for 23 years, and I was sorry that I hadn't leaned harder on her to run for office. I raised the subject again many years later as she approached her 75th birthday.

"Mummy, is there any aspect of your life that you would change, or anything you've wanted to do that you haven't done?" I asked her.

This time her answer came swiftly.

"I would have liked to have been governor," she said softly.

I wondered if she was serious, and she turned her head as if she didn't want me to probe any further. I realized that I had touched upon something deep that was also for her bittersweet. I had no idea that she harbored such a wish, although her mantra had always been "trust the people," which is a good way to begin an adventure in politics.

"You would have made a wonderful governor, Mummy. I wish you had tried," I said. She didn't respond again, and I didn't have the guts to ask her anything more about it.

"Rutgers Honors Mrs. Neuberger, Graduates 8,700" was the headline in the *Daily Register* on May 25, 1979. I learned something from that article that my mother had never told me: She had turned down two requests from her party to run for public office, once for State Assembly and once for Congress. In the article, she urged women to consider running for office: "There is not one single solitary Republican woman in the state senate and never has been, and I think that is awful. Democrats have always done better by women than we have."

My mother would be surprised—and pleased—to know that there are some Republican and Democratic women in the New Jersey state legislature today, and that women hold 20 percent of U.S. Senate seats. She would be disappointed, however, to know that at the moment there is no woman in the New Jersey Congressional delegation, but pleased with a recent development: my distinguished congressman is retiring and two able women are vying for the seat. She was an early pioneer in the movement for women's electoral justice.

Turning to Education

In the final 12 years of her life, my mother shifted her attention from politics to education, perhaps because making much-needed change is such a slow political process. "Politicians always go into the future looking back over their shoulder at the past," she told me once in frustration over a bill's failure. She was a leader in thinking ahead to the future and about what needed to be accomplished, and it was hard for her to wait for people to catch up to her.

In 1970, Republican Governor William Cahill appointed Mummy to a six-year term on the New Jersey State Board of Higher Education, and Governor Brendan Byrne reappointed her to another term six years later. (She called every governor by his first name.) She was elected vice chairman of that board in 1972 and chair from 1975 to 1978. More governors from both parties had appointed her to more terms and different positions than any other woman in state history.

I only saw my mother in action as a member of the State Board of Education, where she represented the Board of Higher Education in its deliberations. To my surprise, she did not hog the limelight as many (often male) board members did. She spoke only when she had something valuable to add to the conversation, and she always kept members moving along to cover the agenda in a timely manner. She knew the board material cold and didn't try to play to the press like other members. She didn't put up with any malarkey—"phoniness, blandishment, overstatement, political rationalizations," as Braun wrote—and always tried to find middle-ground solutions.

My mother valued her work as chairman of the Board of Higher Education more than any other responsibility in her lifetime of service. She loved it especially since it assisted young people of limited means whose parents had no or little education beyond high school. She believed that access to public education was a way out of poverty and into a better life, and she saw these young people as her special constituency, offering them the chance to be the first in their families to graduate college. They had no better champion than her.

In Braun's tribute to my mother, he said that she had "contributed significantly to every advance higher education has made in this state in the last 15 years," such as forcing tougher teacher-training standards on recalcitrant bureaucrats and union representatives. (She even publicly called her fellow members "puppy dogs" for meekly following the Commissioner of Education, who did not support tougher standards.) She also fought hard for expanding services for preschoolers, and I'm certain that if she were alive today, she would have strongly supported President Obama's call for universal preschool education.

I keep the nameplate for her seat in the Department of Higher Education boardroom on a shelf in my office. It says simply "Mrs. Neuberger" on one line and "Chairman" right below it. Perhaps some would say that "Chairwoman" should have been used instead of "Chairman," but this feminist has another view. My mother was tough and showed courage equal to any man's when she fought for better public education—and I like the juxtaposition of the words.

Another's Start in Public Life

When I was 50 and at a loss about how to reconnect with the professional world, my mother gave me a helping hand into public education. She used her considerable political clout to secure me an appointment to the New Jersey State Board of Education. Somehow she sensed that being responsible for K-12 education policy would be a good fit for me. How right she was: like mother, like daughter. An added delight to her help was that we served on the board together, probably its first and only mother-daughter duo. As chairman of the Board of Higher Education, she was an ex-officio member of the State Board of Education, and we attended monthly meetings together in Trenton for almost five years.

Mummy and I tried to keep our relationship at a distance during public meetings, but one time she momentarily forgot our unwritten contract of acting as public servants, not as mother and daughter. She was addressing the board on some matter when I raised my hand to indicate to the president that I wanted to make a comment. I held my hand over my head for several minutes as the president looked elsewhere, and Mummy turned to me and said, "Susie, put down your hand. You're making me nervous." Of course, I did as she said, and my comment vanished into thin air. Despite moments like this one, it was a pleasure to serve with her, given our common commitment to enhancing public education.

Although she always appeared at the board meetings in Trenton, refusing help with the long drive except during the last years of her life, Mummy's incredible energy and health were failing because of crippling arthritis. In 1982, the year she died, I was embroiled in New Jersey's hard-fought struggle over sex education as the go-to person on the State Board. I couldn't turn to her for advice. Had she been able to give it, I believe that, ever the pragmatist, she would have said, "If you think young people need sex education to have a better life, and the only way you can make sure that all youth will have access to it is through a State Board requirement, then go for it." My sense of her support helped me to fight the good fight.

Summary Judgment

My mother's favorite of her many awards was her honorary Doctor of Humane Letters degree from Rutgers University. During the commencement exercises, then-president of Rutgers, Edward J. Bloustein, praised her more than 40 years of "selfless public service." I keep the black velvet mortarboard with gold tassel that she wore on the occasion in my cedar closet, and whenever I see it, I remember her on one of the happiest days of her life. She seemed to smile from the beginning to the end of it. The degree of pride she felt for me on my wedding day equals the pride I felt for her on that day. When Mummy died three years later, we buried her with her Rutgers degree.

After her death, heartfelt eulogies came pouring in from Governor Kean and many others we knew and didn't know, which meant a great deal to our family. They assuaged the pain of her death, consoling us and prompting profound pride in the outstanding public figure we called Mummy. I had once asked her in a quiet moment, "Do you believe that we shall see each other again after we die?"

"No, I believe this is all that there is," she said.

As a public figure, my mother definitely made the most of "all that there is" and filled me, her daughter, with immense pride and humility in her extraordinary accomplishments and legacy.

A Complex Personality

My mother died in October 1982 at the age of 75, and some months after her funeral, I was asked to say a few words at the unveiling of her portrait at the small public library in Lincroft, New Jersey. The portrait shows her seated at a desk, gently smiling, holding her glasses, and wearing a red suit, white blouse, and her favorite gold choker and earrings.

The library is nestled behind tall trees at the end of Lincroft-Middletown Road, a mile-and-a-half south of Sunnyside Farm. That spring afternoon, it was a true community gathering of people who knew my mother well. I was the only family member present.

All of the invited guests sat in rows of standard metal chairs in one of the library rooms. I looked out at their somber faces wondering what I could say to help them realize how important they had been in my mother's life. I didn't want my words to be only perfunctory. I wanted to convey more than our family's thanks for their contributions to my mother's many successes. I wanted to tell my mother's dear, close friends something special about her feelings for them. I paused, looked at all the women and men—some who had worked for her on the farm, some who were close neighbors, and some who were good friends—and suddenly the right words came to me.

"My mother found it hard to say 'I love you,'" I said, feeling as though I was holding each person in an embrace. "I'm sure she never said these words to any of you, but my mother loved all of you. I know she loved you."

I turned away from the podium and while the audience applauded, I thought to myself, *I don't remember ever hearing Mummy say "I love you" to me, but I know she did.*

When I look back on the 52 years we spent as mother and daughter, I find Mummy's love for me strong and vibrant. I do not find it in memories of her physical affection (she struggled to show her love that way), but in the legacy of her passions and commitment to education and public service to change the world for the good.

Early Memories

My mother was born on April 30, 1907, in New York City, the oldest child of Elsie and Samuel Kridel. Her father was a successful businessman, and her mother remained at home overseeing the household servants who raised my mother. When Mummy was eight years old, her parents welcomed a son, William Jacob Kridel, and she felt that her mother stopped loving her from that moment on. She always said she had a distant relationship with her.

One could say that Mummy began life as a Jewish princess, a role she later rejected. She grew up in an apartment on 84th Street at Park Avenue, attended a private girls' school, Ethical Culture, and graduated at age 20 with a Bachelor of Science degree from Barnard College. After three years of graduate work, she married Daddy, and my birth and then my sister's soon followed.

My father's income provided the same lifestyle that my mother knew growing up, perhaps at an even higher level, and wealthy women of my mother's day did not take physical care of their children. They had the means to hand this responsibility off to nannies and then governesses when their children grew older. Mummy had been cared for as a child by a German nanny, and she repeated this pattern after my sister and my births. I simply accepted the fact that our daily upbringing was handed off to the servants, who were kind to us and respected my mother.

I can't recall my first memory of my mother, but I have an old tiny envelope with "For Daddy" written across the front that contains two small cards my mother wrote within six months of my birth. The first one is engraved with my name and includes this note for my father: "This is to tell you that I love you very much, dear Daddy. A big hug and kiss from your little Susan Mary." The second little card is engraved with my mother's name, "Mrs. Harry Hobson Neuberger," and on it, my mother writes:

> Just to tell you again, my darling, how much I love you. The past year was so wonderful. Let us hope that the future years will be good to us. Let us try to make our house a joyous one for ourselves and our lovely little Susan. I'll do my share, I promise. We should thank God for the blessings he has bestowed on us.

Our family's first apartment in New York City was at 1100 Park Avenue on the corner of 89th Street. I have wisps of memories of Mummy in elegant evening gowns coming in for a quick goodnight kiss before she and Daddy disappeared for evenings on the town. I remember her speaking German or French to our nurses and governesses—she was fluent in both—to make sure I didn't understand what she was saying about me.

At Sunnyside Farm, I remember the pleasure of coming into her dressing room and seeing her country clothes hanging neatly in the closet. I would look across to the mirrored wall as she sat combing her hair at the dressing table, which was scattered with perfume bottles and china bric-a-brac that I longed to touch. When I grew older, I noticed an inconsistency between my mother and her dressing table: Although she had her hair and nails done at a beauty salon on a regular basis, she wore minimal makeup and only lined her lips with red lipstick. I always thought she was simply too eager to get to the business of volunteer work.

Mummy always wanted to have a deep tan and on the coldest day of the year could be found bundled up in warm clothing, sitting in a chair with her face up to the sun. She would be smoking a cigarette, which was considered a perfectly normal activity for young matrons at the time. (Fortunately she never developed lung or skin cancer after exposing herself to thousands of cigarettes and hours of sunlight.) I would see her out of the corner of my eye when I was riding my pony in the front field, but I never thought she was looking at me.

Growing Up with Mummy

On our bedroom wall at the farm was a large framed photograph of my mother as a little girl. In it, she smiles sweetly in a party dress and patent leather shoes with a large bow atop her long dark curls. I love the picture, but it gives no hint of the complex person my mother became in later life. Mummy was definitely not warm and fuzzy. Although she had a pet name for me, "Zaabi," which she often used in her letters to me at camp and college and even on my honeymoon, I don't remember her ever giving me hugs and kisses. She certainly never gave me special treatment when I was sick in bed; she left that kind of care to our governess.

I never felt Mummy neglected me in any way, and it took some time before I realized that she was torn by internal conflicts between striving for independence and being a wife and mother. I knew early on that she believed in the importance of getting the best possible education. One morning, we were in the car on Park Avenue and stopped behind a bus with the words "The Brearley School" emblazoned on its back window. "That's the school I want you to go to," she said, "because it's the best girls' school in the city." When I managed to gain admittance in the second grade, she never seemed particularly interested in my schoolwork or asked if I needed help. She appeared at school functions, but only in a perfunctory way.

I never believed that Mummy thought I was particularly intelligent because she didn't ask me for my opinion on subjects that came up in daily life. But years later, she respected my ability to complete a graduate degree in education from Bank Street College, asking me if she could buy me the graduation hood. When I told her that the small, progressive college didn't have such a hood, she seemed disappointed and shook her head. I know she was pleased that I was the first person in our immediate family to receive a degree higher than a bachelor's.

It was hard for her to compliment others, including me. Sometimes she would even apologize about me in front of guests, which made me feel awful. Once when I was about twelve, I came into the library with my hair uncombed as she was entertaining. She looked up at my disheveled head and said to her guests, "Please excuse Susie's hair. I know it looks like a Brillo pad." The words stuck with me, as mothers' critical words often do, and I spent much of my life trying to tame my unruly locks into a smooth pageboy, the hairstyle of all the popular-with-boys girls.

A Role Model

I never thought of my mother as a supporter of women per se, although she was a good women's role model. In order to get ahead and have her views respected, she had to become more like one of the boys. She would have relished the compliment former Governor Byrne once paid her after she died, when he said, "Kay had guts," a description usually applied to men. She would have been a strong supporter of the suffrage movement of the early 20th century, because of her passionate belief in voting rights. But she wasn't overtly interested in the second-wave feminist movement, including the sexual revolution, when it hit the United States in the sixties.

Mummy supported women entering the political arena, but she wasn't able to apply her beliefs to women like me who wanted other types of careers.

Although she was pursuing a career in the public sphere, she encouraged my sister and me to be homemakers rather than working professionals. She was not alone: Marriage was the "career" of choice for most female undergraduates in the early fifties. If it hadn't been for my father's encouragement to find a job after graduation, I might have felt lost.

I had the impression as a teenager that she favored my sister, a beautiful, successful debutante with lots of boyfriends, who never entertained the idea of having a career early in life. I was an unsuccessful debutante with few boyfriends and zero marriage prospects. Mummy's message to me was to get married to a nice Christian boy, which I didn't know how to do. Although she never said anything, I knew that I would fail her if I married a Jewish man, and I couldn't disappoint her. Her beliefs shaped my choices, and I didn't trust myself enough to think independently about issues of social class.

I was relieved when I learned that the handsome, single *Life* correspondent in the Far East who I was curious about was Don Wilson, a good Christian name. I have a feeling that my mother was relieved as well, and I shall never forget her beaming expression the day Don and I married. Her happiness almost eclipsed mine.

Mixed Messages

We never discussed women's conflicts about work and motherhood, but I know Mummy was relieved that after marrying, I devoted myself primarily to raising our two little children, who came along quite rapidly, and being a supportive wife to Don after his appointment to the Kennedy administration. I had looked into becoming a writer for a United States Information Agency magazine when I first arrived in Washington, but I didn't pursue the opportunity once I became pregnant. In retrospect, I might have been able to balance work and family, but perhaps I was subconsciously influenced by my mother's conflicts about work and home life and her ideas about who I should be.

My confusion about the role I should take as a woman surfaced when Bobby and Ethel Kennedy invited me on a presidential trip around the world.

Officially I went as a reporter for *Ladies Home Journal,* but my mother charged that I was going as "Ethel's bridesmaid." She said that I would be stuck with chores like helping Ethel pack and unpack, which disappointed her. I told her that I felt fortunate to be invited and didn't care about my role, even if it involved doing menial tasks.

"Mummy, I enjoy being of service, and if I can be helpful to the Kennedys, I don't think I'm demeaning myself in any way," I said.

Her comment confused me, but then I remembered that she had broken with women's traditional roles to become a leader of worthwhile causes that enabled people to lead better lives. I remember when my eighth-grade Brearley classmates elected me the "most ambitious" in our class, and I felt so important and happy. When I burst into our apartment to tell my mother the news, she said that she was ashamed of me. "Being ambitious is not a worthy goal for any young woman," she said, adding that I had disgraced her. I must have showed my classmates how ambitious or "pushy" I was for them to have selected me.

I was surprised and hurt because I thought that my mother was an ambitious person herself on behalf of the causes she cared about, which included promoting the abilities of women. I promised myself that I would never do anything again in my life that would result in hearing myself called "ambitious."

Years passed as I moved between volunteer work and attending graduate school while raising three children. In 1977, when I was 47, my mother finally took matters into her own hands and suggested that I serve as a member of the New Jersey State Board of Education. She explained that the board set policy for all public schools, and when I protested that I didn't know much about public education since my children had gone to private schools, she assured me that knowing about private education could positively inform the way I viewed education issues.

"You have tutored in public schools, have a master's in education, and are committed to helping poor and minority children advance through education," she said. "You'll make a good board member, and I will try to help get you the seat from Mercer County that Dr. Marian Epstein has vacated."

Since she knew her way around state government in Trenton, I soon found myself taking the oath of office for a five-year term on the State Board. Neither of us realized how working together as a team of women dedicated to better education would bring us closer. Our time together redefined us as equals. Her criticisms about my habit of gravitating to subservient roles dissipated, and she saw me as someone who could make a genuine difference in the world—and she was proud of me.

Losing Mummy

The last years of my mother's life were not easy ones, and old age was not kind to her. Her mind was as keen as ever, but she suffered horribly from arthritic pain in almost all of her joints, particularly in her knees. She lived alone at Sunnyside Farm in a large house on extensive grounds managed by only a staff of four. I once asked her if she would like to come and live with us in Princeton, and she angrily turned me down. She preferred to be independent to the last.

Although she never said so, I believe she really missed my father on whom she depended more than she ever admitted. She missed his good humor and optimism, which mitigated her tendency to pessimism. I once asked her if she ever wanted to have a dinner date with another man in the 12 years she had lived without Daddy.

"No, certainly not," she snapped.

I noticed that Mummy, who had never taken a nap in her life, slept longer in the morning and went to bed earlier in the evening. *She's going to sleep her way into eternity,* I often thought.

Her 75th birthday, on April 30, 1982, would be her last, but we didn't know that.

My sister and I hosted a small party for Mummy on the farm and gave her a book of letters from her family, friends, and colleagues, which were full of stories and praise about her accomplishments. She flipped through it briefly and then set it aside, saying that she'd read it on another day; she wasn't one for reading compliments about herself.

In my letter to my mother on her birthday, I remembered when she visited me at Vassar in November 1948, the day after the election of Harry S. Truman as president and the defeat of Governor Tom Dewey, the pundits' choice. The election stunned the nation. Mummy had entered Lathrop House with my large cardboard laundry case and a box.

"Why didn't Dewey win?" I asked her. She kissed me on the cheek, told me that the box contained brownies, and then said, "Never underestimate the American people." I wrote:

> I cannot remember what else we did and said to each other that day in November, but the picture of you carrying the laundry case and the box of brownies and giving me your perceptions of complex political events has always remained crystal clear. Perhaps because it symbolizes what I have found continually extraordinary about you throughout our years together: your ability to be a loving and attentive mother (and grandmother) to me while, at the same time, having a nearly full-time career as a political leader and politically concerned citizen.

I wrote about how she cared for me in physical and spiritual ways and cared for others. I told her that she taught me the value of helping those who face adversity. The heartfelt words I wrote to Mummy in 1948 still ring true to me 65 years later. Women's perpetual struggle to balance the demands of work and family may never disappear entirely, but I think my mother found that balance.

༄

At a Republican women's luncheon on October 14th, 1982, Mummy had a heart attack and was rushed to Riverview Hospital, in Red Bank, New Jersey. I was in New York City and immediately drove down to see her at the hospital. My last conversation with her before her death only confirmed that she believed my primary role should be stay-at-home mother to my children, even though she herself had ventured out into the world to make a difference.

She looked perfectly healthy propped up against some pillows in her bed in the hospital's intensive care unit. The doctor had assured me that the attack had been a mild one, so I wasn't a bit worried. After we talked for a while, she said to me, "Go home to your children. Take care of them. They need you."

Her closest friend, Connie Ueland, had dropped in and planned to stay and talk a little more. I wish now that I had suggested she leave with me to let Mummy rest, but I didn't. She would be the last person other than hospital staff to see her alive. I certainly didn't expect Mummy to die as I leaned over and kissed her cheek, saying lightheartedly, "I'll be back to see you tomorrow." I wish that I had said, "I love you."

I climbed into my car and drove the hour or so back to New York. My mother's cardiologist called around noon the next day to tell me that Mummy had died of a second, sudden heart attack. I felt bereft, depleted, and so angry that she died alone and I had not been with her.

I called my sister in Grosse Point, Michigan, to convey the sad news and drove back to the hospital. I saw Mummy lying peacefully on a gurney. Her struggles were over: the pain from the arthritis was stilled, and the passions that fueled her public life banked, although I was sure she would have preferred to keep fighting for these causes. She left these causes for me, and in many ways I have walked her path. I whispered goodbye and told her that I loved her very much and always would.

As my mother would have wanted or ordered, I returned to my children to tell them that their grandmother—a public woman who did so much for others, and a private woman who was a good, loving mother to me—had died. True, my mother never told me that she loved me, but when I remember her life as a strong and constant role model and consider the legacy that she left me, I know that she did—and that has made all the difference.

Growing Up

Celery Soup

I was seven years old and alone with our cook in our apartment at 1100 Park Avenue in New York City. The cook, whose name I can't remember, brought me supper on a tray in the playroom. I sat down on a child-sized chair at a child-sized maple table, and she put the tray down in front of me. On it was a spoon and another item: a bowl filled with a thick, white substance, like Elmer's glue. The soup, which had no smell and no character, looked like house paint inside a can. I instantly recoiled.

"What is this?" I asked her.

"This is your supper," she said.

"Yes. What *is* it?" I asked, more insistently.

"It is celery soup. Cream of celery soup," she said.

She towered above me with her hands on her hips. I felt small sitting in my chair. I looked up at her, and she looked down at me. Silence prevailed.

I picked up the spoon, dipped it tentatively into the substance, put the smallest amount on it that the spoon could hold, and placed it in my mouth. I let the soup slide down my throat. It tasted like nothing I had ever tasted before. It tasted *blah, dull,* and I wanted a drink of water to rinse all traces of it from my mouth. But there was no glass on the tray, and I was left with the soup's thickness and strange flavor coating my tongue.

"I don't like it," I said. "Not at all."

"Well, that's all you are getting for supper, so you had better eat it."

"No dessert?" I asked.

"Absolutely no dessert if you don't eat every drop of this soup."

This was not a contest of equals. The cook glowered at me. I was a prisoner in her power. Despite the threat of starvation and no dessert, I continued to look from the bowl to her face, and back again.

"No," I repeated, "I don't like it, and I won't eat it." I wasn't about to budge.

I considered my options as I glanced around the room. There was a bathroom in between the playroom and my bedroom. I immediately planned my strategy: to somehow get this cook person out of the room, make a mad dash to the toilet, dump the soup into it, flush it down, and return to my seat. *Pretty neat way to get rid of the celery soup,* I thought.

As I finished devising my plot, the telephone rang.

"Oh, no you don't," the cook said to me, somehow getting inside my head and, much to my surprise, guessing my carefully thought-out strategy. She ran into the bathroom and locked the door, so I couldn't open it from the playroom, and ran into the kitchen across the hall to answer the phone.

Time was not on my side, and my plan to flush the celery soup away into the New York City sewer system was no longer feasible. I looked around for a place to hide the soup. I opened the closet and decided on the spot that pouring the soup behind the neatly arranged rows of shoes wouldn't work.

Then I spied another possibility: a rectangular radio fit neatly into a space along one of the room's walls. I grabbed the bowl, jerked the radio out of its comfortable spot, poured the soup into the dark space behind it, pushed the radio back, and raced to my seat, placing my empty bowl with the spoon in it on the tray. I felt triumphant.

The cook returned. She stared into the empty bowl. Her face registered complete surprise. She looked straight into my eyes, and I stared right back at her.

"Where is the soup?" she demanded.

"I ate it," I replied.

"Where is the soup?" she demanded again, somewhat menacingly.

"I ate it," I lied.

She unlocked the bathroom door and looked to see if there were any tell-tale remnants of the celery soup on the toilet seat. Finding none, she stopped the interrogation, picked up the tray, and, in a haughty manner, left the room, likely confused that a seven-year-old had defeated her.

Did she bring me applesauce, Jell-O, or junket (a packaged powder that turned into sweet pudding when cooked with milk), the usual desserts offered to young children of my era? I don't remember, but I didn't care a bit. I had evaded the horrible celery soup. I had removed all traces of the hated supper and outwitted the cook—or so I thought.

A couple of weeks later, my mother marched into the playroom and started sniffing.

"Something smells rotten in here," she said to my sister, the governess, and me. She had a sharp nose for smells. She started to systematically make the rounds of the room, sniffing as she went. She didn't leave a stone unturned. She looked behind a bookcase, opened the closet door, pulled the sofa out from the wall, and walked into the bathroom for good measure.

I waited, knowing she was not going to stop until she found the source of that bad odor. She checked the closet, and I felt relieved that I had the good sense to not dump the soup behind the shoes. Eventually, after a five-minute search that felt like five hours, she zeroed in on the radio. I knew she was about to learn the truth. I had thought that the soup would sit behind that radio for years, never disclosing its whereabouts to anyone. I must have used magical thinking to believe that somehow the celery soup would shrink and disappear, leaving no trace.

Even as my mother homed in on the smell, I truly believed that a domineering adult shouldn't force a child to eat celery soup and that "right" was on my side. My mother pulled the radio from its secure place in the wall. It groaned as it gave up its secret.

"What is *this*?" she demanded.

My mother was never intimidated by anything or anyone.

"What is what?" I responded.

"Come and see for yourself," she said, like a detective who finally finds the body.

I looked into the half-darkness and saw the celery soup lying in a round, quiet pool, covered with a thick skin of gray dust. Our governess came over to see the dust-covered mass.

"Oh, that's where she hid it!" she said, looking as if she'd seen a rainbow after a particularly hard rainstorm.

"What?" my mother asked.

Out came the whole story of the celery soup and my leading role. I played my part well: I didn't deny the facts, I didn't burst into tears. I held my ground. I explained that I was in the right: I should not have been forced to eat a food that I obviously didn't like. I said it wasn't right for a grown-up to force a child to do something she didn't want to do.

My mother listened, but in the end, she ruled against me.

"You are going to be punished for this," she said. "You lied not once, but twice, and that is unacceptable. You cannot lie. You will get into lots of trouble if you keep lying."

I couldn't believe that my mother didn't see the righteousness of my cause. She had sided with the cook over me, her daughter. I can't remember the exact punishment she handed down to me. I do know that I wasn't spanked. I was not asked to clean up the soup, which in retrospect would have been a just punishment to fit the crime of deceiving the cook. It would have been good for my soul and probably would have made me think twice about lying in the future.

But the cook and the celery soup weren't the winners in the long run. To this day, I have never, ever eaten a drop of cream of celery soup. Not one single drop.

I won the food fight.

God Save the Queen and My Governess

I have admired Queen Elizabeth II almost all of my life, although not many people know it. When asked about my role models, I never think to mention her and focus instead on Bobby Kennedy and Marian Wright Edelman. But as the queen celebrated her 60 years upon the throne, I found myself thinking about why I have such affection and respect for her. In a strange way, we grew up together on opposite sides of the Atlantic, and the bridge linking our lives was my childhood governess, Mona M. Volckman.

Joanie and I had several nannies and governesses who helped oversee, protect, instruct, and love us from birth until we went away to college. I chafed under this arrangement by the time I was a teen, thinking I was too old for such supervision. But I understood it was necessary: our family lived in only two apartments in New York City over the course of my life—1100 Park Avenue for the early years and then 40 East 66th Street. But our principal residence was at Sunnyside Farm, in Lincroft, New Jersey, where we went every weekend and for three months in the summer. Because we went to school in New York, Joanie and I lived in the apartment during the week with a governess and a cook while our parents lived on the farm. They came into the city a couple days each week, and we returned home to Lincroft on weekends.

The arrangement seemed perfectly natural to us, and I always thought the principal reason for it was my mother's desire to have us attend the Brearley School.

Joanie and I were five and seven respectively when Miss Volckman—or "Volckie," as we called her—entered our lives. The changing of the nanny guard ended with her arrival, and she became a permanent fixture in our household for 12 years. We held her in our affection even after she left our parents' employ when we were in college, and we mourned her when she died in faraway South Africa, where her niece and other family members lived.

I remember when Mummy introduced us to her in the playroom at 1100 Park Avenue. We were aware from snippets of conversation that she was interviewing for the position, and we were eager to see the results. I remember getting up from the floor where I was playing to see who would be our next governess. *Would I like her? Would she like me?*

I saw a well-dressed smallish woman with a cute hat on her head and a warm smile. She radiated high spirits, and I thought having her around would be fun. I had no idea that this woman would become a family fixture or how much I would learn from her, love her, and appreciate her willingness to understand and love me.

"This is Susie, and this is Joan," Mummy said.

I looked at my new governess with curiosity and thought, *Oh, she's smiling. She must like us. She's going to like me, and I will like her.* Somehow I knew that she was going to stay with us. Miss Volckman smiled kindly, took me by the shoulders, and turned me toward the floor-length mirror on the bathroom door. We smiled into the mirror, and I saw us side by side with her arm around my shoulders as if to protect me from anything bad.

"Oh," she said. "You're the difficult one, are you?"

It was a given in my family that Joanie was perfect and I was the troublemaker. Everyone acknowledged this distinction, and it always made me unhappy because I didn't know how to shed the label. (Years later, when I had had an appendectomy, all I kept saying as I awoke from the anesthetic was, "Susie is a good little girl. Susie is a good little girl.")

Volckie smiled as she said this, and I realized that she was teasing me and didn't believe everything my mother had told her. I decided that the description of me couldn't have been all that awful or she would not have accepted the position. On the other hand, perhaps she liked caring for challenging children and didn't want to care for two perfect little girls.

It seemed as if the British Isles came into our world with Volckie's arrival. She was a warm, brown hen of a woman with sturdy shoes, and she spoke every syllable with a perfect English accent. Of Scottish descent, she was the most consummate English person I had ever met in my life.

Volckie's country was her life, and she adored it with a relentless passion. She made it her duty to ensure that my sister and I would come to love all things English almost as much as she did, and over time she used the two English princesses, Elizabeth and Margaret Rose, as a way of fostering this love. The princesses were relatively close in age to me and my sister: Elizabeth, born in 1926, was four years older than I, and her younger sister, Margaret Rose, was exactly my age, born in 1930.

It was natural for Volckie to think that she had come as close as she ever would to caring for the princesses by caring for us—two little American girls from an affluent family who lived on Park Avenue. There were also physical similarities between the princesses and my sister and me: we all had curly hair, light eyes, and fair skin. True, we didn't live in Buckingham Palace, but we had a spacious apartment and a house in the country.

Child-rearing in certain social classes in the thirties and forties meant instruction in good manners, and Volckie decided to use the two princesses as role models to turn us into exceptionally polite, well-behaved little girls. Volckie reminded us about the princesses' impeccable manners. She taught us how to curtsy to our parents and guests and encouraged us to practice on the farm's lawn. When it came to manners, Volckie was a perfectionist. Joanie and I learned how to use our forks and knives correctly according to English standards, to fold our napkins, and never drink our milk when our mouths were full of food. She also stressed neatness, which she considered one of the most important values, and demonstrated how we should keep our clothes neatly arranged in our chest drawers. Later, when she felt it was appropriate, she taught us how to make "hospital corners" on our beds every day.

Volckie also introduced me to and encouraged my love of teatime. She would have deemed it some sort of betrayal of her homeland not to stop every day around four o'clock in the afternoon to have a cup of tea, a British custom. She gave Joanie and me "milk tea," composed of weak tea with lots of milk and sugar. I loved the drink and custom and still stop daily for my cup of tea.

When I first became aware of the princesses, their parents were the Duke and Duchess of York. The Duke of York was second in line to the throne. No one ever imagined he would become king, since his elder brother, Edward, had been crowned king early in 1936. However, in a crisis of the monarchy that shook the English-speaking world, Edward VIII abdicated the throne eleven months into his reign. He renounced the throne to marry the woman he loved, an American divorcée named Wallis Warfield Simpson, whom the Church of England deemed unacceptable as queen.

My sister remembers Volckie crying as she listened to Edward's abdication speech, because she worried for the monarchy's future and believed that the king had brought disgrace on her country. I viewed the abdication without much pity, because radio commentators reported that the king's brother would replace him when he departed. This meant that soon I would be able to more closely follow the princesses' lives. My sister consoled Volckie and assured her that all would be well.

The princesses' father and mother became king and queen of England in a splendid ceremony on May 12, 1937. Volckie woke my sister and me in our shared bedroom in the early light of that morning, so we could hear the proceedings. We listened intently to the small radio placed on the table between our wood-framed beds. There was a hush in the room as we strained to hear every word of the ceremony.

I was thrilled listening to the beautifully clipped voice of the Archbishop of Canterbury as he crowned first the king and then the queen and blessed them. He seemed both close and far away.

After listening to this historic event, the grandeur of which completely enthralled me, there was little holding us back from becoming deeply absorbed in the lives of the princesses. I always played Elizabeth to Joanie's Margaret Rose. (After all, Elizabeth was the heir to the British throne.) Even if Joanie asked for one chance to role-play Elizabeth, I would never allow it. She was much too compliant and good-natured to put up much resistance. I was the eldest, and I was going to play the starring role.

We practiced even more curtsying and dressed alike in clothes especially designed to make little American girls look like the royal princesses. We wore elegant A-line dresses in pastel blues and pinks. Elizabeth and Margaret grew up with corgi dogs, while we had an Irish setter, dachshund, Dalmatian, and pointer to keep us company. Like the princesses, we spent afternoons on the farm riding our ponies, and I made up little plays in which we were the royal princesses having tea with our doll-sized china tea set. Later my sister and I would mark coronation day by playing with painted metal dolls of the king, queen, and princesses dressed in their velvet and ermine coronation robes and jeweled crowns.

I worked hard to perfect my curtsying technique: lifting both arms, crossing one leg behind the other, bending the knees of both legs, extending my hand, bowing my head, keeping my eyes lowered and then rising upright, withdrawing my hand that his or her majesty had graciously touched, and beaming. Despite my hard work perfecting this one act, I realized once beyond childhood that it wasn't going to solve all my problems or get me where I ultimately needed to go in life.

Curtsying was a fun game on the farm, but I lived a sheltered life behind the fences of its fields and had much to learn about reality. Somehow I got it into my seven-year-old head that I was special because we lived on a large farm and had servants who did most of the work in the house and on the farm. We went to school in New York, didn't play with any local children, and filled the void with the princesses, who became our friends.

In July 1939, my mother informed us that King George VI and Queen Elizabeth were coming to the Red Bank train station minutes from our home. I was old enough to realize that this was momentous news and the town would become the center of national attention because of their history-making visit. The monarchs planned to take a train from Washington, D.C., after they had met with the president and first lady, disembark at Red Bank, and transfer to a car headed to Sandy Hook, where they would board a boat that carried them to New York City.

The news of the king and queen's stop in ordinary Red Bank made me delirious with excitement. The idea that I would breathe the same air as royalty was too much to comprehend. Suddenly, those two special people connected to me only through the radio, who were crowned in the cathedral and inspired hours of my imaginative play, were about to become real—and I was going to actually see them in the flesh.

Mummy reported that two little girls would be chosen to present a bouquet of flowers to the queen as she stepped off the train. I immediately decided that my sister and I would be selected for the presentation ceremony. After all, we were close in age to the princesses.

I increased the number of curtsies in my practice routine. I was particularly critical of Joanie's curtsies and made her do them over and over again. I would make impudent remarks to her, such as, "Oh that curtsy will never do," and sometimes I even suggested that I would be the only child chosen for the honor. Of course, my curtsies were perfect and did not require any polishing. No one, especially Volckie, voiced any words of caution that would bring me down to earth. My hopes were high that the selection committee was going to choose my sister and me.

Yet as the day approached, I began to realize that we were not going to get the invitation. I watched to see if some stranger would appear at the gate with the coveted tidings of joy. I listened every time the phone rang, waiting to hear Volckie or my mother say, "But of course, Mr. Mayor, Susie and Joan would be happy to present their majesties with a bouquet of flowers and welcome them to Red Bank."

I was right: the honor went to the mayor's two little granddaughters. We did have choice seating to watch the arrival however. My mother arranged for us to view it from the second floor of a little store that sold newspapers and other sundries across from where the train arrived. My sister and I had a good look at the king and queen when they stepped out of the train—she beautiful in a pale-blue dress with a large, matching hat sweeping up from her forehead, and he resplendent in a military uniform. The two little girls performed their role well, but I was sure that my sister and I would have far out-curtsyed them. The air had escaped from the balloon, and I was disappointed. After all, I had a British governess who schooled my sister and me in the ways of royalty. How could the officials not know about our training and reward its merit?

Volckie's influence in our lives increased when Britain declared war on Germany on September 3, 1939, and she decided to do all she could to ensure victory for her beloved country. I was only nine, but I learned a great deal that year from the adult conversations around me, the daily war reports on the radio, and the newsreels preceding the movies Volckie took us to see. I learned about the Nazis' invasion of Europe, the extraordinary evacuation of British and French troops from Dunkirk, France, and the Battle of Britain, in which the Nazi air force pummeled England with air raids—raining bombs on cities, military installations, and other targets.

I also learned something deeper about the character and courage of the British people and their so-called "stiff upper lip." In newsreels, I saw quite ordinary people standing ankle-deep in the rubble of their homes maintaining that they could withstand any attack and certain that their determination would bring victory.

As the war took hold and we learned to live with it on a daily basis, we played princesses less as Volckie put us to work for the war effort. We knitted squares of khaki wool ("knit one row, pearl one"), which she sewed together to make blankets for the troops. We collected scrap aluminum foil and tried to plant a victory garden behind our playhouse.

Volckie introduced me to the geography of England. I learned about the White Cliffs of Dover that are part of the British coastline. She read aloud from the short verse novel *The White Cliffs*, by Alice Duer Miller, which tells the story of Susan Dunne, a young American tourist who marries a young, upper-class Englishman named John on the eve of World War I. John is killed in France after their son is born, and because of her love for the country, she stays in England to raise him as an Englishman.

The novel's opening lines explained my governess's deep love for her country—a love that I, as an American child, could not fully understand.

> *I have loved England, dearly and deeply,*
> *Since that first morning, shining and pure,*
> *The white cliffs of Dover I saw rising steeply*
> *Out of the sea that once made her secure.*
> *I had no thought then of husband or lover,*
> *I was a traveler, the guest of a week;*
> *Yet when they pointed 'the white cliffs of Dover,'*
> *Startled I found there were tears on my cheek.*
> *I have loved England, and still as a stranger,*
> *Here is my home and I still am alone.*
> *Now in her hour of trial and danger,*
> *Only the English are really her own.*

The war came even closer to me than I could have ever guessed when my father enlisted in the Marines after the bombing of Pearl Harbor. I wanted the war to end in victory for the Allies, so Daddy would come home and Volckie's family, who were in England through the worst of it, would survive. I shared in the euphoria when the war in Europe ended in June 1944 and the war in Japan ended in 1945. I remember exactly where I was when I learned the good news that both had ended in triumph.

Volckie stayed with our family for five years after the war ended, but nothing that she did for me later in my life exceeded the loyalty and love of country that she showed me during those war years. My confidence about the protection that my family's wealth and class afforded me had been shaken by the war, and I realized that there was nothing particularly special about me—all those brave people withstanding the bombings in London every night were far worthier of respect and admiration.

My romance with the royal princesses didn't end with the war. I followed their lives as they grew up and felt especially close to Princess Elizabeth as my life progressed. I watched the television broadcast of her marriage to Prince Philip, the Duke of Edinburgh, in Westminster Abbey in November 1947, and her coronation in the same place on June 2, 1953, when she took the oath to serve her people. I followed the births, lives, and marriages of her four children. Some of my life's major events, including marriage and childbirth, coincided with her own. In 1952, *Time* magazine chose her as "Woman of the Year," a high honor, and I beamed. The caption beneath the lovely image of her smiling face on the cover spoke a new universal truth: "On a hardy stalk, a new bloom."

Volckie had chosen a good role model for me.

Volckie's birthday is on August 7th, and I try to remember each year. But more important, I honor her every afternoon by having my cup of tea, with lots of milk in it, of course.

A Magical Farm and a First Lady

The most important home of my life as a child and adolescent was Sunnyside Farm, which my parents purchased when I was two years old. It was a well-named farm: from my earliest childhood memories to the last time I walked the property to say farewell after its sale and my mother's death in 1982, I think of it as bathed in sunlight. My parents' intense love for the house, farm buildings, trees, flower gardens, and clear brook that bordered the acreage was palpable, and I couldn't have imagined a more beautiful place to grow up.

Sunnyside had everything required for a genuine working farm: a dairy where the milk cows gave milk; shelters for beef cattle; pens for pigs; coops for egg-laying hens; a brick silo, where silage was kept to feed the animals during the winter; corncribs, where ears of corn raised in the fields were stored; a small apple orchard; a large vegetable garden; a rose garden; and a kennel for our dogs. It also had a comfortable stable with stalls for eight horses and a tack room where we hung ribbons won at competitions and shows.

The centerpiece of the farm was a large, white farmhouse with dark-green shutters that was built in 1760. The second floor had five bedrooms and five bathrooms, and Joanie and I shared a bedroom to the left of the handsome staircase that led from the ground floor. We could shut a door that separated us from our parents' bedroom and dressing rooms and thus keep secrets from them. Of course, our governess also lived in this part of the house, so she kept a close eye on us.

We would lie on our single beds and listen to special radio broadcasts that brought history to life: the abdication of King Edward VIII, in December 1936, the coronation of King George VI and Queen Elizabeth, in May 1937, and many New Year's Eve reports from Times Square. We would lean toward the radio to better hear the countdown. (I still don't feel the New Year has properly arrived until I watch the ball drop at that ceremony.)

The farm extended over a spacious 127-acre property. A gentle, babbling brook cut through it on the east and flowed south. Tall locust trees, which we fondly referred to as "The Grove," stood on a rise along the dirt road leading to the brook and formed the highest point of the property. Our family would have picnics in The Grove, and in early June, my sister and I would gorge on the wild strawberries that dotted the rising slope. They were one of the most delectable foods I ever ate, sweeter than the sugar lumps I sucked before feeding them to our horses. After our mouths and fingers were smeared with strawberry juice, we would walk down to the brook to paddle our feet in the cool water, careful to avoid the poison ivy.

Joanie and I would also play "Pooh Sticks," a game I had learned from reading *Winnie the Pooh*. We would stand on the left side of the sturdy bridge that spanned the brook and hurl our sticks upstream as far as we could, and then rush to the right side to see whose stick would finish first after going under the bridge. We would squeal with delight and cry, "Mine won! Mine won!"

We were always creative and happy playing on the lawns of Sunnyside. We would play dress-up and pretend we were getting married. Always the bride, I would wear a long slip—purloined from my mother's bureau—and a piece of fabric for a wedding veil, and carry a sheaf of forsythia. My sister would wear a black tie and high silk hat, removed from my father's closet.

Childhood was a magical time of life for me, and I assumed for children everywhere. I didn't know that not every child in the world collected eggs in the chicken coop and watched the blacksmith put new shoes on her own pony. I took for granted all of the farm's fascinating attractions and never wondered how other little girls around the world lived. I was a little princess in a magical realm.

◈

Christmas at Sunnyside was sumptuous and fragrant. My parents would place a ceiling-high pine tree in a corner of our wood-paneled library a few days before the holiday. There it sat, giving off its lovely odor until Joanie and I were snug in our beds with visions of sugarplums dancing in our heads. I assumed that Santa would trim the tree with Mummy's and Daddy's assistance, but in reality, they raced to trim it on Christmas Eve after Joanie and I went to bed, making sure that the library door was firmly closed, so we couldn't sneak a peek. I could never figure out how Santa could trim that tree with all the beautiful ornaments and tinsel, leave mounds of presents, and then make it to another child's house—but I didn't dwell on it for too long.

Once inside the library on Christmas morning, I always checked to make sure that the same blue-and-gilt star topped the tree. After I found it in place, I would turn to the huge pile of presents (mine always on the right and Joanie's on the left), feeling relieved—since Santa only brought presents to good little girls—and happy for the hours ahead of me in which to tear away the pretty paper and ribbons.

When my mother finally ended her Christmas productions, she agreed to give the star to me, and it topped my tree for years. Eventually, my grandchildren wanted to have Christmas in their own homes (Santa knew their addresses and not mine), so I gave it to my daughter Penny, who faithfully places it on top of the tree in her home.

We had other holiday traditions, including one we've kept unbroken through the years. Every Christmas Eve, the oldest female family member reads the beloved Clement C. Moore poem, "'Twas the Night Before Christmas," to the children before they go to bed. This solemn obligation has fallen to me for many Christmases now, and I have kept faith with my past and my parents' tradition. The simple act of reading this poem touches my heart.

Life at Sunnyside Farm taught me the importance of security for a child—not just the security that comes from possessions, but also the kind that comes from beautiful surroundings. The farm's environment connected me to the life energy that filled my body and encouraged me to skip, run, and laugh. It taught me multiple lessons about hard work, farming the good earth, the vagaries of nature, and caring for animals. I learned that people are dependent on their surroundings; in my case, this included my parents, the household help, and the farmworkers who toiled from dawn to dusk to make our home run smoothly.

But not everything *always* came up roses for me at Sunnyside Farm.

Mrs. Roosevelt Comes to Lincroft

When I was ten years old, I saw First Lady Eleanor Roosevelt up close and personal near Sunnyside Farm. She was a good friend of my godmother, Geraldine Thompson, who lived in a grand house on an estate near us in Lincroft. Mrs. Thompson was an active Republican who worked hard for women's causes. Party difference was not as apparent in the forties as it is today, and women tended to overlook it and work together on social concerns.

Every year, Mrs. Thompson hosted a large pet show at her estate to raise money for local charities. The show had many classes in which animals—mostly the pet dogs and cats of the child contestants—were judged in a large show ring and awarded colored ribbons in various categories, including largest, smallest, and prettiest. The climax of the pet show was a class for pets and their owners dressed in costume to illustrate a literary or other theme.

One September, my mother reported that Mrs. Roosevelt had accepted my godmother's invitation to come to the annual pet show and was going to judge the final children's event: using pets in a creative way. I was thrilled, not because I knew anything about the Roosevelt administration's work helping people dig out from the Depression, but because I would see my first flesh-and-blood first lady, a VIP of some magnitude. I was determined to attract her attention and impress her with my cleverness. I imagined her judging my entry as the best and getting my picture taken with her for the local paper as she handed me my blue ribbon.

I had a wide choice of animals from the farm. One of our sows had given birth to a litter of piglets, and my fertile mind came up with the idea of using one of them to dramatize the well-known nursery rhyme "Tom, Tom the Piper's Son":

Tom, Tom the piper's son
Stole a pig and away he run,
The pig was eat and Tom was beat
And Tom went roaring down the street.

I didn't plan on following every detail of the rhyme—particularly the part "the pig was eat" and "Tom was beat"—but I decided to dress up as Tom and hold a sweet little piglet under my arm. I knew the pig would be scrubbed clean by our farmer and concluded that Mrs. Roosevelt would be charmed by my originality. I imagined that she might leave New Jersey and tell all her friends—and perhaps even the president himself—about the clever little girl in New Jersey who had won the contest by dressing up as Tom and carrying a piglet. I might even become famous.

I was right about originality. No other children had thought of carrying a baby piglet into the show ring, since they had figured out ahead of time that it was dangerous territory. Mrs. Roosevelt entered the ring and immediately dominated it. She seemed to fill the entire ring with her long black coat and her black hat perched on the side of her head. I wondered if there would even be room in the ring for all the children with their animals.

A pet show official ordered me and the other contestants to walk around the edge of the ring carrying our respective animals, so that Mrs. Roosevelt could judge us and the audience, which was lined three deep around the fence, could applaud. I was ready in my bright red-and-green costume, but the minute the farmer handed me the piglet, it began to squeal.

I had not anticipated this possibility and was completely unprepared for what happened next. The piglet squealed and squealed and squealed—each squeal higher-pitched and louder than the one before. The noise was deafening, and the other children, with their perfectly behaved, silent pets, stopped in their tracks. My piglet was stealing the show, but certainly not in the way that I had intended.

Then I heard these devastating words from Mrs. Roosevelt in a loud, clipped accent that no one in or outside the ring could possibly miss: "Will someone please take that pig out of here?" Suddenly from all sides, people ran to obey the first lady's command, and I soon found myself run out of the ring. Our farmer appeared from nowhere, took the squirming, squealing pig out of my hands, and ran back to the truck in which he and the piglet had arrived. I was left outside the ring while Mrs. Roosevelt went back to judging the best contestants. I was crushed.

In the nursery rhyme, Tom came to no good end, and the same could be said of me. Tom was "beat" and so was I. My dream of winning the blue ribbon and receiving it directly from Mrs. Roosevelt's hand vanished. As I stood beside the show ring, I was awash in disgrace, but I had to stay and applaud the lucky winner: a girl dressed up as a scarecrow with a pet crow resting quietly on her shoulder. A picture of the fortunate winner with a beaming Mrs. Roosevelt by her side appeared on the front page of the local paper.

My mother found me in a state of dismay and kindly suggested that we leave the scene. I had missed my big chance to impress the first lady and attain a new height of importance in the eyes of my family and community. I'm not sure why I felt the intense desire to seem important and shine for others, but I did. I wanted to be a big fish in a small pond. I recovered from Mrs. Roosevelt's rebuff, and what occurred in that show ring never changed my deep admiration for her—and I didn't stay mad at the piglet either. It wasn't his fault.

My Riding Life

Riding horses came almost as naturally to me as breathing when I was young. I caught its rhythms from the start, and it made me feel strong and powerful. I loved urging my horse onto the correct lead in a canter and sailing over fences, the higher the better. I was on top of the world when on top of a reliable horse.

I never saw my mother on a horse, but I saw my father ride, compete in horse shows, and hunt (or "ride to the hounds," as this aspect of the sport was called in the thirties and forties). When he went hunting, Daddy was always dressed in correct riding or hunting attire: black leather boots shined to a high gloss with silver spurs attached at the heel; a fitted, black jacket with satin lapels; and a black, silk top hat. It filled me with pride to watch him urge his horse over the jumps.

My father introduced me to the sport when I was five and showed me that it was daring and fun. After giving me the gift of riding for six or so years, he swiftly ended my love affair with it when I was eleven.

❧

Two grooms on Sunnyside Farm, Jim Hanahan and Steve Boland, cared for the horses at separate times and were my first riding teachers. Their lessons came easily to me because I was young, fearless, and confident. Daddy owned both hunters and jumpers, and I learned to ride on a brown-and-white piebald named Prudence. At certain times, she lived up to her name. One week, she decided to test our relationship by bucking me off her back every day. She always did it right in the front field of the farm, a distance from the fence where the groom and sometimes my parents were watching. Prudence and I would be cantering along when she would stop, put her head down, and buck me from her back. I usually landed to the side of her, and since I had let go of the reins, she would make off to the barn. My father made it clear to me that I should get right back on the horse if I was thrown off. The groom would catch Prudence and wait for me to walk back up the field and climb back onto the saddle. For some reason, there was only one buck a day, and then after I returned to her saddle, she became a perfect angel.

One day when Prudence bucked, I flew over her head and landed on my back, looking straight up into her muzzle. She picked up one foot and stepped delicately right onto the center of my chest, and then she picked up her other foot, placed it over my body, jumped over me, and galloped toward the gate, where the groom Jim would normally be waiting. But he wasn't that day, because, sure that she had stepped on my heart, he was running at breakneck speed toward me as I lay on the ground. He scooped me up and started running toward the house, scared to death. He screamed at the top of his lungs and somebody appeared at the front door.

I tried to shout over the din: "There is nothing the matter with me! Please put me down!"

He finally heard me.

"Daddy says I have to get back on the pony, and that is what I am going to do," I said.

Some days later, Prudence stopped bucking me off her back, because I had learned how to deal with the situation. Every time I saw her lowering her head—whether we were walking, trotting, or cantering—I jerked my reins till she threw her head up, knowing I had foiled her plan.

At the age of five, I was riding Prudence when I won my first ribbon at the Monmouth County Horse Show. I was in a class for children called the "lead line class" because an adult—in my case, our groom Steve—walked a child on a pony around the show ring with other contestants. I and the other children knew we would be judged on how well we sat on our ponies and how well we posted up and down on our saddles when we were asked to trot. When the judge requested it, the adults leading our ponies guided them into the center of the ring and lined them up. The judge would walk by, look at us sitting on our ponies with our eyes riveted between the pony's ears (which we all hoped were pricked), and ask each of us to back up our mounts a few steps.

I was excited to ride in the Monmouth County Horse Show, a sizable event. Right before Steve and I entered the ring, he took out a small cardboard book of matches, tore off the matches, folded the cardboard over, and tucked it between the saddle and my left knee.

Steve said, "I don't care what color ribbon you win, but do not let this matchbook drop onto the ground the entire time you are in the ring."

He patted my knee as I pressed down on the matchbook cover.

"Did you hear what I asked you to do?" He stared straight at me.

"Yes. I should not let the cover drop on the ground, even when I am trotting. Is that right?"

"Yes, that's right," he said.

Whatever happened in that ring, I would not allow that piece of cardboard to drop. I jammed my knees into the saddle and straightened my back as Steve walked Prudence and me into the ring. I had never tried harder to keep my knees pressed into the saddle. An important riding rule is to never allow any daylight to show between your knees and the saddle. Steve made sure that I would remember this rule as he took me through my paces.

At the end of the class, I was awarded a white ribbon for fourth place. The rosette was placed on the left side of Prudence's bridle. With Steve in the lead, I rode her out of the show ring where my mother, smiling proudly, greeted me.

"You were wonderful. You rode so well," she said.

But I wasn't interested in my mother's praise or the little white ribbon fluttering from Prudence's bridle. For once, competitive little me wasn't disappointed that I didn't see a bright blue ribbon on her bridle. I was thinking about that little piece of cardboard that I could still feel between my left knee and the saddle. I had followed Steve's instructions as I had promised.

Prudence stood still as I slowly drew my knee back from the saddle, staring intently as I moved it away from the matchbook cover. The intensity of my knee's pressure had glued that cardboard to the saddle, and nothing would dislodge it.

"Look, Steve," I said, "It's still there."

I felt a glow of triumph. I had been asked to do something challenging, and I wanted to show Steve that I did what he had asked me to do. I knew that in the long run, the lesson of disciplining myself to never show daylight between my knees and the saddle would win me more prizes than if I had won first prize in that one class.

The next year at the same horse show, when I was six, I progressed from winning fourth to winning the lead line class on Prudence. She had a blue ribbon on her bridle, and I had a silver cup, the first of many I won over the years. This time, Steve didn't ask me to keep a matchbook cover beneath my knee, perhaps because he was sure that I no longer needed to be reminded not to show any daylight between my knees and the saddle.

From Prudence, I graduated to Golden Jubilee, a beautiful chestnut pony with a prancing step that Daddy bought for me. When I rode her in a show, her chestnut coat glowed in the sun after Jim had curried, washed, brushed, and toweled it dry. Her four white feet were always spotless, and her mane was either braided or combed to show off her neck when she arched it as we rode. Sometimes Jim put a wad of gum under her tail, so she would arch that, too. To this day, I believe we did well because of her classy way of moving; she made me look good whenever we competed.

Once Golden Jubilee helped me beat one of the all-time great United States equestrians, William C. Steinkraus, in one class in a New Jersey horse show. Billy (as he was known in horsey circles) was five years older than I and, as an adult, competed in five Olympic games—winning gold, silver, and bronze medals over several decades. His specialty was show jumping in a ring, and one sunny afternoon in 1941, when I was 11 and he 16, we found ourselves competing against each other in the same horsemanship class.

The class didn't involve any jumping. We simply had to walk, trot, and canter around a ring, back our mounts, and perform a figure eight that required changing leads at key moments. At the end of the first phase, the judge asked Billy and me to change horses, which was a common request if the competition was close. The purpose was to see how quickly a rider would adjust and respond to a horse she or he had never ridden before.

Knowing of his reputation as the best rider, I was excited about the chance to ride Billy's horse. I dismounted and began to take my stirrups off my saddle, so I could transfer them to Billy's. I noticed that Billy didn't look happy, since he likely realized that his feet would be much closer to the ground on my pony than they had been on his own mount. Indeed, his feet dangled far below where they should have rested while I mounted a larger horse and looked in perfect proportion to it.

At the judge's command, we took to the rail, and Billy's horse performed perfectly for me. On the other side of the ring, I noticed that Golden Jubilee was giving Billy trouble. She would not follow his commands to trot and canter. Usually she was a lamb when I asked her to change a gait, but not on this particular afternoon.

With an assist from Golden Jubilee, I beat Billy Steinkraus one afternoon in one insignificant show. The victory became good dinner-table conversation for my parents, and Billy went on to win the ASPCA Maclay Cup and the Good Hands finals at the National Horse Show in Madison Square Garden that November. The twin victories established his preeminence as the finest rider in the nation.

He had a distinguished riding career, becoming the first American to win an individual equestrian gold medal at the Olympics. I'm sure he never thought back to the afternoon when he rode my pony, but whenever I read about his amazing exploits over the years, I found myself smiling: once, in my equestrian career, I had the better of him.

On December 7, 1941, the Japanese attacked Pearl Harbor, and the United States declared war on the Nazis and their allies. I didn't know the effect that this attack would have on my riding life until a few weeks later when I came down to breakfast in the dining room at Sunnyside. I sat down and looked over at my father to wish him good morning. Yet before I could get the words out, he said, "Jim is going to be drafted, and therefore there will be no more riding." Daddy explained that he was hoping to get back into the service, and no one else could care for the horses. At 11, I was not going to be able to fill the void; I barely knew how to muck out a stall and care for a horse on a daily basis.

I could hear from the seriousness of my father's tone that there was no use protesting. He didn't give a lot of orders, and when he did, we paid attention. I realized that the war was going to ask something of each of us, and I did not want to be considered spoiled and selfish. My father did not approve of spoiled, selfish children.

I soon moved on to summer camp and acting, yet I never forgot riding. It gave me a feeling of personal competence unmatched by anything else I did as a child. On a horse, I felt confident about my ability to make my way in the world. Riding was my first real passion, but early passions cool with time, and I never faulted my father for his decision to end my involvement in it. He showed me that there are financial limitations to some activities: a good value to learn early in life. But the fact that he introduced me to and championed riding in my early years conferred the more lasting gift of tenacity.

When I was an adult, a magazine writer described me as "charming but tenacious." My son, Dwight, sent me a T-shirt he had created with my picture and the words "Charming *and* Tenacious," which I loved to wear. I owe a lot of my tenacity to learning and loving to ride.

Camp Arcadia

As U.S. involvement in World War II grew closer, my mother decided to send me to sleepaway camp, which was popular for children of families with means. A Brearley classmate's mother had told her about Camp Arcadia, a summer camp for girls in Casco, Maine.

So in late June 1941—after only peripheral involvement in such preparatory activities as sewing nametags on uniforms and collecting items on the new-campers' supply list—I found myself in Grand Central Station. I was 11, surrounded by mostly older girls, waiting for the train that would take me away from my parents, sister, and Sunnyside Farm for eight weeks. Soon I would arrive in Portland, Maine, and transfer to an open, flatbed truck that would take me to a secluded, private camp on a lake that I had never seen.

Looking back 71 years later, the closest thing I can compare to the experience of that long-ago June morning is the scene in *Harry Potter and the Sorcerer's Stone* when the children with luggage-filled shopping carts on Platform 9 ¾ say goodbye to their parents before boarding the train to Hogwarts. I'm sure that they felt the same confusion, loss, and excitement that I did milling around Grand Central Station.

I stood next to my mother and father, surveying the other girls. I knew no one. I was told that my classmate's parents were driving her to camp, and then I heard my mother, who had promoted going to camp, suddenly backtrack and say, "You don't have to go, darling, if you don't want to go. We can go home."

I looked up at her in bewilderment, wondering, *After all the nametags on all those camp uniforms?*

Luckily, before I could counter, my father overruled her.

"Of course, she's going. This is not the moment to suddenly change your mind. You're going to be fine, and you're going to have a wonderful time," he said.

I had no fear about what the summer held in store for me, but I was worried that Daddy might back down and give in to Mummy's anxieties, because I had seen it happen before.

Daddy is right, I thought to myself. *If I turn back at the station gate, it would signal that I could turn back whenever I was in a new situation.* What he and I didn't realize was that walking through that gate would provide four summers of happiness and contribute significantly to the development of my character.

I started life at Camp Arcadia as a plebe in a cabin with four other girls my age and an older girl, who was our counselor. The hundred or so campers came from up and down the East Coast. One girl arrived from Virginia, and I admired her for having come so far. The girls were like me: white, affluent, private-school students whose parents wanted them to have solid learning experiences in a safe, beautiful setting.

I loved the camp at first sight. The dark-green wooden cabins blended with the towering pine trees. The cabins for the juniors, plebes, and seniors dotted the hillside down from the Main Lodge. The hill melted into a sandy beach at the edge of Pleasant Lake, and the water was always fresh and cool. It was ideal for the swimming and canoeing that formed the core of the summer program. It could be problematic for sailing, though, as the wind was rarely strong enough for us to learn how to sail in difficult situations. (I really liked sailing, except for the many times I was marooned in the middle of the lake in a dead calm.)

George Meylan founded the camp in 1916, and George's daughter, Juliette Meylan Henderson, directed it (we called her "Mum-Mum"). The Meylans owned a large farm that provided fresh food for the campers. Even during the war years, we ate delicious, family-style meals in the dining room. A dessert beloved by all was a "mud pie," a combination of sponge cake and warm chocolate sauce, which we ate with relish on Friday evenings. Only one food restriction was placed on us: at Sunday lunch, we couldn't have the delectable ice cream, freshly churned from cream produced by the farm's cows, unless we had written a letter home and shown the stamped envelope to our counselor during the week. I never missed Sunday dessert. (My mother faithfully wrote me several times a week, and from time to time, I'd get a short note from my father, always written in his beautiful, flowing script.)

I was never homesick. There was no reason for it, because I was up-to-my-chin in exciting activities. From the start, Arcadia's focus on individual effort and accomplishment matched my ambition to succeed. I liked to learn, and the program's structure appealed to this side of my personality. The activities—led by well-trained counselors with different areas of expertise—weren't competitive but rather based on progressing from basic to expert levels. Every Sunday night, our personal accomplishments were rewarded at an all-camp meeting in the Main Lodge, where Mum-Mum called our names and handed us a little felt emblem signifying the sport or activity in which we had achieved a specific level.

The first level gave you a yellow emblem; the second, a white; the third, a red; and the fourth and highest level—an unattainable one, unless you had special talents or spent three or four years at Arcadia—a bright blue. We pinned or sewed the emblems onto our blue felt banners or guarded them zealously and took them home for someone else to sew.

Campers treasured their banners, brought them back to camp each summer, and hung them on a wood stud above their cot. The older campers, and counselors' banners were laden with felt emblems, which motivated me. One could tell at a glance how hard a girl worked at camp and in what sports and activities she excelled. I treasured my banner and enjoyed seeing it fill out from year to year. I was satisfied to know that I had attained a fourth level in swimming, canoeing, camp-craft (which included trips to remote parts of Maine, learning how to camp and survive outdoors), sailing, dramatics, and a few other activities, including *Chipmunk Chatter,* the little weekly newsmagazine written by campers.

I kept my banner in my possession for many years and loved to look at it, because it was like a piece of modern art with its four colors and variety of emblems positioned in intriguing patterns. Over the years, when life's accomplishments were not so immediate, I would look at it and the feeling of accomplishment I craved would wash over me.

My only granddaughter, Olivia, asked to see my old banner after she returned from her first summer at Camp Arcadia, and I discovered that I'd lost it. It saddens me that I can't use my emblems to talk about how our interests are the same or different. I'd like to tell her about my emblems for two American Red Cross certificates: First Aid and Junior Lifesaving. I aced the comprehensive First Aid test, which included learning to stop blood flow using the body's pressure points, and how to use a tourniquet and apply splints for different broken bones. The United States was at war during three of my summers at camp, and doing well on a First Aid test made me feel like I was part of the war effort. I thought I might even qualify as a Red Cross volunteer, offering first aid in case the Nazis bombed my town. (Nothing like a whiff of success to get the thoughts rolling!)

The Junior Lifesaving test was part of the third swimming level, and I thought I was going to lose my life learning how to save someone else's. We learned that it was best to help drowning people by throwing them a life preserver, oar, or log, or rowing a boat and pulling them into it. Swimming to them was a last resort, yet in order to attain the Junior Lifesaving certificate, we had to swim into deep water, remove our clothes except for our bathing suit, and then swim a certain distance more toward a buoy, which marked the drowning person.

For the test, we wore our sneakers and camp uniform, which consisted of a pair of shorts and a short-sleeved, V-neck shirt that was hard to pull over our heads. On the morning of the test, I swam out to a deep place, removed my sneakers and shorts, and tossed them into the rowboat of the counselor who accompanied me. I swam away from her boat, crossed my arms, and grabbed my sodden shirt at its edges. I began tugging it over my head until, when it was at shoulder height, I found that it and I were stuck. I couldn't pull it any farther over my head, and I couldn't pull it back down to my waist.

Water began to rush into the vacuum I had created, and I began to sink. I probably wasn't in any danger, but I felt that death was approaching. I had read that when one is drowning, one's life passes in review, and I was sure that this was about to happen when suddenly my counselor's arm reached down and dragged me up to the surface. Somehow she checked off the test item, and she didn't have to remind me that a swimming rescue could have its pitfalls.

The war occurring outside of camp spurred me to excel in another activity: picking string beans, for which I had an emblem in all four levels. Campers traveled by truck to the nearby farm to pick string beans on its many acres. Adult labor was scarce during the war years, and even small fingers could harvest the ripe beans that would be sent to a local cannery and eventually overseas for the troops. I was excited to do something for my country. After all, my own father had joined the Marines, and other campers' fathers had also enlisted or re-enlisted in the service. We were proud of them.

Once at the farm, we each received a large burlap bag and were directed to the fields. We walked up and down the rows—reaching high and low, in and out—to snap off those bright green beans. When told to stop, we dragged our bags to a big scale to have them weighed (we were paid one cent for every pound).

I remember my first day's weigh-in: I stood next to my bulging bag, which seemed as tall as I was and probably weighed as much. A farmer helped me pull it onto the scale, and I watched the arrow waver until it came to rest on 96. I knew that my friends had picked 90, 92, and 94 pounds, but no one had picked 96 pounds. (My competitive juices were flowing!)

"You did it," the farmer said to me. "You topped the scales. Your 96 is the largest number of pounds picked today."

I felt a wave of satisfaction, but I didn't say a word. I didn't care if he gave me 96 cents or not. I wanted to pick the most beans for our troops (but I also liked to win competitions!).

I climbed back into the open truck with the other campers, and we were soon singing, "We've been working in the bean fields, all the livelong day," a new version of an old favorite, "I've Been Working on the Railroad." The sunset seemed especially pretty, and I felt that we had done valuable work for the war effort.

Although I had made friends at camp and enjoyed achieving ever-higher levels in most activities (except archery and riflery), I couldn't explain why I was not "tapped" for the Honor Society. The most successful, well-liked girls were chosen to be its members because they exemplified "The Spirit of Arcadia," a spirit characterized by campers who were loyal, wise, busy, honest, strong, brave, contented, dreaming, happy, and reverent.

I believed in the Honor Society with all my heart and wanted more than anything to be "tapped" for it. "Tap nights"—when society members came down the hill holding candles, calling out the names of the newly elected members chosen in secret—were two of the most important ones in the camp season. The members would stand outside the cabins of the girls they'd selected and start the ceremony with this song:

Camp Arcadia, our hearts to you, our hands to you.
We pledge ourselves to your success.
Our love for you will n'ere grow less.
Camp Arcadia, our hearts and hands to you.

The society's leader would say a chosen girl's name and then add, "Come with us now in silence." Two members would enter her cabin, take her hand, and light the way—the new girl wearing a bathrobe and slippers—as they walked her up the hill to the Arts and Crafts building. There, the new pledges agreed to live up to "The Spirit of Arcadia" in thought, word, and deed. They also received a pale-blue satin ribbon to wear with pride to breakfast the next morning.

For two summers at camp, I watched this ceremony unfold and never heard my name called. As I turned on my stomach to go back to sleep after the honored campers had walked up the hill, I felt disappointed and angry with myself for failing the spirit of Arcadia standard and jealous of those who had passed it. No one told you why you failed to be tapped, and you couldn't ask. I finally figured out that I needed to work as hard at being a better camper in the spirit of Arcadia as I did at achieving levels in activities. I made a conscientious decision to attain and demonstrate to others the ten qualities contained in the "The Spirit of Arcadia," and this eventually made me a better person. I became nicer to my counselors and the girls in my cabin. If someone asked for a volunteer, my hand was the first to go up. I tried to do as I was asked and not argue back. If, on a camping trip, the counselors needed someone to dig a hole where we could pee or poop, or find wood for the fire to cook on, I volunteered for the chore. The more difficult and unappealing the chore, the more readily I offered to do it.

It was good that I had to wait until the first tap night of my third summer at Arcadia to hear my name ring out in the darkness. By then I had learned a couple of lessons: helping others is a good habit and reaching a much-wanted goal requires persistence.

In retrospect, I wonder why being in that Honor Society meant so much to me. In late life, I've avoided joining exclusive organizations for a variety of reasons and never regretted my decisions. Why did I so yearn to wear the pale-blue ribbon on my uniform blouse, which identified me as someone who had been tapped? At ages 11 and 12, I simply wanted to be a member of the "in" crowd, and this desire eventually helped me become a better person by thinking of how to assist others first rather than care only for myself and my own desires. I also wanted to make my parents proud of me. My reputation as the family troublemaker haunted me, and I decided that a good camp record was a form of redemption.

Around this time, I reached an important milestone at Camp Arcadia: my first menstrual period. I was one of the last in my cabin and Brearley class to get it. I went to what we called "the john" one cloudless day at camp, pulled down my blue shorts, and looked down to see a dark smudge of blood on my underwear. I was the only girl in the long row of toilets at that time of day, but I didn't call out with pleasure. I felt a warm glow of satisfaction start at my head and flow down to my toes. I double-checked the stain on my piece of toilet paper, pulled up my underpants and shorts, flushed the toilet, and ran up the hill as fast as I could to the nurse's cabin. I couldn't wait to trumpet my accomplishment and get the necessary equipment to wear as a badge of honor. I was coming of age.

Summers at Camp Arcadia were satisfying for me and for Joanie, when she, too, started attending. For four blissful summers, I was a happy camper. I never thought of returning for a fifth summer as a counselor-in-training when I turned 15. My interest in acting was growing stronger, and I wanted to improve that skill. After I became a mother, I hoped that my daughters would catch "The Spirit of Arcadia" and avail themselves of the same wonderful experiences. Only one of the two went and didn't like it all—but my granddaughter, Olivia, has spent two summers among the pines.

In 2013, I went back to Arcadia for Parent-Camper Weekend to spend a full day among the girls and take a swim in Pleasant Lake. Much has changed, but much has remained the same: the pine trees; the delicious lake, still relatively unspoiled by housing developments around its perimeter; the genial counselors; the enthusiastic campers; and the feeling of peace and good fellowship. When I told Olivia's friends that I had been a camper in the 1940s, they looked at me as if I'd said I'd been there in the fourteenth century.

Parents and campers had dinner together under the pines, and then the campers gathered to receive their felt emblems. Names were called out for those who earned "The Spirit of Arcadia" honor, but this was done with much less fanfare than when I was a camper. Olivia was selected for the honor in her first year at camp, which showed she certainly had a leg up on me. Like me, Olivia enjoys riding better than anything else at camp, and that strengthens our bond. (She has "a beautiful seat," as they say in the horse world.)

As the moon rose over Pleasant Lake, the campers began to sing the lyrics that I remembered so well: "Camp Arcadia, our hearts to you, our hands to you. Camp Arcadia, our hearts and hands to you."

I looked from the glowing campfire to the stars above the towering pine trees and felt the true, blue spirit of the little place in Maine that influenced my life for the better—and I felt at peace.

Dramatic Stirrings

When I was seven and in the second grade at Brearley, I decided to become an actress. The fourth-grade French class was putting on a play about Joan of Arc—or "Jeanne D'Arc," as we learned to say in correct French. The teacher who was directing the play came into our second-grade classroom, searching for two younger girls to play Jeanne's cousins in the play. She asked our homeroom teacher to pick the girls.

Since we all wore the same school uniform—navy blue gym suits and blue or white blouses—we looked like peas in a pod with no distinguishing features to make us good choices for a play. We didn't have to do a pronunciation tryout to test our French accent. My homeroom teacher scanned the room until her eyes rested on me.

"Come here, Susie," she beckoned.

I walked to the front of the class, and she turned to the French teacher.

"Why not take her. She had drops in her eyes yesterday, and they won't wear off for a couple more hours. She can't read, so she might as well learn some French."

Little did I know that my eye drops would open up for me a whole new world—of theater—and spark my ambition to succeed in it. Off I went with a classmate, whose name I cannot remember, but to whom I also owe the stirrings of my acting ambitions.

When I first heard the story of Jeanne D'Arc, she became my instant heroine. Here she was, a simple peasant girl tending sheep when "heavenly voices" told her that she should put on armor, mount a white horse, lead her countrymen into victorious battles, and eventually crown the Dauphin, Charles VII, King of France. What could be more thrilling for a seven-year-old than the story of a young girl's gaining glory, helping her country, and doing the will of God? My French teacher withheld the other parts of Joan's story: how she was captured and imprisoned by the English, tried by a panel of high church officials, and found guilty of heresy, and how she chose to burn at the stake rather than accept life imprisonment.

At our first rehearsal, the French teacher taught us the only two lines that were entrusted to us: *Bonjour, ma tante* ("Good morning, my aunt") and *Bonjour, mon oncle* ("Good morning, my uncle"). I recited these lines religiously while looking in my mirror at home and riding the bus to and from school—and I begged anyone at home to listen to me. Fortunately, my parents and my governess spoke French fluently, so they could tolerate my demands to practice my accent.

My classmate and I rehearsed walking and crossing the floor of the classroom, extending our hands, and curtsying to the future saint's aunt and uncle. We were directed to smile politely and deliver our lines in unison. After the greeting, we were to stand with the group of fourth graders playing peasants in Jeanne's town. We rehearsed first in the classroom and then on the large, raised stage of the school's Assembly Hall, which could accommodate the entire student body and faculty.

We performed perfectly in rehearsal, although we never practiced in front of a live audience. I felt completely confident—perhaps a bit cocky—and my classmate gave no indication that she felt anything but the same. I had my lines down pat; I had said them without fail every night before I went to sleep. (I'd been told that you would always remember whatever you recite to yourself if it is the last thing you do before falling asleep.)

We wore costumes, kerchiefs tied under our chins to make us seem more like part of a French peasant family. Perhaps the little kerchief had been tied too tightly under my classmate's chin, because she froze when we came onstage during our one-and-only performance. A quick glance at my classmate's pale face convinced me that I alone was going to have to say our lines. Clutching the hand of my mute companion, I said clearly, "Bonjour, ma tante. Bonjour, mon oncle." Then, still holding her hand, I joined the other fourth-grade peasants.

I was pleased with my performance, and in a burst of perhaps too much self-congratulation, I felt that I had saved the day and Jeanne D'Arc's glory by stepping up and delivering those two lines on cue by myself.

After the applause ended, I became a regular second grader again, but something had happened to me: deep inside, I felt dramatic stirrings that I had never felt before. I liked being on the big stage, stepping into the breach, and delivering those lines. I liked having people tell me I had done a good job: perhaps Jeanne's story of personal courage had rubbed off on me. Whatever it was that I did onstage, I knew down to my toes that I wanted more of it.

As if by magic, I felt that I had discovered something special that I could do differently and well. It was a defining moment for seven-year-old me. I had remained calm and composed in a challenging situation, hadn't blown my lines, and followed the directions I had been given without making a single mistake. This feeling of competence and determination didn't leave me after my performance. I decided to become an actress and didn't waiver from my decision for 14 years.

Dramatics at Brearley

My decision to become a thespian wasn't totally unrealistic, because dramatics played a large role in the curriculum at The Brearley School. Our teachers believed in having us begin early reading and performing scenes from great works of drama early, beginning with the ancient Greek playwrights. In late middle school and the upper grades, we memorized passages from William Shakespeare's plays, including many of his greatest soliloquies, and to this day I can remember quite a few of them. It wasn't all Shakespeare: each sixth grade performed a Gilbert and Sullivan operetta, albeit shortened versions of the originals. My class did *The Mikado* and my sister's class, *The Pirates of Penzance*.

Brearley's philosophy for taking on artistic and academic challenges was "Our girls can do anything—the harder, the better." Spearheading the school's dramatic effort were two superb teachers: Ruth Loud and Mildred Dunnock, whom we called by her married name, Mrs. Urmy. She was a real working actress who played important roles in many Broadway plays during the evening and directed our school plays during the day. She was an intelligent, skillful director, and a gracious star to her students when we saw her in a play. If we wrote a note telling her that we were in the audience, she would invite us backstage to her dressing room. Walking through the backstage entrance—a rather dim, dark alley next to the brightly lit theater—reminded me of walking up a church aisle.

My classmates and I would knock on the stage door and find Mrs. Urmy clad in a dressing gown, smiling as we stood mute before her. I would peer behind her to her dressing table with its large mirror with light bulbs down each side, open jars of cold cream, comb, brush, and makeup.

My first acting role didn't catapult me into instant school-play stardom. I had to work my way up the ladder from bit parts in middle school to eventual leading roles in high school. I also started out on the wrong foot: playing male rather than female roles in my all-girls school. I wanted to play the leading female parts to show that I really had talent; playing male parts showed only that I had a loud voice. Nonetheless, it was easy to cast me as a man, since I was slightly taller than my classmates and my hair was short, wavy, and a bit unruly.

In sixth grade, our class staged a version of the famous biblical story "The Book of Ruth." I prayed for the leading role of Ruth and to this day can recite her famous words to her husband revealing her undying love and loyalty: "Entreat me not to leave thee; for wither thou goest, I will go; and where thou lodgest, I will lodge: thy people shall be my people, and thy God my God." I found them to be incredibly romantic and envisioned having the same feelings someday for my future husband.

My classmate Rachel Morgan, who was cast as Ruth, looked as if she had walked right out of the Old Testament, with her long, black hair and olive skin. I didn't even win the part of her husband, Boaz, which went to a taller classmate, Brenda Gilchrist, who because of her height was doomed to play male leads throughout her years at Brearley. I was cast as "a man in the crowd." I hoped against hope that someone would get sick the day of the play and the dramatics teacher would call upon me to be the replacement, but it never happened.

*
Even in seventh grade, when I played another male bit part, in George Bernard Shaw's *Androcles and the Lion*—a challenging play for middle-schoolers due to the great amount of memorization required and its complex ideas—the fire to become an actress did not die. I forged ahead when, suddenly, one classmate broke out of the ranks due to her special acting talent. Ann Whittlessey was not only a brilliant student but also a gifted artist and actress. She always won the leading roles and could play both genders equally well. Our drama teachers could sense her talent from a long way off. Besides playing the Lion in *Androcles and the Lion*, she played Hecuba, the wife of Priam, the king of Troy, in our tenth-grade dramatics club's production of Euripides' *The Trojan Women*. I admired Ann, knew in my heart that she deserved these roles, and was jealous of her. I wanted to be the best actress in the class, and she was a rival I could never surpass.

After a summer at theater school, I made a breakthrough in Brearley dramatics and finally landed a leading role, Helen of Troy in *The Trojan Women*. Helen's physical beauty is renowned for having "launched a thousand ships" and the Trojan War. For the part, I wore a long, flame-colored dress, draped like those on the famous Greek statues in the Metropolitan Museum of Art and the Louvre. There was a Grecian knot in my wavy hair. Euripides' Helen was the most unsympathetic character in the drama: the Trojan women blamed her for seducing Paris and causing the war that led to the death of their husbands, sons, and extended families and the conquest of their homeland. In contrast, the most sympathetic character was Hecuba—the Queen of Troy and the mother of Hector, the great Trojan hero. Ann played her to perfection. Euripides wrote a serious, anti-war play, but it wasn't the message that was important to me at 15 years old. It was the fact that I had finally landed my best part since second grade.

Without question, Ann's performance outshone mine. She played Hecuba as though the weight of all the Trojan War's losses were on her shoulders. Hecuba made Helen look like a spoiled child who lacked basic concern for others, and no one in the audience could possibly feel any sympathy for her. I struggled to find my footing, hoping that somehow I could eek out a little compassion from Hecuba for Helen.

After the play, everyone raved about Ann's performance, but hardly anyone said anything to me about mine. I was envious of her accomplishment, but my family had taught me long ago that envy was a destructive quality; thus, I tried to suppress my feelings.

✦

Another incident twisted like a knife in my heart after the play. My sister's classmate's mother was a famous theatrical agent, and I heard that she was coming to see it. After it was over, I asked my sister to find out if her friend's mother had noticed me and said anything about my performance. I was told that her only reaction was about my deep-set eyes. The famous agent had said, "Oh, you mean the girl who has no eyes?" I really thought for the moment that the world—or at least mine—had ended.

I didn't know how to solve this physical problem. Later, in theater school and summer stock, I learned to apply small touches of white makeup around my eyes so that they would emerge from my face, and I did this faithfully for every performance in college. I suppose I owe the theatrical agent a debt of gratitude for being honest about my facial problem.

Although Ann stole the show from me in *The Trojan Women,* by senior year we were co-starring in James M. Barrie's *Quality Street,* a charming little comedy by one of England's most famous playwrights. The play was about Phoebe and Susan Trossell, two sisters who start a school for genteel children. Ann had the leading role of Phoebe, the ingénue who falls in love with a dashing young soldier. I played the older, somewhat silly Susan, who had no romantic interests and ended up an old maid. It was a character part, and although I wanted to play leading ladies, I ended up doing a good job with it. Ann and I played to each other's strengths, and this time I wasn't jealous. We received many compliments for our performances and were rewarded for them at our class graduation in June 1947.

Brearley offered only a handful of prizes at graduation, one of which was the Fanny H. Phillips Dramatics Prize, named after a well-respected history teacher. I wanted to win that prize to validate the hard work I had put into pursuing my acting dreams. Several days before the ceremony, a student whispered to me that she had seen a list on the head-of-school's desk and that my name was opposite the heading "Fanny H. Phillips Dramatics Prize." I was sure that Ann would win the award because she played much more challenging roles than I did all through school, but the news gave me hope.

I had a wide ambitious streak, and I didn't even ask myself what winning that prize would do for me other than having my name inscribed in the school records. Perhaps I thought it would help me as I went off to college and then onward to an acting career on Broadway. I liked winning, yet ambition was downplayed among young women of my day.

The class of 1947 did not graduate in the Assembly Hall, which was the usual site of Brearley's graduation ceremonies. The ceremony was moved to Hunter College to accommodate the increased audience, as Mrs. McIntosh ("Mrs. Mac" to the students) was leaving to become the dean of Barnard College. Members of the class—all in matching white dresses with red-rose corsages pinned on our left shoulder—sat onstage while the rest of the students sat in rows in the audience facing them.

Mrs. McIntosh led the ceremony, presented the prizes, and gave the only speech—a review of the graduating class's sterling qualities, idiosyncrasies, and, when germane, scrapes and headaches caused by its members. (The most memorable moment of the ceremony came after the prizes were awarded, and Mrs. McIntosh would say the traditional words, "And now Class V becomes Class VI," mentioning each class as it moved up in the school hierarchy until she reached Class XII. Then she paused and turned to the seniors and said, "And now Class XII will become alumnae.")

My insecurity about the dramatics' prize increased as Mrs. McIntosh announced the other prizes. Finally she said, "And the last prize is the Fanny H. Phillips Dramatics Prize." She turned to the table beside her and picked up two similar-looking packages, each wrapped in white tissue paper and tied with simple dark-red ribbon.

Oh, I thought, *the prize is going to be divided and given to Ann and me.* I was right.

"This year, the prize is given to two students in Class XII whose performances through the years have impressed us: Ann Whittlessey and Susan Neuberger," she said.

As I got up from my seat and walked to the podium, I was relieved that the faculty had done Ann and me a favor by making sure we wouldn't be hurt by the decision. I decided they chose this strategy more for me than for Ann. She had never said that she wanted an acting career. I had done everything I could to inform the world that this was my goal. I'm not sure I was a nice enough person to acknowledge to myself that Ann was a better actress than I was and deserved to win the prize outright.

After graduation, Ann chose to go to Smith College, and we talked about becoming roommates if I also went. I decided a few days after graduation that

I would go to Vassar College instead, and I was relieved to no longer have to compete with her. (I didn't realize I would have to continue competing against all sorts of people to attain my goals.)

No one encouraged me as I traveled down the theater path. My Brearley classmates had envisioned a more managerial rather than performing role in theater for me, and they were probably smarter than I was about my talents. The yearbook editors had written a prophecy, "Fantasia à la '47," for the 41 members of our class. The setting was the Elysian Fields, and to this heavenly place the editors brought all the class members together again to report on what they had accomplished in their lives.

In the first draft of the prophecy, which I had somehow previewed, I was the director or producer of a play. The play's star was Bethel Leslie, a class member who had started acting on Broadway when she was 14 and never appeared in school productions. I didn't want to be a director or producer. In fact, I had no idea what a producer did. I leaned on the editors to change the prophecy, since it was not in its final form. I wince to think that I did this rather than accept their verdict on my future. They acquiesced to my request, and in the final version, they made Bethel the director, noting that "on earth she had Broadway tied to her apron strings." As for me, they wrote, "Susie Neuberger didn't need any explaining; she had been world famous as an actress. Even the natives of Borneo had sent a delegation to her agents begging for a personal appearance."

My classmates knew me better than I knew myself. They knew I possessed managerial talent, since I was captain of the winning sports team and ran a successful, school-wide cookie contest senior year. Bethel lived up to the prophecy for her and had a long, successful career in theater on Broadway; I went to her plays and applauded her triumphs.

In the end, the editors and I saw eye-to-eye on one yearbook section. They had designed a chart for each member of the class with the following categories: "Trick of Singularity," "Where Art Thou Found?" "Give Us a Taste of Your Quality," and "Rude Am I in My Speech." Under "Where Art Thou Found?" they listed "in the theater section" for me, acknowledging my obsession with all aspects of the dramatic arts: acting, seeing Broadway plays, reading plays, and writing about theatrical life whenever we were assigned long, historical papers. They knew that my theater obsession had lasted my entire school life, beginning in that faraway French play in second grade.

We were in complete agreement.

Setting the Stage

By the time I was a teenager, I had been pestering my parents for some good theatrical training. A friend from dance class harbored theatrical ambitions, and her mother suggested that I attend the Rollins Theater School, in East Hampton, Long Island. It had a good reputation, and young people with private-school backgrounds like mine attended it. So at 15, I headed off to the Rollins Theater School for my first summer drama-school experience.

Its founder, Leighton Rollins, was an ebullient, round-faced bald man with a fringe of white hair. He looked like Santa Claus and had a great love for the theater. He had organized a group of excellent teachers to instruct youth like me who'd been severely bitten by the acting bug.

During the eight-week session, we were cast in a series of plays staged for local audiences at the John Drew Theater in East Hampton. We lived together in different houses around town and met each day for classes in acting technique, dance, speech, and singing. For the first time, I didn't have to play male parts, since there were as many boys as girls at the school. It was a relief to no longer worry about being cast as a man, like shedding a heavy coat when the spring crocuses first appear.

Upon arrival, we had to perform a monologue for Mr. Rollins and the teachers. I chose one about a young woman standing on the edge of a New York City subway platform who's about to throw herself in front of a train. I wanted to impress my teachers with a monologue on a subject far more dramatic than my narrow, traditional teen life. I thought they'd be impressed by the difficulty of my choice. They weren't, and in an acting class later on, I learned something important—that it's far better to choose monologues about relatable feelings, because you convey more authenticity to the audience.

At our initial tryouts, a student named Eda Fields quickly established herself as the best actress among us with her superb interpretation of a monologue from George Bernard Shaw's *St. Joan*. Like my monologue, it concerned losing one's own life—but Eda's Joan was a real, flesh-and-blood woman ready to lay down her life for her belief in God. She created a powerful portrayal of the brave French peasant girl responding to her English judges, who had sentenced her to life imprisonment. She wore her long hair in braids around her head and stood absolutely still, with her eyes focused on her judges. Her voice grew stronger with every word:

> *I could do without my warhorse; I could drag about in a skirt; I could let the banners and the trumpet and the knights and soldiers pass me and leave me behind as they leave the other women, if only I could still hear the wind in the trees, the larks in the sunshine, the young lambs crying through the healthy frost, and the blessed, blessed church bells that send my angel voices*

floating to me on the wind. But without these things I cannot live; and by your wanting to take them away from me, or any human creature, I know that your council is of the devil and that mine is of God.

Shaw's words touched a part of my adolescent self that yearned to live dangerously and do something grand. I knew deep within myself that I wanted to do something significant in the world to help people. At the same time, I felt that it was overly presumptuous to have these feelings. Who was I to think I could make any difference in the world? My mother and father helped others through their work, but I didn't see anyone my age trying to do so, and I felt that I was too cocky to even dare dream of saving the world.

Shaw's Joan made me realize that some people are willing to die for their beliefs, and Eda's powerful delivery blended her and Joan into one person. While Joan asked me to be bolder than I had ever thought I could be, Eda asked me to be a completely believable character onstage.

That summer we staged *Cradle Song*, a play by the Spanish playwrights Gregorio and Maria Martinez Sierra. Eda won the principal role of Teresa, a child raised by a group of Dominican nuns in a cloistered convent who leaves at 18 to marry. I played a young nun—complete with a long, white habit, large wooden cross around my neck, and rosary beads at my waist—and had only two lines.

I loved watching Eda transform herself into Teresa with every performance. She conveyed Teresa's love of life with such energy that she made growing up among nuns seem ideal for a child. Although I had only a few lines, I was for the first time performing a Broadway-length play from start to finish. I loved the feeling night after night during the play's run as I grew more confident in my acting abilities. I decided that I belonged onstage and found myself caught up in the romance between Teresa and the young man who asks her to marry him. (I, too, yearned for the first signs of romance.)

That summer in Long Island, I studied acting technique—how to accentuate a pause onstage, how to fall, and above all, how to engage other characters so our dialogue sounded like normal conversation. We studied modern dance and singing in the mornings and worked backstage at weekly productions during afternoons and evenings. I learned the hundreds of details that go into producing even an amateur play. I gathered props, helped make scenery, and swept the stage clean with an old-fashioned broom. I never complained about any aspect of the work: this was the theater—the pool with a deep end I wanted to dive into with my heart and soul. If someone had said "jump," I'd have said, "How high?"

My first memorable season of summer theater was upstaged by a huge national event: President Harry Truman's announcement on August 14, 1945, that World War II had officially ended. Like every other place in the country, East Hampton exploded with joy. Almost everyone ran out of their houses and converged on the green—jumping, cheering, and hugging each other with joy.

Although my father had served in the Marines on the home front and was never in danger, I felt relieved knowing that he was really safe from harm and no more atomic bombs would wreak havoc on the Japanese people. I rode on the fire engine—sirens screaming, all through the town—blowing kisses and yelling, "It's over, it's over!"

First Kiss

The Rollins Theater School moved to Lenox, Massachusetts, in 1946, and I with it. The school was located in a spacious red barn turned theater across the street from Tanglewood, the Boston Symphony's summer home. After our day's dramatic endeavors, the other students and I would lie on the lawn at night and listen to the beautiful music wafting on the air.

Progress in almost everything can often be measured in inches, and my second summer at Rollins began to yield some small but pleasing results. I was still, at 16, one of the youngest participants, surrounded by college students trying to find a place for themselves in the theater after graduation. They were always cast in the large parts, but I began to land small roles, which bolstered my confidence.

I was excited to be cast as Mustardseed, a fairy in Shakespeare's *A Midsummer Night's Dream*, and I absolutely adored the part, even though it only had five lines ("And I," "Hail!" "Mustardseed," "Ready," and "What's your will?"). I threw myself into the part so completely that the man playing Oberon, the King of the Fairies, broke in laughter during one performance after I had delivered the line "Ready." He quickly reassumed his king's stern demeanor.

For this part, an unforgettable touch was that I had to *look* like a mustard seed, so I applied bright-yellow makeup to my face, arms, hands, and legs before every performance—and then spent hours removing it with oodles of cold cream and Kleenex. (I thoroughly enjoyed the process.)

I yearned for larger parts to show my mettle, and that old streak of ambition that my mother so disapproved of when I was younger pushed toward the surface. I wanted to be a success, and I believed that what I learned at summer theater was going to help me. I thought it would propel me into leading roles when I returned to high school and then directly to Broadway tryouts, where I imagined I would immediately land a role and then, of course, instant stardom. I didn't realize through these hazy dreams that my parents had already made up their minds that I was going straight to college.

My first role with more than a few short words that summer came with consequences. The play *Berkeley Square* was a romantic drama that greatly appealed to my teenage desire for love. It told the story of a young New Yorker named Peter Standish who in the 1920s is transported back in time to 1700s London to meet his ancestors and falls in love with a distant cousin, Helen Pettigrew.

I had a small part as the maid, but I was determined to make audiences pay attention to me. I decided to create a *real* character, even though she wasn't integral to the play. An acting teacher had told me that regardless of her part's size, a good actress must know everything about her character. So I spent hours writing pages and pages of background about the little maid: where she was born, how she got into a wealthy household, and her hopes and dreams. I felt totally comfortable slipping into character when the curtain rose.

The maid opens the play, and, wearing a long gray dress, white apron, and puffy white cap, I walk around the set's morning room, dimming candles with a candlesnuffer. As the room darkens, Tom Pettigrew, the boorish son of the lord of the manor, enters the room, spies my character, grabs her, and forces a rough and passionate kiss upon her mouth. I wrench myself from his embrace and run offstage, clinging to my cap.

In early rehearsals, the young actor playing Tom had given me only a peck on the cheek, and the director, who was in his twenties, let him get away with it. But when the dress rehearsals started, the director stopped the scene, bounded upstairs to the stage, grabbed me tightly, and planted a deep, wet kiss on my lips. As he gripped me with his right arm around my waist, he moved his left hand up across my breast. I was locked into this position for what seemed an hour and sputtered for air when he finally pulled away.

"Extend that kiss; don't shorten it," he said to the actor. "You're supposed to be a no-good cad, and this is the first instance you have to give the audience some clue to your character."

He turned to me—I who had never before been kissed on the mouth by anyone—and ordered: "And you—you make believe that you like it."

"All right," I said to myself, as if swallowing a large pill, "This is what acting is all about. Do as the director tells you and show that you really like that kiss."

In the spirit of the theater, I knew I had to turn my discomfort into a credible performance, and Tom gave me a wet, passionate kiss for eight straight performances. If I'd had to kiss some unattractive, slob of a boy in real life, I would have been disgusted and refused—but this was the theater. I was ready and willing to do it to bring me closer to my Broadway dreams.

My first onstage kiss led to my first real kiss from a boy offstage. As the summer season drew to a close, Mr. Rollins's grandson—a young, redheaded man named Jerry—asked me to a party in Lenox. I was very pleased, since Jerry was cute and no one had ever asked me on a date, even though I was almost 16. Many of the college students around me were always talking about their dates.

I had no idea why Jerry asked me to this party, but in any event, I took great care with the way I dressed, wearing a pretty plaid taffeta dress with a black velvet choker around my neck. I wouldn't have put it past Mr. Rollins or his wife to encourage Jerry to invite me to the dance. I had a "nice girl" reputation among everyone at the school.

At the end of the evening, when Jerry brought me back to the student residence, he kissed me ever so gently on the lips. My first reaction, which seems rather cold, was: "Oh, good, people can no longer say to me, 'Sweet 16 and never been kissed.'" I knew that turning 16 without having been kissed meant failing an important teenage test. Naturally I believed that all my friends had already passed it with flying colors. I didn't care if I ever saw Jerry again after that evening, but I was happy that during the first months of school I could boast to friends about my first kiss. (Thankfully Jerry—unlike Tom in the play—behaved like a gentleman and didn't press for anything more.)

I loved my two summers at theater school and practiced what I learned when I became an apprentice for two seasons at professional summer theaters. As I was getting ready to wrap up my summer at Lenox, our modern dance instructor, Ingeborg Torrop, a tiny Danish lady with ink-black hair who wore long black dresses, gathered us around her.

"Not all of you will become actors and actresses. But all of you love the theater. You will be intelligent members of the audience. Actors need intelligent audiences. They cannot perform well unless they have intelligent people like you in the audience," she said. She made me realize that I had a role in assuring the future of the theater, whether I was onstage or off. I stowed her sage advice away in my mind and kept pursuing my dream.

Crying for Betty Field

I moved on to a much bigger stage in 1948 when, at 18, I was hired as an unpaid apprentice at the Westport Country Playhouse, in Westport, Connecticut, the premier summer theater in the country. I felt as if I had arrived at the forefront of American theater. As many as 20 starry-eyed college students like me worked without pay doing anything and everything for the sheer joy of being in the company of top actors for the summer. Apprentices were a supply of cheap labor for theater managers. We ate, slept, and breathed theater and received no formal training, but the managers said that we would learn more about the stage in 12 weeks than in our entire college careers.

That promise was good enough for me, and I felt like I was getting closer to my Broadway career. We apprentices painted scenery, scavenged for props, assisted with costumes, and, on occasion, served as assistant stage managers, which included sweeping the stage after each matinee and evening performance. We were cast in small walk-on parts if we were lucky and landed small speaking roles if we were really lucky.

It was a star-studded 1948 season at Westport. Among the acclaimed actors that graced the stage were Betty Field and Thornton Wilder in *The Skin of Our Teeth*, which he authored; June Havoc in *Lysistrata*, by Aristophanes; Tallulah Bankhead in Noel Coward's *Private Lives*; and José Ferrer in *The Silver Whistle*. I was given a small part in *The Skin of Our Teeth*: "The woman in the audience who cries." (I decided that crying in eight performances came close to a speaking part.)

The director told me that my character cries out loudly to mask what the lead character, Sabina, is saying. Each performance, near the middle of Act II, I crept upstairs to the balcony, took my reserved seat, and began to cry loudly (some might say "hysterically") on cue. I arose from my seat and bolted from the balcony to the safety of the theater's first floor. I performed this part to the best of my ability. Acting was like a ladder, and although I was only on the first rung, I believed there were many other rungs ahead.

After one evening's performance, while I was sweeping the stage and setting up the nightlight, the actress Betty Field walked onstage, smiled, and much to my surprise, stopped beside me: "You cried very well tonight," she said and then walked on.

I stopped sweeping and stared after her. *How did she know I was the woman who cried? How did she pick me out of the crowd of apprentices?* To have a Broadway star give a lowly would-be actress like me a tiny shred of recognition was like drinking nectar from the cup of a god.

Managing Sarah Churchill

My fourth and final summer theater was the Falmouth Playhouse in Falmouth, Massachusetts, where I apprenticed in 1949. Of all my summer theatrical experiences, this one had the greatest significance for my family. As a result of my apprenticeship, my father and mother rented a gray house with dark red shutters at 100 Moorland Road to keep an eye on me and offer me a clean, comfortable bed and bath. They soon decided to buy the house as a permanent summer home, and the house on the hill has been used and loved by all family members for the past 60 years. I chose to stay with my fellow apprentices that summer. I had completed my sophomore year at Vassar and was used to communal living, which had few amenities.

When I took up residence at the Falmouth Playhouse, I didn't know anyone in the community. I had chosen Falmouth because its founder, Richard Aldrich, had run another summer theater with a fine reputation in Dennis, Massachusetts. He was married to the famous British actress Gertrude Lawrence, who had won acclaim on Broadway playing the English governess, Anna, in the Rodgers and Hammerstein great musical *The King and I*.

Early that season, I landed a small speaking part in the Anita Loos play *Happy Birthday*. I was a "bar girl," a floozy who hung around bars to pick up guys. I wore a smoky blue, low-cut satin dress, high heels, and a pillbox hat with a long feather that bounced whenever I spoke. Since they were newly minted summer people in Falmouth, my parents came to see me perform. I appeared in the first act, and they joined friends in the lobby during intermission. One friend said to the others, "Harry and K. K. have a daughter in this play." She told them that when she realized who I played, she got genuinely concerned, but told her husband, "That girl can't possibly be a floozy. She is totally miscast."

When my mother repeated her friend's comment to me after the play, I didn't offer much of a defense, knowing deep in my soul that I didn't play the part well. My mother likely recounted the remark to me because she felt that girls who pursued theater weren't of the higher social class that she wanted for my sister and me. She felt that her friends might think I was "sexually loose" because I was pursuing a theatrical career.

Despite my mother's discomfort, I persevered with acting. I discovered that being self-critical was essential to becoming a good actress, and I understood that each performance offered me the chance to be better than I was at the one before. It was my responsibility to improve each time the curtain rose. *No one said that acting was easy,* I told myself. My respect for the craft increased the more I learned about it and understood that a series of tiny steps can lead to a career for people like me who didn't possess innate talent and had to work for every achievement. It was a solitary quest, and I didn't have a mentor to encourage me when I wasn't making progress.

I always knew that my parents didn't approve of my dream. They never gave me positive feedback and believed my pursuit was a passing fancy that I would soon outgrow. I didn't expect them to be enthusiastic about my theatrical work, but they came to Falmouth and rented a house to make sure I was safe from harm and I sensed their concern and love for me.

If even one person I respected had told me that I had real talent, it may have given me the confidence to keep pursuing my dream, even when the going got tough. Since no one did, I kept improving my skills and telling myself that I could climb the mountain alone.

Two plays featuring real luminaries stand out from the Falmouth summer: *The Philadelphia Story,* by Philip Barry, and *Good Housekeeping,* by William McCleery. I had an incident with Sarah Churchill—daughter of the British prime minister and war hero Winston Churchill—who starred for a week in *The Philadelphia Story.* I was the assistant stage manager, helping to ensure a smooth performance, and among my duties was to rap on the actors' dressing room doors and announce the number of minutes before the opening curtain. I felt important keeping the play's performers, especially the stars, on schedule.

One Wednesday afternoon, the stage manager asked me to substitute for him during the matinee performance. His hallowed place was stage left beside the curtain, and I took my position beside the ropes that the curtain man used to pull the curtain at the end of the act. I was careful that afternoon to leave a sliver of space for him to slip into and prepared to give him the cue (a shoulder tap) to close the curtain.

The matinee performance was going smoothly and the second act was coming to a close. The curtain man, George, crammed himself into the tiny space between the ropes and me. He placed his hands on them and waited for my tap. A minute away from the act's end, he suddenly began to hiccup. I started worrying that the audience might hear his hiccups, because they sounded loud, so I tapped George on the shoulder to get his attention. He recognized the shoulder tap and pulled the ropes, cutting off Sarah Churchill's final lines.

She turned her head, drew her mouth into a lion-like snarl, and came running at me, screaming, "You!" Before she could get another word out of her mouth, I said, "Miss Churchill, you have a quick change of costume before the next act. Please go to your dressing room. We shall discuss this incident after the play ends."

I couldn't believe these words had come out of my mouth. I knew I had made a mistake tapping George on his shoulder, but I didn't want to explain what had happened to Miss Churchill. I'd heard that her temper matched her red hair, and I didn't want her to flash it at me. My job was to keep the production moving along. We could have a postmortem after the final curtain descended.

I intended to apologize, but the postmortem never happened. Act III went off without a hitch and the curtain came down correctly at the play's end. Miss Churchill took her bows during the robust applause, and when the curtain came down for the final time, she walked away from me in the wings, changed her clothes, left the theater, and never said a word about the incident. I had learned the meaning of Shakespeare's wise words: "The play's the thing."

Another highlight of the Falmouth summer was the weeklong run of *Good Housekeeping*, which starred Helen Hayes, the "first lady of the American theater." But this production—which featured Miss Hayes's 19-year-old daughter, Mary MacArthur, in her first acting role alongside her famous mother—came to be bittersweet for the entire theater world. After it opened in Falmouth, critics said that Mary had inherited her mother's talent. It then ran for a week at the Westport Country Playhouse after Falmouth and was Broadway bound. But the bright and talented Mary would die from polio six weeks after the Westport run closed. Her sudden death cast a pall over the entire season and hit me hard. I had watched her perform, and our lives had touched each other's. She was my age and looked forward to a long career in the theater, as I did.

Another actress who briefly touched my life also died at an early age. At the end of the Falmouth season, Gertrude Lawrence had come to the theater with her husband, Richard Aldrich, for the cast and crew party, which included apprentices. The successful season was over, and it was time to celebrate. I was feeling relieved and excited and may have had a little too much to drink, which was rare for me. When Lawrence walked up onstage and started dancing, I ran up and joined her. We kicked up our heels for the audience, which responded with wild applause.

Here I am, I thought, *dancing with a great star.*

I was thrilled, and she embraced me when we finished.

"You're a wonderful dancer!" she said.

Well, if Gertrude Lawrence thinks I'm a great dancer, that's something to feel proud about, I thought. Every bit of praise I got for my performing was music to my ears, since I got precious little of it as I plowed along.

I went home late to my parents' house that evening and made some noise entering the house. I was exhausted but not inebriated. The next morning, I woke up to find my father standing at the end of my bed, looking at me seriously.

"Ladies do not drink," he said.

Even at 19, I considered his words law. I'd never been a big drinker and didn't like the taste of alcohol or feeling out of control in a situation, but his comment deflated me. I put stock in his comments, since he rarely criticized me. He was requiring me to be a lady above everything else.

Daddy has picked up on Mummy's tune, I thought. *He doesn't approve of my acting, because it isn't socially acceptable to have a daughter in the theater.*

Playing the floozy (even badly) and getting mildly intoxicated at a cast party convinced even my kind father that I was headed in the wrong direction. Gertrude Lawrence's kind words dissolved in guilt. What was a young, unsure actress like me to do? I didn't have the self-confidence to put my parents' disapproval in perspective, and for the first time, doubt crept into my theatrical dreams.

Gertrude Lawrence died of cancer a few years later, at age 54. I was walking past a newsstand in Grand Central Station when I saw the shocking headlines. In 1951, she had played Anna in *The King and I,* and she and the play were triumphs, and in 1952, she died. I felt a rush of sadness when I saw the headline. Somehow I had bonded with this woman, who had seemed such a free spirit that night when we danced together onstage. She was a star who had shined on me for a moment.

In 1949, the curtain descended on my four seasons of summer stock, and I headed back to Vassar for my junior year. I was a little more realistic about the odds stacked against a young actress like me who dreamed of a professional career, particularly with little to no support from her family. I put on an enthusiastic face vowing to continue.

Theater at Vassar

I arrived at Vassar in Poughkeepsie, New York, in the fall of 1947, an actress-in-the-making with theater on my mind. I'd chosen Vassar in part because its drama department and experimental theater director, Mary Virginia Heinlein, had a reputation for knowing her craft and helping students reach their goals. I hoped she would help me reach Broadway—after all, Poughkeepsie was only a train ride away.

I had wanted to go to the University of Michigan because I had heard that its drama department was the best in the country, but my parents scotched that idea. Good, dutiful daughters of East Coast parents didn't venture into the wilds of the Middle West.

No sooner had I settled on campus than I landed a leading role in the annual freshman play sponsored by Philaletheis (Phil), the venerable, student-led extracurricular organization that had been at Vassar since its founding. It coordinated all the student-led theatrical events and ran productions in the Students' Building, which dominated the eastern end of the campus.

At the tryouts, the student director, Jo Jean Millon, told me that she'd heard about my work in summer stock and was happy I'd chosen Vassar. She had gone to Spence, a sister school of Brearley, and wanted to spend her life in the theater.

"It's great you've come here. You're going to love it, and you'll have all sorts of chances to perform," she said.

What a way to begin, I thought, thanking her profusely.

The chosen freshman play was Thornton Wilder's *The Merchant of Yonkers*, upon which the long-running Broadway musical hit *Hello Dolly* was based. It was set near the end of the nineteenth century. I was cast as the lead female, Dolly Gallagher Levi, a flamboyant, ageless widow who sets her cap for Horace Vandergelder, a wealthy, crusty older bachelor in the market for a new wife.

Vassar in the late forties was still an all-female institution, so the "male" lead went to Frances Sternhagen, who, like me, was chasing Broadway dreams. An exceptional character and comedic actress, Franny played Horace to the hilt—roaring and strutting around stage until he won Dolly's hand. As I watched her perform, the old feelings of competition surfaced in my psyche. Despite all the theater work I'd done over time, I had little confidence in my abilities. Yet Franny seemed to have no doubts about her exceptional talent.

During sophomore year, I won another leading role, this time in *Quality Street*, the same role that Ann Whittlessey, my classmate, had played our senior year at Brearley. While I felt that I had acted the part of Phoebe beautifully, my internal critic told me that I wouldn't have been as good had I not watched Ann perform it first. This was the second leading role I'd landed at Vassar, though, so I felt like I was progressing toward my goal.

College required other adjustments that had an impact on my confidence. I had to compete socially and academically with my peers, and many girls were far smarter than I was—in fact, some were brilliant. I had graduated with a class of 41 students and Brearley didn't rank us by grades, so there was little competition among us. At Vassar, I was surrounded by 200 other smart young women, and I felt the ground move beneath me as I struggled to get my footing.

Social competition among my peers was the most difficult aspect of college life. I arrived at Vassar with no contacts with young men in New York City, especially at the Ivy League colleges. Many of my classmates didn't have any contacts either, but they simply went to mixers at nearby West Point or engineered blind dates through friends, which didn't appeal to me.

Yet rather than allow the social chips to fall where they might and focus on my acting, I struggled with feeling unpopular. I hated weekends, when so many of my friends went off to meet their dates for football games and fraternity parties. If only I'd been more confident that my social life would pick up, even if I had to wait until graduation, I might have worked harder at academics and acting. Instead, I divided my attention between acting and envying my friends' social lives.

The beginning of my junior year, I received another compliment about my theater work: The Phil officers asked me to direct the freshman play, and I chose *I Remember Mama*, by John Van Druten, a major hit of the 1944 Broadway theater season. It was about the daily lives and dreams of the Hansons, a loving Norwegian immigrant family led by an indomitable mother. I felt a special affinity for the Broadway play when I saw it at 14. It centers on Katrin, Mama's eldest daughter, who wants to become a writer. After watching her daughter receive rejection after rejection for her stories, Mama intervenes on her behalf and helps her get published. Perhaps the play revealed my own unexpressed longing for my mother's help.

I loved casting and directing, yet I had to learn by doing. Since the play takes place in Mama's kitchen, mostly around a table and four chairs center stage, I initially put all of the action behind the table. When we finally got to rehearse on the big stage, I quickly realized that I had made a terrible error, as the table got in everyone's way. So I restaged most of the action in a couple of hours and held my breath that the cast would remember the staging when the curtain rose. (They more than met the task, making me look good.)

At the end of my sophomore year, Phil's student officers had selected me as vice president for the coming year, which set me up to run in the college-wide election for presidency of the organization, one of the most important positions on campus. But I hadn't reckoned on Franny, who also decided to run. The election took place late junior year. No one organized a campaign (that would have been "unladylike"), and I certainly didn't have the originality to undertake one. I was lulled into thinking that my successful direction of *I Remember Mama* gave me an advantage. Yet it didn't help enough, and Franny won the election.

I remember kneeling beside a friend in the dining room with my hand shielding my tears after I learned the results. I felt as low as I ever had in my life, and I interpreted the loss as one more signal that my acting career had run its course. It seemed like whatever success came my way in the theater world, Franny was always giant steps ahead of me.

My self-created rivalry with her became real when I heard that Professor Heinlein had told everyone during freshman year that she couldn't wait to get her hands on "that talent." She never showed any interest in me during the one drama course I took with her or came to my student-led plays. My feelings hurt, I decided that if she wasn't interested in me then I was not going to be interested in her department. As petty as it was, I impetuously changed my major from drama to English.

I attribute my self-defeating actions, which dot my early life, to my short fuse and low self-confidence. I couldn't handle competition and took the nearest exit whenever I felt its hot breath on my back. Not having a cheerleader in my corner might have contributed to my reactions to these events. No one was present to pat me on the back and tell me to hang in there.

Fortunately for me, my decision to quit wasn't as devastating as it could have been, since I was finding other paths. By then, I had been writing theater reviews for the student newspaper, the *Vassar Chronicle*, and had read every play printed since the beginning of time, so I decided that becoming a drama critic might be a wise next step.

It wasn't customary in the forties and fifties to encourage young women to pursue careers. My mother wanted my sister and me to marry early and settle down to a nice domestic life, although her own political and public service sent a different message. I always considered having some sort of career after college. Of course, I didn't have an alternative, since I didn't have any semblance of a boyfriend. While many of my friends sported beautiful diamonds on their left hands, the opportunity to marry early was never mine. (Much later, I would say, "God takes care of fools and angels." I was no angel, but I would've been a fool to marry early, since I had no concept of the commitment required by love and marriage.)

My brightest friends were heading off to medical or law school to become pioneers in traditionally all-male professions. I didn't have any desire for graduate school since I didn't think my academic performance was an unqualified success. I went home after graduation to find work, and fortunately my parents pulled some strings to get me an entry-level job in journalism.

My life in theater at Vassar had a nice coda. In June 1951, I directed our class's commencement-week performance for alumnae, seniors, parents, and guests. The one-act play was a synopsis of *Princess Ida*, an operetta by Gilbert and Sullivan, and concerned feminist issues, appropriate for an all-female college.

On performance day, precisely at one of the high points in the action, a plane suddenly flew low over the theater. I was standing in a big ditch in front of the grassy stage, and for a moment I thought I would have to tell the pilot to fly the plane out of its airspace. But then this feeling of knowing when I could or could not change something beyond my control washed over me, and like that moment in summer stock when I confronted the furious Sarah Churchill, I knew I had to make the best of a bad situation.

I signaled my classmates to stop singing and waited patiently for the plane to pass overhead, and then I gave them the cue to commence again. In that moment, I felt the power that accompanies leadership, but I also understood that sometimes simple patience can fix a problem, since problems often resolve themselves. For that reason, I have always loved and tried to remember the advice of the Serenity Prayer:

> *God, grant me the serenity*
> *to accept the things I cannot change,*
> *Courage to change the things I can,*
> *And wisdom to know the difference.*

Much to my surprise, abandoning acting didn't break my heart. I didn't miss the challenging tryouts, makeup sessions, or stage managers calling, "Curtain going up!" I learned the importance of speaking onstage and in public without fear: good life lessons.

Franny Sternhagen went on to become one of the great actresses of our time. We had a long friendship, and I was her faithful follower for many years. Decades after Vassar, I said to her, "Franny, I starred opposite you long before anyone else did!" I remember her graciousness whenever I visited her backstage after a superb performance, and I always kept my visits short, as I knew a long car ride awaited her before she slept. I never felt a shred of envy about her success and was genuinely proud to know her.

Franny once wrote me a note that helped me understand and appreciate what turned out to be my life's work in sexuality education. "You have tried to heal this broken world," she said. Her words were real applause and erased any of my lingering thoughts that I had somehow spoiled my original Broadway dream. Instead, I found a more natural calling.

Journalism and Love

Life at Life

It took me a few months to get my feet on solid ground after graduating from Vassar, but once I did, they pointed me in an exciting new direction. I graduated in June 1951 naïvely planning to use my amateur theater and college journalism experience to become a drama critic for a major newspaper. I had already helped produce plays in summer stock, acted in and directed plays at college, and wrote theater reviews for the *Vassar Chronicle*.

During senior year, I heard that an interviewer from Time Inc. was coming to campus to talk to prospective candidates for its prestigious Editorial Training Program. A successful candidate would be hired as a trainee to spend a year or more learning the nuts and bolts of how the editorial departments functioned, which usually led to a permanent researcher-reporter position on one of its three magazines, *Time, Life,* and *Fortune*. I decided to interview despite my thin journalism résumé, thinking the experience might one day lead to a theater reporting position on one of its famous magazines.

The interviewer was looking for generalists with stellar academic records, yet a quick look at my transcript showed that I was definitely not basking in academic glory. I thought my straight A's in political science might help me, since Time Inc.'s magazines covered current events, and I also decided to stress my theater accomplishments. Yet despite thinking that I had made lemonade from lemons, I didn't receive a callback.

With help from my parents, I landed a good job as the assistant to the food editor of the great daily newspaper the *New York Herald Tribune*. Clementine Paddleford had graduated from the Columbia School of Journalism and worked her way up through the ranks of different magazines until, in 1936, she reached the august position of food editor at the *Tribune*. She was a female version of the day's cynical male journalist—gruff, tough, and remote—and she seemed to resent me from the start, since someone in the front office had pressured her to hire me. She saw me as an inexperienced, pampered young woman, and I can understand her resentment at having to give me a position.

My job was to answer questions from readers who called Miss Paddleford about her weekly recipes. I was definitely not a food maven, so cooking was of absolutely no interest to me. Since someone had always prepared my family's meals, I knew absolutely nothing about ingredients or techniques. My mother had failed to offer any instruction, and her abilities began and ended with scrambled eggs and hollandaise sauce.

I didn't possess the skills to answer questions, and most callers were disappointed that the famous food editor wasn't speaking with them. Miss Paddleford made it clear that I wasn't to bother her with questions, and I'm sure my responses consequently contained many mistakes. She had no patience with me when I made the slightest error and never gave me the benefit of the doubt.

Our desks were located on one side of the large editorial "bull pen," and many young male reporters had to walk past my desk, which was separated from hers by a six-foot-high wall, to get to their own. She might have resented the fact that one of these young reporters would occasionally stop by to talk with me, and this location eventually caused my undoing.

One afternoon, I was talking to a caller about her concern with a recipe when a reporter on his way back from lunch stopped by my desk and cracked a joke. It was funny, and although I tried to smother it, I couldn't stop myself from giggling into the phone.

"You're laughing at me," said the caller. "How can you be so rude? I'm going to call Miss Paddleford and tell her you laughed at me."

Despite my protests and pleadings, the woman slammed down the phone and a feeling of dread came over me. I knew that laughing at a caller would be the cause Miss Paddleford needed to fire me—and I was right. The reader, true to her word, called, and before I knew it, I was shown the door at the *Herald Tribune:* a failure at my first job.

Onward to Time Inc.

In his memoir, Don, kindly called my incident with Miss Paddleford a "hiccup," but it was a blow to my ego. My parents had gone out of their way to help find me the job and I had let them down. It wasn't as if the job was even a good fit for me, but being fired from it had a lasting psychological effect. I felt at loose ends: my academic record wasn't stellar and, unlike so many of my classmates, I wasn't on the path to marriage. My theater career had crashed and burned, and I did not want to go to graduate school. I returned to my parents with my tail between my legs.

Suddenly—and I will never quite understand why—I decided to take some responsibility for my life. I told my parents that they had done enough for me and I would find my next job on my own. I felt at peace and confident that I could surmount my demise at the *Tribune.*

My father, ever the kind soul, suggested I try advertising and meet with the personnel department of McCann-Erickson, one of the largest American advertising companies. I remember shaking my head and telling him that I didn't want to be part of such a necessary but problematic enterprise. I had learned in fabled Vassar professor Helen Lockwood's excellent course, "Contemporary Press," about the incestuous relationship that could exist between magazine editorial and advertising departments. She believed there should be a definite line between these departments so that business would not influence magazine content and had taught me well.

Instead, I made an appointment with the personnel department at Time Inc., and when the interviewer described an opening in its College Bureau, a part of the Time advertising department that sold subscriptions to college students, I leaned forward in my chair and said, "I would definitely be interested." I'm sure Professor Lockwood would have shuddered, but I decided that any job would be a toehold in one of the world's great magazine publishing companies.

This time, the position suited me: I would write letters to college students urging them to purchase subscriptions to *Time* and *Life* to enhance their college experience. Who better to write such letters than a recent graduate of a respected college like Vassar? I was offered and accepted the job without a moment's hesitation.

I reported a bit early to my first day of work on December 1, 1951. Suddenly, a messenger came into the room and began putting envelopes on people's desks. He handed me one with my name front and center and a check for $50 inside. Immediately, I rushed through the door to find him.

"You must have made a mistake. I arrived ten minutes ago. I haven't worked a day for this company. Please take it back," I said.

"Keep it," he said, looking surprised. "That's a Christmas bonus. Everyone gets one."

I couldn't believe my luck ending up in a company that gave bonuses to brand new employees. I took it as a good omen, and my luck at Time Inc. didn't run out. The job was easy for me, and I discovered a new ability: coming up with original, creative ideas that caught people's attention. I realized this a few days into my arrival when the advertising department chief, John Philip Sousa—grandson of the famous composer of "The Stars and Stripes Forever"—invited everyone in our department to a holiday lunch. Although the newest addition to the group, I found myself walking up Fifth Avenue talking to John about an idea I had to improve my work. He stopped in his tracks and looked at me.

"That's a wonderful idea, and I'll talk to [Advertising Director] Bernie Auer," he said.

True to his word, he relayed my idea to Bernie and it was implemented, but the idea per se wasn't the point. John Sousa gave me an early Christmas present: I was 21 years old, and no one had ever complimented me on the originality of my ideas.

Turn in the Road

My work for the College Bureau only got better, and I was asked to organize large-scale parties for education groups, particularly those who held big national conventions in Washington, D.C. It was all about public relations, of course, although the term had yet to be coined. Time Inc. offered lots of food and drink at a convention's end, so groups would be grateful for the company's largess and promote its magazines to their constituencies.

The parties I organized helped me take the next step in my career. At one in Washington, D.C., I met *Time* correspondent Frank McNaughton, an older, well-respected reporter who knew politics like the back of his hand. Time Inc. had asked him to organize a series of television programs at the 1952 political conventions in Chicago. For some reason, Frank took a shine to me and before I knew it, I was given a leave of absence from the College Bureau to become his reporter-researcher on the project.

These television programs—Time Inc.'s first steps into the medium that would soon rule the world and end *Life*'s glory days—have long faded away. But I remember chasing after Estes Kefauver—the Democratic senator from Tennessee who was a dark-horse candidate for the presidency—to sign him for the program. (He carried a broom as a symbol of the housecleaning he'd do if elected.) I also worked on a program about Teddy Roosevelt's 1912 attempt to return to politics as leader of the Bull Moose Party.

Covering the two conventions was like taking a course in real-time politics. I had never before ventured into the nuts and bolts of how to win the required number of delegates at a party convention, and I got a dose of this aspect of the political system by helping Frank produce these programs.

My mother and younger sister attended the Republican convention: my mother as a New Jersey delegate and my sister as a page. There is a prized family photograph of my sister resplendent in red, white, and blue with a straw boater on her head, seated on the shoulder of a delegate and holding a large sign, "I Like Ike."

When the work ended, I headed back to New York City, sure that I would return to my cubicle in the advertising department—yet Frank had different plans.

"I'm going to go see Marian MacPhail [chief of research at *Life*] and suggest she hire you as a *Life* reporter," he said on our trip back.

I was caught completely off guard. This was the job I might have won if I'd been accepted into the Editorial Training Program. It was one of the most sought-after journalism jobs in the company, if not the country—especially for a woman. A Vassar classmate who had been editor-in-chief of the *Vassar Chronicle* was a secretary at Time Inc., where she remained for many years. I felt sorry for her and realized how lucky I was that the same fate had not befallen me.

Frank kept his word, and I soon found myself in Marian's office on the 34th floor of the Time-Life building. A woman of few words, she said that Frank was pleased with my work and offered me a job as a *Life* researcher-reporter starting immediately. She told me to think it over for a day or two and then let her know. As I left her office, I caught sight of some women my age who had come to the magazine through the Editorial Training Program. I was finally getting a chance to move *ahead* of them to the front of the line, but for some perverse reason I nearly decided to stay in my nice, safe cubicle in advertising. My boss, Bernie, soon saved me. I asked to see him, and in his usual kind way, he asked me what was on my mind.

"Bernie, Marian MacPhail has just offered me a job as a *Life* researcher-reporter." Not even waiting for his reaction, I blubbered on: "But I've decided not to accept it, and stay here in advertising."

He gave me a quizzical look.

"This is a job that young men and women dream about. It's important in life to move forward. Don't look back, don't be afraid. If you try, you'll most likely succeed. But first you have to try," he said.

I realized that he was acting like a father, and after I thanked him and walked out of his office, I put my self-defeating habit aside and went back to Marian's office to accept her offer. Nine months after my arrival at Time Inc. and at 22 years old, I became a *Life* researcher-reporter. I was beginning to find a place for myself in the world.

At Last: Life

Marian assigned researcher-reporters to various departments, depending on editorial needs, openings, talent, background, and length of time at *Life*. As a reporter built up a record, he or she could ask to move to another department. Most female reporters were assigned to back-of-the-book departments, and many more males than females ended up on the 34th floor, assigned to national and foreign news.

In 1952, for my first six months at *Life,* I worked on a special issue on the United States economy, the most junior person on a team of four reporters in the Special Projects department. Expertise in economics was not a requirement, fortunately, since I knew little about the topic. The magazine's mission was not to reach the most highly educated, but rather to produce stories that could be read by the largest swath of people. *Life* in the fifties was the nation's best-selling magazine, reaching millions of people a week.

As a reporter for the special issue, I was responsible for outlining, planning, and developing a range of stories, including "Women in Industry," "Successful New Business," and "Leisure Time in the U.S." I did a story on a woman on the assembly line at Johnson & Johnson's factory in New Brunswick, New Jersey, never dreaming this city would one day play a much larger role in my career.

After the special issue, I moved on to become the junior reporter in Editorials, where my annual salary rose from $3,024 to $4,750. In a hideaway on the 36th floor—where Henry R. Luce, founder and editor-in-chief of Time Inc.'s worldwide magazine publishing empire, also had an office—senior researcher Grace Horan and I labored over weekly editorials written by John (Jack) Knox Jessup, the chief editorial writer. I felt as if I had returned to college, but one that required learning a new body of knowledge in the incredibly short amount of time of five days. Each week, Jack would write about a current news topic— like U.S. trade imbalances, the coming national election, or the tax structure—and Grace and I had to cram our heads full of the facts on the subject to check for his accuracy in the full-page editorials he wrote with amazing ease. We had to absorb huge amounts of information in a limited amount of time, using little brown envelopes stuffed full of newspaper clippings that came on command from the morgue several floors below. The clippings contained valuable material, gathered as they were by the editorial trainees, many with Phi Beta Kappa keys.

As the junior researcher in Editorials, I was fortunate that Grace was experienced, knew Mr. Jessup well, and tolerated newcomers. She understood that I was a neophyte about some of the grand issues of the day, accepted the holes in my knowledge, and appreciated my hard-working nature. It was a cold day when the editors had to write a retraction, and it happened only once on my watch, when I claimed that the Korean War was the only war the U.S. had lost. ("No, sir," a reader wrote. "The U.S. also lost the war of 1812.") The printed apology went into my personnel file.

One week, Mr. Jessup went on vacation and Henry R. Luce himself stepped in as temporary editorial writer. Known to be remote, he had earned the accolade "the most influential private citizen in the America of his day." Grace was away, and it fell to me to fact-check his long, difficult editorial. I remember finding four or five facts that needed further discussion, and I had to beard the lion in his den. I walked into his office, hoping my pounding heart wouldn't smother hearing his answers.

"Mr. Luce, I'm Susan Neuberger, the researcher this week as Grace Horan is on vacation. I have checked your editorial several times and found a few points that I want to talk to you about," I said.

He raised his eyes and looked at me from under his dark bushy eyebrows.

"Sit down in this chair, and we'll go over all of your concerns," he said kindly, much to my surprise. We went over every point, and he made my suggested changes without argument. I wish now that I had told him what a privilege it was to work on his magazine, but I missed my moment. While I had handled a challenging situation well, I looked forward to Grace's return.

Working at *Life* was as good as it got for a woman fresh out of college. Most of us felt privileged to work there, not only because the salaries were excellent, but also because the management never questioned any expenditure of funds in pursuit of a story. I remember when one male reporter hired a plane for $2,000 for a couple of hours so a photographer could take an aerial shot of some wild animals in Alaska, and hardly anyone raised an eyebrow.

Once I almost upset the apple cart of generosity when I handed in my expense account with the actual amounts I had spent rather than the generous amounts designated for breakfast, lunch, and dinner. I had placed my expense account on the managing editor's desk when his secretary came rushing out of her office shouting, "Come back here immediately." I was sure I had made some horrendous mistake and walked back toward her.

"What do you want to do?" she demanded. "Do you want to scuttle the system?"

"What have I done?" I said, surprised that I still had a voice.

"You have put the exact amounts that you spent for each meal on your trip rather than the amount the company gives reporters for their meal allowance," she said.

"But I didn't spend $8 for breakfast," I countered. "It's there on the bill: I spent only $2.50."

She was close to exasperation.

"It doesn't matter. Take this back to your desk and mark $8 for breakfast, $11 for lunch, and $18 for dinner in the proper spaces, and then bring it back to me. And don't attach the bills—that isn't necessary. Go do as you're told."

Sure that I was going to get fired for charging the company too much, I was reprimanded for charging too little. Like Alice in Wonderland, things at *Life* were topsy-turvy, but I loved every minute of it.

I met a lot of people at *Life*, including my lifelong friends Eleanor Graves and Caroline Zinsser, who were brilliant, exceptionally talented researcher-reporters. Eleanor worked in the Modern Living department and Caroline in the Text department. Eleanor rose to become the highest-ranking female editor of *Life,* and Caroline was an early feminist activist who kept asking why female reporters at the magazine earned less than male ones. I was so pleased with my salary—when I left it was $8,700 a year—that I didn't even join the union to press for financial equality for women reporters. I'm embarrassed to admit that I probably wouldn't have known what feminism meant and the contributions my female forebears had made for me.

Later, after Caroline and I had left the magazine, I found a new career in early childhood education and followed her footsteps by obtaining a graduate degree from Bank Street College of Education in New York City. Later, she became director of the prestigious Bank Street School for Children and a published author of many reports on early childhood education and books that were historical in nature.

The Party Department

After 11 months in Editorials, I moved to a new department called Parties, which featured a weekly pictorial, "*Life* Goes to a Party," that was about social frivolity. In general, it was the intellectual opposite of Editorials, but it produced a more serious feature called "*Life* Visits," which took the reader into a celebrity's home or business.

The bright young women and men who worked for "*Life* Edit," as it was called, were a lively group who worked well together and had fun on the side while producing the magazine. I wanted friends and romance, as I wasn't getting any younger, and the move to Parties was like going from winter to summer: from serious, major ideas to the lighthearted social nonsense of the day.

I asked for the assignment, because at 24 years old I was beginning to feel like time was running out to find a mate. Regardless of how well my career was progressing, I felt the pull of my generation's raison d'être: marriage and motherhood. Many of my classmates—and my younger sister—were already mothers, and I had served as a bridesmaid in their weddings, caught lots of bouquets, and became a godmother to their children.

When I was assigned to the Parties department, I hoped that I might have the same luck as my predecessor Claire Walters, who met and eventually married the captain of a cruise ship after covering an overnight cruise to Bermuda. Would I, too, find romance covering a *"Life* Goes to a Party" story? Not likely, I soon realized, although I did cover a slumber party given by the daughter of the New Jersey Commissioner of Education, in Princeton, a town to which I would move some ten years later. But my position in the Parties department did ultimately have romantic results.

When I was able to find a party or an interesting visit, my job was to keep track of the photographer's film rolls and take good notes for captions and text blocks for the editor. A cardinal rule was to never supplant the photographer by taking one's own pictures and to keep out of camera range, regardless if the building you were standing in was collapsing or a bomb went off right beside you. That was the moment for which *Life* photographers ached: creating a picture that was the equivalent of 1,000 words. They were the best at capturing the world in its glory and sorrow, and it was a privilege to carry their camera bags when they made the frequent request.

Once I even had the pleasure of working with Alfred Eisenstaedt, dean of the world's professional photographers, on a story about a 12-year-old's birthday party. He was a darling, dapper little man with a charming German accent, and everyone called him Eisie. He broke the rules and allowed me to snap a photo of him running a three-legged race with one of the children, which made the back cover of a book about children's birthday parties derived from a series I planned. I was always pleased to see my photo credit below a picture of one of the world's legendary photographers.

The *"Life* Visits" feature often covered important people and celebrities, but occasionally ordinary people were the subject. I spent one Saturday night chronicling the Myles Standish family of five, in West Hartford, Connecticut, with photographer Esther Bubley. The story, "*Life* Visits: A Family's Saturday Night," became an eight-page spread in the November 8, 1954, issue and earned a mention in the sought-after "Editors' Note." The note explained that Mrs. Standish—after watching her five-year-old son run upstairs not once, but three times—sighed to reporter Susan Neuberger, "I wish you'd come every Saturday night—those children never looked so clean in their lives."

⁓

While I was covering other people's parties and making friends for *Life*, I was also looking out for myself in an audacious, strategic way. The grapevine of reporters and photographers revealed the existence of a *Life* foreign correspondent in the Far East bureau who was single, handsome, and eligible. His name: Don Wilson. I began to do what all good journalists did: gather information about him, and every bit of it delighted me.

This man was about five years older than I was; upon graduating from Yale, he was immediately accepted into the Editorial Training Program. He was a rising star among the foreign correspondents; best of all, he was tall, thin, handsome, intelligent, and amusing. Although he'd had some mild flirtations with other *Life* reporters during home leaves, he hadn't married any of them.

I pulled most of this information out of the Parties department editor Stanley Flink, a dashing figure himself. Stan had married Mary Hilson, the daughter of my father's Wall Street business partner, and he knew and loved to talk about Don, since they had both graduated from Yale around the same time. Without knowing it, he fed my interest in this stranger half a continent away. I was growing more and more intrigued and wanted to meet this man when he returned to the New York office.

I also pried some information out of Jun Miki, a Japanese photographer who was back in New York from the Far East bureau after working with Don. Miki and I covered a possible *Life* feature on the cast of the Broadway hit *Pajama Game,* which opened in May 1954 and ran for over 1,000 performances. Early in the run on a summer Sunday, the cast held a party on a privately owned island near New York City. Miki was assigned the story, and together we clambered over the rocks while the cast members let loose and leapt from rock to rock with incredible grace. I was much more interested in finding out more about Don Wilson than I was about how the cast was feeling about their day off, and he fed me some tasty tidbits.

Miki went back to Japan, and when next he saw Don in Korea, he told him that a female reporter in the New York office had asked about him. My cover was almost blown, but Miki said that he couldn't remember my name. And before he left for Japan, he dropped one last piece of interesting information: Don was coming back to New York in December on a month's home leave.

Long after we had met, Don said that when he arrived back at *Life*, he asked the national affairs editor, an old friend, to name the most attractive, single women reporters.

"You didn't make the list," Don reported.

Even though we were married, I felt snubbed, but then I calmed down and smiled: the otherwise intelligent editor had gotten it wrong.

Much as I loved my job at *Life* and did it well, I did not see "Susie Neuberger, Girl Reporter" as a lifelong career. My generation's pull toward marriage and children was too strong, and no one talked about the possibility of having both a marriage and career at once. Although I had some role models who balanced work and family, many of the women reporters, especially those covering worldwide breaking news, were older and single.

My mother's message to me was certainly about getting married. Her words about ambition being an inappropriate quality for young women had left their mark. I didn't have enough confidence to see myself as a professional married woman, and in retrospect, I wish I had.

Old friendships are old friendships, and they are particularly strong when there is a Yale connection. One late afternoon in early January as dusk was settling over the city's skyscrapers, I looked up from my desk outside Stanley Flink's office for a brief second and noticed a tall, thin figure in a trench coat striding past me. Bursts of laughter and shouts of "Stanley!" and "Don, old chap! How are you? Welcome home, my boy!" swept through the door like a ferocious wind gust.

I had to get into the room.

Don: Beginnings

I made up a lie to get into the room for an introduction to Don.
    I had only the narrowest of time frames, perhaps minutes, in which to meet him. If I didn't think creatively, he might leave my editor Stan's office—where I had heard them laughing and talking for almost an hour—and disappear forever into the maze of offices at *Life* magazine, which housed many other young, unmarried female researchers and reporters like me. Or, for that matter, he might disappear into the vast landscape of New York City, never to emerge again. I had to think fast, and my mind went into overdrive.
    I gathered up the large layout of the story I was working on, juggled the pages so they wouldn't fall to the ground, rose from my desk—not even tak-

ing a moment to check my hair and lipstick—and marched into Stan's office.

"Stan," I said seriously, "I'm sorry to interrupt, but I have some questions about the layout, and I need the answers right now in order to meet our deadline."

I was lying through my teeth. Stan turned his head away from Don—whom I recognized, having already seen pictures of him in stories that had appeared in the magazine's "Editors' Note"—and looked at me with surprise.

"Really?" he asked. "I didn't know we were under deadline with this story." (We weren't, of course.) "Fire away," he said, and then he added, "Oh, by the way, Don, this is my researcher, Susan Neuberger."

I pivoted away from Stan, my heart pounding, and said as casually as I could, "Oh, hello, glad to meet you. *Sorry* to interrupt your conversation with Stan."

Another lie: I wasn't a bit sorry, and since I had created the scene, I had to dream up some lame questions to ask Stan in order to remain in the room. Stan believes to this day that while I was asking those questions—which I desperately hoped were showing off my researcher skills—Don was appraising me in my form-fitting, pink angora sweater and liked what he saw. If this is true—and Don always vehemently denied that it was my form rather than my clear, concise questions to Stan that attracted his attention—I would have been deeply embarrassed. Had I been given advanced warning that I was going to meet Don Wilson on that December afternoon, I probably would have worn something less form-fitting, like a blouse.

Stan answered my questions, and I thanked him, picked up the layout, gave a quick smile in Don's general direction, and left the room. I went back to my desk not knowing what would follow and hoping my pulse rate would slow down. What followed was wonderful and life changing: Don left Stan's office, stopped at my desk, and chatted with me. He remembers that it was about the news of the world, Broadway shows, movies, and so forth, but I recall none of it, probably because of the increased adrenalin coursing through my veins. Had Don asked me, upon leaving Stan's office, "Would you like to spend 54 years of your life with me?" I would have answered, "Yes. But first, let me grab my coat."

Such is the power of immediate and intense physical attraction. However, he didn't ask me.

After a few minutes, I said that I needed to get back to that story deadline, and Don uttered what he later called the "fateful words": "I'll give you a call, and we might have a drink."

"Fine," I replied, but I remember feeling skeptical. I didn't know if this man I had so wanted to meet, because he seemed to possess the qualities that made him right for me, was a person whose word could be counted on. But he kept his promise and called the next day to ask me out for a drink. I was elated: the white lies paid off with exactly the result I had wanted. Dreams do come true: I had a first date with Don.

We agreed to meet after work at the large, circular marble structure with a flat top known among Time Inc.-ers as the "fish bowl," which was on the ground floor of the Time-Life building. Don didn't keep me waiting. He wore a heavy, fur-lined trench coat, looking as if he had stepped out of central casting to play the part of the handsome foreign correspondent. After we smiled a greeting to each other, he reached out and took my left arm and tucked it protectively in the space he created under his right arm as we headed out the door for a drink in a nearby hotel.

From a distance of almost 60 years, the evenings of the next three weeks that followed are a blur, but they were filled with Don. His presence overshadowed everything else, although I did my work at *Life* and explained to my family why I wasn't coming to the farm on weekends. I was living in the family apartment at 40 East 66th Street, where our faithful English-born housekeeper, May Will, who had traveled to Australia and then to America, lived in a tiny room off the kitchen. She was completely discreet, and the beginnings of my relationship with Don were safe with her.

When January's end loomed and the days of Don's leave dwindled to a precious few, I told him I would accompany him to the airport to say goodbye. He had talked about the possibility of my coming to the Far East to visit him for a month in the spring, and although it posed some hurdles, I accepted with alacrity. He mentioned that he would meet me in Japan and then we would visit Hong Kong and Singapore, where he was living with Dwight Martin, the chief correspondent for *Time*, and possibly go to Indochina.

During our trip in the cab to what was then called Idlewild Airport—which years later would be renamed for John F. Kennedy after his assassination—Don said, "You're going to need a visa to Indochina in case we decide we want to go there. The government requires it." In that moment, he was the general, and I was not about to disobey his command.

After we kissed and hugged goodbye and before his plane was even in the sky, I grabbed the first taxi I could find and asked the driver to take me to the Indochina Consulate in mid-Manhattan. Upon arrival, I paid the driver and ran up the steps as quickly as I could, afraid that the clock was ticking and the Consulate would already be closed for the day. I burst through the doors and asked the person at the reception desk for the necessary papers to get a visa. They were easy to fill out except for one line, "Purpose of Trip." Of course I wanted to write "Love," but I decided that I wouldn't be doing myself any favors with this response, so I wrote a quick lie, "Education," and pushed the completed papers back across the desk to the officer.

I nearly waltzed out of the Consulate, pleased that I had followed Don's instructions and looking forward to writing to him about my accomplishment. I wanted to assure him: I intended to visit him in May, I was a person of action who didn't allow grass to grow under her feet. I had taken seriously weeks of getting to know each other, and ours was not a brief dalliance. I wanted Don to realize that I thought he was attractive, intelligent, and fun to be with, and that I was happily falling in love with him. Most of all, I wanted our romantic idyll to continue. In the end, it didn't matter that although my visa was approved, we didn't visit Indochina! It was the immediate action that I took that pleased us both.

Some hurdles had to be overcome before I could get on the plane the last day in April 1955. "Nice young women" didn't travel to see their male friends for an extended amount of time *before* they were married. I'm sure that many did, but if so, it wasn't public knowledge. It didn't happen in my particular social circle, and the reason was quite simple: nice girls did not have sex with their boyfriends until they were married. They were supposed to be virgins on their wedding night, although this restriction didn't apply to young men. In the days of my youth, abstinence before marriage was the rule—or so I believed—and I'm sure a reason so many of my women friends married right after college was because they didn't want to wait any longer to have sex.

Going to visit Don in the Far East for two weeks unaccompanied by another adult or even a friend was tantamount to holding up a placard with the words, "I'm going to sleep—and have sex—with my boyfriend." Of course, since Don and I were both adults—I was 25 and he was 29— this was our intention. If this relationship didn't resolve into marriage, however, there was the added pressure of my being labeled as a "sexually promiscuous woman." (Don, of course, wouldn't have been called a sexually promiscuous man.) There were also whispers that women who broke the abstinence-before-marriage rule were "loose," and men would date them only to have sex with (but not marry) them. Some of these ideas seem like incredibly old-fashioned strictures today and make me laugh as I remember them.

Serendipitously, I did have a chaperone of sorts, at least on my flight to Japan: Mrs. Herbert Semler, the mother of my former Brearley classmate, Gay. Her brother, Peter, was involved in government work in Japan (probably the CIA), and she told me that her mother was planning a trip to see him in May. *Bingo!* I had an older woman to give me some cover, thin as it was. I began mentioning Mrs. Semler's name whenever I told friends and colleagues that I was headed to the Far East.

Even better than Mrs. Semler was the invitation from Frankie MacDonald, who had become a good friend at *Life*, to be a bridesmaid in her wedding in Honolulu, Hawaii, in early June. It was a stretch to talk about this obligation as the reason for my solo trip, since it came at its end, but it still worked to explain why I was going on a voyage alone to meet a man. My explanation may have fooled some, but certainly not all.

My parents were good sports about the trip, determined not to stand in my way now that I had finally met an eligible bachelor. My mother insisted on using her considerable political clout in the Republican Party to ensure that my name was listed at U.S. embassies on our route, so I could tap into the power of the American government if problems arose. In retrospect, I shudder to think that she called in such powerful artillery to protect me from harm: being with Don and both of us working at *Life* might have been enough if something had happened.

What appealed to me most about Don was that we shared the journalism profession and a powerful interest in politics and world affairs. Years after we married, when we lived in Washington, D.C., I heard Mary Bunting, then the president of Radcliffe College, speak about how professional women could have a fulfilling family life. Her message for solving the work-family dilemma was for women and men in the same profession to marry. She offered two reasons why: they could share a common vocabulary, which would help them understand their respective goals, and they could share a social circle that would form a cohesive, supportive environment. I knew Don and I would never lack for a topic of conversation.

Once, a friend whose marriage dissolved after 25 years asked me what I thought was the glue that kept my marriage to Don together. Without giving her question the thoughtful response it deserved, I quickly answered "politics." (Sometimes immediate responses are the truth.) From the moment we married and I switched my political affiliation from Republican to Democrat, we embraced a mutual passion for U.S. politics and elections, and world events in which our country was involved.

We shared our common interest in the world on our month-long trip through the Far East in May 1955, which Don claimed I called our memorable "pre-honeymoon." I wouldn't have changed a bit of it. Before I took off from New York, he sent me a Western Union cable, using "cablese"—a form of language known mostly to foreign correspondents. It couldn't have been more welcoming: "Barring last minute balloon ascension eyell be Haneda Airport May third eight ayem. Love, Donsan." (Japanese names usually had "–san" at the end, so Don was using the lingo of the day. In Japanese, I would be called "Susiesan.") The rather cryptic "balloon ascension" part of his message meant barring some fast-breaking news story that he would have to cover for the magazines, which almost happened when the Bình Xuyên, a large band of Vietnamese rebels, rioted in Saigon. Somehow someone else covered the story, and he flew to meet me. Don often recounted this tale years later to prove that he had chosen me over a possible lead story in *Life*. He made the right choice.

Our first moments together proved a bit awkward: Don had somehow used his magazine credentials to meet me at the foot of the stairs of my Pan American flight when it reached Tokyo. I had to take leave of Mrs. Semler, which was a bit sticky, and I was momentarily unprepared to handle the handsome U.S. Army Major who was standing right beside Don. Due to my father and mother's involvement, the Major had met my flight, saluted briskly, and offered me any services, starting with a ride into the city.

One thing at a time, I counseled myself, while smiling at the two men and Mrs. Semler and praying for divine guidance. I thanked Mrs. Semler and bid her a warm goodbye, and she blended into the crowd. I turned my attention to the Major, thanking him for his efforts and assuring him that Don would escort me into the city. I added that I would be in Don's good hands for the rest of my stay in Tokyo. The Major did not protest, probably thankful that he didn't have to spend the next few days keeping a watchful eye on us.

Don seemed patient throughout these comings and goings, and I rewarded him properly with a warm kiss when we were finally alone in the back of a Tokyo taxicab headed to the Imperial Hotel.

I wish all young lovers could have the chance that Don and I had to travel together to a strange and wonderful part of the world, getting to know each other and building the foundation for a longer, deeper relationship.

Don, who had lived in Tokyo between stints covering the end of the Korean War, knew so much about the country that he gave me a daily tutorial on some aspect of it. I was a rapt student to his teachings. We took a one-day trip to see the Kamakura Buddha and then drove to the Izu peninsula west of Tokyo and stayed in a lovely inn at the foot of Mount Fuji, the highest mountain in Japan. As Don wrote in his memoir, "We took hot baths, wore padded brown kimonos, slept on tatami mats, ate sushi for the first time, and toured the rural areas. We tramped around little villages in a green countryside where we were the only Americans in sight." I still feel the magic of the moments we spent exploring Japan and spending time alone together without the pressures of the modern world to distract us.

We also visited the ancient capital of Japan, Kyoto, where I was fascinated by the throngs of rosy-cheeked little children, smartly dressed in their navy blue school uniforms. They visited the temples and museums en masse and stared at me, a long-legged American woman with blonde hair. Don had the foresight to buy a handful of prints by the 19th-century artist Utagawa Hiroshige—famous for his "One Hundred Famous Views of Edo"—at rock-bottom prices before the art cognoscenti gobbled up his work. Those prints, which have hung in all the homes we've lived in, always take me back to our trip in the ancient, mystical country.

Besides his intelligent and delightful company, other aspects of Don's personality pleased me during our drives through the Japanese countryside. He never hesitated to ask someone for directions when we were lost, and I found this endearing and certainly different from other men back in the States, who usually insisted they didn't need any help. He was also extremely polite to the innkeepers and deferential maids, who helped us with our baths and bedding. I liked every single aspect of his character and was completely smitten by this man on our first journey together.

I didn't realize it at the time of my journey to see Don, but the trip foreshadowed my later dedication to ensuring that young people would have knowledge about and access to birth control and contraception in order to prevent an unwanted pregnancy. Acting on my mother's advice, I visited a Planned Parenthood clinic in lower Manhattan and was fitted for and purchased a diaphragm, a device that would keep me "safe" from becoming pregnant. Birth control and contraception were primarily female concerns in the 1950s, unless one's male partner was adept and, more important, willing to always use condoms whenever he was having sex. (The famous playwright, George Bernard Shaw, called the development of the male condom "the greatest invention of the 19th century.")

I don't remember ever having a conversation about protection with Don before or during the trip, and that would probably have been the norm for most unmarried couples. Devices to ensure protection in the late 1950s were few and far between: the pill and other forms of long-term, hormone-based contraception didn't exist until the 1960s and 1970s, and women had to rely on the diaphragm. One had to use it with consistency and care to ensure protection, and I guess I did. Never having had a pregnancy scare contributed to my conviction about the importance of teaching young people honestly and correctly about all forms of contraception. Contraception added immeasurably to my pre-honeymoon.

My romantic and sexual feelings for Don are not evident in the scrapbook I made after our trip. Although the book's leather binding disintegrated, I have its 35 double-sided pages neatly encased in clear plastic sleeves, but they are dreadfully dull. They focus on the facts and omit my growing feelings about Don. Here I was traveling thousands of miles—taking a risk with both my heart and my reputation for a journey with a man I barely knew who had swept me off my feet—and I didn't include any feelings of love for him. Was this natural reserve? Was it my upbringing, which discouraged discussion about feelings? Was I protecting myself from disappointment and rejection, should Don, in the end, decide I wasn't the woman he wanted to marry?

I included only a few pictures of us together, even though we were virtually living with each other for weeks. The idea of traveling and living with a man to whom I wasn't married may have embarrassed me—or may have made me shy about revealing it—and I hid the relationship in a cascade of pamphlets, small photographs, airplane ticket stubs, and baggage claim checks. My carefully printed, handwritten captions never reveal my guilty secret: having a sexual relationship with a man to whom I wasn't even engaged!

I thought if I kept Don at a distance in the scrapbook—except for one little picture of me sitting on his lap, looking as if I was about to kiss him—I would speed his interest in asking me to marry him. (It didn't.) I had always heard "play hard to get" when it came to a man, but I certainly hadn't played hard to get when it came to Don. After two weeks, I was ready and willing to follow him to the ends of the earth—at least to the Far East, which was almost the same distance in the mid-fifties.

I wish I had a record of my growing feelings toward Don. I remember our trip in a haze of happiness. I'm sure it had its ups and downs, but we were young with no responsibilities, and Don was a good leader and I a good follower. The days were sunshine-filled, and we swam a lot—I bought my all-time favorite bathing suit in Hong Kong, a purple American-made Cole of California. One of my most treasured pictures is of Don and me washed up in the foam of Hong Kong's Repulse Bay, our faces wreathed in smiles.

I didn't want our trip to end, but it did. Having to attend my friend's wedding in Honolulu was a good way for it to end. It was something concrete to look forward to when I left Don; I couldn't allow myself to dwell on the sadness of leaving him. I knew that I would face a lot of tough questions upon returning home still a single woman: "Well, what happens now? Are you going to get married? Do you love him? Does he love you?"

I definitely had marriage on my mind at the end of our travels, but it takes two people to bring this concept to a reality, and I left behind a man in Singapore who wasn't ready to make such a commitment. My scrapbook ends with a whimper, and I hid my concerns, writing, "The flight home was wonderful, and I ate lunch with a member of the Portuguese Embassy … weather delayed our flight and around 9 p.m., with leis still around my neck, I landed at Idlewild Airport in New York, NY, U.S.A."

In his memoir, Don concluded his chapter about our trip in similarly enigmatic fashion: "When Susan arrived back in New York, she quickly found that her cover was blown (as I think it should have been). Her visit with me was top news around the office, and she was badgered with questions about the romantic highs and lows. She found the interest amusing and fielded most of the prying questions."

I could have better ended my scrapbook by confessing the intense sadness I felt on my journey home after our idyll had to come to a close. Don referred in his memoir to one incident relating to it that we joked about through the years. He writes that on my first night away from him after five weeks, I went out for dinner with the pilots of my Pan Am flight to Hawaii, who had taken pity on me because I cried the whole first leg of the flight to Manila. What I didn't know at the time was that he was equally miserable about my having to say goodbye and leave him, which leads to the packet of love letters.

Love Letters from a Distance

I found the packet of letters in a shoebox within a shoebox in a plastic bin in my basement, and I wish I had found them before Don died. The 50 letters had been hidden from plain sight for 40 years, and I only discovered them when I was looking for the letters I wrote to Don after our Asian adventure together. I had completely forgotten that I had saved his letters along with some cables, postcards, and even short memos he had sent in late November 1955, when we briefly worked a floor apart at *Life*. I had felt the need to save every word Don wrote to me, and on rereading them, I know why.

These neatly typed letters, written when Don was 29 and 30, are passionate, rueful, charming, intelligent, sexy, funny, serious, and wise—all at the same time. Some are exceptional travelogues that outdo any published guides. When I carefully reread each of them, I feel as if Don is in the room with me again. They are like a new gift of love, even though he died two years ago.

❧

Don wrote me about two letters every week after we met at *Life* and he left for nine months to work as the magazine's chief correspondent in the Far East. "I've probably written more words to you than all the rest of my correspondence put together in the past ten years," he said in one letter. "In fact, I write a lot more for you than I do for *Life*. It's so much more pleasant, too."

All of Don's letters arrived on company stationery from *Life*'s international office in Singapore. He wrote to me from many faraway places, and his words transported me across the globe to Melbourne and Darwin, in Australia; Phnom Penh, Cambodia; Jakarta, Indonesia; Sarawak, Borneo; and a little place in the Australian outback called Alice Springs that enchanted him. He called visiting there "something of a Mecca-like experience":

> Population about 3,000, it sits halfway between Darwin in the north and Adelaide in the south. It's surrounded by the McDonnell Ranges and there is a color to the area that exists nowhere else in the world. The closest approximations are Arizona and New Mexico, but the colors around "The Alice" (for that's what it's called) have a certain softness, almost pastel to them that I don't believe exists in the American desert areas.
>
> The Alice is a true frontier town, even today, and the pubs are filled with characters who go by the names of "Jack the Dogger" and the like. They wear the great wide-brimmed Australian bush hats, speak of 'roos (for kangaroos), Billys (in which they boil their stew), a swag (which is the bedroll they use), going bush, which means staying alone too long in the wilds and going off one's rocker, etc. The language in this unsettled part of Australia is the most colorful brand of English I've yet encountered.

After our pre-honeymoon, his letters became much more passionate, loving, and overtly sexual. He changed his initial greeting from "Dearest Susie" to "Darling," "Darling Angel," "My Darling Susan," "My Blonde Angel,"

"Dearest Plum," "Dearest Soft-as-Silk," and similar lovely nicknames. Each letter ends with the same steadfast phrase, "All my love and kisses, Don."

These post-idyll letters also reveal Don's endearing nickname for me, "Mophead," which derived from my unruly mop of hair. He mentions it in his first letter after we said goodbye in Singapore on Sunday, June 5: "I thought about the way you almost bury your wonderful steel-wool head in the covers in the morning and then peep over at me. Our bodies come together (almost automatically) and then you invariably say, 'We must get some more sleep.' But I don't think you ever really mean it."

He ends his first letter to me after I left with words that anyone in love would want to hear: "Goodbye for now, Sweetheart. It was the nicest five weeks of my life." He also notes that he told his colleagues at *Life* that he was "fatigued" with the Far East and wanted to come home. I decided, of course, that this meant only one thing: he wanted to come home to be with me.

Most of Don's later letters have one or two sexual references, and sometimes I blush when I read them. He was comfortable talking about sex and didn't hold back about our lovemaking, but in deference to him and my old-fashioned sense of propriety, I will disclose only one detail. In an August letter, he wrote, "I think you've got a better body than Marilyn M—honest." I can't resist sharing this for posterity, as everyone knows that Marilyn Monroe had one of the most desirable figures in human history.

Don's comments should be put in some perspective. He was far more sexually experienced than I was; I had had few romantic and sexual adventures and wasn't curious to learn about the art of sex from books, which in retrospect would have been good, since learning something new about a subject never hurts. I knew that he'd had several affairs; part of the ethos of being a foreign correspondent was to be sexually involved with many women, and Don would write to me about his colleagues' exploits on a fairly regular basis. I deduced that he was not immune to the same ethos, and I'm sure that he was having his share of casual carnal fun before we met. He enjoyed and played the role of correspondent to the hilt, and old habits die hard.

But after we spent five weeks together, things began to change. I certainly was in love with Don and had no intention of getting seriously involved with another man, but it was harder for him to accept that he might have to change his ways. The idea of a permanent commitment frightened him, and the pushback was to have a brief affair or even a series of affairs to prove that he was still fancy free. It didn't take him long to test these complicated feelings—perhaps three days after I had left town—but he did have the decency and remorse to write me about the experience.

> I finally broke my celibacy last night and must report to you—always candid, that's me—that it really wasn't so hot. A strange face on the pillow next to me, and I almost shuddered. Actually a very nice British girl whom I once liked, but you've ruined me. I bundled her off. I am now settling in for another long period of celibacy, which may last for several months.

I can't remember my reaction to Don's confession, but perhaps I backed off from giving him a lecture. He offered me a compelling fig leaf to compensate for his poor behavior: a rendezvous in Hawaii on his trip home "if you're not married by then." He wrote:

> I would love nothing better than to stop for a week on one of the lesser-known islands of the Hawaiians and make love to a certain dame who seems to blot out all other dames. Do you think you could get away for a week? And do it secretly so no one would know where you're going? That way we could fly back to New York together. Advise me on this, angel, and please examine all possibilities.

Don kept mentioning the idea in his letters, asking, "How about Hawaii?" In one, he said that if I met him in Hawaii, we could recreate the "biggest thing since the beach scene in *From Here to Eternity*," a 1953 movie in which Deborah Kerr and Burt Lancaster engage in passionate lovemaking on a gorgeous expanse of beach. In the rush of desire to be with him, I could see myself accepting his invitation and then later realizing that my parents and bosses at *Life* would view my going away again as completely crazy.

I was always concerned that Don's interest in me was purely sexual, and that he didn't consider me as his future wife. His urging me to dash off to another rendezvous on a magical island simply confirmed that I might be no more to him than a sexual object. (Now that he is no longer here, I wish I had thrown caution to the wind and joined him for our own movie-like scene.)

Although the sexual aspects of Don's letters are pleasing to me now from such a distance, I prefer the parts about the tenderness and love—whatever that crazy word means—growing between us. Early in August 1955, he wrote:

> Have I told you too how big the void gets sometimes without you? … I miss talking to you and getting into continuous arguments as I try to enforce my ideas on you and you gently brush them aside. I miss you as a partner in swimming and someone to talk to over a nightclub table. I miss admiring you in your clothes—you dress very well—and in your purple bathing suit. I miss you reaching out and holding my hand when we're out walking.

Don's letters weren't only about externals: at times he showed shrewd insight into some aspect of my personality that caused me problems and may have troubled him. On August 30, from Singapore, he wrote:

> You know, I feel that I know you very well in certain ways, and I can completely understand this fatigue business with you. You are a wonderful girl and, underneath all my gags, I admire and respect you for the way you try to be nice to everyone. But perhaps what I was always trying to say to you in Japan and Hong Kong was that you give too much of yourself to others. It seems to me that people who do that tend to lose their individuality and their sense of "myself" when they try to please all the people that they know.

Soon Don was homeward bound. He had taken my decline of his invitation to rendezvous in Hawaii in good humor, saying, "Well, angel, I can't deny that I'm disappointed about your apparent decision not to attend the meeting at the summit of Hawaii." He also, without asking my opinion, turned down an offer to become *Life*'s bureau chief in Bonn, Germany, which must have been hard to do. While a career-advancing opportunity for him, it would have set back the pace of our romance.

Don was looking forward to seeing me again, but some of his words were contradictory. He wanted to stop over in San Francisco with a view to deciding if he might want to live there someday (*with me or without me?* I wondered). But he couldn't contain his excitement at coming home and working in the New York office, although he worried he would be only a small fish in a big pond and lose the luster he had gained working solo all over the Far East.

Some of his excitement bubbled over in strange ways, such as in his letter of October 25, when he proposed the location of our first meeting.

> Darling, I want to meet you someplace screwy in NY, and I've pretty well hit upon the Port Authority Bus Terminal. You see, the day I arrive will be taken up with Mother and Father anyway in Montclair. They will also meet me at the airport. So the next day I will drive in from New York and park atop the Bus Terminal. If you are downstairs at the information booth at an appointed time, I can sweep you into my big masculine arms and kiss you.

Our letters crossed each other, and Don didn't know that I had finally moved out of my parents' place and rented an apartment six blocks north at 52 East 72nd Street. His last letters kept up a steady drumbeat of his excitement to see me. In October, he wrote about cutting down his days in Hawaii.

> Due to the fact that it will be dull, bleak, and cold without you, and the attendant parties of December lie before me, and I hope you haven't made a date for every night in December already because, darling, a certain Bill Holden-type [a sexy, lanky movie star of the time, whom I always thought Don resembled] recently returned from the Far East and has hopes of monopolizing your time.

"Hurry home, darling," I wrote to him. "Shall meet you on deck at the Port Authority building or the middle of Times Square, if you prefer that setting. Still cannot quite believe that 'D-Day' [my play on the World War II date] is in sight. Please don't postpone it to Washington's birthday—all my love."

I hope that my embrace of Don upon seeing him was warm and long. It was the least he deserved after writing me all those beautiful, loving letters. As for these love letters, I wish I had kept them front and center in my life, not hidden away in a shoebox within a shoebox. Don and I should have reread them each year on our wedding anniversary and made them a permanent part of our marriage. They would have enriched our relationship and love life and triggered conversations not only about our past, but about our present and future.

Hang on to your love letters, e-mails, and texts. Even in your eighties, you'll enjoy rereading them and experiencing the wonderful feelings that love can bring.

Home Again

Don came home; we went from the passionate highs of 1955 to the more problematic lows of 1956, and the flow of letters stopped. We worked a floor apart from each other in the office. He became a writer in the "Newsfronts" section, which was as confining as his job as a foreign correspondent had been liberating. He spent his days writing text blocks and photo captions and submitting his work to an exacting copy editor named Joe Kastner, who could have taught an elephant to write good copy if he—the elephant—had enough time.

Don's personal life was also different: no longer did he live in a gracious home in Singapore with several servants tending to his needs. He had an apartment in the city, and I probably wasn't sufficiently sympathetic to the difficulty of the transition for him.

I always thought Don was a natural writer who could write about any topic with grace and ease, but *Life*'s formulaic text blocks proved difficult for him to master. His lack of confidence made him miserable and rubbed off on our relationship. At the same time, I had a new assignment in *Life*'s Education department, which was an excellent fit for me.

Our love affair floundered for a while, and it was a natural comedown from the intensity of our adventure in Asia and the pent-up longing we felt during our months of separation. Later, in his memoir, Don wrote that upon his return he considered me "the love of my present and future life," but his actions didn't prove his words and I didn't see it quite the same way. I was scared to death that what had happened between the two of us a year earlier might happen for him again with another pretty researcher. Time Inc. was full of smart, stunning women who no doubt saw what I saw: a handsome, smart, charming, funny, single man who wasn't at all ready to settle down.

I threw myself into my new assignment. The Education editor, Norman Ross, was committed to having a new story assigned, photographed, edited, and laid out for the back of the book each week. He worked at a demanding pace that somehow I was able to match, although I was despairing about Don and dating some men on the side to make him jealous.

By day, I was responsible for researching stories about what was new and important in the education field, tapping sources to get advance information on curricula, teaching methods, vogues in student dress and habits, and other aspects of the education world. By night, I was living in my new apartment while Don lived in another rental, both of us feeling angry and unloved.

I felt incapable of surmounting my difficulties with Don. I wanted to get married and he didn't, even though we were smitten with each other. In retrospect, we'd only been together a brief year. I had wanted to marry Don before I officially met him, but I had a ruinous history of becoming angry with myself, perverse, and mistrustful, and then walking away from challenging situations—a patently self-destructive streak in my personality. I had walked away from pursuing an acting career, and now—even though it was completely disadvantageous to what I wanted most in the world—I began to seriously think of walking away from Don.

Thanks to my pediatrician, Dr. Albert Santi, I began to see an elderly psychiatrist who thought I was "confused at the highest levels." His acknowledgment of my confusion reassured me that nothing was seriously wrong with me, except that I had a bad habit of making decisions that worked against what I wanted. My weekly conversations with him and his sage advice on how to keep my relationship moving forward kept me centered and prevented me from blowing my future with Don.

When I finally reported to him that Don had asked me to marry him and I agreed, he said goodbye on the spot.

"That's a perfect ending for our talks together," he said, a smile encircling his face. "You must be so happy, and I am as well."

He moved forward in his chair and looked me straight in the eyes.

"Don't you ever come back again."

He had viewed his role as that of a marriage broker, helping me bring my relationship to a successful conclusion, and I was pleased that he didn't regard me as one who needed extensive therapy to resolve her problems. I've always felt a debt of gratitude to this doctor whose advice steadied me when I needed it most.

About a year before this happy turn of events, the editors at *Life* realized that Don's skills lay in the field as a political correspondent and national affairs reporter and not in the office as a writer. They gave him the chance to cover the Democratic and Republican conventions and then offered him his dream job: Bureau Chief of *Life* in Washington, D.C. The offer saved our relationship, and Don leaped at the chance of becoming head of a bureau that consisted of three photographers, six correspondents, secretaries, and an excellent darkroom.

In his new role, he covered the 1956 Democratic and Republican conventions, which took place in Chicago and San Francisco. He suggested that I fly out to meet him at the end of the Republican gathering; he'd rent a car, and we'd drive across the country together. This time I accepted his invitation with alacrity, remembering how well we'd traveled together in Japan; I hoped another trip would build on the good memories.

The conventions were pretty tame, as the Republicans again nominated their 1952 winning ticket of President Eisenhower and Vice President Nixon. Although we didn't know it at the time, the results of the Democratic convention in Chicago augured well for our future. Although the Democrats nominated Governor Adlai Stevenson for president and Senator Estes Kefauver for vice president, Senator John F. Kennedy stole the show and was catapulted onto the national stage. Little did we realize that four years later Don would join the Kennedy campaign and help JFK become president.

I decided that since we were traveling in America and not incognito in Japan, we should pretend to the outside world that we were a married couple. I also decided that wearing a wedding ring would help us through registration hurdles at different motels on our transcontinental journey (keeping us safe from prying eyes and smirking motel owners). I bought an inexpensive gold band and enjoyed the feel of it on my third finger.

We drove in a gray Buick convertible and went back to doing what we loved: soaking up history and relaxing with each other. We stopped at many places: an expensive family-run ranch in northern California, where a horse I was riding tossed me off its back; Reno, Nevada, where Don walked into a gambling parlor and walked out an hour later with $700 in winnings; Yosemite National Park, where the aspens were turning gold in the September light; and Abraham and Mary Todd Lincoln's home in downtown Springfield, Illinois, from which he left in 1861 to become the 16th president of the United States.

Don had a lifelong love affair with U.S. presidents and loved learning more than he knew about them, and he was an excellent teacher for me. He particularly liked researching Woodrow Wilson, as he wrote his senior thesis at Yale on him and people always asked if he was related to him. I enjoyed being part of the learning process and wearing the gold ring on my finger. When we got back to New York City, off it came.

Don took over as *Life*'s bureau chief in Washington, D.C., in early 1957. He settled himself in an adorable, small, pea-green house on the corner of 29th and Olive streets in Georgetown. He even found a housekeeper and cook, Louise, and set up a typical bachelor pad with her help. We took turns commuting to our bachelor/bachelorette apartments every weekend.

In the shoebox containing the love letters, I found an American Airlines plane schedule with flight departure and arrival times between Washington, D.C., and New York. I also found a sweet note attesting to his pleasure about our get-together in Washington: "What a great weekend! Darling, you are still as wonderful as ever, and now I know why I missed you so much. Now I can think of you in terms of Mt. Vernon and General Lee as well as in terms of Kyoto and Hong Kong." But even better was Don's memoir passage about this moment in our relationship: "Susan and I commuted every weekend to be together, and there was no diminishment in our love for each other. So what the hell was I doing? Susan was wondering the same thing."

The wondering came to an end on the morning of January 14, 1957, three days before my 27th birthday. Don hadn't come up for the weekend, but he called to say that he had Monday off and would it be all right if he came up for the day? It was fine with me as I had the day off. I didn't think he had an ulterior motive, even when he walked in the door around 10 o'clock in the morning carrying a purple orchid in a white, see-through box. That should have been the tip-off: Don was not prone to buying me flowers.

We were sitting on the sofa and he gave me the orchid, which I put on the coffee table, and then he reached over, took my hands in his, and said the words that I had longed to hear him say for two years: "Susan, darling, will you marry me?" Without waiting a single second, I said, "Of course," and broke into peals of laughter, and then we both burst into tears. After calling our respective families (I had never met his), we went to the movies. I don't think Hollywood would have approved of this rather ordinary ending—we did buy a bottle of champagne to toast each other and our future—but it felt fine to us.

Happy Ever After

It finally happened, and it could have been a feature in the Party section of the magazine, "*Life* Goes to a Party: The Wedding of Susan Neuberger and Donald Wilson." Don and I were married on Saturday, April 6, 1957, in New York City. We had a traditional wedding at St. James' Episcopal Church on Madison Avenue and 71st Street. I wish that we had been a little more adventurous and married on that beach in Hawaii that was so alluring to Don, yet our families would not have followed us there. (Many years later, our son, Dwight and Deborah Davis were married on Orcas Island in Puget Sound, Washington. We flew there in a single engine plane and enjoyed a somewhat non-traditional but wonderful wedding.)

The church rector, Dr. Arthur Kinsolving, performed the traditional Episcopalian marriage service, and I have kept the white booklet, from which he read the simple ceremony, next to my prayer book in my bureau. When I found Don's love letters, I also found a little cardboard box with the initials "NW" in silver, forming a circle on top. Knowing that the bride and groom gave tiny pieces of fruitcake wrapped in foil to each wedding guest to sleep on the night after the wedding (to bring the newly married couple good luck), I opened it quickly. No cake, but I slipped the empty little box into my bureau drawer right next to the booklet. I liked the way the designer had the "N" and "W" touching each other.

I finally had the gold ring that I had so wanted, and it remains right on my finger where Don placed it that Saturday in April. When we married, men didn't wear or want wedding bands, but on our fortieth wedding anniversary, I gave Don a wide gold band from Tiffany's engraved with his and my initials and the date, April 6, 1997. I presented it to him over dinner after we went back to St. James' with our three adult children and their families to retrace the scene of our marriage. He loved wearing the ring and never took it off. After he died, I removed it from his finger, and from time to time I wear it around my neck on a gold chain. It brings back many happy memories of our love and life.

What made the wedding special was the fact that ours was an office romance—finally we could proclaim it to the skies—and everyone at *Life* felt that he or she had played a role in it. We invited all 50 of the editorial staff, and they had a wonderful time enlivening the staid, old Colony Club with their drinking, dancing, and toasting. Dwight Martin—the *Time* bureau chief in Singapore who had shared his elegant house with Don—was an usher, replete in a morning coat, which must have been uncomfortable for someone used to wearing only shorts and a shirt. We named our son after Dwight because of his many kindnesses to us at the beginning of our love affair.

Stan Flink was at his funniest and most charming, taking full credit for our relationship, since he had made the introduction in his office. And my mother was happier than I had ever seen her in my life. I kept looking at her, especially when I was dancing with Don.

"Have you ever seen my mother look happier?" I whispered to him over Lester Lanin's music. "She thought that I would never get married. She thought I would be an old maid." I planted a kiss on the lips of my rescuer—and my mother's savior.

༄

We went on a lovely, relaxing honeymoon at Half Moon Bay, a resort on the north coast of Jamaica, but it wasn't quite as electric as our pre-honeymoon. Our bodies were good friends with each other by that point, and it isn't easy to re-create first passion. But we learned some facts about each other, one of which was my proclivity to seasickness. One day we took a canoe ride on the usually calm, turquoise waters of the bay. The wind came up, the waters turned choppy, and the canoe bounced and bounced in the little waves. When we returned to shore, looking for a touch of sympathy, I admitted to Don that I felt seasick. He looked at me with astonishment and said, "If I had known about this problem, I might not have married you." I thanked my lucky stars that we hadn't taken any canoe rides during our time together in Asia. (Much later in our lives, Don had to contend with my problem of seasickness when we sailed with the Kennedys, and on one trip I threw up at Bobby Kennedy's feet. Kennedys abhorred weaknesses of any sort. That time he responded with gallantry and cleaned up the vomit without a reprimand.)

Our two-week honeymoon came to an end on April 21, 1957. When the plane landed at Washington National Airport and we arrived suntanned and happy at 1229 Olive Street NW, I stood on the pavement looking up at its pea-green exterior, thinking, *You'll be spending more than every other weekend here now.* I was grateful that both the house and, more important, its adored owner were finally mine.

Washington

Lady-in-Waiting

Jacqueline Lee Bouvier Kennedy was one of the first people I came in contact with as a newly married woman in Washington. I had first crossed paths with her as a teenage girl. It was the 1947 debutante season in New York City, and 17- and 18-year-olds like Jacqueline Lee Bouvier and I were plunged into a round of balls during Christmas vacation. We had both completed our first months at Vassar. I caught sight of her at one of the balls at the Waldorf Astoria, resplendent in an off-the-shoulder, emerald-green satin evening gown with a bouffant skirt. Other debs like me were wearing white dresses with corsages above their left breasts. Jackie wasn't wearing any flowers. Holding herself in a regal way, she was walking up a grand set of stairs and, behind her, two young men dressed in white tie and tails. She smiled confidently and commanded the eyes of everyone on the balcony.

She is a queen, I thought. I knew I'd never have the sophistication to walk so confidently up the grand staircase. I'd be too preoccupied staring at my own feet so I wouldn't trip on my dress.

Jackie and I grew up no more than a few blocks from each other in apartment houses on the Upper East Side. We had never met but went to rival, all-girl independent schools within blocks of each other near the East River. She eventually went away to Miss Porter's School, in Farmington, Connecticut, but I stayed at Brearley through twelfth grade.

Our lives finally intersected when we arrived at Vassar in the fall of 1947. My sightings of her on the leafy campus were few, but we did share one class: French. It was a sophomore-level class, and Jackie spoke the language fluently. I did not. Professor Madame LeLavandier doted on "Mademoiselle Bouvier" with her perfect pronunciation and accurate grammar. I could never roll my tongue around the language as impressively as Jackie did, and I imagined that she would have no trouble speaking French to President Charles de Gaulle. (I didn't suspect that it was merely a matter of time.)

Jackie often came to French class in riding attire with highly polished boots. The rest of us, mere mortals, wore pedal pushers and twin sweater sets. We surmised that she had stabled her horse somewhere off campus and either came from riding to the midday class or returned to it when it was over. Her savoir faire was dashing, somewhat forbidding, but spoke of her confidence.

I struggled to gain confidence, and from the start of college I felt there was an outsized competition for position based on beauty and dates with young men. I didn't have either, especially dates. Much of the talk those first months at Vassar was about the debutante balls and which men from which colleges were going to be your escorts. I had never invited a man to escort me to a ball, and I struggled to learn how to do it.

Jackie, on the other hand, was hailed as the "debutante of the year" by the society press. I admired her poise and composure, knowing I could not in a hundred years be worthy of such an accolade. But she possessed more than glamour—a talented, serious student, she chose to leave Vassar and spend her junior year at the Sorbonne in Paris. Another classmate and one of my closest friends, Shirley Lewis Oakes, chose the same path. She and Jackie shared an apartment free from the rules of our all-women's college with its curfews and limits on male visitors.

The thought of spending a year abroad to widen my horizons never crossed my mind, since I was still tied to my parents' apron strings. Shirley's letters recounted stories of her and Jackie's romances with dashing men from exotic countries. I spent my boyfriend-free days directing the freshman play, *I Remember Mama*, and writing theater reviews for the *Vassar Chronicle*. Her accounts of dashing men gnawed at my perceived inadequacies.

When Jackie's junior year in Paris was over, she decided not to return to the cloistered halls of Vassar. She transferred to George Washington University, in Washington, D.C., where she could live with her family. I heard that she said she wasn't coming back because Vassar was for "little girls," and I believed her comment applied directly to women like me, spending our last year on campus with its curfews and restrictions. Jackie had bigger dreams.

Life after graduation turned out to be less formidable than I feared. I lived in New York City and surprised myself with my resiliency after getting fired from my first job, and soon landing a better one at *Life*. Jackie graduated from George Washington University and became the "Inquiring Photographer" for the *Washington Post*.

After our brief careers in journalism, we both married: Jackie to Senator John F. Kennedy in 1953, and I to Don in 1957. Shirley was a bridesmaid in both weddings. Jackie's wedding to the dashing bachelor was immediately dubbed the "wedding of the year," and pictures of her dancing in a gorgeous gown and flowing lace veil appeared in newspapers coast to coast. She had captured the most eligible bachelor in America. I read every news story. Having a friend who was a bridesmaid in the "wedding of the year" made me feel as if I was in Jackie's fairy-tale orbit, if only for a moment on its shimmering edge. Furthermore, there was already talk that the senator might run for president, giving *Life* an unprecedented opportunity to do many stories about him and his new, beautiful bride.

Don and I were married in a smaller-scale ceremony that was certainly not covered by the paparazzi of the time, but I was happy with my choice of husband. At 27, I was among the last of my peers to marry; I had not only finally passed my generation's "marriage test," but I was in love with and had married a handsome foreign correspondent. I moved to Washington with Don, never imagining that my life would reconnect with Jackie's again or how his new position at *Life* would serve John Kennedy's presidential ambitions.

Soon after my arrival, someone in Senator Kennedy's office who was savvy enough to realize that *Life* magazine connections were important for a man with presidential ambitions connected the Vassar dots. Jackie called shortly after our arrival to ask if she could come for tea at my house. What I remember most were my preparations for her visit. I spent hours sprucing up our Georgetown townhouse. The Kennedys were living in an elegant, red brick townhouse, and our little house on Olive Street suddenly felt uncomfortably shabby. Since I couldn't magically change Don's modern furniture to eighteenth-century antiques, with which I surmised Jackie had undoubtedly furnished her home, I decided to make everything in our house sparkle.

When Jackie arrived, she looked around the house, searching awhile for the right word to describe it.

"Oh," she said. "Isn't this pristine?"

I felt as if her huge, dark-brown eyes, which she focused on me with piercing intensity, could read all my insecurities. For a terrible moment, I wondered if she had watched me climb the ladder to wash down the doorway the day before her arrival. I had a feeling that if our teatime were a tryout for a play, I wouldn't receive a callback.

I was at ease during only one part of her visit. Don had called in advance of Jackie's arrival to tell me that Senator Kennedy's book, *Profiles in Courage*, had that day been awarded the Pulitzer Prize for history. Jackie hadn't heard the momentous news, and her dark eyes grew even wider as I told her. She asked for the phone to call her husband's office to confirm it. I was relieved that I could be the bearer of such important news, since I had no confidence in my ability to make small talk.

Lady-in-Waiting

❧

I didn't see Jackie again until after each of us had had a child: Caroline was born in November 1957, and Dwight in the spring of 1958. When our children turned three, we were both invited to join a playgroup of about a dozen mothers and babies from the Georgetown area. Jackie came with her little daughter frequently, and I became more comfortable talking with her about child-rearing issues. Although she never put on airs, I felt a distance between her and the rest of us, as if she were waiting for her starring role in the drama of the United States presidency.

My husband and I had become friends with Bobby and Ethel Kennedy during this time, and when Senator Kennedy announced his candidacy, I urged Don to consider taking a leave of absence from *Life* to become part of his campaign. I believed that we might have a chance to play a part in the Kennedys' unfolding pageant.

Senator Kennedy claimed his election as president of the United States on a cold, clear November morning. I watched from the audience as he stood onstage in the local high school in Hyannis Port, Massachusetts, with Jackie beside him, nine months pregnant in a royal purple coat. She smiled as the president-elect announced, "We look forward to a new administration and a new baby."

I suddenly remembered what Jackie had advised our mutual friend, Shirley, about one of her boyfriends: "Marry him. He'll be king, and you'll be queen." I wondered if she, too, had planned to marry a king, as it appeared she was ascending a throne. I also wondered if Don might play a part in the administration, and I, as his wife, a small role in the First Lady's entourage.

A few weeks later, Don was appointed deputy director of the United States Information Agency in the Kennedy administration, and we were caught up in a round of inaugural balls. Jackie was more elegant than a movie star in her slimming, white-chiffon sheath, which she had designed herself. (It's now part of the permanent collection of First Ladies' inaugural gowns at the Smithsonian, National Museum of American History. The dress I wore to those balls—a shell-pink satin skirt and sequined lace top made to order by Madame Paul of Georgetown—hangs in a cedar closet in my basement.)

My role as a lady-in-waiting was about to begin, as a rumor made the rounds of our playgroup that Mrs. Kennedy—the form of address newly required of all of us—wished to transform our group into a proper school for Caroline at the White House. The rumor became reality, and Mrs. Kennedy asked me to help her organize the White House school and find an experienced person to become its head teacher. I was flattered that she offered me a chance to be of service to her. I wanted to impress Jackie with my professional abilities and to shine for her.

Mrs. Kennedy wrote memos to me in her distinctive handwriting on yellow legal pads about all aspects of the proposed school. She explained what she wanted in a head teacher: a willingness to be circumspect and to understand the delicacy of working in the White House, trustworthiness and experience teaching young children. I traveled to New York City to talk with the head of the Lower School of my alma mater about a prospective teacher and arranged a meeting with Alice Grimes, the Brearley kindergarten teacher who Mrs. Kennedy eventually selected.

As the school's opening day approached, I set up carpool arrangements for the mothers. No one ever complained when asked to drive the carpool to the White House through the southwest gate, given the chance to see President Kennedy talking to the children around the swings on the newly fashioned playground. On occasion, a mother would ask to shift her carpool duty, so she could go to the hairdresser before picking up the children.

The creation of the White House school was but a footnote in the history of the Kennedy administration, yet serving Mrs. Kennedy was as satisfying to me as anything I had ever done. I was realizing that I was more suited to the role of a professional than to that of social charmer, that I was more comfortable in service than in leading others. Serving Mrs. Kennedy was meaningful, and I finally felt comfortable in my skin.

One afternoon, after the school was running smoothly, a White House messenger came to my front door with a gift from Mrs. Kennedy. It was a framed print of the south side of the White House, where the school's rooms were located, with an American flag flying from the top. Mrs. Kennedy had inscribed a note of thanks on it:

> This flag should be flying for you—for behind that balustrade is our little school—and all your dedication to it has done more than anything to bring happiness to its resident pupil—and peace of mind to her mother!
>
> With such appreciation—Affectionately, Jackie

I read the inscription several times, knowing instinctively that the little print would forever be among my dearest possessions. It was the only object I would ever receive from Jackie, and I have kept it on a small stand on my bedside night table for 40 years. I consider it a medal of sorts for public service, which I believe is the highest form of service one can perform in society. I never showed the print to my mother, though, or told her how I'd kept it close to me. It may have reminded her of my choice to be a lady-in-waiting.

After the assassination of her husband in November 1963, Mrs. Kennedy returned to New York City. Although she later married Aristotle Onassis and lived briefly abroad, the city was her home. My family and I had moved back to the city when Don left President Lyndon Johnson's administration. Again, Jackie and I lived within blocks of each other on the Upper East Side. From time to time, I would see her walking around the reservoir in Central Park, wearing large, dark glasses and a silk scarf over her head. Not wanting to break into her reverie, I would drop my eyes and continue my run—always in lady-in-waiting mode.

We came face to face in Prague some years later, in 1993. I had heard that she and her companion, Maurice Tempelsman, were at the same hotel where my friends and I were staying. I wasn't too sure I wanted to see her. Many years had passed since I helped her set up the White House school, and I couldn't think of anything to say to her.

One morning, the decision was taken out of my hands. I had returned from an early morning walk around the city and was dressed in an ordinary, tomato-colored raincoat and old pair of running shoes. I was sitting on a small sofa in the hotel lobby, waiting for my friends to join me for breakfast, when the elevator opened and I glimpsed Jackie and Maurice walking into the lobby. I was mortified by my appearance and immediately ducked my head, hoping she wouldn't see me. As I sat with my chin tucked into my chest, I saw a pair of shoes moving slowly toward me. They stopped directly in front of me, and I heard her feathery voice say, "Susie [pronounced Soozie], is that you?" Jackie had caught me flatfooted, and I knew I had to stand up and have a conversation with her. She introduced me to Maurice, an instant charmer, and we talked about the beauties of the city.

Back in the States and musing on having seen her again, I realized that Jackie and I had changed as women, and I felt a closer connection to her. We had both become working girls: she a book editor at two prestigious publishing houses and I director of a sexuality education organization at a state university. She had embraced feminism, given an interview to *Ms.* magazine, and spoken out for women's equality. I marched for women's reproductive rights and advocated for pregnancy prevention services for teenage girls. I felt more secure about my beliefs and abilities. The distance between us had lessened a little, and I felt that Jackie and I might actually have a conversation of equals, should we ever be together again.

Jackie died in 1994 of non-Hodgkin's lymphoma a year after I saw her in Prague, and I miss her. Sometimes a memory concerning my mother returns when I think of her. My mother would often ask me when I was a young adult, "Susie, why do you want to be someone's lady-in-waiting?" Her remark troubled me because I knew it was partly true. Only later did I realize that my relationship with Jackie perfectly represented my mother's anxiety about my tendency to play a subservient, lady-in-waiting role to others more powerful than I.

In different ways, they both helped me realize that some women do service for others while in the limelight, and others do service as ladies-in-waiting.

A Washington-Plus Wife

U.S. INFORMATION AGENCY's deputy director Donald M. Wilson has an invaluable asset in young, elegant, efficient wife, Susan. Favorite of official Washington, she studies French, teaches remedial reading in spare time, runs a well-organized household *and* attends to the growing pains of son Dwight, 6; daughter Kate, 5.

As the Kennedy administration rolled along, I became something I never thought I'd be: a social butterfly. My principal job was spending my evenings with Don at countless private and diplomatic parties in order to enhance the image of the New Frontier as distinct from the older, more staid Eisenhower administration. Married women of my generation were expected to do their share as social butterflies, but I was doing it in spades in Washington. I was caught up in the social whirl without giving it much thought. I'm sure many women envied my position, but it was expected of me and I could not complain. If I hadn't on occasion caught a glimpse of the White House, the Washington Monument, or the Capitol beginning in late 1961, I might have thought that I was still in New York City doing features for "*Life* Goes to a Party." The major difference between my life at *Life* and the social whirl of official Kennedy Washington was that Don and I were at the center of the parties and journalists were reporting on our activities—not the reverse.

The social whirl began almost as soon as President Kennedy took the oath of office and didn't taper off until everything ended in Dallas. We had moved into our first post-married home at 4237 Garfield Street NW, a small, charming colonial perched on a hill only 15 minutes from downtown D.C. By election time, we had two young children and Don, as deputy director of the United States Information Agency (USIA), was charged with serving as second in command to Edward R. Murrow, the famous CBS war correspondent who signed on as USIA director. Ed and Don were charged with implementing the administration's policies to reshape our nation's image around the world to one that was admired.

I relied on a series of live-in au pairs, who usually came from abroad for a year's stay with us to ostensibly learn English and help me take care of our children, although we did our best to see them as much as we could. Although shopping had no allure for me, I spent an inordinate amount of time purchasing floor-length evening gowns and short cocktail dresses, but even more on having my hair coiffed. I would have it cut, colored, straightened, blow-dried, teased, combed, and sprayed into the bouffant look so popular back then. As for my party clothes, I benefited from my friendship with Ethel Kennedy, who kindly suggested that I use her dressmaker, Madame Paul, who designed perfectly fitting clothes that her army of couturiers spent nights sewing in time for clients' parties. Amazingly, Madame Paul never had her clientele wear similar outfits. I can still remember my two favorite evening dresses: a bright-pink, ribbed silk number that I wore when I was photographed dancing with Bobby Kennedy and a pale-green satin dress with a dramatic off-the-shoulder drape, which I wore to a White House dance.

I look back with some horror on the many hours I spent trying to beautify myself for social events rather than focusing on more important tasks like caring for my family, community, and country—but administration officials' wives did what we were told. My role models were Ethel; Nicole Alphand, the stunningly svelte wife of the French ambassador to the U.S.; and, of course, Jacqueline Kennedy, who appeared daily in the press wearing a different—and ever more elaborate—new gown and hairstyle. My life may have sounded glamorous, but it was full of pressure since I had to keep everything on an even keel at home and be ready when Don appeared in his official, chauffeur-driven car to whisk us away to another social occasion. Washington was a punctual town: events started on time and ended promptly so administration officials could be at their desks early in the morning.

Part of the arrangement in Washington's social circles was to reciprocate and give parties, although not necessarily on the same scale. A couple—mainly the wife—was judged by the quality of the dinner parties they hosted and the importance of their guests in the Washington hierarchy as well as by their table settings, seating arrangements, meal creativity and choice of wine and, most importantly, the quality of their guests' conversations.

I had never given a fancy dinner party in my life before arriving in Washington, so I learned by observation and the belief that practice makes perfect. I knew I couldn't go wrong if I followed Jacqueline Kennedy's lead. One of the hallmarks of the Kennedy White House was the use of round tables that seated ten people at state dinner parties, which was a break from tradition. I followed the first lady's lead and used special, floor-length linen tablecloths for round tables; low, round bowls of flowers as centerpieces; carefully planned seating arrangements that recognized guests' ranks; place cards at every seat; and small, gilt wooden chairs.

Perils of Being a Hostess

Early in the administration, Don and I were invited to a dinner party hosted by Rowland Evans, a highly regarded *New York Herald Tribune* columnist, and his delightful wife, Kay, who became a good friend and would later join us on Bobby and Ethel Kennedy's 1964 trip to Europe. Ethel and Bobby, who had been appointed attorney general, were invited to the same party, and he was the guest of honor. Bobby, who was more comfortable with people he knew, took Kay aside when he arrived and asked who she had seated him next to. When she told him, he said, "I want to sit next to Susie Wilson." Kay, a little annoyed at having to change her elaborate seating chart, whispered to me, "That's certainly a compliment for you." She was surprised, since she didn't think Don's rank granted me a position next to the newly minted attorney general, and she didn't know that I possessed enough charm and conversational skills to engage her guest of honor. Nevertheless, Bobby and I had a nice time chatting about our respective little children and some issues of the day.

I had learned by then that conversations were the lifeblood of these diplomatic parties. Night after night, as I sat between two men with important positions, I was under pressure to keep them interested in my conversation. I once asked Ethel, who could talk a flock of birds down from the trees, for advice on how to start a conversation with a new dinner partner.

"Turn to your right [the most important guest was to a woman's right] and quickly ask your dinner partner, 'What do you do?' That should take you through the first course and halfway through the main course. Then, as he quickly tries to finish his salad because dinner is being served, turn to your left and ask the other man the same question."

"And what happens if his answers only take me through the salad course?" I asked, eagerly dropping her advice into my memory bank.

"Probably won't, and you can say things like, 'Oh, that sounds so interesting, please tell me more,' and by the time dessert is done, he'll be winding down."

I realized that the burden of a good conversation was really on the other person, but it still wasn't easy for me, and I always judged a conversation's success on whether the person I was talking with laughed at appropriate moments. (One reason I was initially attracted to Don was because he often laughed at the things I said, which deepened his connection to me.)

Ethel's tips worked to perfection most evenings, and I employed them frequently, but they didn't work out quite as planned at one of our first dinner parties in our new house at 5105 Lowell Lane NW, which we moved into in late 1962. Don and I were hosting dinner for 30 people in honor of Adlai Stevenson, the U.S. ambassador to the United Nations. Ambassador Stevenson was seated on my right, and after Don had welcomed our guests, I turned to him ready with the question, but he quickly asked, "What do *you* do?" I panicked: *Had he heard Ethel's advice to me? Had he instructed her?* He smiled reassuringly, and I decided to tell him the truth: "Oh, Mr. Ambassador, you may not believe me, but that was exactly the same question I was going to ask you!" His face melted into a soft grin, and we were off exchanging answers.

Despite my private tutoring from Ethel, I never had great confidence in my conversational abilities. Raising two young children often prevented me from keeping abreast of fast-breaking news, and I didn't dare give my opinions about current events to people who were involved in forging them. Of course Don, because of his position, was always on top of every subject under the sun that arose during a dinner party. I always marveled that he was never at a loss for words, which took the pressure off me.

I never dared speak at the Hickory Hill Seminars that Bobby organized for members of the administration with the leading thinkers of the day. We felt honored to be invited, and Don had confidence in his knowledge of history and current events to ask pertinent questions. I assumed that I wouldn't even be able to form an intelligent question, and I would have choked trying to get the words out of my mouth. I can feel the fear of having host Bobby say to me, "Now, Susie, let's hear from you," but he restrained himself. I wasn't the only woman scared to speak at important dinner parties; almost all of us Washington wives were working so hard to help our husbands keep up with the challenges of their jobs as well as care for our children that we didn't have time to work on ourselves.

Although I wouldn't have had the word for it, sexism was rampant during the early sixties and alive and well in the Kennedy administration. Bright, powerful women were not cabinet level appointees; they were their wives—and women were judged on their charm rather than their suggestions about policies. One evening I was invited to a small, informal dinner in the family dining room of the White House. A good pal of the president's asked him when he was going to "do something for women." Quick as a flash, as was his habit, Kennedy replied, "I'll do something in the second term, but first I have to get re-elected." His answer reflected the mood of the country rather than his own views about increasing opportunities for women. But hopes for a second term under his leadership and more programs enhancing the roles of women died in Dallas on November 22, 1963.

A Brief Shining Moment

In 1962, I became the executive "chairman" of a special benefit for the Lt. Joseph P. Kennedy Jr. Institute in Washington and the Kennedy Child Study Center for Retarded Children in New York City (no one in the early sixties questioned the use of a masculine title to describe a role held by a woman). Ethel gave me the opportunity to organize the benefit in Washington as an amusing way to thank me for my help on our round-the-world trip in February; the Kennedys liked to test their friends' mettle and keep them on their toes, so she decided to put me to the test once again.

The family started the organizations in memory of two of Joseph and Rose Kennedy's children. Their son Joseph P. Kennedy, Jr., a naval aviator, was killed when a plane filled with explosives that he was piloting blew up over the English Channel. Their daughter Rosemary suffered from developmental delays and was institutionalized for much of her life.

Ethel and her sister-in-law, Jean Kennedy Smith, decided to hold the benefit on September 25, 1962, to raise funds for the organizations. It would preview a performance of the Irving Berlin musical *Mr. President* at the National Theater. What set this benefit apart from many others in Washington, D.C., was the promise that President and Mrs. Kennedy would attend the performance, and it would be followed by a supper dance at the British embassy for the most expensive ticket purchasers.

The First Lady was the benefit's honorary chairman and I, as Mrs. Donald M. Wilson, was the executive chairman for Washington (three women served as executive chairmen for New York). I knew I had been given the position because of my friendship with the Kennedys, not because I possessed any particularly outstanding skills. As executive chairman, I coordinated the executive committees and a general committee of 150 women in Washington and New York and oversaw planning for the theater performance, the 16 pre-theater dinners at the homes of the cream of Washington society, and the fancy supper ball for 600. I had so much to do that I never stopped to worry about whether I would fail or succeed. The Kennedys were the American royal family at the time, which made my job easy. When I asked people for a favor, they responded with alacrity, and although I didn't realize it at the time, organizing the benefit played to my strengths: working hard, recruiting and keeping people involved, carrying out innumerable requests, and attending to details quickly with good humor.

My friendship with Ethel gave me instant credibility, and I was pleased when legendary White House correspondent Helen Thomas, of United Press International, wrote that the "nagging details which go with a Washington event are being handled in part by Mrs. Donald M. Wilson, wife of the deputy director of the USIA." She mentioned my worldwide trip with Bobby and Ethel and then added a line I liked: "Susie Wilson is New Frontier all the way." The press often characterized the New Frontier as youthful, vigorous, and energetic, and Thomas must have thought I possessed these qualities.

I am amazed today when I look through my scrapbook of the event and see the letter President Kennedy wrote to me and the committee on White House stationery, with "Mrs. Donald M. Wilson, Committee for the Benefit of Kennedy Homes for Mentally Retarded Children, Washington, D.C." printed at the bottom. His letter, which was included in the benefit program, revealed his deep interest in what was then called "mental retardation," which he considered the "number one child-health problem" in the nation.

Media coverage of the benefit was intense: articles began appearing in early spring in the Washington papers and in the national press by summer. *Vogue* and *Town & Country* magazines ran features on the fashionable women involved in the benefit. The New York papers reported on ticket requests, which came from as far away as Paris, Monaco, and Ireland. People lucky enough to buy top-priced tickets were flying in for the evening from New York, Chicago, and other major cities.

We sold out the benefit weeks before the performance and raised $90,000, a large sum of money for the time. Our goal had been $70,000—$35,000 for each beneficiary—but the Kennedy family decided to donate the additional

$20,000 to the city's United Givers Fund. The Kennedy glamour definitely put the benefit way over the top. Ethel with her captivating smile and the charming Jean Kennedy Smith appeared in many photos relating to the benefit. I was pleased to be included in some of the stories, especially in one by Betty Beale, the society columnist of official Washington, who wrote for the *Washington Star*. She reported on the first benefit committee meeting at Ethel's home on March 9, 1962:

> It looked as though the who's who of Washington feminine society under the Kennedy administration had assembled in the Robert Kennedys' drawing room. ... The good-looking, young wife of the Deputy Director of USIA launched into the whys and wherefores of what promises to be the most brilliant, most glamorous, most newsworthy benefit ever held in Washington.

Not bad press! *Time* magazine's review of the evening called it the "sveltest, splashiest, most scrambled-after social affair that the nation's capital has seen in many years." It reported that the only letdown was the musical, but all of us involved in the effort were excused from the poor review since we were responsible only for the events before and after it. The benefit is a blur in my mind; I was so focused on making sure everything went off without a hitch, but I do remember President Kennedy never looking more handsome or Mrs. Kennedy lovelier. Their guest for the evening was Alice Longworth Roosevelt, the spirited daughter of Republican President Theodore Roosevelt who announced that she had temporarily become a Democrat during the Kennedy administration. It was a star-studded evening in every way, and it all went smoothly even though it rained. (We ordered up 20 golf-size umbrellas to shield guests going from theater to cars to dinners.)

After the event, Ethel instructed me to carry out one final detail: sending flowers in Steuben vases to the 16 Washington wives who gave the pre-theater dinner parties and to committee members who had gone beyond the call of duty. Later that day, a florist's assistant appeared on my doorstep holding a box. I thanked him, closed the door, and took out one of those Steuben vases filled with spring flowers. They were from Ethel, whose note read:

Dear Mrs. President:

    Jean and I want to congratulate you on somehow managing to get across to the world that you are entirely responsible for the unheard of success. You are—Therefore it's all yours next year.

She signed it, "Busloads of hugs and kisses from the assistant to the aide of one of many." The "Mrs. President" referred to me, and I was appalled when I read it, initially fearing the worst: *Had I indeed hogged the limelight? Had I not given Jean and Ethel their due when I spoke about the benefit? Why didn't they realize I couldn't have done anything without them?* I immediately called my florist and asked him to send two bouquets of the most beautiful flowers to Jean and Ethel. I dictated heartfelt notes of thanks, emphasizing that there would have been no benefit without them.

After I reread the note, I calmed down; I realized its tone reflected Ethel's sly humor and sense of fun. Ethel did pay me a compliment weeks after the benefit was over: "Susie, you are all set up now to run the opera benefit." This was high praise, because the Washington opera was the cultural icon of old guard Washington, but I had no desire to plan another benefit without the Kennedy women leading the way.

Assessing Achievements

In 1965, Letitia (Tish) Baldridge, who was Jacqueline Kennedy's respected social secretary, wrote a story called "The Capitol Wife-Plus" for *Cosmopolitan* magazine and coined the term "Washington Wife-Plus" (or "WWP"). She defined a WWP as "a woman who really wants to help her husband and who gains ego-satisfaction from his accomplishments. … While basking all the time in her husband's glory, she suddenly finds that she is basking in a goodly share of her own." She aimed to draw some conclusions about the qualities women needed for success in Washington's social circles. Her piece ran with the subhead, "In the nation's capital, where affluence is less important than influence, and the personal touch more potent than the political, the Solon's secret weapon is often his charming wife. An insider reveals the subtle ways of the Washington wife who helps her husband succeed without the appearance of really trying." (A "solon" is a government official, diplomat, or congressman living in Washington.)

By then, the Kennedy administration was sadly history and Lyndon Johnson was president. I was one of the five women featured in her story, all of whose husbands, like Don, served in both administrations. Her description of a WWP fit who I wanted to be at that time of my life like those elegant, long, white kid gloves that I wore with evening dresses to State Department dinners. She identified me and the other WWPs as "the wife of," using only our husbands' first and last names. I was oblivious to the fact that I wasn't identified as an individual but as Don's wife, which is what society asked of me.

The flattering photograph that ran with the story shows Don, me, and our children Dwight and Kate on the staircase of our second home in Washington, at 5105 Lowell Lane NW. Dwight is holding a book and apparently showing off his reading skills, and Kate is reacting to the story. Don and I are in evening clothes and my hair is freshly coiffed; the children are dressed in their pajamas and bathrobes. The caption reads: "U.S. Information Agency's deputy director Donald M. Wilson has an invaluable asset in young, elegant, efficient wife, Susan. Favorite of official Washington, she studies French, teaches remedial reading in spare time, runs a well-organized household, and attends to the growing pains of son Dwight, 6, and daughter Kate, 5."

These words describe the woman I wanted to be at that time of my life, yet when I read the story many years later, I am proudest of its mention of my volunteer work as a remedial reading tutor. There were many poor African-American families whose children went to inadequately funded schools in Washington, D.C. Teachers needed volunteers to help students who had fallen behind in reading, and I found a program that placed me in classrooms as a volunteer tutor.

I will always remember one of my students, Jessica, a tall, gawky second grader with curly hair who was struggling to learn to read. I worked hard to find interesting ways to pique her interest in the written word, but was never successful. We met twice a week in a tiny closet at her rundown school. She was always interested in knowing about what she called "whitey's world," and to satisfy her curiosity, I asked the principal permission to drive her to our house for supper. The principal granted my request, and one afternoon, I brought her to our large, bluestone house surrounded by mowed lawns and large trees. As it was springtime, the azaleas were in bloom and the trees were full of new greenery. I had no idea how Jessica would react to this change of scene from the cramped noisy streets of her inner city neighborhood.

When I pulled into our driveway, she uncurled those giraffe-long legs of hers, pushed open the car door, and stepped outside into a virtually unknown world. My banal words "Welcome to our house" died on my lips as I looked at Jessica, who seemed absolutely dumbfounded.

"Oh, it is so quiet here," she said. "So quiet."

As she took in the quiet, I imagined the world she had left: tiny rooms with thin walls, beds shared with siblings, radios blaring music, black-and-white TVs flickering, cars racing by, and even a burst of gunfire or two as night fell.

Years later I was reminded of Jessica when I became educated about the high rates of unplanned pregnancy among African-American teen girls in the United States, due in large part to their growing up in poverty without much hope of escaping it. I often wondered if she had become one of the statistics and hoped that another tutor had come into her life and helped her learn to read and thrive at school, since a good education is critical to escaping poverty for a better life.

Travels with the Kennedys

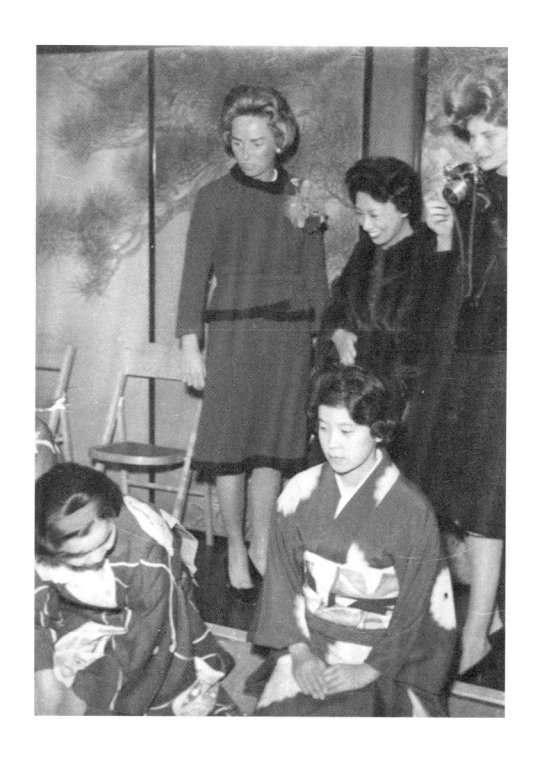

In December 2012, I attended a luncheon at the Robert F. Kennedy Center for Justice and Human Rights to honor the 2012 Robert F. Kennedy Laureate. My children and I had set up the Donald M. Wilson Fellowship at the center shortly before Don died. It funds the annual salary of a young person who wants to dedicate her or his life to bringing Bobby's dreams to fruition, and Kerry Kennedy, his beloved daughter and the center's president, showed her gratitude by inviting me to stay closely involved in her organization's work. I was especially pleased to be sitting at a table with her. Once the eight other guests were seated and we introduced ourselves, she said to everyone, "Susie and Don Wilson were my mother and father's best friends and were always at Hickory Hill. Susie also went on the month-long trip with my parents around the world." She urged me to tell the guests about our trip's highlights.

I was honored that she had called Don and me her parents' best friends. Bobby Kennedy was among the fastest-rising young stars on the political horizon in the late fifties and early sixties, and after John F. Kennedy won the presidency, he and Ethel topped the list of the people everyone wanted to know. They could have had any friends they wanted, but they championed loyalty, and Don and I were among their first friends in Washington.

We were close friends before and throughout Kennedy's presidency and until his and then Bobby's assassinations. Bobby and Ethel's daughters Kathleen and Kerry attended Don's memorial service, where Kathleen spoke, and Ethel sent us an enormous vase of beautiful white flowers that graced the center of the table at the reception.

When Kerry asked me to speak to the guests, I told some of the stories I'd been telling friends and colleagues for years about my round-the-world trip with her parents in February 1962. I had been recounting them for decades, because I wanted to share with others why Bobby and Ethel were such incredibly good people and outstanding ambassadors for America. At the end of the luncheon, one of the guests said to me, "Your tales made us laugh, but I felt my eyes fill with tears knowing what our country lost when Robert Kennedy was killed." Tears filled mine.

I realized, as I often have, what a privilege and inspiration it was to be Bobby and Ethel's close friends. They provided Don and me with joy, laughter, unbelievable fun, and countless opportunities to learn during our many hours with them at Hickory Hill, their expansive estate in McLean, Virginia, where little children and big dogs perpetually surrounded them. Most of all, they changed the direction of our lives by asking Don to join John F. Kennedy's presidential campaign. We saw in Bobby and Ethel the most universally admired qualities in human beings. Ethel would say that only Bobby possessed these qualities, and she basked in the light he cast, but they both shared and admired the same qualities in each other.

The Parking Lot

I met Ethel Kennedy in a parking lot off Connecticut Avenue in Washington, D.C., on a quiet Friday afternoon in June 1957, a couple of months after my wedding. Don and I had moved into his Georgetown house on the corner of 29th and Olive streets. I was running some errands, and as I got out of my car, a woman brought her open convertible, brakes screeching, to a dead stop right beside me. As she flung open her car door, I immediately knew it was Ethel Kennedy, the wife of Robert F. Kennedy, who was making daily headlines as the chief counsel of the McClellan Committee on Capitol Hill. The newspapers carried stories about his relentless efforts to investigate improper and possibly criminal practices by union labor leader Jimmy Hoffa. Ethel, who by that time had four young children, attended the hearings almost daily with one or more of her children, so she was frequently photographed and easy to recognize. She was also usually smiling in photos, but not that morning. When I saw her get out of the car, she looked desperate.

"My daughter fell off her horse. I think she broke her leg. Will you help me carry her into the doctor's office?" she asked.

"Of course," I said. "Tell me what to do."

She told me to link our hands together as she coaxed the little girl to slip onto our "chair." As she slid her arms around our necks and climbed aboard, I learned that the girl's name was Kathleen. I marveled that she didn't even whimper as we carried her into the nearby building. (I hadn't yet learned that "Kennedys don't cry," regardless of the intensity of their pain.)

I stayed with Ethel and Kathleen for about ten minutes until I was convinced her injury wasn't severe. Ethel, a naturally friendly and curious person even in difficult moments, asked for my name and some details about my life. I told her that I was the wife of Don Wilson, who headed the *Life* magazine bureau in Washington, and that we lived on Olive Street. As a nurse arrived to carry Kathleen into the doctor's office, I slipped out without a second thought that anything further would come of our brief encounter.

In these first moments with Ethel, I could feel the excitement of her presence, her directness and genuine interest in people, asking them about themselves rather than talking about herself. This directness was a fundamental aspect of her personality, as was, I would learn, her highly-developed sense of fun. I didn't realize that my chance meeting with her would turn out to be one of the most serendipitous moments of my life, and that some of the happiest and saddest moments of our lives would flow from it.

I was wrong that nothing would come of our meeting in the parking lot, and Ethel called the next morning, a Saturday, inviting Don and me for a swim at Hickory Hill. I accepted with pleasure and off we went to begin an exciting and enduring friendship.

From the distance of decades, I remember that first afternoon and other afternoons to follow: the sun shining as we walked through the back door of their elegant Georgian mansion and down the hill to the swimming pool full of children. Ethel standing in the middle of the pool like a mother hen with her eyes on her chicks, who were splashing, running, diving (mostly cannon balls), and having a perfectly marvelous time. Sometimes Bobby was present; when he arrived, the children would jump lickety-split out of the pool and throw themselves on top of him. It was sometimes hard for him to smile because of his work, but the minute he heard his children calling "Daddy, Daddy," his face would break into an ear-to-ear grin as he collapsed on the hillside, letting his pack hug and then hug him some more. He would then head into the pool where the fun and games would pick up once more. The dogs, some bigger than small ponies, would bark loudly as he and his kids roughhoused until the sun set and it was time for supper.

The Kennedys' humor—sometimes self-deprecating, deadpan, and needling—affected everyone in the best of ways, and after taking in the scene that first afternoon, Don and I agreed that we wouldn't want to be anywhere else but poolside at the Kennedys. From that June day in 1957 until we left Washington in 1964, Don, I, and our children Dwight and Kate, after they were born respectively in 1958 and 1960, went to Hickory Hill almost every weekend and occasionally during the week. We would arrive for swimming, tennis, touch football, charity benefits, and black-tie dinners. These dinners mixed glamour with chaos, for example, when a cabinet officer or high-ranking member of the administration, often in his tuxedo, would end up unceremoniously pushed into the pool by another guest, most likely one of Bobby's old college friends.

It didn't take me long to realize that our lives might move in a new direction—toward government service—and in late 1959, I came up with an idea that would change the trajectory of our lives. I suggested to Don, who adored politics, that he make a bold move and ask Bobby Kennedy if he might join John F. Kennedy's campaign effort. In his memoir, *The First 78 Years*, Don acknowledges my influence: "Susan [which he called me from the time we met until he died] had urged me to join the [Senator's] presidential campaign, but I was not sure I wanted to give up my interesting and well-paying job as the Washington Bureau Chief of *Life*."

I probably persisted, trying to fully explain the opportunities for him, and Don eventually spoke to Bobby over lunch at the Metropolitan Club. He was receptive to the idea, saying that the Kennedy camp would love to have Don join the press operation, a perfect place for him. He suggested that Don wait to make his final decision until after the Democratic convention that summer of 1960.

Don told me about his conversation with Bobby a couple of days after I gave birth to our second child, Katherine Loudon Wilson (Kate), in George Washington University Hospital. I was thrilled—or I should say doubly thrilled: first with the birth of our adorable little girl on January 6th, and second with the clear pathway that Bobby had laid out for Don to become involved in the presidential campaign. (When Kate was born, on Epiphany, a friend wrote, "May she always be a gift to you," recognizing the day, according to the Christian Bible, that the Three Kings brought their gifts to the baby Jesus in the manger. She has fulfilled its promise.)

We knew that those who signed on to a campaign in its early stages and performed well were usually in line to secure a position in the administration if that candidate won. I never doubted that Kennedy would receive the Democratic nomination, which he did on the convention's first ballot, proving that he was the overwhelming favorite of the delegates. Don asked for and received a leave of absence from Time Inc. and became an assistant press secretary for Kennedy's presidential campaign.

After the campaign, he became deputy director of the USIA, which was another perfect fit for him. He was offered the position before Edward R. Murrow became director of the agency, which had 40,000 employees worldwide. Ed, as he always wanted to be called, thought so highly of Kennedy's call for service in the New Frontier that he gave up his lucrative position at CBS to become director. He accepted Kennedy's nomination of Don to be deputy director before he even met Don rather than fill the position with someone he personally knew. Don was honored and thrilled to be part of the Kennedy administration, and one of its youngest members. This would never have happened if I hadn't pulled into that parking lot.

World Traveler

My invitation to travel with Bobby and Ethel came out of the blue. In early 1962, the president asked Bobby, then attorney general, to take an around-the-world trip to acquaint leading officials in key countries with the new administration and its policy plans. Bobby called Don and asked him if I could join them on the trip. (Don couldn't be included since he was working hard in his new position.)

Bobby said that Ethel would like a pal on the trip to help her with its formidable logistics. It would last all of February and cover 30,000 miles with 11 stopovers in 28 days. The schedule included visits to Tokyo; Hong Kong; Jakarta, Indonesia; Bangkok, Thailand; Saigon, Vietnam (for a meeting on an airport tarmac); Beirut, Lebanon; Rome, Italy; West Berlin and West Germany; The Hague; and Paris before a return flight to Washington, D.C.

Bobby decided to emphasize the importance of youth and spread the message of the New Frontier in America. President Kennedy had used the phrase in his acceptance speech at the Democratic convention in 1961. He had said:

> We stand today on the edge of a New Frontier—the frontier of the 1960s, the frontier of unknown opportunities and perils, the frontier

of unfilled hopes and unfilled dreams. ... Beyond that frontier are uncharted areas of science and space, unsolved problems of peace and war, unconquered problems of ignorance and prejudice, unanswered questions of poverty and surplus.

People around the world looked forward to learning about it from the brother of the handsome, young U.S. president.

At the time, our children were four and two, but we had an excellent nanny from Germany who told me that she could easily handle their care, and Don was present to supervise. Bobby and Ethel were leaving seven children behind in McLean to do the president's bidding.

The night before our departure, the president and Mrs. Kennedy invited Don and me to a small farewell dinner for Bobby and Ethel in their private quarters at the White House. Mrs. Kennedy may have seen our trip's schedule or was aware of the speed at which this couple traveled, because as she said goodnight to me, she whispered some advice: "Susie, be sure to take vitamins with you. You'll need them." I appreciated her concern; I made it through the month without vitamins by feeding off Bobby and Ethel's infectious energy.

My role on the trip was a dual one: I went not only as Ethel's pal but as a credentialed journalist. Don always believed that Bobby had set up a meeting for me with Bruce Gould, the editor-in-chief of *Ladies Homes Journal*, to help me earn money to defray the trip's expense. He never confessed and I didn't ask him, but a few days before our scheduled departure, I found myself in Mr. Gould's New York City office as he suggested that I cover the trip for his magazine. Although my credentials were thin and I'd never written a major magazine piece, he hired me for $3,000 and suggested I take a camera along to photograph highlights. (If I had little experience writing long magazine articles, I had even less as a photographer, since *Life* usually left taking photographs to its award-winning photography staff.)

I had so much to do in such a short amount of time that I didn't give much thought to what lay ahead or what I was leaving behind. The Kennedys' invitation was a compliment, and I was determined to please them. I was being handed the chance of a lifetime to see the world through Bobby and Ethel's eyes.

Although it seems unimaginable today in the world of large press contingents, our traveling party had just ten people: Bobby and Ethel; John Seigenthaler, Bobby's administrative assistant; Brandon Grove, a State Department staff liaison; four American reporters; a TV cameraman; and me. (Brandon devoted a chapter of his book *Behind Embassy Walls*, which covered his successful State Department career, to our trip and described me as a "close and high-spirited friend of Ethel's.") We traveled on commercial airlines without government security personnel, although some appeared from time to time along the way.

If there was a test for being "high-spirited," I came close to failing it at the start. Our first stop was Hawaii where the "fun" began when Bobby, Ethel, and I went for a spin in a small sailboat on the Pacific Ocean off Honolulu. The Kennedys are strong sailors who like to keep their sails full. We were squeezed together on a small boat, with Bobby at the tiller and Ethel holding the sheet (the sail's rope). I didn't have a responsibility since they hadn't yet tested my sailing acumen, but I knew enough to know that we were moving with the wind at our back and had a long way to return to shore. I also knew that if you had concerns about the Kennedys' plans, it was best not to voice them aloud.

The shoreline was receding fast when Bobby looked at Ethel and said, "Let's swamp the boat." Before I could utter a word, he jibed the boat, which turned on its side and filled instantly with water. As it began to sink, Bobby and Ethel looked at me and said, "Better start swimming." I took one look at the distant shoreline, where I could hardly discern a building, and instantly recalled what I had learned during my sailing lessons at camp.

"You go right ahead," I said, trying to sound casual. "I learned that it's better to stay with the boat."

No sooner had the words escaped my lips than a U.S. Coast Guard powerboat—no doubt assigned to keep an eye on the attorney general—appeared to haul us in. I always believed that Bobby knew about the Coast Guard's nearness and decided to swamp the boat to give us a thrill. Undoubtedly someone in that Coast Guard boat had tipped off the press, because a story about Bobby and Ethel's sailing "misadventure" appeared on the front page of the *New York Times* the next day. The reporter referred to me as "an unidentified woman with the Kennedys," which annoyed my mother to no end.

"Why are you just going along as the lady-in-waiting?" she wrote to me later. "You don't have your own identity." (My identity problem rearing its ugly head again.)

Ever the politician, even 3,000 miles away, she wanted to read my name in the newspaper of record. It didn't matter to me, because I was moving at such a fast pace—meeting new people, helping Ethel learn Japanese phrases in time for our arrival in Tokyo, taking notes like the journalist I was supposed to be, and trying to keep my beehive hairdo (the style of the time) from falling to pieces—that I wasn't thinking of anyone I had left behind.

Soon after, I almost failed another test more serious than the sailboat escapade when I nearly embarrassed the Kennedys and myself in front of a large television audience in Japan. Ethel preferred to accompany her husband to events, but she agreed to do a couple of them alone, including a live broadcast of a tea ceremony, practically a sacred rite in Japan. The wife of the American ambassador to Japan had planned the appearance as a way of introducing Ethel to the Japanese viewing audience. I was invited to participate in the ceremony with her.

We arrived in the studio minutes before the program was to begin and were told to kneel side by side on two cushions before the camera. A production aide placed a cup of what I surmised was Japanese tea and a plate of what looked like a delectable French pastry in front of each of us. My mouth watered at the pale-pink icing shimmering under the bright camera lights. *How delightful, something deliciously French to go with the unsweetened tea*, I thought, forgetting for a moment that I was in Tokyo, not Paris.

When the director cued us to take a bite, I beat Ethel in our race for the cakes and bit down on the tantalizing morsel. "*What* have I put into my mouth?" I shuddered. It tasted like a combination of paste and fish, and I couldn't swallow or spit it out before the huge live audience tuning in to watch the famous Mrs. Kennedy drink tea. I realized that the "cake" was made of dried fish paste, and I had no choice but to swallow it without

A favorite picture taken by a photographer for the *Times of Trenton* to accompany the story, "Women Who Have Made a Difference," published in December 1995. I was one of eight local women whose contributions were noted.

My father in two different guises that reflect important aspects of his life: *left*, in his uniform as a First Lieutenant, Field Artillery in World War I, and, *below*, in his Class of 1917 Princeton alumnus reunion jacket. He earned the Distinguished Service Cross for "extraordinary heroism" in France and raised copious sums of money for his university from his classmates.

My mother at two of the proudest moments of her life: *left*, giving a nominating speech for the vice presidential candidate, Henry Cabot Lodge, at the 1960 Republican National Convention and, *below*, receiving her honorary Doctor of Laws degree from Rutgers University in 1979. Part of the citation read: "Few in this or any state can equal your forty-four year record of selfless public service in penal reform, law enforcement, and higher education."

Life photographer Leonard McCombe, with whom I was on assignment for the Party section, took this picture during a brief moment of respite from my duties.

Life photographer Eliot Elisofon took these pictures of Don and me standing before the Great Buddha of Kamakura in the Kanagawa Prefecture in Japan during my five-wefi visit to the Far East after we had met in the office in New York City.

We were married in St. James' Episcopal Church on April 6, 1957.

For a month in February 1962, I traveled around the globe with Bobby and Ethel Kennedy as a friend and journalist. The goodwill tour began with a stop in Japan and included one in Rome, where the brother and sister-in-law of the recently inaugurated, young president had a private audience with Pope John XXIII.

Left, Bobby and I enjoy a good laugh at a Washington, D. C. dinner party. This picture appeared in *Vogue* magazine. *Below,* Don and I joined other friends on several exciting (and sometimes hazardous) sailing trips with Bobby and Ethel off the coast of Maine.

Early in our children's lives. *Left to right*, Kate and Dwight in the leaves in Washington, D. C.; Kate (*third from the left*) in her role as a soldier in the New York City Ballet production of *The Nutcracker*; Penny in a tree in Princeton; and Don, Dwight, and me on my father's small powerboat, *The Katy Did*, in Quissett Harbor, Falmouth, MA.

Above, my parents in midlife. *Right*, my sister, Joanie, and I dressed for the wedding of her eldest daughter, Hope Woodhouse, and Richard Canty in September 1983. The wedding was the final event at my parents' beloved Sunnyside Farm in Lincroft, NJ. They had died in 1970 and 1982.

Kate dancing in the ballet *Ravenna* at the Pacific Northwest Ballet, Seattle, WA, in the 1980s; Dwight holding a friend's son in the U. S. Peace Corps in Honduras, November 1982; and Penny when she was a ski instructor in Aspen, CO, in the winter of 1989-90.

The family welcomed our children's loving spouses: Dwight married Deborah Davis on September 28, 1991, on Orcas Island in the San Juan Islands in Washington State; Kate married David T. Breault on June 15, 1996, in New Preston, CT; and Penny married Richard A. Falkenrath on September 4, 1999, on Martha's Vineyard.

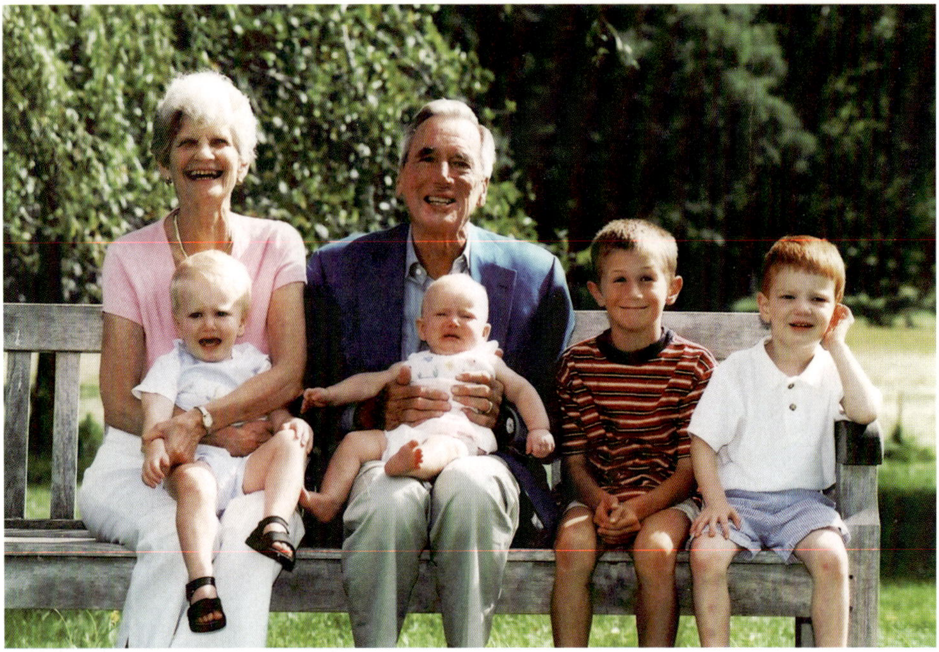

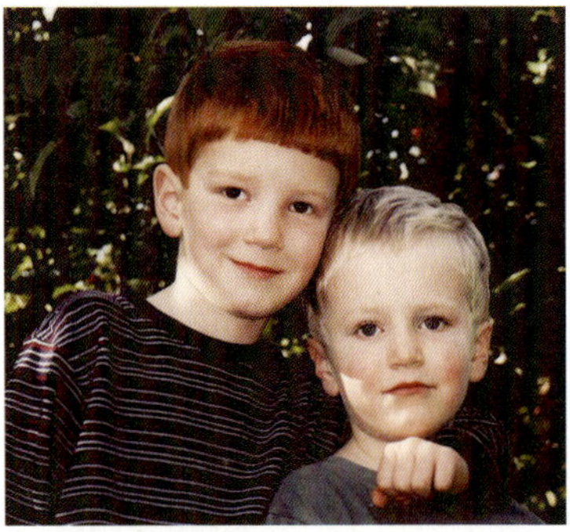

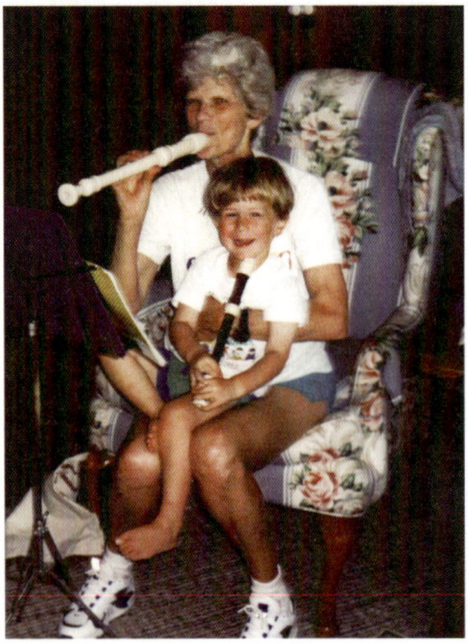

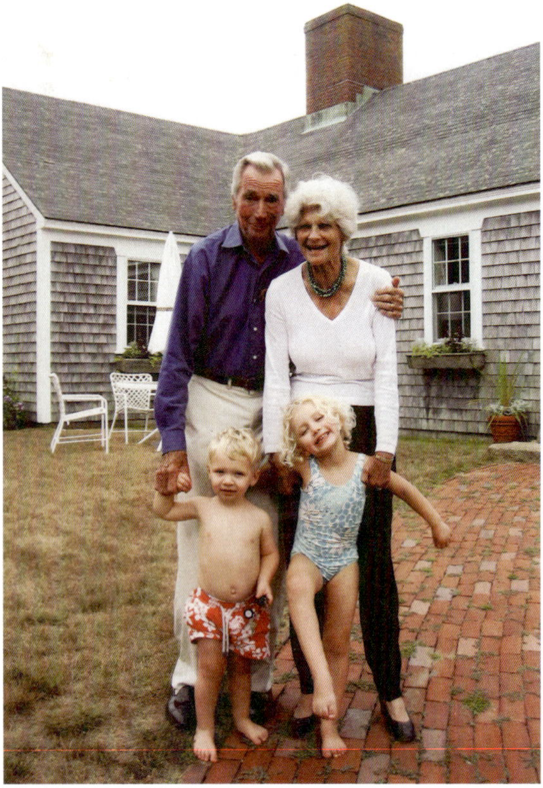

Above, the family gathered to celebrate Don's 80th birthday at Mohonk Mountain House in New York. Each of us wore a T-shirt with a picture from one of the chapters of his memoir, *The First 78 Years*. *Below*, my daughter-in-law, Deborah Davis, designed the T-shirt for my 80th birthday celebration when we convened on the Vineyard. The T-shirt read, "Can you keep up with Susie?" and showed a young woman in full flight.

Don and I, all smiles through the years, including my all-time favorite of him with his arms b‹ind his head.

Left, we celebrated our 40th anniversary in New York City in 1997 by returning to St. James' Church and running down the stairs, recreating that special moment after we were pronounced "man and wife." *Above and below,* Don doing what he especially loved to do: swimming in the Atlantic Ocean at the Vineyard (1991) and traveling to faraway places in Asia, such as Angkor Wat in Cambodia (1997).

Right, Jacqueline Kennedy Onassis was the guest of honor at a fundraiser at our home in Princeton in September 1980. She came on b)alf of her brother-in-law Senator Ted Kennedy, who was running for the Democratic nomination against incumbent President Jimmy Carter. *Below*, giving support to the Obama/Biden ticket at a fundraiser in New York City in September 2008, I post for a picture with Dr. Jill Biden, whose husband, Joe, was the candidate for Vice President on the Democratic ticket and Michelle Obama, whose husband, Barack, was running for president. They (we) won!

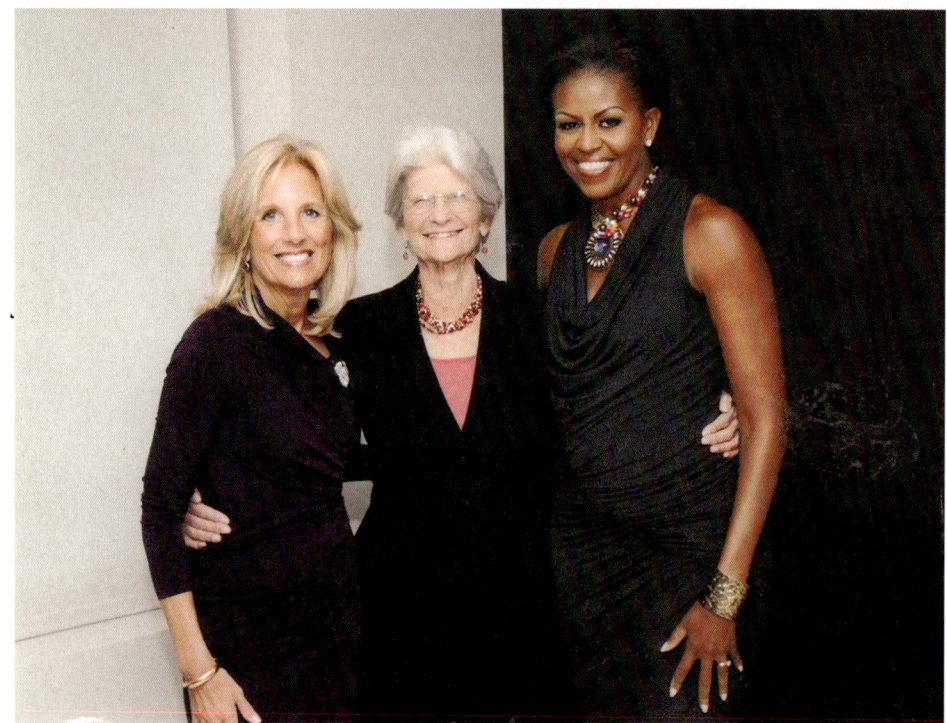

Right, New Jersey Education Commissioner, Fred G. Burke; State Board of Education President, S. David Brandt; and me, a member of the State Board from 1978-1983. *Below*, the staff of the Network for Family Life Education, now Answer, on the campus of Rutgers University in 2004, with the editorial board of *Sex, Etc.*, our teen-to-teen magazine and website. For the past 20 years, *Sex, Etc.* has reached millions of young people in the U. S. and other countries with honest, accurate information about sexuality and sexual health.

The gathering of the Woodhouse and Wilson families to celebrate the wedding of my sister's younger daughter, Amy, to Richard Tobey Scott in Maine, September 2000.

Above, in July 2006, the family gathered for the last time at 4574 Province Line Road in Lawrence Township, where we lived for 40 years. We named the gathering "Our Farewell to the House" wefiend. Pryde Brown, a professional photographer and former neighbor, took this wonderful family photograph. *Right*, Dwight snapped this picture of Don and me on the small patio of our condominium in Constitution Hill in Princeton, only 1.8 miles to the east of Province Line Road. The picture was taken only two months before Don died in November 2011.

A photograph that appeared in August 2008 in the *Vineyard Gazette* above the headline: "At Age 78, She Has Achieved a Doctoral Degree in Running, Not to Mention Life." I am wearing my number for the Chilmark Road Race, a 3.1-mile race that I have run for many years and am still running.

gagging in the process. As I did, I looked over at Ethel, who was smiling pleasantly as though she had indeed eaten a French sweet. Always the perfect politician's wife, she drank a sip of tea and took another bite, much to the director's delight.

Since I was the only other woman on the trip, I was afforded some special privileges. Instead of staying in a hotel with the rest of our group, I could stay with Bobby and Ethel wherever they stayed, whether it was presidential palaces, ambassadors' residences, or guest houses. The palaces in Jakarta and Bali, in Indonesia, were intriguing: intricately decorated, with carvings reflecting the country's culture and objects handcrafted by local artists. In Jakarta, we stayed with President Sukarno, leader of the Indonesian independence movement and his country's first president. After a restful night behind mosquito netting on a comfortable wooden bed, I greeted Ethel in the dining room for breakfast.

"It's going to be a race to see who gets to the food first. Us or the ants," she whispered, pointing to a column of tiny ants crossing the snow-white tablecloth.

After having traveled with the Kennedys for several weeks, nothing much deterred me, and I beat the ants to my breakfast.

The Kennedys enjoyed putting their friends in uncomfortable situations, but the teasing and challenging would stop shy of a complete loss of face. Toward the end of our stay in Jakarta, we attended an elaborate and endless formal dinner hosted by the Indonesian attorney general, who wore a military uniform. Bobby believed that an attorney general was the chief enforcer of a nation's laws and should not be associated with the military. He wanted to show his disapproval by refusing to attend the dinner, yet he was persuaded to go. After suffering through it for an hour, he wanted to leave, but Brandon Grove whispered to him that it would be impolite to do so before watching the elaborate entertainment planned by his host.

After barely sitting through a performance of the national candlelight dance by a group of Indonesian dancers, Bobby saw his way out. We had heard that the Twist—the American hip-swaying dance craze that was raging around the world—had been banned in Indonesia: a couple could be jailed if caught performing it. Bobby seized the moment and, to my complete amazement, he announced that Brandon and I were going to demonstrate the Twist to the guests.

Failing to follow his order was akin to treachery. I reached out to the six-foot-five Brandon, who was growing paler by the second, and we walked to the stage to do a few steps, barely making any gyrations before slinking back to our seats. The Kennedys and our gaggle of press applauded wildly, and then Bobby said goodnight to our host. I sighed with relief knowing I had escaped a night in a Jakarta jail, which would have been a dramatic change from the presidential palace. Bobby commented on this moment in his book about the trip, *Just Friends and Brave Enemies*: "Susie obliged brilliantly, while Brandon, mumbling bitterly about his image [in the State Department], produced a genteel and polished Charleston."

The atmosphere among our band of travelers, which was led by our merry maker-in-chief, Ethel, was mostly lighthearted, but Bobby had serious duties to perform for the president, including making speeches and meeting with world leaders. He especially enjoyed speaking to young people. He wanted these future leaders to embrace a vision of the New Frontier and change the world for the better. He burned with a controlled passion and love for his country and spoke eloquently about the ideals our democracy was founded upon. The challenge of the day, as he saw it, was a struggle between freedom and communism, and he championed freedom whenever he spoke.

Early on in our trip, at Waseda University, in Tokyo, I saw the first expression of his deepest beliefs. Bobby had been invited to speak to the Japanese college students, but he received advance warning that a leftist group might disrupt the session. Ambassador Reischauer warned Ethel and Bobby that they might be in danger, but Bobby never backed away from promoting American ideals.

In the student auditorium, we found a seething crowd of 3,000. A heckler rose and started using communist propaganda points to criticize America, and then the lights went out and Bobby's microphone went dead. Undeterred, he grasped a bullhorn and spoke in response extemporaneously for 20 minutes on the meaning of freedom:

> Let me just tell you what the United States stands for. ... We were born and raised in revolution. ... We believe in the principle that government exists for the individual, and the individual is not a tool of the state. ... We in America believe that we should have divergences of views. We believe that everyone has the right to express himself. We believe that young people have the right to speak out and give their views and ideas.

The audience calmed down, and at the end of the speech, we joined Bobby onstage to sing the Waseda University song. His interpreter had given us a phonetic version, but it was still hard to read, so we tossed it aside and came into our own at the song's end, chanting, "Waseda! Waseda! Waseda!" The audience erupted in cheers and the incident became one of the biggest press stories about our trip. I had never seen such a raw display of courage before, and I understood in that moment the risks that activists must take and what is needed to sway an audience.

Bobby and Ethel taught me how to take chances as I observed them handle incidents like this one. Many audiences on our trip admired American courage and cheered Bobby when he encouraged them to boldly stand up to their repressive governments. Few people in my life until that point had applauded me for being outspoken; I had been taught that women would be more successful by being polite than by speaking up. Yet here, before my eyes, Bobby was telling audiences to speak out for their beliefs, and I believed he was also directing his advice to me.

Bobby and Ethel's deep Catholic faith influenced some of our trip's activities. During free moments, we visited hospitals, orphanages, and schools run by Catholic nuns. These visits opened my eyes, as I had missed the lesson from my family, schools, and religion about what it meant to be poor. I had never understood the circumstances in which poor people lived or met those who were working with them to remediate that poverty.

One day in Hong Kong, we visited a slum where hundreds of poor families lived in shacks with corrugated iron roofs. We went inside one tiny room, and I expected to see people in an unkempt living space. Instead I saw an immaculately kept room with a scroll on the wall and below it a little vase containing a single orange flower. The children standing before us were neatly dressed, and their parents bowed respectfully before their American visitors. I realized then that materially poor people could appreciate beauty and order and feel pride in themselves regardless of their economic situation.

Bobby frequently spoke about the "other America where the poor live" and how the affluent often "surrender personal excellence and community values to the mere accumulation of material things." His was a voice urging people to think of those who needed help.

After leaving Asia, we stopped briefly in Beirut, Lebanon, and Rome and then headed to West Berlin, the German city split down the middle after World War II. The West German-controlled half lived in freedom while the East German-controlled half lived under communism. The Russian leader, Nikita Khrushchev, had closed the border between East and West Berlin in 1961, and the communist government had erected a crude cement wall topped with barbed wire. Tanks guarded it to keep residents from escaping to freedom.

We arrived on a freezing cold day unprepared for the weather's effects. As Bobby drove through the streets in an open car, wearing only a thin overcoat, we could see him practically turn blue before our eyes. We visited the wall, noting the wreaths, flowers, crosses, and pictures of the brave East Germans who had died trying to jump over it to freedom. When Bobby made his opening remarks in City Hall Square before 180,000 cheering spectators, Ethel, ever mindful of his welfare, crept up behind him and massaged his back to increase his circulation.

The next day, February 22nd, Bobby gave a longer, more memorable speech at the Free University of Berlin, noting that it was the 230th anniversary of George Washington's birth. Comparing freedom and communism, he used strong language to condemn the East German leaders for erecting the wall. He quoted the Robert Frost poem "Mending Wall," noting that the poet had also recited a poem at President Kennedy's inauguration.

> *Before I built a wall, I'd ask to know*
> *What I was walling in or walling out*
> *And to whom I was like to give offence*
> *Something there is that doesn't love a wall,*
> *That wants it down*

The audience cheered wildly, and I saw some wipe away tears. In the speech, he also spoke about our trip.

> Over the past few weeks, my wife and I have traveled many thousands of miles—across the United States, across the Pacific Ocean, from Japan along the Chinese coast, down to Indonesia, across the Indian Ocean, across Pakistan, up through the Middle East, through Italy—and now we arrive in the free city of Berlin. Nothing has touched us as much as your reception for us here today.

He went on to say:

> I have seen men and women at work building modern societies so that their people can begin to share in the blessings of science and technologies and become full members of the 20th century. Social progress and social justice, in my judgment, are not something apart from freedom; they are the fulfillment of freedom.

Bobby taught me the essence of leadership: to inspire people to be better than they thought themselves to be. To his audience in the shadow of the wall, he talked about racial injustice in America.

> For a hundred years, despite our claims of equality, we had, as you know, a wall of our own—a wall of segregation erected against Negroes. The wall is coming down through the orderly process of enforcing the laws and securing compliances with court decisions, an area where my own responsibilities, as attorney general, are heavy.

After a journey of long days and short nights, covering tens of thousands of miles, Bobby was urging an American audience not present to do and be better.

That evening, Mayor Willy Brandt, of West Berlin, hosted a dinner for the Kennedys, a party that Bobby stayed at until the end. He asked to go into the kitchen afterward to thank the people who prepared the food he had enjoyed. (I saw him do this often on the trip.) He was as comfortable talking to kitchen workers as he was to leaders in palaces.

I remembered Bobby's visit to the kitchen that evening when I heard the first report in June 1968 that he had been shot in the kitchen of a Los Angeles hotel, ending a life that held such promise for millions around the globe; I was crushed at the cruel irony.

Coming Home

We flew home to the States, and when the plane landed in Washington, D.C., the door opened and all the Kennedy children bounded down the aisle of the airplane and flung themselves on their parents. Don followed at a more leisurely pace, holding a large sheaf of flowers to welcome me home. In Paris on the last night of our trip, we had gone to a *son et lumière*, a sound and light show, where we learned about the city's great monuments while they were bathed in spotlights. As we gathered our possessions preparing to leave the plane, Ethel called to us, "See you later for the *son et lumière* of Washington." She made all of us laugh, as she had throughout our journey.

All good things come to an end, and I had been looking forward to seeing my good, patient husband and our dear little children. It was hard to return to earth, though, after feeling I had touched the stars with Bobby and Ethel. They had changed my life, showing me how to be bolder and do more for the world's poor, just as they had lifted the spirits of millions around the world, giving them hope for a better future.

Encore, Encore

Two years later, in June 1964, General Maxwell Taylor, who was chairman of the Joint Chiefs of Staff, invited the Kennedys to commemorate the 20th anniversary of the D-Day landings at Normandy. The American landscape had changed dramatically since Bobby's world trip in 1962: his brother had been assassinated in November 1963, and although he served as attorney general in the Lyndon Johnson administration, he was understandably miserable, depressed, and worried about the country's future. He saw the trip to Europe as an opportunity for renewal.

The Kennedys decided to take their three oldest children, Kathleen, Joe, and Bobby, Jr., to the historic event and scheduled visits to other places in Europe. They invited me, the alum of the world tour, and their close friend Kay Evans to join them. As we climbed aboard a military aircraft to cross the Atlantic, Ethel confided to us that she was in the early stages of pregnancy with their ninth child. (That baby, Matthew Maxwell Taylor Kennedy, known as Max, was born nine months after the trip). Pregnancy was a normal condition for Ethel, and she never let it slow her down or dim her buoyant personality.

The ceremonies at Normandy were moving, and we walked past the graves of the Americans who had died on the beaches. They were marked by crosses and other religious symbols, and I remembered the poem "In Flanders Fields," by Lt. Col. John McCrae, with its opening lines: "In Flanders Fields the poppies blow/Between the crosses row on row."

Ethel, her three children, Kay and I visited Paris, Venice, Capri, Greece, and Rome before meeting up with Bobby, who had stayed behind for some meetings in West Berlin. Ethel had a system for traveling with children: one day for sightseeing and then the next day off, preferably at the beach. The system worked well, although the kids occasionally showed extreme energy, such as the time that Joe and Bobby Jr. climbed a lamppost in full view of the American ambassador at the embassy in Paris.

I had met Pope John XXIII on my trip around the world in 1962. On this trip, there was a private audience at the Vatican with Pope Paul VI. At the end of our visit, Ethel said in her usual teasing way, "Susie, *you* [meaning you Episcopalian, you] have met *two* Popes. When are you going to convert?" She was semi-serious, having told me that she would get a place in Heaven for converting non-Catholics to Catholicism. I quickly reassured her that her many good deeds, faithful adherence to doctrine, and large family guaranteed her automatic entrance, and she didn't need to add a convert to the list.

I wasn't an acceptable candidate for conversion anyway. When we saw the official picture taken of Pope Paul with us, I looked fine in my black dress and black veil, but instead of looking at the pontiff himself, I was looking directly at the camera. Ethel, with her quick eye, reminded me that I should have been looking at the Pope. Fortunately her daughter Kathleen or sons Joe and Bobby weren't looking at him either, and I've always felt that she helped smooth over my faux pas.

After we reconnected with Bobby, we traveled to Poland—first to Warsaw and then to Częstochowa—to see the famous portrait of the Black Madonna. The Polish people, who were devout Catholics, adored the Kennedys and treated them like rock stars, crowding the streets and cheering wildly at all our stops. I believe they equated the loss of President Kennedy with the loss of their freedom to the Soviet Union and wanted to express their sympathy to Bobby.

One Sunday, the crowd engulfed the American ambassador's black limousine, in which the Kennedy family was traveling after attending morning mass. I was riding in a car directly behind it with Kay and Jackie Kennedy's sister, Lee Radziwill, whose husband was a descendant of a distinguished Polish family. The ambassadorial car was enormous, and as the crowd surged toward it like the sea, the driver finally stopped so no one would get hurt. Promptly, Bobby, Ethel, and their three children all climbed up on the roof, and he spoke to the throngs below, opening with the comment, "This is the way we always come home from church!" And they looked completely comfortable.

We rolled down the windows inside our car, which was stuck in the crowd, and listened to the cheers. We couldn't see anything, but the noise was deafening. The incident was a triumph, yet the American ambassador complained that the Kennedys had made dents in the roof of his car. He didn't make too many friends for America, but Bobby and Ethel certainly did. The Polish people started singing a marvelous song, "Sto lat," which means, "May you live one hundred years." They hadn't sung it to their premier in years, but they sang it lustily for the Kennedys.

Our stopover in London on the way home was equally moving but much quieter. The British government was building a memorial to honor President Kennedy, and we drove to see the site at Runnymede, the 188-acre meadow along the river Thames that was a sacred place in British history. It is where in 1215 King John sealed the Magna Carta, the foundation of English liberties that greatly influenced the creation of the U.S. Constitution. The British felt it was an ideal place for a memorial to honor the slain president, who had many connections to England.

Queen Elizabeth formally dedicated the memorial in 1965 in the presence of Jacqueline Kennedy and her two children. As part of the ceremony, she deeded the one acre of land on which the memorial stands to the U.S. in perpetuity. The stone reads, "This acre of English ground was given to the United States of America by the people of Britain in memory of John F. Kennedy."

I experienced the same wonders traveling with the Kennedys on this trip as I did on my first with them: excitement, enthusiasm, the desire for knowledge, the endorsement of freedom, and, in Bobby's speeches, the call for change. This trip abroad gave him the confidence to push forward again in search of a better world. In September of 1964, he resigned from the Johnson administration to run for the U.S. Senate and was elected senator of his newly adopted state of New York. Those cheering crowds he had encountered throughout Europe had been instrumental in his decision.

"Wow, what a ride!" exclaimed astronaut John Glenn when he climbed out of his space capsule—and I thought exactly the same thing when I returned from my world trips with the Kennedys. I also felt a responsibility to put into practice what Bobby tried to teach the world; this led me to begin my efforts to help those in need. When we returned to the States, I undertook small acts: tutoring Jessica in Washington, D.C., and later larger ones: working for the New Jersey Office of Economic Opportunity in Trenton when we moved to New Jersey.

I didn't go on Bobby and Ethel's trip to South Africa in 1966. I can only imagine the setting and the legendary words he spoke to the large crowd in Cape Town on June 6. His speech, known as the "Ripple of Hope," sounded like the many I had heard him give on our trips. He said:

> Every time [a person] stands up for an ideal, or acts to improve the lots of others, or strikes out against injustice, he sends forth a tiny ripple of hope, and crossing each other from a million different centers of energy and daring these ripples build a current which can sweep down the mightiest walls of oppression and resistance.

I have tried to live these words, sometimes overtly and sometimes quietly, to show Bobby and Ethel my gratitude for the chance to travel the world with them.

A Farewell to Two Leaders

I was in Washington, D.C., on Friday, November 22, 1963, the moment the nation learned that President John F. Kennedy had been shot. I was in my car, driving to my hairdresser on Connecticut Avenue when the announcer broke through on the radio to read a bulletin from the Associated Press wire: "There is a report that President Kennedy has been shot in a Dallas motorcade this afternoon," he said.

I started driving straight to Don's office at the USIA, believing that he would put the lie to this newsflash of unbelievable horror. I turned up the volume on the radio and looked around to see if there were any other signs that the earth was shaking beneath me. It was a warm, beautiful day beneath a cerulean sky. Everything seemed normal when it was exactly the opposite.

I barged into Don's office, but I didn't belong there; Don was now in charge of the USIA's handling of this ghastly news event, since its director, Ed Murrow, was sick at home in Pawling, New York. As deputy director, he and his colleagues worked nonstop through the night transmitting millions of words and pictures to news outlets around the world, trying to explain what we couldn't understand ourselves—that our young, dashing, inspirational president, who had told us to "ask not what your country can do for you—ask what you can do for your country," had been killed by an assassin.

I was bereft and numb, but Don could offer me no consolation. What happened next is one of my least proud moments: instead of driving immediately to Hickory Hill to offer comfort to Bobby and Ethel, I turned to ice, stupidly assuming that they would want to be alone with their grief. The ensuing guilt I felt taught me a lesson: when anything terrible happens to someone you love, go immediately to that person. Sympathy and empathy are all that a friend needs at a time of crisis, and these emotions do not come tied up in a pretty package.

I went home and tried to explain to my five-year-old son and three-year-old daughter that "Caroline's daddy has been killed by a bad man with a gun and is in Heaven now with the angels." In their sweet ways, they offered me a tiny drop of balm and seemed to accept that what I had said was perfectly plausible and the world was still spinning on its axis.

Everyone in the administration was inconsolable for months, if not years, to come. Don and I were invited to the White House to pay our respects, kneeling before the flag-draped casket that rested on the same bier as Abraham Lincoln's casket had in the imposing East Room. I kneeled at a prayer bench in front of the casket and mumbled a prayer. The mass card for the president, which I have kept for 50 years, was inscribed with the simplest of prayers: "Dear God, Please take care of your servant John Fitzgerald Kennedy." An excerpt from his first and only inaugural address was printed beneath it:

> Now the trumpet summons us again—not as a call to bear arms, though arms we need—not as a call to battle, though embattled we are—but a call to bear the burden of a long twilight struggle, year in

and year out, "rejoicing in hope, patient in tribulation"—a struggle against the common enemies of man: tyranny, poverty, disease, and war itself.

Don and I stood for hours in long lines with thousands of other citizens to see the flag-draped casket once again as it lay in state in the U.S. Capitol and President Kennedy's little children touched it to say farewell. We went to the state funeral and Requiem Mass at St. Matthew's Cathedral and later to Arlington Cemetery, where President Kennedy was laid to rest. Jacqueline Kennedy's decision to put an eternal flame at her husband's resting place acknowledged her acute sense of history and was one of the most beautiful acts of love that I have ever witnessed. She was determined to carve a place of importance for her husband in American history, even though the fates had robbed him of the time to prove his full potential as a great president. She—and the choice of an eternal flame for his grave—signified the respect in which she held his presidency, the love she felt for him, and her belief in his legacy.

Farewell to Camelot

After her husband was killed, Jacqueline Kennedy said of his time in Washington, "Once there was a spot for one brief shining moment that was known as Camelot," and for one brief shining moment, Don and I were part of it. We were incredibly fortunate to have shared in this rare moment in American history. The high point for Don came during the Cuban Missile Crisis when he substituted for an ill Murrow. For 13 days in October 1962, he served as a member of the National Security Council Executive Committee, EX-COMM, a group of the highest administration officials on whom the president relied for advice and counsel. After the crisis's resolution, the president gave Don a silver calendar mounted on an ebony base, and it was his proudest possession. It hangs framed in the library of our Constitution Hill home.

Don turned 40 on June 27, 1965, and resigned earlier that year from the government to accept a job at Time Inc. He knew that President Johnson would never appoint him to a higher position in the administration, given his Kennedy ties. We had to leave the city and the dear friends we loved. I knew

I would miss it all, especially being at the center of the political world and having my husband's hands on the pulse of power in order to make the world a better place.

As we were getting ready to leave, I realized that I had never shown our children the great, enduring monuments of Washington. To make up for not teaching them about our country's history, I hustled them into our station wagon, and in the space of a couple of days, we saw George Washington's home, Mt. Vernon; the Jefferson, Lincoln, and Washington monuments; the Capitol; all the museums; and everything in between. I would not recommend this tour to anyone with young children, but I wanted them to have some memories of the city that Don and I had called home with such joy and incredible sadness during the early years of our marriage.

Being part of the Kennedy administration was like living in a Disney movie—until the magic ended with the assassination. In a way, it had all been too perfect and unreal, yet we were young and hopeful that we could make a difference for our country and the world. I don't think Don ever recovered from the event in Dallas, which of course was only compounded five years later when Bobby was killed in Los Angeles. He had such high hopes for another position with a second Kennedy administration, perhaps as an ambassador to a small country, but that was not to be.

The assassination also ended the social whirl that I had been swept up in and offered me a chance to hang those evening dresses away in a dark closet and look for something more substantive to do. Bobby Kennedy had already pointed me in the direction of working to reduce poverty among American families, and I never looked back as we packed up and left Washington.

The Last Trip

Nineteen sixty-eight was one of the darkest years in American history, marked by the assassinations of Martin Luther King, Jr., and Robert F. Kennedy and violence in the streets of Chicago during the Democratic National Convention. But it had also been a brief year of hope for our family when Don joined Bobby's presidential campaign.

Bobby announced his candidacy on March 19 in the same Senate room where his slain brother had announced his quest in the winter of 1960. He set up a potential three-way race between him, President Lyndon B. Johnson, who won re-election in 1964, and Senator Eugene McCarthy, who had captured the support of the vocal anti-Vietnam War movement. At the end of the month, President Johnson stunned the nation by announcing that he wouldn't run for re-election, turning a difficult three-way race into a two-man one that favored Bobby.

Don, with my enthusiastic encouragement, jumped at the chance to join Bobby's campaign—not only because of his overwhelming devotion to him as our good friend, but because he believed that Bobby was the person who could reignite the hopes of the New Frontier. In 1965, Don was given another leave of absence from Time Inc. to join Bobby's campaign. His first job was to work on television spots in preparation for the primary elections.

The first two months of Bobby's campaign had its share of ups and downs. His victory in the all-important California primary on June 4 would have helped his campaign finally gain momentum. But Bobby's quest came crashing to an unthinkable, horrible end in Los Angeles early in the morning of June 5, when Sirhan Sirhan shot and killed him as he exited the ballroom and entered the kitchen at the Ambassador Hotel.

Don had been in a room at the hotel with some of the Kennedy family, feeling elated after the victory, and had maneuvered himself downstairs toward the front of the stage, where he joined the small group waiting to escort Bobby out of the hotel after his victory statement. In his memoir, he describes what he witnessed: "I was perhaps 50 feet behind [Bobby] when I heard the shots. I pressed forward and saw [him] lying on the ground, being attended to by his bodyguards. I walked back, and, by chance, ran into Ethel, who cried, 'Take me to him.' I did so."

Bobby never regained consciousness and died 26 hours later with Ethel's arms wrapped around him in his hospital bed. The hopes of the millions who supported him for president died with him at that exact moment. He died on

June 6, which was our son's birthday. My children and I were in our apartment on 72nd Street in New York City when I heard the news on television. Dwight was at my side, and I told him what had happened. He said to me in his sweet, ten-year-old way, "Oh, Mommy. You will never forget Bobby because he died on my birthday." He was right, of course, but what he didn't know was that I would think of Bobby not only on the anniversary of his passing, but at countless times throughout my life.

Don returned ashen-faced and crushed to our New York City apartment, and I gave him every ounce of my sympathy. For the second time in our lives, someone we had served and loved was cruelly snatched from our lives—our dreams of making a difference through public service shattered in an instant by a gun's bullets and the world plunged again into deep mourning. I believe that the Kennedy assassinations forever ended Don's desire to continue in government service. He always said those years of service were the best ones of his life, and he had thought they would never end.

Don was an honorary pallbearer at Bobby's funeral on June 8, which was held at St. Patrick's Cathedral in New York City. He stood for several hours with other friends and colleagues beside the casket as it lay in front of the altar in the giant cathedral. As I dressed for the funeral, I realized that the last time I wore black was in 1964 for a happy event: a private audience with Pope Paul VI in Rome. The weight of the loss of our dear friend was unbearable.

Bobby's younger brother, Teddy, gave the perfect eulogy for him. It combined many of the inspirational ideas that his brother spoke about during his short life, which had so inspired me. Teddy, his voice breaking, ended the eulogy with the following words:

> My brother need not be idealized, or enlarged in death beyond what he was in life; to be remembered simply as a good and decent man, who saw wrong and tried to right it, saw suffering and tried to heal it, saw war and tried to stop it. Those of us who loved him and who take him to his rest today, pray that what he was to us and what he wished for others will someday come to pass for all the world. As he said many times, in many parts of this nation, to those he touched and who

sought to touch him: "Some men see things as they are and say why. I dream things that never were and say why not."

After the service, the mourners boarded a private train in Pennsylvania Station that carried the casket to its permanent resting place in Arlington Cemetery in Washington, D.C. It was my last trip with Bobby.

It was a sun-dappled afternoon, and the train moved slowly in recognition of the thousands of citizens—of all ethnicities and races, economic strata and ages—who lined the track to say goodbye, wave an American flag, and salute him. Their collective grief silenced all of us inside the train, and I will never forget those six hours we spent together, with the late-afternoon sun streaming through the windows.

I felt as if the sun stayed in the sky longer than usual that day, refusing to set in its normal pattern. I thought that if the trip did not end, we would never have to leave Bobby—but leave him we had to do, in the ground at Arlington Cemetery with the sun finally slipping into evening.

I looked back at the sturdy white wooden cross that marked his grave and promised him that I would try to do the work he had asked each of us to do. As Don and I walked together down the grass to the limousine, I felt some comfort for Bobby, because I knew he was a good Catholic who believed in the promise of an afterlife. No one in my estimation had ever lived the highest tenets of Catholicism as faithfully as Bobby. I found comfort for Ethel in knowing that she was carrying his last child, a daughter named Rory Katherine Elizabeth, born six months after her father was buried.

Don and I returned to Bobby's gravesite for memorial masses several times after that final trip on the train. We sang his favorite songs of the sixties, read his inspiring words, saw his resolute, ever-faithful and loving wife, and watched his children grow into fine adults carrying on his vision.

I have not forgotten Bobby Kennedy. I believe our country and world would have been better had he lived and been elected president. Until I die, I will work to keep alive his vision for our world and never be afraid to share the belief echoed in the Alfred, Lord Tennyson poem "Ulysses," which was engraved on his Mass card: "Come, my friends, Tis not too late to seek a newer world."

Moving About

The Manhattan-Princeton Axis

The word *peripatetic* has always intrigued me, and traveling from place to place accurately defines the period of time when we were living in two different places: our weekend home in Princeton and our apartment in New York City. I am not at all sure whether the effects of moving from place to place—the continual packing and unpacking of belongings, the new schools and friends—were positive or negative in the long run. Some would say we had the best of both worlds with a city apartment during the week and a country home on weekends, and if we had taken a family poll, the suburbanites would have been in the majority.

It was hard to leave Washington, but like so many of our friends in the administration, we had to move on after the assassination. Don had reasoned that his new job at Time Inc. dovetailed well with the international work he'd done at USIA, and since I had chosen the "Mommy track," supplemented by some volunteer work, his career was paramount. We agreed on Princeton as a place to call home, since we both had New Jersey roots. My mother was also an influence: "Go to Princeton," she urged me, "It has a university, which will add a dimension to your lives that other suburbs cannot." She was right, and we never regretted the choice.

We rented a much-too-large, yellow, neoclassical house at 100 Mercer Street in the heart of Princeton, complete with white pillars and spacious back and front lawns. Don commuted to his job, which didn't exactly turn out to be his cup of tea. Although he was a good sport, he found it hard to rise at seven o'clock each morning to take two trains and a subway to work in mid-Manhattan and do the reverse each evening, often not returning until nine o'clock, long after the children were in bed. The idea of moving to New York City began to creep into our thoughts.

We were also restless. It was hard to readjust to being ordinary people and not at the center of government power. I used to return to Washington every six months to have my hair cut by my favorite hairdresser, which seems ridiculous now when Manhattan beckoned with its many competent stylists. It was also hard to get going socially again, as Washington had provided us an established structure for making friends and having fun.

Welcoming Penny

Don immediately decided to join the local country club, which surprised me. We had never joined a club in Washington; we didn't have to when the Kennedys' Hickory Hill summoned us each weekend. I didn't want to become a country club wife and wanted no part of that life, but my mixed feelings about our new life in Princeton led to something tangible and wonderful: the decision to have another child. It was something of a bold move: we already had two lovely children, ages five and seven, who had adjusted nicely to our new community. I often attribute the decision to have a third child to a conversation I had with Bobby Kennedy.

"Susie," he said to me at dinner one evening after his brother's assassination. "What would have happened to my mother had she only had two children?"

I knew instantly what he meant: the eldest brother, Joe, had been killed during the war, and the second eldest sister, Kathleen, had died in a private plane crash four years later; both were in their 20s—and their deaths were never far from his mind. If we ever lost Dwight and Kate, we would cease to be parents and have no more children to love. Bobby's parents had had seven children to console them after the death of the eldest children. Don and I discussed what Bobby had said, and we both thought that having another baby might also help us to readjust to our changed lives.

Our third child and second daughter, Penelope, whom we called Penny, was born in April 1967, to the entire family's delight. A story about her name made the rounds of friends and family: she was named for one of Don's former girlfriends, with whom he had had a romance long before he met me. I also received some credit for giving our new baby the name, which I liked a great deal; I felt no jealousy of his former flame.

Everyone greeted Penny with much joy, even her older brother, Dwight, who was sad for a while because, as he had confided to me, "I was hoping for a boy to play baseball with." Always a good sport and a kind soul, Dwight adjusted, and I tried to lengthen our baseball practices on the back lawn between breast-feedings.

Shortly after Penny's birth and two years after our move to Princeton, we decided to move to New York City to reduce Don's commute. At almost the last minute of our Princeton life, a real estate agent suggested that we look at a rental property in Princeton that we might like for weekends, a gracious house at 4574 Province Line Road (actually in Lawrence Township). We fell in love with the house at first sight and decided to keep one foot in the community.

The promise of returning to Princeton each weekend helped Dwight adjust to the big city, although he hated having to wear a coat and tie to the proper school he attended. Katie was happy in New York, as it meant a chance to study at the School of American Ballet—the New York City Ballet's prestigious school for prospective dancers, which accepted her when she was seven. Don especially benefited from the move, since he arrived home early enough to enjoy seeing his three offspring before bedtime. I was a city girl at heart and glad to return to my old hometown, where I was sure to find plenty of interesting volunteer work to balance life with a new baby. I even managed to get used to driving to Princeton every Friday afternoon with the three children and our au pair, adjusting to weekend life and then piling everyone into the car for the Sunday evening drive back to the city.

I couldn't have managed our lives in two places if it hadn't been for the au pairs, who became a part of our family. We began the custom of having an au pair to help with childcare and light housework when we lived in Washington, after Dwight and Katie were born, and we continued it for many years. Each au pair stayed with us for a little under two years: Crystal came from Germany, Mieke from the Netherlands, Ösa from Sweden, and Helen, Aurelia, and Brenda from England. I am still indebted to them for their help as we went back and forth like yoyos between Princeton and New York City, renting different apartments up and down Manhattan's East Side.

Katie was particularly close to Helen, and when she left us to return to England, she invited Katie over for a two-week summer visit. She flew to London by herself at age ten to visit Helen, who took her to see some of England's great sites. Andrea Jayne Ridilla, of Pittsburgh, was another admired au pair. We hired her in 1979 when she was 23 and pursuing her master's degree in music at the Juilliard School for aspiring and talented musicians, and she lived with us rent-free in exchange for helping to care for Penny. (Dwight was then at boarding school, and Katie's life was consumed by ballet and schoolwork.) Andrea became part of our family, and even while she was coming into her own as an international oboe star and music professor at Miami University in Ohio, we never lost track of each other: to this day, she always calls me on my birthday from wherever she is on the globe.

We moved every two years, renting three different furnished apartments, which was like changing horses on a carousel each time the music stopped. But I climbed off the wooden horse every time and moved to the next place without giving it much thought, always hoping to turn the new apartment into a comfortable home. Our moves came to an end in 1974 when we finally bought an apartment at 1050 Park Avenue at 87th Street and stayed until Penny graduated from Brearley in 1985.

Our Constant North Star

Sailors of old relied on the North Star to find direction on the ocean, and our house at 4574 Province Line Road became the constant North Star in our lives. We rented it in 1967 when Penny was only nine months old and jumped at the chance to buy it when it came our way, since we had come to love it so much.

The house brought with it a set of neighbors that could never be matched. Our closest ones were Sally and Tony Maruca, who lived to our right, and Tom and Mary Lee Jamieson, who lived to our left. (Katie called them the "hard-core neighbors.") Others who lived in close proximity over the years were Yolande and David Harrop, Ann and Sid Harwood, Scott and Hella McVay, Alissande and Fletcher Satterwhite, and Mary and Bob O'Leary. Marian and Harry Heher lived further south on Province Line but were definitely considered part of the neighborhood, which Hella called "better than Mr. Rogers'," because it was exciting and real, whereas Mr. Rogers' was exciting but on TV. There were also 29 children around the same ages who came and went, and we had the space for them to congregate, play touch football games, and have fun.

When we told all our wonderful neighbors that we had bought the house, a member of the talented group—who remains anonymous to this day—wrote a poem of welcome. The opening verse sets the tongue-in-cheek tone:

> Not far from here, there's a big house that's white.
> It's the one that automatically lights up at night.
> In years to come, where Cruice once stood,
> The Wilsons may come to live here for good.
> Great for us, but imagine their plight
> Having to deal with home ownership day and night.

Our home came with a touching story: it was built 70 years earlier as a gift from a groom to his bride. The bridegroom had commissioned Rolf Bauhan, the eminent architect of the day, to design the home, and it must have been one of the largest and most gracious of its time. It was whitewashed brick with a two-car garage and a step-down living room off the center hall downstairs and six bedrooms and four baths upstairs. It was set back from the road on ten acres of spacious front and back lawns, which contained a swimming pool and a pool house with a cupola. An awning-covered terrace adjacent to the living room made it easy for our guests (and the deer) to admire a rose garden and a splashing fountain.

Don worked hard to find the stone sculpture of a fish that he placed in the fountain and fiddled and fiddled to make sure it worked properly each spring when he refilled the pool. I fiddled with the rosebushes, which afforded me an annual battle to protect them from black spot, Japanese beetles, towering trees that blotted out the sunlight, and deer that found them delectable. I eventually replaced the roses with small boxwoods, which didn't require six hours of morning light and weren't on the deer's menu. Don and I spent many pleasant hours reading under the terrace canopy and watching our kids run happily with their friends on the lawn, prompting in me warm feelings of happiness and gratefulness for all our good fortune.

I remember the neighborhood kids' pickup basketball games at our net in the paved courtyard and the touch football games on our front lawn that included jumping over or colliding into the three-foot high boxwoods that lined our brick front walk. (The considerable crashes effectively destroyed Don's beloved bushes, and I had to replace them with low-growing, hearty pachysandra that withstood dramatic end-zone catches.)

One summer afternoon some years before we sold the house, I was in the backyard and heard a car drive up. I walked into the paved courtyard and saw a gray-haired older woman open the door and step out. I had never seen her before in my life.

"I am Molly Beurkle from Arizona," she said. "This is my house, which was given to me when I was married—as a wedding present." I instantly put two and two together and greeted this woman who had materialized out of nowhere.

"Oh, yes, I know the history of the house. Welcome. I am so glad to meet you. We love your house," I replied.

A younger woman emerged from the car, and Mrs. Beurkle introduced her as her granddaughter. "I know I should have called in advance, but I'm here for a short amount of time," she continued. "Can I please show the house to my granddaughter? She has heard so much about it, and it is where her mother grew up."

I did a quick calculation of the state of the house, decided it was in pretty good shape, and ushered her up the back porch and into the kitchen. "Please make yourself at home. It is your house, too," I said. "Explore to your heart's content. I don't want to intrude. Take lots of time. I'll be in the backyard."

About an hour later, Mrs. Beurkle and her granddaughter reappeared. I offered tea, but she shook her head and then looked at me with an air of puzzlement. "But my dear, you've made no changes," she said. I was startled but then realized that she spoke the truth: We hadn't made any major changes to the house at all.

"Why should we?" I said. "Who would want to change perfection?"

Mrs. Beurkle smiled warmly, and I knew I had chosen the right words to describe the house that had been her wedding present. She died some years later, having never returned to see it again.

When we decided to sell the house after living there for 40 years, some realtors said that had we made some changes, such as modernizing the kitchen and bathrooms, we would have been able to increase the asking price. But for Mrs. Beurkle's sake, I'm glad that we didn't. The house did us proud, and to this day I feel pleasure when I recall the parties and good times our family enjoyed there.

I cannot forget Dwight's Fourth of July parties for his 50 Yale classmates; our 25th wedding anniversary bash, with people from our wedding party coming from distant points; or the communal Thanksgiving in 1980, when each neighbor cooked a dish for the feast and we cleared the living room of furniture, piling it up in our garage, to set up round tables and chairs so everyone could eat together. I also can't forget our neighbor Tom Jamieson's 50th birthday, when all the guests came as celebrities who lived in 1930, the year he was born (Don and I were the Duke and Duchess of Windsor); the gathering of the "January 17th Birthday Club" (my birthday); or our annual "Smiles of a Summer Night" party to celebrate Don's birthday.

We couldn't have given any of these parties without Team Clemens, a merry band of caterers led by Ilse Clemens and her talented and helpful family members, including her sister-in-law, Jordy, and, on occasion, depending on the size of the party, her husband and son. If catering were an Olympic sport, Ilse and her team would have won the gold. Nothing deterred her and her helpers from ensuring that the assemblage—the larger, the better—enjoyed delectable food and good wine and had the best possible time.

Don and I threw a "Goodbye-to-the-House Party" in May 2006 when we sold it and downsized to a condominium in Constitution Hill in Princeton. We held it the day before the movers came to carry off our many cardboard boxes and furniture. My creative friend Anne Reeves had suggested that for the invitation I superimpose an excerpt of a lovely Mary Oliver poem on a photograph of the house. It read:

> *Goodbye, sweet and beautiful house,*
> *we shouted, and it shouted back,*
> *goodbye to you, and it lifted itself*
> *down from the town*
> *and set off like a packet of clouds…*

The party was the perfect way to thank our house for all the happiness it had given us, and for always being the constant North Star to which we returned with such pleasure. And no one seemed to mind balancing their drinks and themselves on the packed boxes.

The World of Work

I never went back to journalism, although the many skills I learned from it served me well in every other job I undertook in my life. I became interested in public education and child and family poverty when we lived in Washington. I'm embarrassed to admit that after receiving what was considered a good education for a woman and attending church on a regular basis, I didn't know much about poverty in my own country, and I knew even less about it in others.

Bobby and Ethel cared about the needs of the poorest people, because of their Catholic upbringing, which stresses people's responsibility to care for the poor, especially as the Gospel according to Luke says, "To whom much has been given, much will be required." After traveling with them and seeing the work of the good nuns in hospitals, schools, and community programs, I began to understand that I, too, had the responsibility to take a more active role in understanding the multiple reasons for family poverty where I lived. In Washington, I became a volunteer in a program to help poor children improve their reading skills, and then I moved to New Jersey determined to work in an anti-poverty program while raising my three children.

After settling into our house in Princeton, I traveled to our state capital in Trenton for a part-time volunteer job with the New Jersey Office of Economic Opportunity (NJOEO), the newly created, statewide anti-poverty program. Its director, John C. Bullitt, was a friend of ours from the Kennedy days, when he was assistant secretary of the Treasury. He helped me become the assistant editor of the program's quarterly newsletter, *Opportunity*, and I wrote stories about local federally funded anti-poverty programs.

I once drove to Newark to interview the director of one of the city's anti-poverty programs that had received grants. This young African-American director didn't spend much time on small talk. While I sat down on the wooden chair in his bare office, he immediately began to give me his views. Looking me straight in the eye, he voiced many of Newark residents' needs, which weren't being met by the program. For a moment, I felt he was blaming me for the sad conditions in which so many African-Americans were living. He stopped for a minute, sat down behind his desk, and looked at me again.

"I'm warning you and all those people at their desks in Trenton who are in charge of this program, that the federal money coming into the program here is too little, too late, and not making a difference in the life of Newark residents," he said.

His voice began to rise: "If the people's demands for better public housing and the end of failing schools are not met, people are going to riot and take to the streets. Let me repeat: there's going to be rioting right out there on Springfield Avenue."

When I returned to our office, I reported what he said to John Bullitt, but he dismissed the man's prediction of a riot.

"You must have heard him incorrectly. I doubt you're right, and please do not write what you heard," he said. But riots for economic justice and more political control did erupt in Newark in the hot summer of 1967, and the rioters marched right down Springfield Avenue. The Newark riots were front-page news, and our director missed the story and an opportunity to intervene through governmental action before they began.

Bullitt's dismissal of the Newark director's words lingered with me. They reflected the view of an affluent white man who was essentially out of touch with the African-American community in the largest urban center in the state that he was trying to help. There was a disconnect between the people making policy and the people who could benefit from it, and it was an important lesson for me to learn. The experience shaped my thinking when I began my work helping poor people to achieve better lives through sexuality education and teen pregnancy prevention efforts.

Overall, I gained a lot of respect for the state government workers who tried to find solutions to the serious problems affecting poor people. I always disputed Ronald Reagan's remark that "we fought a war on poverty and poverty won," which was insulting to those suffering its ill effects. As I moved about the state, I saw the difference that federal money could make: Head Start for young children, low-income housing for homeless families, and job training for unemployed men. True, the outcomes weren't perfect, but nothing ever is. We are still fighting these same battles about the need for federal programs in 2014.

As I reported on these stories, I realized that I wanted to do something more valuable than writing about poor people who needed assistance. I wanted to dig deeper and get involved, not write about others making efforts. I was becoming aware of the dichotomy between telling and doing and recognizing the need for both elements to solve a problem.

In New York City, I discovered a nonprofit organization called School Volunteers that gave me the opportunity to work directly with schoolchildren in a poverty-stricken area of New York City. The organization placed women like me in schools in East Harlem and the Lower East Side, where children in the early grades were falling behind and failing to learn to read. It was assumed that someone with a college degree could teach children how to read, which I realized wasn't correct once I became more acquainted with the reading process.

We were provided training to enable us to understand the pernicious effects of growing up in circumstances that poverty dictated, such as inadequate housing and failing public schools, and to help children living in such circumstances. Once assigned to a school, we pulled the child out of class for special tutoring in a resource room. Working with the classroom teacher, who always seemed so relieved when we walked into the room, I'd do my best to remediate some of the students' weaker skills and encourage their excitement for reading. Many of the children used idioms that didn't appear in the little books they were given to read, and so they made many mistakes when reading out loud. Though I tried to teach them that "reading is talk written down," they didn't see it that way, and my frequent corrections probably contributed to their insecurities. At the time, most of the classroom reading books had pictures only of white children. *The Bank Street Readers,* which showed pictures of African-American children for the first time in publishing history, were a godsend, and my students' faces lit up whenever they saw themselves in these books.

I was anxious at first about going directly into poor African-American neighborhoods. A friend and I were assigned to a school at 128th Street, in East Harlem, and her husband, a prominent official at the United Nations, drove us there the two mornings a week we volunteered so we wouldn't have to take the subway or bus into unfamiliar areas. I'm ashamed to think that I wasn't more courageous, but later, when I worked as a teacher's aide in P. S. 30, I did take the subway without incident.

Teaching children to read was definitely not easy, but sometimes the white-led education and testing establishments made the going even tougher for them. Elizabeth Moulton, another school volunteer, and I decided to point out some of the problems that reading-test designers inflicted on poor, African-American children. We wrote an opinion piece, "The Unfair Tests," which appeared on the *New York Times* opinion page on September 18, 1971. We had studied the standardized reading tests taken annually by 600,000 mostly poor, minority, elementary school students in New York City, who scored far below the more affluent, white students in the suburbs.

"The tests may be suitable for children raised in Pawling or Pelham [white, wealthy New York City suburbs] or in Kansas or New Hampshire," we wrote, "but they are patently unsuitable for children raised in East Harlem."

We explained that the vocabulary, illustrations, and values in the tests' stories related to middle-class backgrounds and experiences, with little or no connection to poor children's actual lives in the city. We recommended that they not have to take these tests "in their present form again, and at the very least, the tests must be redesigned to give the children a better chance." We never knew if our article drew any responses, but today's standardized tests are more sensitive to the vocabulary and educational needs of poor urban children.

Moving on to Graduate School

I felt I needed more instruction in the reading process and in the techniques for and philosophy of teaching young children. At the Bank Street College of Education on the Upper West Side, a graduate school that specialized in early childhood and elementary education, I found the Cary Leadership program, which offered a new pathway for minorities and women to become school leaders as principals, primarily in urban schools. African-Americans and Latinos had been shut out of leadership positions in the early 1970s, even though school populations were overwhelmingly composed of minorities. The traditional route to becoming an educational leader in public schools was through the classroom, which meant years of teaching. The Cary Leadership program offered participants an opportunity to leapfrog over classroom hours directly into leadership positions.

I applied to and was accepted into the program in 1974. Although it seems highly unrealistic looking back, I thought I might become principal of an urban elementary school. I also believed that graduate school might help me become more active and integrate everything I had learned from my work experiences.

Bank Street's progressive mission was to train its graduates to forge change in the stodgy, traditional public school system. Thirteen people were selected for the Leadership program that year, 11 were African-American or Latino/a, and two were white (I and another woman, Margaret Cohen). Margaret had been a public school teacher, but I had only my minimal volunteer experience.

The program offered me a life-changing perspective: as one of only two whites in a program that lasted almost two years, I began to understand how it felt to be a minority. The African-American woman who headed the program spent 99 percent of her time mentoring the minority students. It was a good experience for me — I realized how alone a minority person feels, and it made me more sensitive to diversity issues.

I soon learned that teaching wasn't only about pedagogy but also about students' social and emotional growth and development. Until I arrived at Bank Street, I had heard no one discuss the importance of helping students develop character, relationships, and values. Bank Street's approach was a revelation to me and influenced my later work in sex education.

Instead of writing a master's thesis for the program, I became part of a National Teacher Corps effort to turn around a failing public school, P. S. 179, on the Upper West Side. The mission of the Teacher Corps was to forge partnerships between universities and these schools to train teachers to be more sensitive to the background and needs of poor, minority students. There was a huge gulf between white, middle-class teachers and their poor, black students, and it needed to be filled with promising new ideas to encourage better teaching.

I joined the Teacher Corps team at P. S. 179 and engaged in a variety of tasks, ranging from writing a newsletter for teachers to running a resource room to working one-on-one with classroom teachers. It was challenging to assist some of the tenured teachers; most were older and marking time before they retired. They weren't interested in improving or making changes to help their minority students. One teacher in particular bothered me; during the winter, she had the children dressed and ready to go down to the school bus at two o'clock every afternoon. The bus didn't leave until three, so the children sat like bumps on a log in their chairs—all bundled up in their outdoor clothing in the overheated classroom doing nothing constructive. When I asked her why this was the case, she said, "So they'll be ready at three o'clock when the buses come."

"But aren't you cutting out an hour of instruction in their day? Many of these kids are behind in reading. Could you read out loud to them while they sit there or have them get dressed closer to three?" I asked.

I did my best to hide my annoyance, because as an intern I had absolutely no power or influence on her. She had tenure and was simply going through the motions of teaching, and no federal program in the world could have changed her point of view—but it changed mine toward tenure. I came to believe that it was wrong to tenure teachers for their entire careers after their having taught for only three years, which was the longstanding procedure in the city's public schools. (I held fast to this view when I became a member of the New Jersey State Board of Education, which set school policy. Although because of pressures from the teachers' unions and professional organizations, we never took the issue of teacher tenure head-on while I served on it. I regret it.)

I learned some other long-lasting education principles in graduate school: the importance of balancing theory and practice, how to change direction if necessary to teach a concept, how to make a lesson for an elementary-age child more concrete and less abstract (I once had a fifth grader walk 5,280 feet to understand the length of a mile, and I did a lot of cooking with second graders to help them learn math, reading, and writing). Most of all, I learned the importance of listening to and trusting the views of children, even little ones, because they had something valuable to say that could help you teach them.

I also learned critical lessons during these years in inner city schools; one was that poor children carry burdens that more affluent children don't have to face. Many of my students were the children of single, teen mothers, who were trying to juggle caring for them while completing high school or their GED. Many were growing up in fatherless households and cramped apartments where they didn't get to bed until late in the evening and arrived at school sleep-deprived the next morning. They often didn't have materials at home to help them with their homework. The children I worked with were spirited, funny, concerned, bright, and caring, like my children, but because of the complex economic and social circumstances and lack of policies to overcome poverty, they came to school with strikes against them.

I found that teaching these children was hard and exhausting, and when I came home, I would often be sharp with my own children because I didn't have any gas—or patience—left in my tank. "Why are you so mean to us?" one of my children asked on one occasion, and the question made me feel awful, and even more emotionally exhausted.

I didn't know how or didn't have the patience to explain the world's inequities to my children. I tried to portray the gulf by writing another article, "Two Worlds Separate and Unequal," which compared the last day of my daughter's second grade at Brearley with graduation day for the second graders at my East Harlem school. The privileged children were leaving school for enriching summer experiences, yet the East Harlem children were going to spend their summers on the hot city sidewalks. The two worlds were separate and unequal. The article was never published.

With my Master's of Science in Education in hand, I graduated from Bank Street in 1976. I had learned a tremendous amount about the educational and social needs of poor children. I wasn't sure how I was going to take what I had learned and make a difference, but I did know that my two-year-long bus and subway commute across Manhattan's east and west sides was finally over.

I was determined to never forget the schoolchildren I had met along the way, especially Denise Brown, a second grader in East Harlem. We were working on her reading skills one morning, and she was looking at the names of the colors red, green, blue, and brown written on pieces of paper to test her sight-reading ability. Suddenly she looked up at the blackboard where some of the children's names, including hers, were written. She grabbed the piece of paper with the word "brown" off the desk, dashed to the board, and held it up against her last name, "Brown." She looked at it a couple of times and then turned her head with all its little braids and yelled, "I can read! I can read!" I ran over and gave her a big hug. "Yes, you can!" I said in equal delight. My memories of Denise and the other children stayed with me as I fought for sex education and other public school improvements years later in Trenton.

Bank Street's Cary Leadership program was based on a faulty premise: that the entrenched public school establishment would be flexible enough to allow people without classroom teaching experience into educational leadership positions. Some of my class members were able to become principals, but not me—a middle-aged white woman who had never taught a day in her life. I looked for jobs in private schools but decided not to pursue becoming a second grade teacher—not because I didn't respect the job (teaching is the hardest job you'll ever love), but because I didn't think it would be a good fit for me at my age. Penny was nine years old, too young to leave every day for a full-time job, even one with a schedule similar to hers. I didn't yet know that an opportunity to serve on the New Jersey State Board of Education was soon coming my way.

Our Midlife Crisis

I was once asked to list the ten most important memories of my life, beginning with the most important. It didn't take me more than three seconds to write down "Penny's hand." It was an incident that threatened our entire family, but most particularly our daughter Penny, who was eleven at the time. Don was 53, and I was 48.

From the beginning, I sensed that something was seriously wrong with the bump that appeared out of the blue on Penny's left hand. I had never seen anything quite like it: a swelling in the bone a few inches below the base of her middle finger. I first noticed the bump as Penny and I were crossing a street in Washington, D.C., in 1978. I had reached out to take her left hand when I looked down and saw it. Penny and I were spending a week of her spring vacation in Washington seeing the sights with her friend and classmate Kate Howard; Kate's older brother, John; and their mother, Karen, who had become a good friend of mine.

We were learning and having fun, seeing monuments and museums and playing games in the evening in our room at the famous Watergate Hotel. The highlight of the trip had been visiting the Supreme Court chambers and having lunch with Justice Byron White, who had been appointed to the Court by President Kennedy in 1962. But Penny's hard little bump cast a slight shadow over moments like this.

As we were saying goodbye in Princeton, Karen pulled me aside and said, "Don't forget to take Penny to see the pediatrician about her hand." I promised her I would, but I didn't keep that promise. I couldn't find anything relevant in my bible of childcare by Dr. Benjamin Spock, and so I ignored the growth. I ignored it and kept thinking, "It will go away tomorrow." My mind indulged in magical thinking, telling me that since the growth had appeared overnight, it would disappear overnight. I didn't want to frighten Penny by constantly looking at the bump or feeling to see if it had grown larger, softer, or harder. I didn't want to know the truth.

The summer passed and the growth remained about the same. Penny was going into sixth grade, and in late August I took her to her pediatrician, Dr. Norman Katz, for her annual physical exam before the school year started.

"What is this?" he asked me, studying the growth as he touched it.

"A little growth that has been there for a while," I replied.

Dr. Katz could have reprimanded me for not bringing Penny to see him sooner, but instead he did something even more chilling. He spoke the truth: "This is serious," he said; "it's a growth in the bone. You must go to a specialist, an orthopedist, and have him look at it. He'll have to take a scraping of the bone and examine it under a microscope."

He wrote down the name of a local doctor, Robert Dunn. "You must make an appointment with him immediately," he said. The emphasis was on "immediately" and I heard his message. Poor Penny seemed frightened, but I assured her that everything would be all right. No one was able to assure me that it would be all right, and suddenly I was wracked with guilt. I had lulled myself into thinking that nothing was wrong with my daughter, and now my inability to face the truth and take action had placed us on the edge of a precipice. The lump or bump, I finally realized, must be a tumor.

I told Don the scary news. Soon all three of us were in Dr. Dunn's office, where he anesthetized Penny's hand, sliced the back of it open, took a scraping of the swelling in the bone, which looked like a bump, and then sewed her hand up. Penny was given a sling, which helped her feel better about her ordeal.

"Don't worry, hand tumors are usually not malignant," the doctor said. His words were better than a sling for me, and I believed him. Of course, my feelings of dread were replaced by relief.

A couple of weeks passed, school started, and I took comfort that we hadn't heard from Dr. Dunn. Don, Katie, Penny, and I had gone back to our usual routine of living in the city during the week and in Princeton on weekends. Dwight was in Spain on a gap year after completing his sophomore year at college.

One morning in early November as I was about to get out of bed, Don sat up and said, "Susan, the doctor called me yesterday. Penny's hand tumor isn't benign. It is malignant." The force of his words actually propelled me out of bed, and I found myself standing in the middle of the room looking straight at him. Don kept right on talking, telling me that the Princeton doctor, so sure that the tumor wasn't a malignant one, hadn't sent the samples off to a local pathologist for immediate analysis. When the results finally came back indicating a malignancy, he was so ashamed of himself that, although it was a Saturday morning, he drove the samples to the pathology department of Columbia Presbyterian Hospital in upper Manhattan for a fast second opinion. The New York pathologist confirmed that Penny's tumor was an "osteosarcoma"—a malignant, cancerous bone tumor that usually develops in adolescence, often when a teen is growing rapidly.

Don told me that Dr. Dunn had given us the name of a highly regarded hand surgeon, Dr. Harold Dick, at the Children's Hospital of Columbia Presbyterian; we were to make an appointment to plan how and when he would remove the tumor. We both decided on the spot not to tell Penny. It was a decision made to protect our child, but in retrospect, it might not have been in her best interest. (Working later in sexuality education convinced me to share news bad or good with kids, although in an age-appropriate way.) Without her, we went to Dr. Dick's office, where he told us that he would have to remove the middle bone and middle finger of Penny's left hand.

"No one will ever notice," he said reassuringly. "I will rearrange her three fingers together so well that no one will ever notice the other finger's absence."

All that sounded tolerable until he added, "She'll have to have some scans to make sure the cancer hasn't already spread to her lungs, the usual pattern for this type of tumor."

He gave us a date for the surgery, which was about a week before Thanksgiving. Dr. Dick, a Princeton alumnus with impeccable medical credentials, was courteous but all business.

Don decided that he would take responsibility for learning all he could about hand tumors in order to be as knowledgeable as the doctors, and I was to keep life normal for Penny. I did the best I could by informing family members, key people at the Brearley School, neighbors, close friends, and fellow employees. We went through the same process that countless other parents go through when they receive a life-threatening diagnosis for a child: feeling confusion, disbelief and panic; confiding in others; going from doctor to doctor hoping for a miracle; desperately trying to keep everything normal for the stricken child; and praying—at least I did—that when we woke up from the nightmare, the world would have returned to normal.

In our case, we ended up taking a train to Georgetown Hospital in Washington for a set of X-rays to determine if the cancer had spread to other parts of her body. "It's probably already too late," the technician in the radiology department whispered to me as I helped Penny lie down on the X-ray table. He was wrong. The X-rays and the MRI taken at Mt. Sinai Hospital the next week showed no further abnormality. We were overjoyed that we had somehow escaped the bullets that had been whizzing around our heads.

I don't remember whether Don contacted Senator Ted Kennedy or vice versa, but Teddy knew all about this form of cancer since his son, Teddy Jr., had lost his lower leg to the aggressive tumor five years earlier at 12 years old. He completely recovered and was back on skis in a short amount of time. Teddy offered Don not only consolation but also means to action. He gave him the name of the same physician at the National Cancer Institute (NCI) in Washington who had helped him and said he would call in advance to give him Don's name.

The NCI doctor asked our Princeton doctor to send Penny's slides to Dr. David Dahlin, a renowned pathologist at the Mayo Clinic in Rochester, Minnesota, whose specialty was bone tumors, for yet another opinion. I remember watching Don hang up the phone after talking to Teddy, thinking, "Teddy has made it his mission to take care of everyone who served in his brother's administration, including us," and I felt an intense rush of gratitude.

As part of keeping everything normal at home, I was at Bank Street working on a project when the office phone rang. It was Don, and his voice sounded different as he spoke words that I never thought I would hear: "Susan, Dr. Dahlin says this is not a malignant tumor. This is not a malignant tumor," he repeated, as if I hadn't heard him the first time. I had never before experienced the waves of joy that spread through my body. I couldn't have moved even if I had willed myself to do so. "Everyone says that when Dahlin makes a diagnosis he is *rarely*, if ever, wrong—and he is absolutely certain that this hand tumor is not malignant."

It is amazing how life can turn around in a moment. We proceeded cautiously, knowing that another round of tests would be done when the bone was removed from Penny's hand—and we still had the wretched task of telling her that she would lose her finger. I had never done anything so raw, so honest in my life, and I was terrified. I had to tell her the truth, and yet to the core of my being I wanted to shield her from it.

We told our loving, trusting daughter that she had to go to a special children's hospital where she would undergo an operation to remove that bump in her hand. We told her that we would stay with her throughout the operation, and that everyone would be kind to her and do their best to make her well. We told her that she would meet Dr. Dick, a surgeon who knew how to fix problems like hers. We made plans to journey to the hospital in upper Manhattan, where Penny was admitted.

She was sitting in her hospital bed in her room at Children's Hospital, made cheery with paintings on the walls and furniture in bright primary colors. I helped her undress and slip into a hospital gown decorated with brightly colored animals. Don stood by the window, and I knew the time had come for me to tell her the truth before a nurse or Dr. Dick would speak with her. I sat down on the bed next to her and put my arm around her, dreading what I had to say.

"Penny, darling," I said. "When Dr. Dick takes that lump out of your hand tomorrow, he is going to have to take away your finger in the middle, too."

A wildness filled her eyes, and they opened wider than I had ever seen them. Confusion, then disbelief, then fury and horror crossed them. Her shriek must have been audible for miles, and then came her cascades of tears while both Don and I hugged and kissed her. Suddenly the room was full of people telling her stories about others with three or even fewer fingers on their hands, and how well they had done in their lives. Don and I simply took turns hugging and kissing her until her last teardrop ceased. Not until much, much later did we tell her about the threat to her life that the little lump in her hand had caused.

The operation went well. Don, true to his promise, had researched every aspect of hand tumors and learned that some hand surgeons replaced a finger that was removed with one from a cadaver. He wanted Penny's hand to be as normal as possible, but I was willing to bet that in due time, our Pen would adjust to having three fingers. Dr. Dick did not want to consider anything but complete removal of the finger, so the entire bone could be analyzed. He assured us once more that the way he would reposition the three fingers would make Penny's hand look almost normal. Dr. Dick did not disappoint. Neither did the pathologist, who came back within hours of the operation with the reassurance that the tumor was benign, as Dr. Dahlin had first reported.

I reacted to all this good news in a way that still makes me marvel: I had always slept through the night without once awakening; when I hit my 40s, the pattern had changed and I would wake up in the middle of the night thinking about some aspect of my life. The night after the pathologist confirmed that Penny's tumor was benign, I slept straight through without waking once.

Penny adjusted to the new hand that Dr. Dick had sculpted for her. She referred to herself with a sweet laugh as "three fingers and a thumb." Not content with his surgery, Dr. Dick wanted to give Penny a course of chemotherapy.

"But why?" I asked Don. "The tumor wasn't malignant, all the scans were fine. Why would he want her to lose her nice, thick blonde hair and feel nauseated for many weeks?" I was determined that this child of ours was not going to have to suffer anymore.

Don agreed with me and said he felt Dr. Dick was "hedging his bets" and wanted to make sure that if any microscopic cancer cells existed elsewhere, they would be knocked out. Don talked to Dr. Dick, who agreed that it was all right to go forward without the chemo, but recommended that Penny have a chest X-ray every six months for a few years to make sure there were no more growths. We agreed. I trembled when we went for those checkups and didn't relax until Penny was officially discharged after having X-rays over the course of two years.

It is funny what one does in the aftermath of a crisis. I was zealous in our preparations to keep life normal for Penny after the surgery. She had decided that she wanted to learn to play the clarinet. When I realized that she was going to have only three fingers on one hand, I asked a musician friend if any instruments required only three fingers on the left hand. "The French horn and the trumpet are the only two instruments that meet your requirement," she said. I thought of the neighbors in our apartment building and decided that the French horn might be the better choice, to which Penny agreed. After the operation, she took lessons and played it with zest for some time, even taking it with her to France on a junior-year abroad program and playing in a brass group at college. The memories of the crisis in Penny's young life and the midlife crises that Don and I experienced as parents often creep back into my thoughts when I hear the plaintive sounds of a solo French horn.

A River Runs through It

"No One Is Alone," is a song from Stephen Sondheim's musical *Into the Woods*, and during this crisis we saw the healing truth of these words. We never felt alone, only swaddled in love from family members, neighbors, friends, and people we didn't even know. Penny felt the love especially from her family and school—and it was remarkable to watch its expression in so many different ways.

Liza Lee was the head of Penny's middle school during the crisis, and she stepped up to explain to Penny's classmates about her tumor and operation. Liza is one of those people who innately know the right words to use in the most difficult situations, because she speaks directly from the heart. Everyone in the class wrote a letter to Penny, and Liza delivered them to her at the hospital throughout the crisis. They ranged from the hilarious to the serious, but they were all exceptionally kind.

Penny's classmates told her, "It doesn't matter about physical appearances; it only matters about your heart." They reassured her that "nobody will notice, no one goes around counting fingers," and "you are the same Penny no matter what." One classmate told her that she knew other people who had lost fingers ("My babysitter had two fingers off, and I didn't notice"), and another told her "the same thing happened to my brother's friend; now he is as good as ever, climbing a 25-foot rope in 10 seconds."

The notes from Penny's teachers showed me that teaching children is the highest of callings. One taped a penny in place of our daughter's name; another wrote to her about her own son, two years older than Penny, who was in the hospital for five months and decided to become a doctor after his experience. "When you are both older and you meet someday at a school dance, you can compare hospital experiences," she wrote, giving Penny confidence that boys were going to like her even if she had a different hand.

The French teacher wrote her a note in French, but thoughtfully translated it into English in case she wasn't up to doing the translation herself. But it was Liza who summed up what everyone was saying in their own delightful ways: "Dearest Penny," she wrote, "All I can say is that you are a very well-loved person, and your classmates said that they weren't worried about the way your hand will look—because they never noticed how your hand looked before—because hands aren't something you notice in other people."

I arranged all the letters in an album with plastic sleeves so Penny could remove them easily if she wanted to reread them. I gave the album to her in April 1997 right before her 30th birthday celebration, 20 years after the crisis had passed. I wrote a letter to accompany it, which said in part:

> What struck me most about the letters is how full of love they are for you and how easy you make it for people—both your peers and adults—to love you. I thought that a reminder of the feelings you engender in others might warm you on your 30th birthday. I also thought it might be nice for you to see how well you faced up to a potentially life-threatening experience. From it you should gain confidence for the future.

I added that if she didn't want to keep the album because it brought up too many sorrowful memories, I would understand and make her another from the multitude of pictures we had taken of her since her birth. Years later, when I asked her to let me see the album again, she unearthed it from a box in her basement, leading me to think that she had kept it in the dark. Her children—Olivia, now 12, and Reed, 10—might be interested in learning about what happened to their mother when she was their age and the bravery she showed surmounting it. From her courage, they might gain courage. From the example of how her friends, family, and teachers rallied in her behalf, they might see the importance of love for others in life.

Some of our dearest friends and neighbors performed memorable acts of kindness during those long November days. Karen Howard would have slept on the floor of Penny's hospital room had I asked her. Sally Maruca altered Penny's woolen gloves so they would fit comfortably over the three fingers of her left hand; Mary Lee Jamieson asked the nuns of Sacred Heart to pray for Penny, telling me that she knew everything would all right; and Nina Maruca,

Sally's daughter, who had babysat for Penny in Princeton, drew a picture from the book *Charlotte's Web*. In the novel, Charlotte, the spider, saves the life of Wilbur, the pig, by spinning a larger-than-life web and writing "Some Pig" in his pen at the state fair. Nina did an adorable drawing of a spider's web and wrote "Some Pen" across it. Sometimes a picture is worth a million words. I framed her little work of art and gave it to Penny to keep forever.

I didn't know how to handle the love that flowed like a river to us from so many sources. It made me uncomfortable not knowing how to say thank you to the many who showered it upon us. I kept thinking, "We're going to have to give a huge party, a ball maybe, for everyone who has done anything to help us through this." The Rev. Hayes Rockwell, the rector of St. James' Church, where Don and I had been married, set me straight. He came to see us at the hospital the night before Penny's operation. I told him that I didn't know how to thank people for their kindness.

"You need to be a receiver as well as a giver," he said. "If people can't feel their gifts are received, they will no longer have the impetus to be givers."

No one had framed the giving-and-receiving relationship with such clarity, and I appreciated his counsel. Have I always embodied it? Probably not.

☙

Some years later, after we had settled into our house on Province Line Road, Don decided to build a tennis court. We had ample space behind the pool and its little house with a cupola. I never questioned his desire to build the court. He loved to play tennis and was good at it. He also knew that I didn't want to spend much time at the country club. After it was completed, the court looked as if it had resided in the space for generations. Our neighbors and friends thoroughly enjoyed it, as did Don and I, and sometimes I would quip that Don resolved his midlife crisis by building a tennis court.

Our real midlife crisis was Penny's hand. At Christmas, Dwight came home from Spain to complete the family circle, and Katie, who had been living with her friend on the West side and studying at the School of American Ballet, joined us at the apartment. I hired a professional photographer to take a picture. I wanted pictorial evidence should the tumor return in a malignant form that Penny had lived with and been loved by us. The picture shows that as a family we dealt with a life-threatening situation and survived. Of course we were plain lucky that we knew Ted Kennedy, who had led us to Dr. Dahlin, and had a great deal of support. I have always had compassion for other parents who have gone through a similar crisis with a beloved child that did not end as happily as ours did.

Penny recently sent me the album that I made for her so I could once more read through the letters, which made me laugh and shed a few tears. Among them I found a letter from Dr. Dick. He had written to Don on February 20, 1979, and was pleased to report that all was well with Penny. "I would like to take this opportunity to congratulate your wife and yourself for a very sensitive and thoughtful parental guidance to your beautiful daughter during this life crisis," he wrote. (I admit that I had a one-sided crush on Dr. Dick during those weeks because of what he did for our daughter.)

I went on the Internet to see if I could find out what Dr. Dick was doing today, and I discovered sadly that he had died in 2011 at the age of 77. His obituary reported that illness had dogged his life, which may explain why he wanted to order a round of chemotherapy to make sure that we had not overlooked any possibility of the cancer's return. I e-mailed Penny about his death and sent her his obituary.

"Thanks so much for sending that," she wrote to me. "It doesn't begin to do the man justice. He was such a gifted hand surgeon and left me with the legacy of his fine work! Thank you, too, for finding him and giving me the finest surgeon, and making that process the best it could be under the circumstances."

I sent a gift in Dr. Dick's memory to the Department of Orthopaedics at Columbia University in thanks for his helping us resolve our midlife crisis. I do not look at Penny's hand very often now, but when I do, all I see are her engagement and wedding rings on the new middle finger that he had created for her.

Sexuality Education

Too Young: Waiting to Learn About Sex and Babies

On a warm April afternoon in 1938, I crouched on the bank across the road from the mailbox at my family's farm in Lincroft. I had picked a spot that hid me from passing cars and anyone in the house who would realize that I was not playing on the lawn. Huddled in the wildflowers, I wrapped my arms around my knees and waited.

Any moment now, the postman would deliver the mail. It was Friday, the day *Life* magazine usually arrived, and I was determined to get my hands on that April 11th issue. My mother had told me that it would contain a story with photographs showing a baby's birth, but she said that I couldn't see it.

At eight years old, I had spent many hours on our working farm. I knew that cows had calves because of bulls, pigs had piglets because of boars, and chickens had chicks because of roosters—but I didn't exactly know *how* babies were made or born. Deep inside, I sensed that there was something powerful, even scary, about it.

"Why can't I see the story?" I complained to my mother.

"You're too young to know about such things," she said. She turned away from me, eager to be rid of my pestering. Immediately, I started plotting to steal the magazine.

I crouched in the wildflowers knowing that I could be punished for breaking a whole list of rules, yet I remained glued to the dirt, waiting, confident in my plan. *I should know about the birth of a baby. I know animals have babies, so why can't I learn how people have them?* I thought.

The postman's truck appeared and slowed to a halt beside our mailbox. He placed an armful of letters and what looked like the magazine into it and then drove off. After carefully looking both ways, I dashed across the road and opened the box. Pushing aside the letters, I grabbed *Life,* stuffed the magazine under my shirt, and raced toward our house. (I felt lucky—no one saw or stopped to question me about the bulge on my chest.)

In seconds, I bounded upstairs to hide in my parents' bedroom—the last place I thought my mother would look for me—and slipped behind an upholstered chair with a high back. I collapsed onto the floor and pulled *Life* from under my shirt. I felt triumphant, but as I opened the magazine, my mother's long arm reached over the back of the chair and my head and she plucked it from my hands.

"And that," she said, "is mine, thank you, and not for you. Now run off and read a book or play with your little sister."

I felt deflated and confused. *Had she watched me the entire time? Why on earth did I think I could fool the lioness by hiding in her den? Would I never learn how babies are made?*

Three years later, I was returning home on a train from Camp Arcadia when some older girls approached my three seatmates and me.

"Do you know how babies are made?" the ringleader asked.

She perched on the arm of my seat like a mother bird poised to feed her young. I couldn't offer an answer, but suddenly I felt like that baby bird with its mouth wide open for the food. Her smile turned serious and her voice became a mysterious whisper: "Your mummy and daddy are in bed, and then your daddy puts his 'thing' in your mummy's 'hole.' Nine months later, out comes a baby."

Things? Holes? No one had taught me the names of girls' and boys' parts and this was terrible news. *Why,* I thought, *would anyone want to do that? Why would anyone want to make a baby? Babies are nice. Wasn't there some other way?* Before I recovered enough to ask her a question, the mother bird departed. The four of us grew silent, cowed by the strangeness of the information we heard.

Hours later, the train arrived in New York City and I was met by one of our farmers, who drove me home to Lincroft. The hour-and-a-half drive seemed endless. When, finally, the car crunched over our gravel driveway, I jumped out.

"Mummy!" I yelled, tearing up the flagstone path to the front door and yanking open the screen door. "Where are you? I have something awful to tell you."

My mother emerged from the library looking shocked by the anxiety in my voice as I grabbed her arm. "This older girl on the train told me that you and Daddy do something in bed that makes a baby in nine months," I blurted out. "This isn't how babies are made, is it Mummy? Please tell me that it isn't."

My mother's silence was deep, and so I knew the awful thing was true. I feared that I would remember what I learned on that train whenever I saw my parents together. She asked me about my summer at camp, to calm me, but I refused to discuss that and ran upstairs to try to adjust myself to the news alone.

Early in the fall of 2013, I stopped at an author's table at a popular children's book festival in Princeton. She had written a little book with charming illustrations naming the parts of a child's body.

"It's for young children," she said.

I leafed through the book.

"You don't include the names for the reproductive parts?"

"No, I didn't."

"I'm a sex educator," I said.

"Ah, of course," she said. "I couldn't, I wouldn't—they are so young."

"What better time," I told her. "The information won't hurt them. It will make them feel respected and proud."

I replaced the book on the table, thanked her for her time, and recalled the little girl hiding among the wildflowers—waiting, wondering, and needing to know.

Public Efforts to Fight the Good Fight

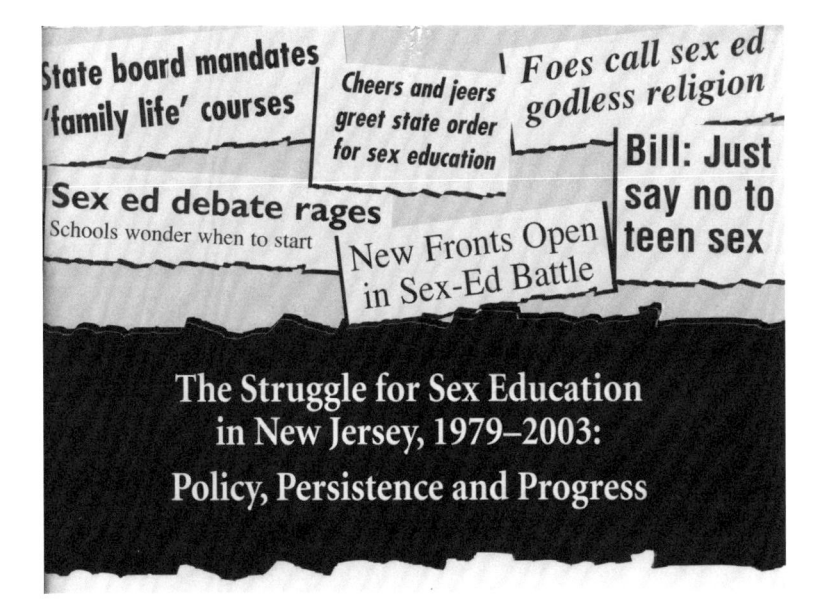

> **State board mandates 'family life' courses**
>
> **Cheers and jeers greet state order for sex education**
>
> **Foes call sex ed godless religion**
>
> **Sex ed debate rages** — Schools wonder when to start
>
> **New Fronts Open in Sex-Ed Battle**
>
> **Bill: Just say no to teen sex**

The Struggle for Sex Education in New Jersey, 1979–2003: Policy, Persistence and Progress

"*Sex, Etc.*"—two words in brilliant-red capital letters leap out from a piece of stained glass that hangs above the window in my home office. You'd have to be blind not to see them. I received the stained glass as a gift on October 23, 2003, at a conference held by the Network for Family Life Education (now known as Answer), the national comprehensive sexuality education organization that I led for 23 years.

More than 400 sexuality educators and advocates had gathered to celebrate the 20th anniversary of the passage of the New Jersey State Board of Education's requirement that family life education be taught to all public school students. It may have been the largest gathering of sexuality educators in United States history, and the buzz of excitement in the room was palpable.

This gift is precious to me: it represents my more than 30 years of work in the state and national sexuality education movement, which began when I was a member of the State Board of Education and helped create and pass the family life education policy. I continued this work when I became the executive coordinator of the Network for Family Life Education, situated in the Graduate School of Social Work at Rutgers University, where we helped to implement the policy in local New Jersey school districts and protected it from opponents—primarily religious and politically conservative groups that didn't think sexuality education could help students lead safe, responsible, and healthy lives. At the Network, I also created what I feel was my major contribution to the sexuality education movement in the U.S.: the *Sex, Etc.* magazine and website written by teens, for teens, on sexual health.

Beginnings

I would never have dreamed that the most important work of my life outside my family would be sexuality education. My own sexuality education at home and school was woefully weak, and I didn't have the expertise to help my two older children receive a much better one. (I tried to do better with Penny.) When I began working in the field, I certainly didn't know how to help young people or realize the full importance of sexuality education and its tie to other national issues: child poverty, teen pregnancy, HIV/AIDS, to name a few. In fact, I would never have become engaged with the subject if Governor Brendan T. Byrne hadn't appointed me to a six-year term on the New Jersey State Board of Education, which set policy for the state's public schools in approximately 600 districts. The State Senate confirmed my appointment on July 11, 1977.

My mother and father taught me about public service at an early age, although they demonstrated it by participation not talk; and other people built on its importance through the years. I leaped at the opportunity for Don to serve in the Kennedy administration even before Senator John F. Kennedy had been elected president, because I saw the possibilities of public service for him. I was crushed to think that the assassination might end our chances of service. When my mother suggested that I consider serving on the State Board, I saw a renewed chance of service to the public.

I liked serving on the board from the beginning, even when I saw the immense piles of reports with lots of numbers and complex statistics that I had to read in preparation for the monthly meetings. The combination of carrying out state law and making education policy clicked for me. I also liked my fellow board members, many of whom had ties to public education, served on local boards, or observed their children as they went through the system. (My children were educated in private schools.) I tried to be a quick study when it came to the issues, and after former State Senator Anne C. Martindell had written to the commissioner of education in a letter of support for me that it was "irrelevant that she is Kay Neuberger's daughter and Don Wilson's wife," I worked hard to prove her right.

The Crucial Question

Not long after I began my term, the state's commissioner of health, Dr. Joanne Finley, presented to the board her annual report on child and adolescent health. Dr. Finley, who had led a Planned Parenthood affiliate and held a master's degree in public health from Yale, didn't mince words that January afternoon in 1979. She said that the state's teens had rising rates of unplanned pregnancy, abortion, and sexually transmitted diseases (STDs), and that ignorance was at the root of these health problems. She asked the board to take concrete action to improve the state's public school sex education programs. At the time, the programs were scarce, if they existed at all, and caused intense controversies at local school board meetings, which prevented their further development.

"Schools are a promising avenue for conveying vital information to children and adolescents about sexuality," Dr. Finley said. "Please do not shrink from your responsibility to provide a 'thorough and efficient education' for New Jersey's students. So many will benefit if you are willing to bite this bullet."

She sat back in her seat, and there was silence throughout the room. Her obvious concern for the students, whom I had sworn in my oath of office to protect, struck a chord with me, and I wanted to know exactly what she thought our next steps should be. I didn't feel a bit reticent as I leaned forward and said, "Dr. Finley, at what age do you think students need to know how their bodies work?" It was an awkwardly phrased question that indicated my unfamiliarity with sexuality education, but I wasn't afraid to ask it.

"By age ten," she promptly answered. She meant that by fifth grade, all students should know about human reproduction and how to protect themselves from unplanned pregnancy and STDs. She thought that accurate, age-appropriate information was a necessary first step for children in the early grades.

After my question, the silence returned; no other board member waded into the sticky wicket of sexuality education. Dr. Finley and her staff gathered up their papers and left the room, and Paul Ricci, the board president, promptly appointed a five-person subcommittee to suggest improvements to state sexuality education programs. He leaned in my direction.

"I would like Susan Wilson to chair the subcommittee," he said.

I am sure he handed this role off to me because I was the only person who had asked Dr. Finley a question. Years later, when I spoke to young people at conferences, I would say, "Be careful what questions you ask. The answers can change your life. The answer to a particular question about sexuality education that I asked at a public meeting reshaped the direction of my working life, changing it positively for me—and I hope for the public good of others."

The next morning in Princeton, Don asked me what my plans were for the day. In his wildest dreams, he couldn't have imagined my response.

"I'm going into New York with you, but I'm going to the Time-Life morgue," I said. (Research materials for Time Inc.'s magazines *Time, Life,*

Fortune, People, Sports Illustrated, and others, dating back to their beginnings, were stored in the morgue.)

"Why? Whatever are you going to do in the morgue? It's full of those little tan envelopes stuffed with newspaper clippings," he said.

"Yes, I need to read through a lot of clippings," I replied. "I've been asked to chair a subcommittee on sex education, and I know absolutely nothing about the subject. I have to learn what I've committed myself and the board."

He smiled one of his nice smiles and wished me good luck.

"I may need it," I said.

When the woman who ran the morgue returned with only two boxes of clippings about sex education, a wave of relief washed over me—but it was only momentary. After reading about all the controversies over sex education in school districts across the country, I realized that I had grabbed a tiger by the tail—and the tiger regularly snarled.

Shaping a Statewide Policy

For the next 26 years, I had the unique experience of helping to shape statewide policy on sexuality education and then helping school boards and educators to implement it in their classrooms. Not many people can claim that they made and then implemented a policy, and in a way, it was like seeing the bud of a rose open and burst into full bloom.

The sexuality education subcommittee decided to change the policy's name from "sex education" to "family life education" to encompass a wider range of curricular topics than sexuality, including "the physical, mental, emotional, social, economic, and psychological effects of interpersonal relationships; human development, sexuality, and reproduction; and strengthening family life." The shift in terms was key to getting the policy accepted by politicians and the public, and defused some of the controversy that began at the start.

The report on sexuality education that my subcommittee requested from the State Department of Education found that many school districts were unwilling or unable to adopt sex education programs in previous years because of local controversies that tied up progress at board meetings. The subcommittee recommended that the state board pass a policy *requiring* family life education in all public elementary and secondary schools. Specifically, our policy required that K-12 family life education—we feared using the actual word "sex" might cause increased controversy—cover, by the end of eighth grade, human reproduction, child abuse, incest, and STDs. By the end of twelfth grade, the curricula would cover all of these topics, plus preparation for marriage and family planning. Parents had the right to inspect and review the curriculum and to remove their children from the program if they felt it was in conflict with their religious or moral views.

The subcommittee outlined a course of study that some years later would be recognized as "comprehensive sexuality education" by a leading national organization, the Sexuality Information and Education Council of the United States (SIECUS). Many groups advocated this course of study which included instruction on both abstinence and other forms of protection from unplanned pregnancy and STDs. Opponents favored instruction only about abstinence and the bare minimum about contraception, usually its failure rates.

The state board anticipated some controversy over the requirement, but never at quite the level that came barreling at it. The good news, however, was that the reliable and respected Eagleton Poll at Rutgers University found that 78 percent of state residents favored sex education and a majority favored requiring it for all public schools. This information gave a majority of board members confidence that we could withstand the controversy swirling around us, that we would prevail and schools would implement the program, making New Jersey the second state in the nation to institute such a requirement in public schools.

Public Extravaganzas

Despite forebodings and editorial comments against it, the board passed our subcommittee's recommended policy by a vote of 7 to 1, the word "requiring" soon shook the rafters and caused storm clouds to gather. Despite the policy's assurances that parents could remove their children from parts of the program that conflicted with their moral or religious views, our opponents were adamant in their protests. Clergy, parents, and groups like the League of American Families and Right to Life argued that sex education should not be taught outside of the family, and that the "mandate," as they insisted on calling it, would cause children and teens to engage in sexual activity. (Opponents used the word "mandate" because it conjured an image of the heavy hand of government curtailing people's rights to make their own decisions. They wanted to persuade the public to oppose the "mandate," because it was a state government requirement that came without the funds needed to aid local districts with its implementation.)

As a public body, the State Board of Education was required by law to hear public comment on the policy. The challenges came with a suddenness and virulence that surprised most board members and the political establishment in New Jersey. It is one thing to read about controversies in the newspaper and quite another to hear at close range in a committee room the distortions and invectives hurled by opponents. As public servants, we had to exhibit self-control and patience, allow citizens to make their points during hearings, and give equal weight to each argument—pro or con. Whenever a member of the public spoke in support of the policy during those tense hearings, it came as a wave of relief.

Sometimes it was hard to keep a straight face when opponents charged that teaching students about contraceptive use "would enable them to prey on younger children," and that sex education would "include such unwanted subjects as abortion, masturbation, homosexuality, bestiality, frigidity, and impotence." I couldn't believe that someone actually thought that public servants would create a policy with the ulterior motive of hurting children. It dawned on me that some opponents sincerely held the views they were espousing. I realized that it was going to take a lot of time, effort, and patience for them to be able to understand my and my fellow board members' viewpoints and the reasons why we wanted to adopt the policy. I learned too that our opponents operated out of fear: fear of losing their children and fear of change. It was a valuable lesson.

The Phil Donahue Show

My experience listening to these opponents trained me well to speak on television and radio programs when I had to go head-to-head with a member of the opposition. In these situations, it was important to acknowledge the opponent's views but then try not to tear him or her apart. I learned that it was more productive to make my own points than to become mired in the opponent's arguments, because the latter didn't advance the discussion.

I remember one moment when I took unfair advantage of my opponents. The producer of *The Phil Donahue Show*—one of the most widely watched daytime TV programs at the time—had invited me to fly to Chicago and appear on the program after the national media had picked up on the sex education controversy in New Jersey. I looked forward to being interviewed by Phil until I realized that he had invited *five* opponents—all members of New Jersey Concerned Parents—to fly from New Jersey to appear on the same show. I knew the ratio wasn't exactly in my favor, but I thought it showed that Phil knew I could handle the situation.

We were waiting in the wings to go on stage when I felt something mischievous bubble up inside me; I turned to Mary Smith, the group's president, and said, "Mary, I have an idea. When we go on the show, you argue my side, and I'll argue yours." It wasn't nice, but I couldn't help it, and poor Mary looked so horrified that I quickly said, "Don't worry, I was only kidding to relieve my stress." She grimaced and turned away from me. I knew that I could easily have argued her side, but she couldn't have possibly argued mine because her views were based on emotions, not facts.

The show went smoothly. The best part was that the audience made all the points that I usually made—only with valuable, personal examples—and all I had to do was sit back and smile while they made them. Mary and her group grew more and more dispirited, and I was glad for them when the hour-long show ended. I could have stayed for at least another hour as long as that supportive audience had stayed with me.

I received about 20 letters from viewers of the show who mostly opposed my point of view about the value of sex education. What I said hadn't changed their minds, but I detected a willingness to be more open to some of my points. I felt that I had planted seeds that might grow into actual changes in attitudes. I answered each letter, because I wanted to respect the writer's effort to share his or her opinions with me. Had I not been part of the public hearings, I don't know if I would have developed this sensitivity.

True Child Advocacy

In April 1980, the State Board held another extensive public hearing at which more than 120 proponents and opponents of the requirement testified for nine hours. To accommodate the crowd of spectators, the meeting was moved to the State Library auditorium. Opponents included the lobbying arms of the state's major education organizations—the New Jersey Education Association, New Jersey School Boards Association, and New Jersey Association of School Administrators—which were against the mandatory nature of our policy.

I was mulling over the effect their opposition might have on the policy when I put in a telephone call to board president Paul Ricci the Sunday before the meeting. His wife, Margaret, answered and said that Paul was on his tractor. "When Paul has concerns, he climbs aboard his tractor and goes off to plow the fields," she said. Her reassuring tone made me smile.

Paul called back several hours later, and I said, "Paul, these education interest organizations always say that they're working on behalf of the state's children, but here they are with family life, retreating behind the idea that the board has exceeded its statutory responsibility. What do you think of that?"

Again, my naiveté almost got the better of me: why would I think organizations that trumpeted how much they cared for children would stand tall on sexuality education? They cared more about posturing before the public than about how our sexuality education policy could help students. Paul reassured me that the policy was worth fighting for, because it was on behalf of the students. His words helped move me past a discouraging moment.

Paul showed that same common sense at an incident that occurred at the meeting in the state library. Catherine Denk, who was with New Jersey Concerned Parents, interrupted the session several times by shouting at board members about the outrageous effects the policy would have on children. The state police were called, and finally, to attract even more attention, she sat down in the middle of the auditorium floor, hoping that Paul would sign a complaint against her, and that photos of her being carried out by burly policemen would be all over the news, winning her sympathy.

Paul immediately understood the ploy and what she wanted and called a recess to allow tempers to cool. The room emptied, and Denk sat alone on the floor surrounded only by her allies, air slowly escaping from her balloon. When the hearing resumed, she departed, sensing no support for her dramatics. Paul taught me some important skills on how to be a genuine child advocate and a calm leader in a crisis.

I had a few other low points during the legislative battles. The media, led by *Newark Star Ledger* education reporter Bob Braun, kept the controversy at a boiling point. His opening salvo was a January 1979 column, "Sex Ed Spells Trouble When It's Mandated," and his criticism of our policy only got worse after that. Once I pulled over to the side of the road to read one of his columns only to burst into tears by the time I finished it. I respected him and had counted on his support, but in public life, one has to accept differing opinions, even from those considered allies, and grow—or shrivel up. I was glad no one saw my tears, and I never allowed myself the luxury to cry about the issue again.

The Lion's Den

The New Jersey Legislature was soon drawn into the struggle. In May 1980, in response to demands for action by New Jersey Concerned Parents, the Senate Education Committee held a one-day hearing on the policy. Normally someone from the State Department of Education would testify on an incendiary issue, yet no one from the Department stepped up to the plate. All eyes turned to me, and I didn't have a choice: I was going to testify on behalf of the board since I had chaired the subcommittee. The time had come for me to become the board's public face.

I felt calm and unafraid. I knew sexuality education was worth fighting for, because so many people had told me that it had prevented them from making life-changing mistakes. I knew that if I didn't become a leader and give the policy the support it deserved, the State Board might lose the battle and thus forfeit its ability to improve students' lives.

Prior to the hearing, I had one less serious and female concern that I raised with the young woman who served as the staff liaison between the board and the State Department of Education: "What does one wear to testify at a Senate hearing?" I asked.

"If you have a [nun's] habit in your closet, I suggest you wear it," she replied. "I think you'd look great in it."

I laughed at her joke, which helped me to relax, and decided to wear a plain suit with no distracting jewelry and little makeup.

Help comes in different forms and ways, and a public information officer at the State Department of Education reached out to me as I was getting ready to testify. She wrote me a little note on pale pink paper with a sketch of a rainbow and the words "There can be no rainbow until the storm has passed." Her note read:

Dear Susan,

My mother once sent me this poem when I was confused with a personal problem. I'd like to share it with you now. Read particularly the last two stanzas before you go into the lion's den on Thursday.

The poem, by an unknown author, was titled "Don't Quit," and the last verse read:

Success is failure turned inside out—
The silver tint of the clouds of doubt,
And you never can tell how close you are,
It may be near when it seems afar;
So stick to the fight when you're hardest hit—
It's when things seem worst that you mustn't quit.

The poem and her note gave me the extra ounce of courage I needed; I gave my testimony along with many others and felt buoyed by the experience.

Learning to Compromise

The Senate Education Committee asked us to make certain changes in our policy, and we knew that if we didn't agree to some compromises in this late-stage battle, we might very well lose the war. The Governor's office had asked State Board president Paul Ricci and me to meet with the legal counsel, Dan O'Hern, to again explain why the board supported this policy so strongly. We went to O'Hern's office and calmly went over what our investigation of local school boards had revealed: that, because of these programs' controversial nature, the local school boards couldn't implement sex education programs on their own.

"I see the purpose and reasons why you have created this policy," said O'Hern, who was later appointed to the New Jersey Supreme Court. Back on West State Street, I told Paul that I thought we had won that round—and I was right: the Governor's office signaled to the Democrats in the legislature that they should not vote to overturn the policy.

I learned a great deal about the legislative process from my work on the policy. I told anyone who would listen that "opponents of family life education never sleep," and I knew they would be back to find another way to block the policy, which they did in 1981, when, to prevent implementation of the policy, New Jersey Concerned Parents brought a suit, *Mary K. Smith et al. vs. P. Paul Ricci et al.*, in New Jersey Superior Court.

The New Jersey Supreme Court moved to take the case directly. Deputy Attorney General Mary Ann Burgess argued the board's position, and on May 25, 1982, the court handed down its decision, 7-0, unanimously rejecting the appellant's points and finding no constitutional problems with our policy.

The decision made the front page of the *New York Times,* and I was thrilled to read the article, because it showed that the board had exercised its powers wisely and correctly, and young people would receive sexuality education that would benefit them. The *Times* quoted me in the last paragraphs of the story: "Susan Wilson, a board member who supported the requirement, said the court's decision parallels the sentiments of the overwhelming majority of parents. She added that the program would 'help young people lead responsible and healthy lives and prepare them to assume family roles.'"

I knew what satisfaction and happiness felt like when I read those words on the front page of one of America's great newspapers. The opponents appealed to the U.S. Supreme Court, which refused to consider the case for "want of a substantive federal question."

Another Governor's Office Meeting

I would continue to fight for the family life education policy, but not from my perch as a member and vice president of the State Board of Education. (I had been elected vice president in 1981.) Republican Thomas H. Kean was elected governor in 1982, the year my six-year term ended, and my reappointment was on his desk. The rumor was that I would not be reappointed to another term because of my leadership on the sex education policy, which his party had opposed. Governor Kean also did not believe in "education mandates." What mattered more to me than reappointment was the status of the policy, which was scheduled for full implementation in September 1983.

I needed a one-on-one meeting with Governor Kean, and for assistance I turned once more to my Republican mother, who used her political clout and arranged a meeting for me with the governor at his State House office. He greeted me cordially, and after some chitchat, I said, "Governor Kean, I know you'll be deciding soon whether or not to reappoint me to the State Board. I've liked serving on the board and feel useful, but the family life education policy is more important to me than another six-year term. Its implementation will mean a lot more to the young people in New Jersey than my reappointment. I'm asking you to allow the policy to go forward in local districts, as is happening as we speak."

My speech was long, but I meant every word. The governor didn't respond or ask me any questions about my strong feelings on the policy. He is a courteous man, and after some more general discussion, he thanked me for coming and said he would think about what I had said. I walked out of the State House wondering if I would ever return.

Governor Kean did not reappoint me to the State Board; he replaced me with Dr. Gustavo A. Mellander, the president of Passaic County Community College. However, he allowed the state's implementation of the policy to proceed. I had won a critical round in the battle, but the children and parents of New Jersey were the real winners. *Star-Ledger* columnist Bob Braun, who had brought so much grief to the board during the battle, summed up my tenure in his column entitled "Board Losing a Sensitive, Dedicated Education Advocate":

> Wilson gained notoriety—and enemies—from her advocacy of the family life education mandate. She was its strongest supporter, its most traveled campaigner. Probably more than anyone else in the state, she believed the process of education could end human misery associated with abuse and ignorance of, and disrespect for, human sexuality … She understood children and their needs probably better than any member of the board.

I found his words comforting, and still do. Bob has remained a friend through the years. He is much more of a cynic than I am about the potential of education, especially sexuality education, to make a difference. Even after weathering the public education battles, I believe that high-quality sexuality education programs can make a positive difference in young people's lives.

The State Board of Education reauthorized the policy in 1985 and again in 1990. Seventy speakers, many still opposed to sexuality education programs, testified at the first hearing, but in 1990, no one testified against it. Our powerful opponents had not disappeared; they were simply lying low, waiting for the right moment to strike again.

When I left the State Board of Education, I asked Education Commissioner Fred G. Burke to write a letter of recommendation for me, and he wrote a gracious one about my work on the board. One line he wrote has always stayed with me, because it so accurately describes the deepest parts of my being: "Susan burns with a passion that is rare in public life."

When I was a younger woman, these words might have made me uncomfortable, because I didn't understand that it was perfectly all right for women like me to be ambitious and to care deeply about and work hard for a cause. After we fought the good fight for the policy, the compliment bolstered me as I prepared to move on. The sexuality education movement had taught me not to be afraid to lead and stand on my own two feet—not as a daughter or wife, but as my own person.

A Home at the Network for Family Life Education

I loved my public work on the State Board of Education but was not downhearted when it ended, as I knew that when someone shuts a door, a window can open. I was lucky to find in the nonprofit sector a window that allowed me to continue my engrossing, purposeful work in sexuality education.

Early in 1983, Estelle R. Robinson, who was director of the Center for Community Education at the Rutgers University School of Social Work, provided me the opportunity I was seeking. She had created the New Jersey Network for Family Life Education, a loose collection of state organizations that supported the family life education requirement. Its executive coordinator, Roberta (Bobbi) Knowlton, was doing a superb job assisting school districts in implementing the board's policy, but she didn't have time to do the necessary fundraising to keep the Network afloat. When she stepped down in 1984, I stepped into the role. With little managerial experience and a great desire to work on implementing the policy, I became the executive coordinator of a sexuality education program at the state university. It was exactly the right spot for me.

Under Estelle's astute direction, I learned to be a manager and found that it was right up my alley. Management, she told me, was a little like cheerleading, and I liked coordinating the dozen or so statewide organizations that supported the policy. I discovered that I possessed an inherent ability to come up with new ideas and raise the necessary funds to implement them. I used grants from New Jersey foundations and the state and federal governments in a variety of ways to strengthen the public's awareness of the importance of family life education, including collaborating with the Children's Defense Fund (CDF) on a national teen-pregnancy prevention media campaign. The Network distributed several different clever CDF posters that were created by one of the top advertising agencies, and I secured a million dollar's worth of donated billboard space to showcase them in key spots around the state. My favorite poster was of a male teen holding a baby and staring at his unseen audience with a grim face; the tagline read: "An Extra Seven Pounds Could Keep You Off the Football Team." One day on my way to the office, I almost drove off the road when I saw a billboard of the poster staring down at me as I rounded a corner.

Soon after I became executive coordinator, the Network started publishing a newsletter, *Family Life Matters,* for teachers who needed advice and ideas on how to teach sexual health. It contained regular features, including discussion starters, editorials, lesson plans, and general articles that teachers could use in the classroom with students or to further their own knowledge about how to teach sexuality education in different settings. We mailed 7,000 free copies of the first issue and eventually built a paid circulation of 2,200 educators and other youth-serving professionals across the nation.

When the HIV/AIDS epidemic finally broke wide open, we took action to train New Jersey teachers how to teach about STDs as part of family life education. We convened a panel of educators and specialists in adolescent medicine to discuss HIV prevention, and it concluded that public education's role was to present all reasonable options and not restrict discussion to abstinence. Our opponents, who had been defeated in their efforts to prevent implementation of the statewide policy, decided to undermine the intent of the requirement to provide balanced instruction and reshape it to their views and values. They believed that all sexual behaviors should be restricted to marriage and wanted a statewide requirement that only abstinence be taught whenever the word "sex" was mentioned in sexuality education class. Statistics showed that more than half of high school students were having sex before graduation, so we knew that, rather than teaching only abstinence, the best, most realistic messages should be to avoid unplanned pregnancy and STDs by using contraception and condoms.

Impressed with our panel's recommendations, the State Department of Education awarded us a $70,000 grant to conduct HIV-prevention training for New Jersey educators, which was quite a coup for a small organization. I hired the best family life educators in the state to design a uniform training module for teachers. From 1988 to 1989, we trained more than 1,200 educators in both HIV prevention and other sexual health topics and left an indelible mark on statewide instruction. I often departed my house at dawn in a station wagon piled high with materials to hold trainings across the state.

Stress-Abstinence Legislative Battles

Since our sexuality education opponents rarely slept, I finally got smarter in 1989 and built the Coalition for Comprehensive Family Life and Sex Education, which was an alliance of 34 organizations. Our mission called for members to testify at legislative hearings, publish op-eds and letters to the editor, and lobby legislators to express our opinions on sex education legislation. I coordinated our efforts to defeat legislation that would require all family life education programs to stress abstinence and limit discussion of contraception, including condoms, only to their failure rates. Young people needed encouragement to use two forms of contraception to protect against both pregnancy and STDs, and we were certain that if students heard only about the failure rates of condoms when, in fact, the effectiveness of proper use was high, many would simply fail to use them.

We won three battles over stress-abstinence legislation in the State Legislature but lost the fourth—and the war. The chief supporters of the stress-abstinence legislation were Assemblywoman Marion Crecco and Senator Gerald Cardinale, Republicans supported by New Jersey Right to Life, New Jersey Concerned Women for America, and the New Jersey Catholic Conference.

The media embraced the story, and I frequently had to debate Assemblywoman Crecco on television and radio. Her appeals for abstinence were heartfelt, and I had to be careful not to overpower her with facts, which weren't her strong suit. She would repeatedly say that all teens should be abstinent until marriage, and it was hard to convince her that this was a religious point of view, not the view of secular school boards concerned with student health.

A friend of mine watched me debate the assemblywoman and said, "I felt sorry for you. It was as if you were debating Kleenex." I realized the good advice of a speech coach who once told me, "Smile at your opponent; then face the camera and make your own points."

From 1992 to 1994, we battled the Crecco/Cardinale stress-abstinence bill in the Assembly. Supporters and opponents converged on Trenton on May 27, 1993, for the Senate Education Committee's first hearing, and there were so many witnesses—55 on the supporting stress-abstinence side—that the committee couldn't hear them all.

The committee chair was Senator John Ewing, a moderate Republican from Somerset County who could be sharp and outspoken. I had asked to meet with him privately before his committee's public hearing and bring three African-American students from Trenton Central High School with me to discuss the bill. (Senator Ewing represented a rural area where few African-Americans lived.) When I brought the students into his office, it might have been the first time he had ever talked with African-American teens. He sat quite dumbfounded while they told him about the many teens who were having unprotected sex and becoming teen parents, and why stressing abstinence in health class would be unhelpful. He asked them what might prevent teens from having babies at an early age, and they said honest information about contraception.

It is hard to know when or how a person changes his mind, but Senator Ewing changed his mind about the stress-abstinence legislation after that meeting. Once the hearing started, he introduced an amendment that required sex education courses to stress all prevention methods as well as abstinence, and it was a tremendous but short-lived victory for our coalition. The original bill's supporters quickly pushed through an amended bill on the Senate floor that restored the original stress-abstinence language, and when it came up for a final vote, it narrowly passed.

A Rutgers lobbyist and expert on counting votes sat behind me as I watched the final vote tally. "Don't worry," she whispered. "If Governor Florio vetoes the bill, the Republicans don't have the votes to override it."

"Are we going to snatch victory from the jaws of defeat?" I asked her. She nodded affirmatively.

We campaigned to persuade Governor Florio to veto the bill, and he did, calling it a "political intrusion" on curriculum development. But we had to sit through the Assembly and Senate deliberations once more as stress-abstinence supporters tried to override his veto. Senator Ewing's decision to break with his party and withdraw his support for the bill was central to the outcome, and he did not vote to override the veto. The opponents' attempt to impose their views on local school districts' curricula failed.

In February 1994, I gave a party at my home in Princeton to thank Governor Florio and Senator Ewing. It was a freezing cold day, and a sheet of black ice covered the back and front yards. I had to figure out how to get the guests of honor into my house without asking them to walk over ice, although they had much experience treading carefully in their political lives. After what they had done for the Network and the Coalition, I would have found any way—even hiring a magic carpet—to bring them inside and thank them for helping us win the stress-abstinence battle. By moving cars around, we were able to bring them in through the garage to hear the cheers of the many celebrants. I was particularly happy to see that both men had placed the needs of the children, parents, and teachers of New Jersey ahead of partisan politics.

The stress-abstinence battles continued into the late 1990s, but Governor Christine Todd Whitman would have none of them, so the programs were safe during her time in office. She was committed to a balanced program that included information on both abstinence and contraception. During her re-election campaign in 1998, her political advisors urged her to accept the federal abstinence-only money that was available for states, and she reluctantly took the New Jersey allotment with the proviso that it be used only in community programs, not in public schools.

When Governor Whitman left for Washington in 2001 to become head of the Environmental Protection Agency in President George W. Bush's administration, Senator Donald DiFrancesco became acting governor. We faced an upward battle with him, as he had voted already for the stress-abstinence bill, but we kept up the pressure. With Whitman's departure, our work continued without her support, and we were in danger of losing the final stress-abstinence battle. Coalition members knew it was only a matter of time before our opponents pushed their case again in the state legislature.

Concurrent with the legislative battles, the Network developed a K-3 curriculum, *Learning About Family Life,* which was highly controversial and ahead of its time. The State Board policy required elementary schools to provide family life education in an age-appropriate way, so we developed for the early grades a curriculum of 43 lessons constituting a distinct story line to offer schools a sensible start to family life education. The story line was built around an elementary school teacher who is pregnant and, by the end of the story, gives birth. It included short lessons about the proper names of reproductive anatomy, how sperm meet up with an egg, and how babies are born into the world ("a woman's vagina stretches like a turtleneck sweater"). The curriculum was designed as a large book filled with delightful lessons and illustrations, so children could view the story as the teacher read it aloud.

Fearful parents and other opponents of our curriculum, which was developed by early childhood education and developmental psychology experts, trotted out the major argument they had used against the State Board policy: that it would encourage young children to have sex. The curriculum was purchased by some districts, including Irvington, near Newark, where Claire Scholz ran one of the most comprehensive family life education programs in the state, and West Windsor, near Princeton, where K-12 school nurse Janice Bartolini embraced the idea of introducing family life concepts in the early grades. The curriculum, age-appropriate and accurate as it was, failed to sell because of its potential for controversy. The publisher, Rutgers University Press, rather than allow its popularity to slowly build, abandoned the curriculum, scrapping hundreds of copies. I believe, to this day, that it could have been successful with better marketing and a more patient publisher. The Network's program manager, Ann Schurmann, wrote an excellent booklet on the reasons for K-3 education, *Baby Steps: Implementing Family Life Education in the Early Grades*, but even it failed to move many school boards.

Around this time, our K-3 curriculum, comprehensive sexuality education, and the New Jersey family life education policy, as well as my leading role in it, came under a sly but savage attack in a 16-page article by Barbara Dafoe-Whitehead that appeared in the *Atlantic Monthly* magazine. "The Failure of Sex Education" was so inherently clever, and seemingly well supported by research, that I feared it would jeopardize all the good work that we had done in New Jersey—and turn gold into dross. However, we were able to survive it and move on. The next idea we generated at the Network became a success beyond our wildest dreams.

Star in the Firmament

Our most important new activity in the late nineties transformed the Network and provided a new way to deliver sexuality education to young people.

I owe a debt of gratitude to Bonnie Parker, the founder and director of a teen health clinic in Princeton named "HiTOPS" (a bow to a favorite teen shoe). The clinic had created a teen council composed of local teens who used skits to communicate sexual health messages to their peers. My thoughtful, intelligent staff and I began mulling over the concept of peers helping peers and came up with the idea of creating a free newsletter written by teens, for teens, on sexual health.

I took the idea directly to a group of teens at a summer program that had invited me to speak about sex education. I stood at the podium on a warm summer's day before a sea of young women and told them about our new idea.

"Would you and your peers be interested in reading such a publication?" I asked. "If any of you think this is a good idea, please speak with me at the end of the session."

I sat down after my talk and waited until the program's end, honestly believing that at most three or four young women would approach me. The program ended, I looked out into the audience, and it was as if the Red Sea had parted and everyone on the Egyptian shore was coming across to the Promised Land. I saw dozens of young women move toward me in a wave.

"Oh, please do this," one began. "Teens talk to each other all the time about sex, and a lot of it is wrong." Another added, "Adults are so uncomfortable with this topic. Parents don't talk to us, and teachers are shy about the subject, too." The young women's desire for accurate information was palpable as they made their appeal to me. I became their advocate on the spot and knew we should move ahead with the newsletter.

One of the first teens we worked with came up with the name: *Sex, Etc.* With an initial grant of $20,000 from the Office of Prevention of Developmental Disabilities in the New Jersey Department of Human Services, we chose our first teen editorial board. The board worked with Nancy Parello, an experienced journalist with a heart of gold who left the *Bergen Record* to join the Network, to prepare the first issue, which we shipped to selected New Jersey high schools in early 1994. (I chose to make it a free publication, because I knew its name might prevent some school boards from purchasing it for teens.) We published *Sex, Etc.* three times during the school year, and I raised the money to keep it free and fulfill the ever-increasing requests for copies.

We published bold stories on topics encompassing abstinence, safer sex, dating violence, pregnancy and teen parenting, and gay, lesbian, bisexual, transgender, and questioning teens. Our first issues also included our popular "Ask the Expert" section, a feature in which an adult expert answered teens' pressing questions about sex and sexuality.

Sex, Etc. was an instant success. We shipped 30,000 copies to New Jersey schools in 1994, our first year of publication; 150,000 copies the second year; and 300,000 copies the third year. By then, thanks to a grant from the Educational Foundation of America, we began national distribution of the newsletter to public schools, health clinics, and community agencies with teen programs. Total annual distribution rose to 700,000 by 1997, 1.3 million by 2000, and 2.2 million by 2003. (For much of the data in this chapter, I am indebted to the excellent history, *The Struggle for Sex Education in New Jersey, 1979-2003: Policy, Persistence and Progress,* by Philip E. Mackey, Ph.D.)

In 1997, *Sex, Etc.* went online at Sexetc.org, and one of our most popular features was "Ask the Experts," where teens could email their pressing questions about sexual health to our panel of sex educators and medical professionals for timely, medically accurate responses. By 2003, our experts were answering 15,000 questions a year, with about 75 percent from teen girls. The volume and content of the questions showed that teens were not getting the comprehensive sexuality education they needed.

The response to our website was astonishing: by December 2003, our visitors had grown to 24,000 a day or 8.7 million per year. When we redefined our mission in 2005 to focus on our teen-to-teen project, our aim was to reach 15 million teens per year—or half of all teens in America. Reaching such a number was highly unrealistic—I needed a major national foundation like the Ford or Carnegie to support it—but goals are made to inspire, and I loved the idea that in pre-Internet days half of America's teens might read *Sex, Etc.* Comments from young readers kept rolling in, telling us that our honest, accurate information helped them practice safer sex, remain virgins, or simply avoid life-changing mistakes.

Another comment about the newsletter that sticks with me came from a young woman who found it on a table in a health clinic in Georgia and wrote to our office. "I love my son, whom I had when I was only 16," she wrote, "but had I been able to read the story about contraception, I would not have had him."

The *Sex, Etc.* newsletter, which eventually became a four-color magazine, reached more than a teen audience. Educators and other youth-serving professionals read it before distributing it to teens or using it to enhance classroom lessons. One day I received a letter from a nun who taught health education at a Catholic high school. She used *Sex, Etc.* in her class but suggested only some stories for her students. The Bishop of her diocese found out about the newsletter and ordered the nun to cancel her subscription. Fearing for her position as a teacher and possibly as a member of a religious order, she followed his dictates but wrote: "Please send my subscription to my residence. Then I can learn what young people are interested in knowing, and I can take that information into my classroom and improve my teaching."

Meeting Mrs. Clinton

There is one moment in *Sex, Etc.*'s history that I won't soon forget. The National Campaign to Prevent Teen Pregnancy, a bipartisan effort to reduce the high rate of pregnancy among American teens, was based in Washington, D.C. In 1997, its president, Sarah Brown, asked then First Lady Hillary Rodham Clinton to preside at its celebration of national programs that showed promise in reducing teen pregnancy. *Sex, Etc.* won the category of "successfully involving teens in finding solutions to teen pregnancy," and I was invited to bring four teen editors with me to the event. It was pretty heady stuff, not only for the teens but also for me, since the first lady's recognition would be unbelievably good publicity for the newsletter.

I had met Mrs. Clinton twice some years before. The first time was at a

Children's Defense Fund (CDF) conference when she chaired its board. Marian Wright Edelman, the president of CDF, the largest child advocacy organization in the country, told me that she wanted me to meet Hillary. The room was filled with hundreds of people as she brought me to her and said, "I want you to meet Susie Wilson, a child advocate from New Jersey." As I put out my hand, another child advocate pushed in front of me and bent Hillary's ear for what seemed like a half hour. Not knowing how to elbow this woman out of Hillary's space, I moved away and missed my opportunity to meet her.

The second was not much better. When Bill Clinton was running for president, I and other enthusiasts organized a large fundraiser in Princeton and invited Mrs. Clinton as the guest of honor. I believe it was the first speech she gave for him at a fundraiser outside of Arkansas, and the crowd filled the large ballroom of the Hyatt Regency Hotel. I was responsibile for introducing Mrs. Clinton, and I worked extremely hard on that introduction—but not hard enough, because I mistakenly said that she had graduated at the top of her Yale Law School class. After she walked to the podium from the wings of the ballroom stage and the applause ended, she corrected me: "Yale doesn't rank its students. I want to make that absolutely clear." I walked off the stage properly admonished, vowing to be more careful the next time I introduced her or anyone else.

I wasn't thinking about that painful moment when I escorted the four *Sex, Etc.* teens through the East gate. I was excited about being in the White House with them. One of the teens was chewing gum, and I said (more as a mother than a magazine publisher), "Do me a favor please and take the gum out of your mouth." He did, but to this day I'm not sure where he put it.

We went into the East Room and I was excited to be in the beautiful rooms that Mrs. Kennedy had restored with such superb taste. I saw the former governor of New Jersey, Thomas Kean, and went over to introduce him to the teens. He was the president of the Campaign's board of directors and would assist Mrs. Clinton in presenting the awards.

I sat down and waited for my turn to accept the award. I had been given instructions to walk to the center of the stage when my name was called, listen to Mrs. Clinton read the citation, shake hands with her and Governor Kean, have my photograph taken with them, and return to my seat. I was sure I could follow the instructions and smile happily at the audience.

Everything proceeded on course until I realized that Mrs. Clinton wasn't going to mention the name of our newsletter. She wasn't going to say "*Sex, Etc.*" She started talking about "teens talking to teens," but didn't say that they were helping their peers receive honest, accurate information about sexuality. She kept going around in circles and even gave the newsletter as bland a title as she could—one that never would have attracted any teen readers.

"The name of the magazine is *Teen Talk*," she said, and I groaned as all sorts of thoughts ran through my mind: *The kids are going to be so disappointed she won't use the proper name…maybe it is because of the recent Monica Lewinsky debacle…her staff is protecting her and afraid to have her use the word "sex."* At the same time, I kept telling myself: *keep smiling, keep smiling…don't let her see your disappointment.*

I have a broad smile that looks natural in the picture of me with Mrs. Clinton and Governor Kean, which is now framed in my living room. I kept smiling through the rest of the program, even when we were standing around after the ceremony drinking warm punch, eating store-bought chocolate chip cookies in the State Dining Room, and using paper napkins. The first lady and governor were long gone, and I was happy to round up the teens and head for the doorway. As we began to walk down the red-carpeted hallway, I apologized to them.

"I'm sorry that Mrs. Clinton didn't use the name of the magazine—that she couldn't bring herself to use the words, '*Sex, Etc.*' You deserve better for your hard work."

No one responded for a few moments, and then Katrina Braxton, who was an especially good editor, said, "No, it's really OK, Susie. Not to worry. We aren't writing *Sex, Etc.* for the First Lady. We're writing it for the teenagers of America."

I flashed Katrina a big grin and put my arm around her shoulders as we went through the door and into the sunlight.

"Of course, how right you are," I said.

When I think about *Sex, Etc.*, I think of the dedicated, hardworking, serious-minded teen editors who wrote for it. They came from diverse backgrounds and different parts of New Jersey. Some were already excellent writers while others were beginners, but under the skillful and nurturing eyes of our successive staff editors—Nancy Parello, Ellen Papazian, and Lucinda Holt—everyone's writing skills improved. Many of our teens went on to study or follow careers in public health, and several graduated from the Harvard School of Public Health with doctoral degrees. It isn't always easy in life to make a difference, but I am convinced that the *Sex, Etc.* teen editors did.

Passing the Torch

The years passed; I turned 75 and realized that I had spent more than 25 years in the sexuality education movement. Right next to me at the Network was my sure-to-be-successor Danene Sorace, our program manager, and I believed the organization would lose her many talents if I didn't move on. My good husband had turned 80, and my grandchildren were growing up. It was time for me to leave the work I had loved so much.

I had led the Network for more than two decades, proving that for once in my life I could stick to the same job. As executive coordinator, I used all the skills I had learned in other positions along the way, particularly my reportorial skills at *Life* magazine, and exercised leadership abilities I didn't know I possessed. The Network had an outstanding staff, and the hardest task for me was to move out of their way and let them show off their talents.

During my tenure, I raised funds from 26 state and 53 national foundations and corporations, secured grants from several governmental departments, and obtained donations from many individuals and friends. I proved to myself that I was my father's daughter as an enthusiastic fundraiser and my mother's daughter as an education activist with sound political instincts.

Sex education found me, and not the reverse—and I feel blessed that it did. It dovetailed nicely with my concerns about reducing child and family poverty, a huge subject that does not lend itself to magic-bullet solutions, and ensuring that all children receive a top-notch education to help them make their way in the world—issues that I learned to care about thanks to my two principal mentors, Bobby Kennedy and Marian Wright Edelman. As a long-time leader in the sexuality education movement, I learned these four valuable but simple lessons:

1. It takes a village;
2. It takes vigilance and hard work;
3. It takes listening to the people, especially young people, one wants to help; and
4. It takes courage.

The sexuality education movement made me much more comfortable talking about sexuality with my friends, children, and grandchildren. In the early years of my work, Don used to say to me as we were preparing for an evening with friends, "Susan, don't talk about what you do tonight." I weighed his advice but didn't always follow it. When I turned dinner conversations around to sexual topics, I found that everyone was energized and participated in the discussion. Now people openly acknowledge at dinner parties that I am an expert on sexual issues and ask for my advice, although I'm quick to say that I am an educator, not a licensed therapist.

Penny benefited from my ability to talk more openly about sex with her than I did with my two older children. She told me that she always insisted her partner use condoms and would not consent to sex if he didn't have any. I must have been doing something right.

I urge all of my children to talk with their children about sex and recommend age-appropriate books, but I sometimes miss opportunities, too. My grandson Reed came into my office one day when he was six and read the words "Sex, Etc." on the stained glass.

"Grandma," he said, "you sure have a lot of things with the word 'sex' on them. Why?"

I was so pleased that he could read that I didn't follow up with an obvious question: "So, Reed, what does the word 'sex' mean?"

When I left the Network in December 2005, the staff gave me a unique gift: a beautiful, two-inch, yellow-and-white gold charm of those two words, "Sex, Etc.," that had figured so prominently in my adult life. I wear the charm on a gold necklace with pride on important and appropriate occasions. A *New York Times* reporter who profiled me referred to it in his story as "bling." Once I forgot I was wearing it on the New York City subway and quickly put my hand to my throat to cover the words, since a lot of people were looking at me. When I'm not wearing it, I put it in my safe-deposit box at the bank, where it rests among my few treasured pieces of jewelry. But because of its uniqueness, I do wonder who will want to inherit it and to whom I shall leave it in my will!

In reality, though, the true treasures were the Network staff, my successors as director, Danene and later Elizabeth Schroeder, and the others I met along the way, including leaders of national organizations: Michael Carrera, the founder of the Carrera Teen Pregnancy Prevention Program of the Children's Aid Society; the Rev. Debra Haffner, of SIECUS; and James Waggoner, of Advocates for Youth. There are also sexuality educators in schools and community organizations around the nation who used our magazine or promoted our website; participants at our national conferences and trainings; the early childhood and elementary school teachers who I taught at the Kean University summer program; and the teen editors who turned *Sex, Etc.* into a shining star.

These people need never reside in a safe-deposit box, because they are part of me.

Running

My Running Life

It wasn't exactly love at first sight, but running and I have been in a steady, pleasurable relationship for the past 30 years. I started doing it for exercise to keep my body in good condition as I neared 50. I was juggling so many family-work balls that I could devote only a short amount of time to caring for myself, and the notion of rising early, dashing out for a quick run, and returning before anyone realized I was gone was most appealing.

Later, I caught the amateur running wave that swept the nation in the late nineties—before many women started racing in older-age categories—giving me a chance to participate, win, and get a high from the sport.

I liked the democratic nature and simplicity of running; all I needed was a pair of running shoes, which usually lasted for months. Running also suited my tendency toward persistence and perseverance, and I committed myself to it the same way I did to sexuality education—like a dog refusing to give up a bone.

It took me some time to run my first mile, which was half a mile from our house on Province Line Road and back again. Two of my neighbors, Sally Maruca and Mary O'Leary, took up the sport the same time as I did, and we started running together. Mary was a much faster runner than Sally or I, and we basked in her glory. Running gave us the opportunity to indulge in what we called "runners' talk," private conversations about serious matters that we never divulged to anyone other than our running partners. These conversations saved me from spending time in a therapist's office.

During the nearly 20 years I commuted between Princeton and New York City, I often ran around the Central Park reservoir. My route took me past the New York Road Runners Club on East 89th Street, and I stopped by a couple of times to learn about their road races, which took place mostly in the park. It was my first brush with the possibility of racing.

I had been introduced to competitive running at the highest level when Don and I saw some world championship track-and-field events. I was inspired to try to compete (on a considerably lower level) by watching the most outstanding runners in the world do the same.

In 1980, with Sally and Mary, I ran my first race that was closer to home: Pam's Party Run, which was ten miles on the towpath along the Delaware and Raritan Canal. The run was a fortieth birthday present from Roland Machold to his wife, Pam. Each mile was designated with a pink balloon, and the runners wore pink T-shirts and were treated to dinner at the Kingston Firehouse, where the run ended and our husbands appeared out of nowhere (for the spaghetti dinner, I suspect).

I tasted victory for the first time in that race, coming in third in my age category, much to my surprise. The win gave me a taste of the fun of athletic competition, which I hadn't engaged in since high school.

In the seventies and eighties, running and tennis became vehicles for feminism and women's liberation (Billie Jean King epitomized this movement), and the passage of Title IX guaranteed high school and college women the right to participate in the same sports that were open to young men. Suddenly male runners began to realize that women are runners, too, and many female athletes began to compete.

The L'eggs Mini-Marathon, a series of 6.2-mile road races for women sponsored by the L'eggs hosiery company, was the first of its kind. The race's tagline expressed one of my most firmly held beliefs: "Who Says Women Can't Run the World."

The Vineyard Race

My favorite race is the Chilmark Road Race on Martha's Vineyard, in which I have competed 14 times. The 3.1-mile long race proceeds over a series of undulating hills on Middle Road from West Tisbury to Beetlebung Corner in Chilmark on the south side of the island.

If the Wilson family were to call any place in the world our summer home, it would be the Vineyard. We've rented many houses there over the years, mostly in Chilmark, which is a more casual and informal part of the island than the fancier Edgartown. What makes it even more special to our family is that Penny and Richard Falkenrath were married there over Labor Day weekend in 1999, an unforgettable wedding attended by many family members who navigated the difficulties of traveling to an island off the coast of Massachusetts.

Given my affection for the Vineyard, I naturally gravitated to this annual race, and I have won it in my age group ten times in my sixties, seventies, and eighties—setting records in the 70- to 79- and 80- to 98-year-old categories. But records are made to be broken, and my eight-year record of 32:57 for women in their seventies was broken in 2013 by 17 seconds. As a small consolation, I continue to hold the record of 43:18 for women in their eighties and older, which I established in 2012, although another woman in her eighties is bearing down upon me.

Don always checked the scores when they were posted, and if I won my age group, he would raise his arms in victory. In 2008, I told a *Vineyard Ga-*

zette reporter who interviewed me after the race that I was going to reward Don for his faithfulness at the finish line by sharing my prize with him: lunch for two at the Farm Neck Golf Club, a locale he enjoyed. "My husband has to live with this woman who runs all the time," I told the reporter.

Don didn't make the race the last three years I have run it, and I missed seeing him smile warmly and raise his long arms in a kind of victory salute as he shouted out the good news.

Runners like to have birthdays ending in zero because it means they can move to the front of another, potentially easier category. Although older runners beat younger ones all the time, age is still an important factor. I was looking forward to turning 70 and moving to a new age category in 2000. To celebrate, I gave myself a different kind of birthday party; I invited a group of friends from my Princeton marathon days to join me for the race: Lynn Lederer and her husband, Peter Johnson, Mary Weeden, and Betsy McKenzie and her husband, Bob Ridolfi. They and Penny journeyed to the Vineyard to run my beloved Chilmark race with me.

Peter bought everyone T-shirts emblazoned with "We're With Susie," and one for me that read, "Happy Birthday, Susie. I'm Susie." My dear running friends—all younger and faster—made a wedge to give me space on the usually crowded, hilly course and then stood aside so I could cross the finish line before they did.

Almost every time I run now, I realize my good fortune in being able to put on my running shoes, go outside for a run, return home in a little less than an hour, take a shower, and then get on with the day. Many friends and acquaintances have suffered joint diseases and had their knees and hips replaced. Many now need canes and walkers to go about the basic business of walking from place to place. I sympathize with them and admire their patience and acceptance of their new physical states. I know, too, that the time will come when I will no longer be able to enjoy the wonderful feelings of freedom and happiness that running imparts.

On my eightieth birthday, my family came to Chilmark for the race. This time they wore T-shirts adorned with a big number "80" that my daughter-in-law, Deborah, had designed. She drew the lithe figure of a girl with a ponytail running across the top of the zero and the words "Can you keep up with Susie?" (Deb ordered shirts in both pale and bright pink, my favorite color. I wear a small, bright-pink one during the day and a large, pale-pink one as a nightgown.) My grandson Sam ran Chilmark in 2012 and finished way ahead of me. Maybe a Wilson family member will keep up the tradition of running the Chilmark Road Race in future years. That would make me happy.

The Long Arm of Running

Running has helped me see the world not as a tourist but as a native of the country, and I have left my footprints not "on the sands of time," as Henry Wadsworth Longfellow urged, but on many of the world's dirt paths and paved roadways. I have run in Vietnam in Asia; in Cairo, Egypt, in the Middle East (which probably wasn't the smartest thing to do in a Muslim country); and in Athens, Rome, Paris, London, Edinburgh, Barcelona, and Helsinki in Europe. These runs connected me to other runners on the planet and strengthened my connection to ordinary people everywhere.

When I run in these countries, I am not the government leader, diplomat, or wealthy businessman riding to work in a fancy black limousine. I am not the worker on the motor scooter or bicycle doing her best to provide for her family. I am more the woman who must get from place to place on foot, because walking is the only form of transportation she can afford. When I run, I feel as if she and I are the same person—and I cherish that feeling of unity.

Once I saw some Tanzanian women in East Africa walking alongside the road, carrying huge baskets on their heads. I expected to see furrowed brows and pained expressions, but instead I saw faces wreathed with smiles. They seemed happy to be alive and walking along the road, and they taught me a lesson: to accept what I have and to not continually strive for more.

Now that I am in my eighties, I mostly run alone as my friends have dropped away and I would only slow down younger runners if they were to run with me. Peter Johnson and I run four or five miles together most weekends, but we are not too enterprising about finding new friends to run with us. If we could, we would cure the running injuries of two special friends, Bob Harris and Oyé Olukoton, who used to run with us on our "Funny Farm" route, five to seven miles over the hills and dales of the Amwell Valley, north of Hopewell, New Jersey. While running it, we would see lower Manhattan skyscrapers on crystal clear days and pass a farm with no fences; we laughed at the boldness of the animals that would cross the road and break our run.

Bob developed a bad back and Oyé bad knees, and eventually they decided it was easier on their joints to use workout equipment at home. I accepted their verdicts but still missed running with them, especially because Bob had introduced the game "Bring a Factoid" for our runs; it required a careful reading of the news to come up with an extraneous tidbit to tell the other runners. It kept us focused on our brains rather than on our feet, which was often a relief.

Sometimes I run 5K races, and there seems to be one every weekend for a good cause. On occasion I join my much younger friend Isabella de la Houssaye and some of her children in the weekend races they run for admirable causes. Isabella is a world-class, ultra-endurance athlete who always wins her under-50 age group; sometimes she doubles back to run with me to the finish line, showing kindness to an aged runner.

Still Running

"Are you still running?" is a legitimate question to be asked at my age. Most people assume that my answer will be, "No, I'm not," followed by an explanation involving age or injury. The question surprises me, as I think people would be more likely to remember my sexuality education work than my pastime as a runner.

"Yes, I'm lucky to be able to still run," I reply.

I'm always unsure of what this question is really about. I usually explain that I am so slow that I have never put excessive pressure on my knees or hips.

Sometimes I add that my steady weight may also be a factor. I wish I had a more satisfying response, but I don't. I am never offended by the question, and it often comes from people who have sustained serious problems with their joints—and they have my sympathy. Given the law of averages, I know that the day may come when I cannot lace up my shoes, and I shall be sad when that day does arrive. In the meantime, I am part of a longitudinal study of runners that the University of California at Berkeley is conducting, and after the researchers analyze their data, they will draw conclusions and report them.

Today on my morning run, I thought of a moment almost 13 years ago when Penny and Richard were expecting their first child, and Don and I our fourth grandchild. I had been running over the hills of a corporate campus to avoid car fumes on the open road when I looked up and saw a bluebird swooping across the trees. It was probably a male, as it was a bright shade of blue. When I got back from the run, Penny called to say that she was in labor and suggested we travel to Washington for the baby's arrival, which we did. Our first and only granddaughter, Olivia, was born that evening, and I have always associated the bluebird with her.

In the early thirties, "The Bluebird of Happiness" was a popular song containing the line "Where there is hatred, show a little bit love." One of my wishes for Olivia is that she comes to understand the joy of spreading love to others.

Coming to Terms with Running

When I was leaving the Network for Family Life Education in late 2004, I organized a "Passing the Torch Party" for my successor, Danene, on November 7, which was Marathon Sunday in New York City. My good friends Lynn and Bob Johnston graciously offered their beautiful home in Princeton for the party. I found a powerful-looking torch of almost Olympic size at the local hardware store and festooned it with ribbons.

The party drew 150 people, and although I protested that I didn't want running the marathon to define my life, I have come to terms with it as a metaphor for my devotion to sexuality education and women's health and reproductive rights. My neighbor Scott McVay, a poet, managed to blend the two passions nicely and came to the party with a charming poem in hand:

> *How fitting! How apt!*
> *How utterly appropriate!*
> *That the New York City Marathon*
> *Should be run today*
> *As the torch is passed*
> *Who won? We know already.*
> *Our neighbor, friend Susie*
> *has run the long race sans break,*
> *the long-distance race where*
> *many falter, snap & stop*
> *long before heartbreak hill*
> *(that's Boston, I know).*
> *So few have an issue*
> *so few a life's work*
> *so few stay the distance*
> *so few endure.*

With accuracy and poetic charm, Scott had tied the work that I loved doing with the sport that had also become precious to me. His poem helped me to accept the intertwining of these two passions in my life, engendering in me the peace of acceptance.

Running and my sexuality education work have made a profound difference in my life. I had loyal, steadfast companions with me on both journeys. They provided me with sustenance when I needed help.

Slow Is the New Fast

A good friend brought me a new running shirt that she found at a triathlon exposition, a place where I would never be seen. Its message, "Slow Is the

New Fast," makes me smile, as it aptly describes my present running speed, which some might describe as one level ahead of walking. At a recent 5K race, a spectator took one look at me and called out, "Slow and steady wins the race," which lifted my spirits. Should injuries come calling, I always have walking in my back pocket.

An injury came calling in November 2013 as I was *walking*, not running, to my morning class at Princeton. I tripped on uneven pavement on Nassau Street and fell, breaking my left elbow. The orthopedic surgeon, Dr. Jon Ark, who did an excellent job pinning it back together again, used the word "crushed" to describe the break. I'm convinced that had I been wearing my running shoes instead of a pair of leather flats, the accident would not have occurred. My grandson's comment about the event almost made it worthwhile: "You showed true grit, Grandma." I was lucky: the elbow could have been a hip or a knee.

Sometimes I walk the not-quite two miles that separate my condo from the heart of Princeton, and I enjoy this mode of movement almost as much as running. I often walk into the Princeton cemetery to the place where Don's ashes are buried to let him know he is in my thoughts.

One morning as I was walking home from his gravesite, the question that so many still ask—"Are you still running?"—popped into my head. As I passed the many markers, I began to smile. *Why not put the question on my gravestone, after I join Don?* I thought. Then the answer would be clear and unambiguous.

A Marathoner's Tale

On Sunday, November 2, 1997—at age 67—I ran the world's largest race, the New York City Marathon, which attracts both Olympic runners and novices like me. I was one of about 40,000 runners to get an entry number for the 26.2-mile race. I never thought I would run a race of this distance. I had stood on the sidelines during a couple of marathons, watching ordinary runners of my caliber pass by, elated by the crowd's cheers. It was their faces wreathed in smiles rather than grimacing in pain that led me to think, *I can do this, too, and I should try.* Or perhaps it was those competitive, ambitious impulses of mine that kept emerging even when I thought I had them under control.

The marathon began on the upper deck of the Verrazano-Narrows Bridge in Staten Island and ended in Central Park in Manhattan, where I had taken my first steps outdoors as a toddler. In between, my feet touched the ground in the boroughs of Brooklyn, Queens, and the Bronx.

◈

If I don't give you my marathon time right now, it will hover over these pages like a dark (or otherwise) cloud, and I want it in proper context. Some weeks after I finished the race, which I recovered from with only a sore toe and some blisters, I boarded a plane to Seattle to see Dwight. As I sat down and reached for my newspaper, the pilot's sonorous voice cut through the rustlings of passengers preparing for the lengthy flight: "Good morning, ladies and gentlemen. Our flying time to Seattle this morning will be 5 hours and 18 minutes."

I snapped to attention, tightening my grip on the newspaper. *That's my marathon time,* I thought. For a moment, I felt as if the pilot was exposing my not-so-fantastic time to everyone on the plane, but then I calmed down after realizing that it had taken me the same amount of time to run 26.2 miles through the city's five boroughs as it would the crew to fly 2,436 miles across the country. (Actually, I ran nine seconds longer: 5:18:09.) Another consolation was that a 37-year-old male had finished only eight seconds ahead of me, and I finished two seconds ahead of a 39-year-old female. I hadn't stopped once during the race at a port-o-potty or the water stations, preferring to grab a cup from a volunteer, swirl the water in my mouth and spit it out, or swallow a mouthful or two while running.

I wasn't the last to finish by any means; many runners took six or even seven hours to complete the course in what had been dubbed the "Monsoon Marathon," because it rained heavily during much of the race. The weather didn't aid runners like me in the back of the pack; the temperature was high in the early stages and plunged later on during a cold front, leaving us shivering by the end. My finish time certainly didn't matter to my loyal college roommate, Genie Havemeyer, who read through every single name to find mine among the thousands of finishers listed in the *New York Times* special marathon section that was published the Monday after the race.

Training Regime

Preparing for the New York City Marathon was a little like getting a Ph.D. in training for and running a race, and Phyllis Marchand, the 57-year-old mayor of Princeton Township who had completed a couple of them, persuaded me to try when she gave me a New York City Marathon T-shirt for my sixtieth birthday. Phyllis and I and three other friends—Mary Weeden, 47, and husband-and-wife team Peter Johnson, 50, and Lynn Lederer, 47—decided to train together. We followed a six-month regime created by the New York City Road Runners Club, and our collective goal was quite simply for *all* of us to finish. We ran six days a week, increasing our distance each week and completing longer runs up to 20 miles at a time on weekends. Peter correctly summed up our philosophy about the endeavor: "Being together is more important than stretching our capabilities." Lynn said that "runners' talk" kept us going—the group discussed books, politics, every bit of fashion (from running gear to black tie), food, kids, schools, jobs, and religion … sometimes disagreeing, but always taking our minds off our feet. ("Runners' talk is good for the sole," Lynn quipped.)

The days leading up to the marathon soon dwindled to a precious few, and we waited with anticipation for our notification of acceptance to the race. All our training would have been in vain without it. Everyone except me had received his or her notification, and I was nervous that something had gone wrong with my application. One day I saw an envelope in the mail bearing the return address of a woman completely unknown to me. Sometimes I toss unfamiliar letters like this into the recycling bin, but something told me to open this one. It was my official notification, along with a note from a psychiatrist who lived on the Upper West Side. She said that my registration had been stuck to hers, and she guessed that I needed it. On such small acts of random kindness from strangers our lives depend.

During the last few days before the marathon, we put the finishing touches on our training. On Friday, we took a final two-mile run to complete the regime, and the next day I treated myself to a professional pedicure. (I knew my feet would have to work hard for me on Sunday.)

One final task on my to-do list was to select my T-shirt for the marathon. I read that it made good sense to attach your first name in large letters on the front, so people could cheer you by name. I also knew that it was fun for runners behind you to read some words or see pictures that would describe more fully who you were. I placed "Susie" in large black letters on the front of my shirt and, to amuse my fellow runners, a page from *Sex, Etc.* on the back. (Many approaching from behind me said, "Slow down, please. We want to read what's on your back." After they saw the two words, *Sex, Etc.*, they would speed up to pass me.)

I spent Saturday afternoon alone watching one of my all-time favorite movies, *Chariots of Fire*, which is about the 1924 Olympics in Paris and two great runners, Eric Liddell, a devout Christian from Scotland who runs for the glory of God, and Harold Abrahams, a Jew at Cambridge who runs to overcome prejudice. The film's title comes from the William Blake poem "Jerusalem," which became a famous British hymn that I sang during my years at Brearley. Its message always stirred me:

> *I shall not cease from mental fight*
> *Nor shall my sword sleep in my hand*
> *Till we have built Jerusalem*
> *In England's green and pleasant land.*

The hymn seemed appropriate for Sunday's task.

Marathon Sunday

I felt prepared to run the marathon. Throughout the long training period, I kept thinking, *One day at a time.* Each time I finished a 15- or 20-mile training run, I made a mental checklist of what I needed to do to be ready for race day. When I became discouraged, Peter would remind me that only one percent of women my age even attempted to run a marathon, and it increased my tenacity.

The weather forecast for the marathon was dismal for runners: warm with intermittent showers and a cold front by evening. I trimmed a plastic garbage bag to wear over my running clothes and carried two small white ones to protect my shoes from becoming sodden at the staging area. (I neglected to stuff an extra pair of socks in my fanny pack, which would have saved my feet from blisters.)

The marathon start time was 11 o'clock, and our well-organized band of five had hired Mario Musso, a retired Princeton Township policeman, to drive us early in the morning to the official drop-off place near the Verrazano Bridge. The crowd was so huge that our quintet became separated. Phyllis and I set off together hoping to find the others, but we didn't see them until after we crossed the finish line, hours later.

We walked past hundreds of runners clad in khaki-colored garbage bags, who looked like an alien army from another planet. Most of us had already shed the white plastic bags around our feet as we sloshed through the vast sea of mud at the staging area. Phyllis wanted to go as close as possible to the starting line, but I didn't want to be bowled over by the throngs of fast runners congregated at the start. I found a good place toward the front and then bid Phyllis farewell and much luck.

I took off my garbage bag and tossed my sweatshirt into a pile of never-to-be-seen-again items that the marathon staff would donate to homeless shelters in the city. I replaced my garbage bag and said two short prayers: "Guide my feet while I run this race," and "Dear God, be good to me. The sea is so wide, and my boat is so small."

I felt alone and in need of protection for the miles that lay ahead. I thought of my children—especially my daughter Kate, who was worried about my running the race, and who would sit for hours that day in front of the TV saying, "Go, Mom! Go, Mom!" (I know her cheers made a difference.) I planned to meet Don, Penny, and her friend, Phil, on First Avenue after I came off the 59th Street Bridge. Phil and Penny were going to run the second half of the marathon with me, and I looked forward to seeing them—but first I had to run 13 miles alone.

I looked around and realized that indeed I knew no one. Each runner standing on that piece of pavement on the bridge was alone with her or his thoughts, waiting for the mayor to, with a shot from the starter's gun, release us to undertake this major challenge in our lives. We sang (or attempted to sing) "The Star Spangled Banner," which energized me, and then the gun resounded in the damp air; in a rush, I and the other thousands began to run.

During the early part of the race in Brooklyn, I thought about May Will, my family's faithful housekeeper, who commuted from Brooklyn to Manhattan each day to take care of the family apartment before I moved out on my own. She had the gumption to leave her home in Australia at 18 and journey to America knowing no one. My memories of her helped the miles go by. By the time I arrived in Queens, I was certain that I could finish the race and nothing was hurting. *You don't have to do this again,* I thought as I approached the 59th Street Bridge. I felt more lighthearted and relaxed, and I began to enjoy myself knowing that I didn't have to train for and run another marathon again. (Once really was enough!) Running is simply placing one foot ahead of the other, and I kept doing that as the miles passed.

The crowds were warm and generous, and putting "Susie" on my shirt had been a good idea. I loved hearing my name called out in the misty air. I crossed the bridge and ran right through a downpour that was cascading like a waterfall off the bridge and onto First Avenue. Don was standing right where he said he would be, clad in a huge green poncho with his arms wide and a broad smile upon his face that would have lifted anyone's spirits. I stopped to talk to him briefly and bask in his warmth, but I wanted to be off as quickly as possible—I needed to "husband" all the precious seconds that I could.

Penny and Phil appeared—he wearing a bright yellow sou'wester—and I bid Don a fond farewell and told him how to find the finish line at 66th Street and Central Park West. The three of us then completed the run up the length of First Avenue. The three-deep sidelines of rain-drenched spectators were an inspiration, and I knew that running that day was preferable to standing for hours for a quick glimpse of a loved one. At least I could keep moving, watch an ever-changing kaleidoscope of scenes, and hear shouts of encouragement. The crowds along First Avenue are famous for their enthusiasm, and runners benefit from their cheers.

With 21 miles behind me, I turned left to follow the course across a sliver of the Bronx. As I began my run down Fifth Avenue toward Central Park, I suddenly heard, "Mrs. Wilson! Mrs. Wilson!" I turned my head and caught sight of Lisa Downing, Penny's childhood friend and Brearley classmate who lived in Harlem and had braved the elements to cheer me on. Her face lit up in a wide grin as she jumped up and down, waving her arms wildly. She rushed to embrace me and offer me her down coat, since the weather had turned cold, but I didn't take it, although I had unwisely jettisoned my garbage bag and felt the chill. Lisa's presence warmed me, as did that of another Harlem spectator, who took one look at my aging face and possibly slumping body and cheered me on with, "You go, girl!"

I picked up my heels and headed down Fifth Avenue, preparing to turn into Central Park around 93rd Street. As we made the turn, a spectator handed me a Hershey's Kiss, and I did something I had read ten times over not to do: take food from someone on the sidelines. But with only a handful of miles to the finish line, my senses had taken leave of themselves, and I quickly opened the silver wrapper and popped the Kiss into my mouth. I know the spectator meant well, but the candy must have come from a Halloween celebration years before. It was as hard as a rock and tasteless. *Serves you right,* I said to myself as I spat it out.

Almost immediately, I was in Central Park, and that made all the difference. It was like coming home, and I knew the park would hold me close and give my ebbing strength the boost it needed to cross the finish line six miles away. Some days before the race, Phyllis had referred a *New York Times* sports reporter covering the marathon to me for an interview, since I was older and running it for the first time. The reporter, Jeré Longman, had asked me what I thought it would feel like when I turned into Central Park on my way to the finish line.

"I remember learning how to roller-skate in Central Park," I said. "When I began running 15 years ago, I started around the reservoir. It is sort of my backyard." Then I added, "You'll see people at their best. I think it will be a transcendent experience."

Longman had quoted me in his piece, and I remembered my comment to him as I started the last six miles. This is the toughest part of the race for a novice runner, who has to rely on adrenalin, cheers from the crowd, physical strength, plain guts, and whatever's left in the tank to push through to the end. Penny's presence meant a lot to me during those six miles, and she encouraged me every step of the way, often pointing to me and telling spectators my name and age!

We turned toward 66th Street off Central Park South, and I saw that the crowd had dispersed. The water and Gatorade stations had been torn apart, but the clock at the finish line was still functioning as I approached it alone. Penny and Phil, who didn't have numbers, peeled off and allowed me to cross the line as 5:18:09 flashed. A picture of me crossing it shows me practically flat-footed with only a wisp of a smile on my face.

I didn't fall to the ground and kiss the pavement, as I had seen so many runners do on TV; I felt a sense of completion rather than elation. An official handed me a silvery Mylar cape for warmth that I draped over my shoulders, and I ran on to find Don, who was nearby. He wrapped his arm around my shoulders and told me that he was glad to get out of the rain, and I understood his weariness: waiting five hours for someone in a downpour was too much to ask of anyone, even a loved one. Don had played such a small part in my training that he couldn't really share in my quiet pleasure at the moment of its conclusion.

He and I headed to Nina Maruca's apartment not far from the finish line, where she offered me a bath in her small tub, and as I sat there soaking up the day, the enormity of what I had done hit my body. When I tried to get out of the tub, my legs turned to rubber and I started to panic—*My legs have gone. I won't be able to get out of this tub*—but then I calmed down, got on my knees, and willed my legs to make one final effort to sustain my weight as I rose.

Fellow runner Mary Weeden soon joined us for dinner at a nearby restaurant, and we headed home afterwards. It had been a full day, and all of us had met our collective goal of crossing the finish line. We were happy to have completed the marathon, but melancholic that we would no longer share the hard work, effort, and intensity of reaching our goal. Success has both its pleasures and sadness.

I received a heap of congratulatory messages, all of which were deeply appreciated, but as I said to whoever offered one, "I put one foot after the other, and you can do it, too"—and I meant it. Some weeks later, I received a special gift: a glass paperweight in the form of an apple slice, from Tiffany's, the familiar skyline of the city etched on it along with my name, the date of the marathon, and my time. It was from Joanie and it is a significant memento.

Initially, when I received praise from others for completing the marathon, I had been afraid that they might define my life by this experience—and that's not what I wanted. Running was an exercise that had simply expanded over the years to include making new friends, competing, and having fun. I wanted others to view my life as more beneficial to people. Eventually I learned to see my accomplishment as something that not many women my age would attempt to do and to accept the compliments.

I was pleased to have run the marathon but happy when my life returned to normal. A few days afterwards, my dear friend Marian Heher dropped off a small gift with a note, and I have kept her note in my wallet all the years since the race. It reminds me of our wonderful friendship, which ended when she died of uterine cancer in 2005.

Always perceptive, she wrote: "Dear Susie, this is to remind you every year of the fantastic marathon—an incredible accomplishment. I am awed by your determination and grit! Love, Marian." In turn, I will always admire the calm and courage Marian showed in facing her death, a much more important statement about character than running a race—even a marathon.

A Road Not Taken

After I left the State Board of Education in 1982, I was feeling a bit at sea about where I should direct my public service efforts when my good neighbor Tom Jamieson, an attorney who often appeared before the Lawrence Township Planning Board, brought me two books about local government. He put them down on my kitchen table and said he didn't know if I'd be interested in serving in local government, because the issues were multiple and different than those that came before the State Board. I interpreted his gift of the books as a consolation prize for having lost my seat on the State Board.

I had never thought about actively running for a local public office like the township council or seeking appointment to the planning, zoning, or school boards—and no one had ever suggested that I would be good at it. My mother, the family politician, had been appointed to state government positions but never proposed that I consider running for office. I always assumed that Don would go into politics because of his experience in the Kennedy administration, but he never voiced any interest in it and loved his job as corporate vice president of Time-Warner.

Tom didn't suggest that I actually run for office—had he done so, I would have valued his opinion, as he was highly regarded in the community—but he did say that if I was interested in serving on the planning board, he could help me. I knew that his word was gold and his support would almost guarantee that I would be seriously considered for the position.

I had felt somewhat qualified to serve on the State Board of Education, but I wasn't too sure about my qualifications for the planning board. But since it was the only offer on the table, I gave him the go-ahead to suggest my name should a seat open up, and about six months later, I was appointed to a four-year term on the Lawrence Planning Board.

I had been spoiled by my experience on the State Board of Education because its mission dovetailed so well with my interests and experience. Not so with the planning board: I found little to grab on to with the exception of authorizing more affordable housing opportunities for low-income families; but as hard as I tried, I couldn't wrap my head—or my heart—around stormwater drainage. To make matters worse, our meetings took place in the evenings, often stretching past 11 p.m. I was relieved when my term ended, since family planning interested me more than town planning, and the morning after my last meeting, I sat up in bed and said out loud, "It's over."

In the late winter of 1987, Nancy Stults, who was then president of the National Organization for Women's New Jersey chapter, paid a call on me at home. We had met when the State Board of Education was trying to pass its family life and sexuality education policy. Nancy was a strong supporter of our effort and had organized her NOW constituency to do the nitty-gritty work that advocates do to taste success on an issue. She was an outspoken, hard-driving leader, and I respected how well she harnessed her forces. She understood that one of the reasons I supported sexuality education was to help prevent and reduce the need for abortions.

With the candles still burning on the dining-room table where Don and I had been having dinner, Nancy sat down and pitched me the idea of running for Congress against our district's incumbent, Christopher Smith. By then, Smith, the former executive director of New Jersey Right to Life, had served four two-year terms in the House of Representatives, having first won election in 1980 in the wake of the Reagan Revolution. He was on his way to becoming the most vocal opponent in Congress of abortion rights, maintaining that it should be illegal in all cases, even if the life of the pregnant woman was in jeopardy or if pregnancy was the result of rape or incest. He led the successful fight against providing abortions in military hospitals and was instrumental in Congress's passage of a law banning partial-birth abortions. His other views were moderate: he was a consistent supporter of veterans' aid and the global expansion of human rights. He was difficult to paint into a corner.

Nancy knew that my efforts to require sexuality education in the public schools as a way to reduce the need for abortion would make an interesting counterpoint to Smith on the campaign trail. A staunch Roman Catholic, Smith favored abstinence-only-until-marriage rather than comprehensive sexuality education, which included accurate information on contraception as well as abstinence.

She understood that I would be able to challenge Smith's one-size-fits-all view on abortion and might persuade voters, especially women, to support a candidate who would promote better sex education policies to decrease abortion rates. Unquestionably, prevailing in such a campaign would be a long shot. Smith had already been re-elected four times by ever-increasing numbers.

Don sat at the table while Nancy made her pitch, and after she finished—and without a by-your-leave from me—he immediately told her that he was strongly opposed to her idea mainly because of my political inexperience. He turned to me and said, "If you do this, you'll get no more than 37 percent of the vote, like everyone else who has run against Chris Smith in the last four elections, and you'll spend a lot of your father's money to no avail."

Don left the dining room, and his words lingered. I felt disappointed that we hadn't had a longer conversation where I could have rebutted some of his arguments. He had a lot more political savvy than I did. I was always the one with the passion, and he, the reasoned response. He didn't ask me how I felt about Nancy's suggestion. He was used to speaking for both of us and was confident that I would see the good sense of his argument.

I thanked Nancy and apologized for Don's quick response to her suggestion.

"You've paid me a compliment by coming here and suggesting that I run for Congress. Obviously, as you've seen, I will have a problem getting Don's support if I chose to run, and it would make the venture even more problematic. His arguments do make sense."

I asked what she thought the next steps should be if we kept the door open. She said she would draft a memo outlining the reasons why I should run and how the campaign would shape up, and I saw her out the door and thanked her again. I returned to the dining room and blew out the candles.

As promised, Nancy dropped off a handwritten, four-page memo detailing what I'd need to do to seek the Democratic nomination to run against Smith in November 1988. She added some comments about my accomplishments and character, showing that she understood my attributes better than I did myself:

"You have repeatedly demonstrated an extraordinary way of dealing with people and issues and chosen to work in a public arena with difficult public-policy concerns—if you can effectively navigate issues through the New Jersey school hierarchy, you can use those skills to run for Congress. ... I honestly believe you will be an excellent candidate and a great congresswoman. ...Thank you for your courage in considering this."

The truth of the matter was I didn't have the courage to stand on my own two feet and explain to Don why I wanted to try running for Congress. And despite Nancy's belief in me, I really didn't have enough confidence in myself to take the plunge.

"In life, you only regret the things you do not do," Joseph P. Kennedy, the father of Jack and Bobby, once said—and his words ring true to me today. The chances were good that 37 percent of the vote was too high a bar, but I would have demonstrated that I had the determination to do something difficult and possibly awakened a constituency of people who did not agree with Chris Smith on abortion and other issues. Losing wouldn't have bothered me, but I couldn't summon the fortitude to take the chance when it was offered to me. I would have had to stand up to Don, it is true, but he would have come around and offered his help. Dwight, who was living in Seattle, had offered a supportive hand and even sent me a T-shirt that read, "Run, Sudi, Run." (Sudi was his nickname for me.)

Twenty-five years later, I'm still angry with and disappointed in myself. Whenever I have the opportunity now, I encourage women—even those with light credentials—to run for political office. I urge them not to muff any chances that come their way and to create their own chances. In 2013, in a blue state, the New Jersey congressional delegation was all male, despite excellent recruitment efforts by both political parties and academic institutions like the Center for American Women and Politics at Rutgers. (At one point, I realized that I had sent a financial contribution to every Democratic woman serving in the U.S. Senate. There were only a handful of them, but it made me feel good to help these women run for political office and win.)

I was 58 when Nancy came calling, and she never came again. I have a sheet of paper stickers with the words "Susan for Congress" that she had created for me as an enticement and sign of her belief in me. The white lettering is centered on a warm red background. It was bittersweet to find them, and I don't plan on throwing them or her campaign plan away anytime soon.

Helping Women Run

I never got another opportunity to run for political office, so I turned to helping others, especially Hillary Clinton, the first woman with a serious chance of gaining the Democratic nomination and running for the presidency. In 2008, she won more primaries and delegates than any other woman in political history. I can say with pride that I helped her to achieve this stunning accomplishment.

It felt completely natural to work for a highly qualified woman running to become the first female president of the United States. Voters in states with primaries could choose between a qualified woman and a qualified African-American, a unique and monumental achievement for our country. (I personally noted this political landmark by placing two bumper stickers—one reading "Hillary" and the other "Obama"—side by side on my old Audi station wagon. I have never seen a bumper like it in all of Princeton.)

Obama's supporters wanted him to become the first African-American president, but I was more naturally drawn to working for the first female candidate. No matter who won, it would be a win-win situation for democracy. At the end of the day, I concluded it was harder for a woman than an African-American man to gain the highest office in the land because political power has been under control of the male establishment in the United States since the nation began.

I happily volunteered for Clinton in the spring, summer, and early fall of 2008 when she and Obama went head-to-head over the Democratic nomination. Because the Texas primary was critical to Clinton's efforts, my friend Lynn Johnston and I went to Dallas to work for the campaign for a week. Being a campaign worker is the least glamorous job in the world, especially if you're not a techie with an iPad attached to your navel. It consists of making endless phone calls, distributing literature, clutching street maps, knocking on doors to drum up enthusiasm, cleaning the always messy campaign-office kitchen, and sweeping the floor.

The best, or worst, part of working on a campaign is waiting for the results, and it's better to head out of town before they come in, in case they are disappointing. Lynn and I left the Dallas office in the afternoon of primary election day after making lots of phone calls urging Clinton supporters to go to the polls. We flew home in time to hear that she had won the Texas primary vote but lost to Obama in total number of delegates. (We hadn't been involved in the delegate aspect of the campaign, so we settled for half a political loaf.)

After Dallas, I moved on alone to volunteer in Indianapolis for a week and again did what was asked, which frequently was sweeping the floor. Obama beat Clinton decisively in Indianapolis, and I could have predicted the ultimate result after seeing the endless lines of African-Americans and other supporters waiting to hear him when he came to town to give a speech. I witnessed the pride that African-Americans of all ages across the nation felt in having one of their own run for president. Obama easily won the Indiana primary.

With the nation's eyes on the crucially important Pennsylvania primary, I moved on to Lancaster to knock on doors and make phone calls to rally support, sweep the floor, and clean up the kitchen. All of the volunteers' efforts were rewarded when Clinton won the Pennsylvania primary by a decisive margin—her last major win before she lost the nomination to Obama.

Hillary Clinton may have the inside track to the presidency on the 2016 Democratic ticket. Should she decide to undertake this formidable task and I am still on my feet, I shall once more volunteer in the primary states to help elect our first woman president. I happen to think women should have the same chances as men to run the country and will succeed and fail in about the same proportion. (Although I'd be willing to put my money on women edging out men by a nose.) Women have already led and are leading other countries, so having a woman at the helm of the greatest democracy and military power in the world is indeed achievable.

We need women leaders to help bring peace to the planet and create a better world, especially for our children. From what I have observed, women are generally more compassionate and less competitive than men and much more willing to find pragmatic solutions to problems rather than endlessly talk issues to death and refuse to compromise. As I learned from a lifetime of travels to many places around the world, and especially during my week with our son Dwight in Honduras, if given the power, women can unite in the struggle for the basics of life: clean water, good schools, quality health care and food, and access to contraception to control the size of their families and find a way out of abject poverty.

Women leaders will make mistakes, but I believe that should Hillary Clinton become president, she will inspire women everywhere to create a better world. If she decides not to run, perhaps in some future time, my children, grandchildren, and great-grandchildren will help another woman become president of the United States and remember that their mother, grandmother, and great-grandmother helped one woman's effort in 2008.

That will be worth all the sweeping.

Family Ties

Parenting Times Three

It was June 1958, and I was alone in my room at George Washington University Hospital. I had awakened from the anesthetic I'd been given to lull me "to sleep" during the final stages of labor with my first child. Somehow through the mists of the end of the birth process, I heard, "You have a son, and he's fine." I recalled that much upon waking, but neither Don nor my little son were in my room. I experienced the first moments of motherhood alone.

I had brought a copy of Dr. Spock's *Baby and Child Care* with me, with its principal message to mothers, "You know more than you think you do." Some kind soul had placed it on top of the metal table beside my bed. Dr. Spock played a special role in my life, which accounts for why I had faith in his advice. When he was a young resident at a New York City hospital after graduating from Columbia University's College of Physicians and Surgeons first in his class, he was the attending pediatrician at Brearley. If a child was sick, she couldn't be readmitted to school without his first checking her ears, nose, and throat in his office at the school.

Dr. Spock was well over six feet tall, and looking up at him as he held his flashlight to look down my throat while I said "Ahhhh" was like looking up at a giraffe. He was a kind doctor with a deep voice and smiling eyes. We lived in fear that he would find the trace of a lingering sore throat, stuffy nose, or earache and would call one of our parents to come and take us home in disgrace. Happily, Dr. Spock never had to look down on me and utter the words, "I'm so sorry, but you're still sick and have to go home."

I pulled myself up to reach for his book, since I didn't know anything about this most important job that I was about to undertake. All my life I had depended upon credentials to certify my knowledge, but nothing vouched for my ability to parent. I would have to learn by doing, because I didn't want to fail the darling little son I had brought into the world.

I had an ace in the hole as I started on the adventure of motherhood. At *Life*, I had helped write a series of stories about how to give developmentally appropriate children's birthday parties, and for some unfathomable reason, I concluded that knowing how to give these parties prepared me for mothering. I was also excited about catching up with my peers, who'd been procreating successfully for years. I reasoned that if they could raise children, I could do it, too, and so I went into motherhood at 28 confident, with Dr. Spock never far from my side.

Don was a loving parent, but he didn't play as large a part in our children's upbringing as he might have if social norms of the time had required more participation from men. Back then, a mother was the principal parent and a father was the breadwinner—and Don took that job seriously and did it well. His work hours were long and intense, and he liked to relieve stress on the weekends by playing paddle tennis and golf.

Dwight and Kate saw much more of me than they did Don, but by the time Penny arrived, he had realized what he'd been missing. He started driving Penny to her riding lessons on the weekends; afterward they'd stop at Cliff's, a little hole-in-the-wall restaurant, to eat lunch and talk of "many things:
Of shoes—and ships—and sealing-wax—Of cabbages—and kings," as Lewis Carroll wrote. Don, like Penny, was the third child and especially close to his mother, and his relationship with Penny gave him a chance to experience the same feelings of togetherness that he and his mother had shared.

The demands of living in two different places gave me little free time to spend with my children, which was a loss, but someone had to keep the ship afloat. I was the stricter parent; Don slipped Good & Plenty candy to Katie and copies of *People* magazine to Penny while I made sure that homework was done and clothes were picked up. We were lucky parents—our children never caused us grief, although Dwight once said that what we didn't know hadn't hurt us, leading me to think that they had experimented with marijuana more than we realized.

Parenting is like childbirth—you tend to remember the good moments and forget the painful ones. (The memory of the only time I hit one of my children, on the cheek, has never disappeared from my consciousness.) We kept the kids busy: Dwight at sports, Katie at ballet, and Penny with riding lessons and eventually a horse. Of course, since we commuted between homes, they were always on the move, and they didn't have a solid peer group in either location with which to interact and possibly be influenced by in negative ways.

If I could change one aspect of my parenting it would be my bad habit of encouraging my children to emulate others rather than be themselves. It wasn't kind to them and made them insecure about their own abilities. I wanted my son to become a lawyer, because I thought lawyers made a difference in our society, but Dwight would have none of it. He finally looked me straight in the eye and said, "Mom, you go to law school." He was right to push back.

I've always regretted sending Dwight off to boarding school when he was only 14. His middle school ended in eighth grade, and we didn't offer him the chance to go to high school in the city and live with us at home. We didn't ask him what he preferred and assumed that boarding school was best, since Don had attended Deerfield Academy and our friends had sent their children off to these prestigious schools to prepare them for Ivy League colleges. In addition, my father had gone to Phillips Exeter, and the idea of Dwight following him there was exciting.

Dwight chose Exeter, but Don called it a "cold nest" after listening to him describe his first year. I felt ashamed and wanted to apologize to Dwight for confining him to a school that wasn't particularly nurturing. Would he have been happier if we'd kept him in our warmer nest? He never considered sending his only child, Eli, away to boarding school.

Similarly, I wonder if I ever gave Katie the chance to stop leading the double life that resulted from attending both a demanding ballet school and a private school. (She was a good sport about it.) Finally, when it was Penny's turn, I relaxed and let her do whatever she wanted without interference, and she stayed home with us until after completing grades K-12 at Brearley. My attempt to balance work and family resulted in my placing a lighter hand on her shoulder, since I was focused on her and on my professional duties. But Penny made me feel better about my mothering when I acknowledged to her one day that I saw myself as a workhorse.

"No, Mom," she said. "You're a show horse, too." I like to think she meant I won a blue ribbon.

My children's grades received too much of my attention. Many parents in our circles indulged in the good-grades game, and I wanted to join it. My academic performance was nothing to boast about and my parents hadn't pressured me, so why was I pressuring my own children? My old drive to succeed raised its ugly head again, only this time it was directed at my kids.

Dwight was a naturally good student, and he obliged my insistence on high marks, but I wonder if he missed the forest for the trees by focusing more on achievement than on enjoying the course content. When he graduated from Yale magna cum laude and was elected to Phi Beta Kappa, I was so happy that it makes me shudder now. His perspective was healthier than mine: to make sure I didn't trumpet his accomplishment to my friends, he told me that he was the last person in his class to be elected into the society.

Katie joined the group when she graduated summa cum laude from Trinity College in Hartford, Connecticut. Dwight and Kate showed me how little respect they had for their PBK keys when they asked me to keep them in my safe deposit box so people wouldn't see them. I recently returned the keys to their rightful owners, but there's a good chance they threw them in the trash. In their attitudes is a late but necessary lesson for their mother: academic honors don't mean much in the overall scheme of life. Other ingredients, like self-confidence, empathy, compassion, and hard work—definitely hard work—are much more important.

Dwight

My memories of the children shift like the patterns of a kaleidoscope. It is impossible to halt the changing patterns and pick out one moment that crystalizes each child to me. With Dwight, I don't remember ever exchanging a cross word with him. That may sound almost too good to be true, but either he was deft at turning my critical comments aside or we were truly soul mates on issues that mattered. Was my persona such that he feared telling me the truth about his feelings, especially if it was painful to hear? Did I rear a child too polite for his own good?

Once he told me that he was known as the odd man out among his six college roommates because he made his bed every morning, a residual habit from his upbringing. "Dwight, you're in college," I said. "If you don't want to make your bed, you don't have to, and I'll never know it." To this day, I don't know if he stopped making his bed.

Dwight and I usually drove from the city to Princeton every Friday afternoon and when he was around 11, we devised a one-time game that was certainly not wholly original but gave us a lot of fun. We decided to try find a license plate from each of the 50 states, and all roads to Princeton and the town itself were fair game in our search. For reasons that impressed me, Dwight always memorized the plates that we had seen and exactly which ones we still needed. We were intense about this game and elated when we checked a state off the list: finding Texas, New Mexico, Montana, or Iowa—usually on the streets of Princeton—brought yelps of joy. The last license plate that we found was Hawaii, the 50th state, and we cheered and shouted as if the Princeton Tigers basketball team, our favorite, had won the NCAA (National Collegiate Athletic Association) championship. As we grinned at each other, I felt a connection with my son that is hard to describe in words: as though we were one.

We only played the game once, but sometimes when I am alone in a car, I start to play it again in a desultory sort of way. It isn't nearly as much fun because Dwight isn't sitting in the front seat beside me.

Dwight and I played Scrabble through the years, he piling up the points and beating me handily with several seven-letter words in a single game. With the spirit of a community organizer, which is how he sometimes describes himself, he never trumpeted his wins or refused to give me another chance to beat him. He could have been a professional Scrabble player, but instead he established a series of social justice businesses modeled on the international, cooperative spirit of the Peace Corps, bringing computer technology to the poor in India (One Roof) and uniting people from different countries to work on common projects in the United States (Collabriv).

He once used a Scrabble analogy to describe me: "From A to Z, from start to finish, Mum, I've been blessed by your 'passion,' a seven-letter word worth at least 70 points in my book." I could write exactly the same to him, only he would find a way to play all seven letters, and I wouldn't.

Katie

We had a family joke about Katie that grew out of a game we played when the children were young: "If you were an animal, what animal would you be?" We decided that Katie was a porcupine, because on occasion she could throw her quills, knowing that beneath them was a most tender, loving, and appreciative heart.

Katie had a challenging childhood. At seven, she was accepted into the

School of American Ballet and balanced the demands of dancing instruction with her schoolwork at The Chapin School in New York, one of the most demanding academic schools for girls in the city. I don't know how she did it. Knowing the competitiveness of the dance world, Don and I felt that a solid education would be a good backup for her, but the pressures of attending two schools at once may have contributed to her throwing her quills from time to time. I have nothing but admiration for her hard work and dedication all those years.

Katie completed all 12 years of ballet school and graduated from Chapin on time with her classmates. Several colleges accepted her, but she decided to pursue her dancing dream and join the corps of the well-regarded Pacific Northwest Ballet, in Seattle. Five years later, she decided that she had come to the end of her ballet career and enrolled in college to major in psychology. She earned her master's in social work and has helped many young adults in her therapy practice. I have never spoken to any of Katie's young patients, but I have a feeling that they, like me, have benefited from her loving heart.

Once when I broke my ankle climbing over a snowbank in New Brunswick in tall, gray leather boots, I sent an SOS to Katie in Massachusetts to come and give me some TLC. She responded with alacrity, even though she was deep into her graduate studies at Smith College. I was sitting in the kitchen when she came through the back door.

"Oh, Katie, you came," I said.

"Yes, Mom, as fast as I could. How are you feeling?" she asked, peeling off her winter boots and coat.

"I'm much better. Thank you, darling," I said.

"Well, Mom, if you're feeling better, then up on your feet!"

We both burst into laughter because we knew that I would have uttered exactly the same phrase had our positions been reversed. My children knew that I didn't accept excuses for anything, particularly when they were sick. Katie's presence cheered me up, and I appreciated her good humor and gentle skewering of my approach to mothering.

My parenting style could also be gentle. I always remember the night Katie came home with a request related to an art history project at Chapin.

"Mom, we went to the Metropolitan Museum today, and each of us picked out one object that we have to re-create at home," she explained.

When I asked her to describe the object, she pulled out a postcard of an intricate Persian carpet full of brilliant colors. As the magnitude of the assignment dawned upon me, she added, "I stopped at the stationery store and bought a roll of paper and a box of paints and colored pencils. We can unroll the paper on the dining-room table and re-create it. Right, Mom?"

I couldn't say no to my exhausted, dancing daughter, so Katie went to bed and I pulled an all-nighter recreating the Persian rug. When I handed the rolled-up paper to her as she left for school the next morning, I kissed her goodbye and made a suggestion: "Darling, next time choose a tea cup." As I lay my head on the pillow that morning to catch a quick few hours of sleep, I concluded that motherhood is about sacrifices, large and small.

Katie inherited her Dad's ability to write special messages in letters and holiday cards. For my 70th birthday, she wrote me a letter about a special memory "that meant so much to me and captured what you gave to me unconditionally as a child and adolescent." She described how she felt upon returning to our New York apartment after school each day, ringing the doorbell, and hearing the excitement in my voice as I opened the door to greet her. We would walk to the kitchen for a warm, soothing cup of tea and cinnamon toast and discuss the happenings of her day. She wrote that she loved our special time together because "it nurtured my soul and my deep connection to you."

Anywhere, anytime, I'm still ready to share tea and sympathy with Katie.

Penny

Penny was born seven years after her sister, and dogs and horses made up for her lack of siblings near her age. When she was young, she defended and loved the worn-out horses that stood in all weathers near the Plaza Hotel in New York City. As a young adult, she adopted a black Labrador retriever on Martha's Vineyard, luring him away from his indifferent owners. He came to live with Penny on Long Island when she worked for a newspaper, and to give her a break, I would invite Zack to "Summer Camp at Princeton" for several years.

We didn't know Zack's exact age, but we saw that he was growing older, and one July when he came to camp, we discovered that he had a cancerous tumor. When he stopped eating and drinking and death was imminent, Penny came immediately. We gently lifted him into the car and drove to the vet, who told us that Zack was ready to die. The vet asked Penny if she wanted to be with Zack when he gave him the shot to stop his faintly beating heart so he would die quickly. She said that she wanted him to have the shot while she was holding him in the field, since he so loved running outside in summertime. Later, Penny told me how meaningful it was that I had held her when we sat in that field: "You held me up and taught me how to grieve, talking about our Zack and urging me to write about one sweet dog's impact on our lives."

Some years later, she had to face the death of her second Labrador, Trudeau, who developed cancer of the mouth. This time, she declined my offer to be with her when the time came for him to die. "No, Mipper," she said (using an extension of "Mip," a nickname all three children used for me). "I can manage Trudeau's death alone this time." And she did.

I used to worry that, given her gentle spirit and loving heart, Penny might be grief-stricken when Don or I died, but she handled her father's death with a strength first tapped, perhaps, when she held her beloved dog in her lap in a field as he died peacefully.

Penny grows more self-reliant as she grows deeper into motherhood, doing an excellent job balancing work and family. She followed her sister into social work after a fling with journalism, obtaining master's degrees in social work from Simmons College and education from the Harvard Graduate School of Education. She carved out a part-time job at the Jewish Board of Guardians in New York City when, after some years in Washington, D.C., she, Richard, Olivia, and Reed settled in the Riverdale section of the Bronx.

When I observed how pressure-packed her life is caring for two young children, holding a part-time job, and managing a large house, I suggested that she try the Mommy track. I had always believed in the necessity of my girls' obtaining an education and the skills needed to work and support themselves, but I suggested that she no longer follow this dictum if she was under too much pressure. "No, Mom, I like to work very much and intend to keep doing it," she said. I wasn't expecting her reply, and she reminded me that your children can always surprise you. The seeds you plant blossom in ways you wouldn't dream.

Love, Always

Jacqueline Kennedy said that if we fail to raise our children well, it doesn't much matter what else we do in our lives, and there is great wisdom in her words. As a parent, you aren't given a report card at the end of the journey; you can only hope that you raised children of whom you can be proud.

Our good-hearted, loving children did grow up, move away, marry, and become parents themselves, and Don and I were delighted. In a recent conversation, an old friend said something that startled me. She has a lovely daughter who's raised two children and holds a top position at a company.

"Amy loves her children," she said. "This generation loves their children more than ours did."

"Do you mean they tell their children they love them more than we did?" I asked.

She said yes, but added that as a generation, we didn't love our children as deeply as the next generation does—and I found that troubling. My children are warm and fuzzy with their kids, and every other sentence, they tell them that they love them. I confess that Don and I never did that, and I did spend a lot of time working to help other people's children, for which I feel some guilt. I'm not sure I would have been a better mother if I hadn't worked, though, since my passion for helping others would have rumbled beneath the surface, making me difficult to live with.

Nevertheless, I wish I had said "I love you" more to my children as they were growing up, and for all the times that I didn't say it, let me say it now: "I love you, Dwight, Katie, and Pen—always have from the first instance I saw you, and always will."

Becoming a World Citizen

I had met a world-class traveler in Don, and we placed our feet on many countries of the globe, visiting the capitals of England, France, Italy, Greece, Germany, Spain, Brazil, and Hungary, as well as out-of-the-ordinary countries like Egypt, Honduras, and Vietnam. We traveled to five continents (missing only Australia and Antarctica), and these journeys were a way for me to learn more about global political, economic, and social issues.

A family trip to Honduras brought me face-to-face with some of the world's poorest people. Dwight joined the Peace Corps after graduating from Yale in 1981 and was sent to that country in an attempt to improve the lives of 180 men, women, and children in the small rural community of El Tablon, some eight hours by bus from Tegucigalpa, the capital city. One of his tasks was to help the residents plant vegetable gardens to vary their basic diet of rice, beans, and a little meat.

I was a bit concerned about this assignment since Dwight was reared primarily in New York City, and I had never seen him put his hands in the dirt, but he spoke excellent Spanish and communicated well with the villagers. He also had a warm personality, enjoyed people of all ages, and encouraged everyone to work cooperatively to solve problems. He especially liked teaching English at the region's first high school, which he traveled to by horse, much to the amusement of the village children.

I will never forget spending Christmas of 1982 with Don, Penny, and Dwight in El Tablon. The residents welcomed us by building the first latrine in the village on a hill overlooking a pretty but polluted stream. It was the only water source for the villagers, and many of them suffered from low-grade infections because of it. We lived among them in a community of 40 identical adobe huts, each whitewashed with a thatched roof. Don and I slept in our own hut on a small wooden table that prevented any movement, and Penny bunked with her "bro," as she called him, in his hut. Without any artificial light, we went to bed at sundown and awoke to the early morning cacophony of chickens, donkeys, cows, cats, and packs of hungry, mangy dogs that greeted the day.

I still remember so much about our trip, including the distant, taciturn men heading to the fields at daybreak to scratch out a meager living growing coffee, corn, and beans and chopping sugarcane. The frequently smiling women were missing nearly all of their front teeth due to repeat pregnancies that had drained their bodies of calcium. They were not downhearted though, and like mothers everywhere, they hoped for a better life for their children. "I shall never go to the United States, but perhaps one of my children will someday," one of them, Melba deMacias, told me. I've always hoped that some of the children—Maricela, Lorena, Maria, Elvin, and Tavo—went on to lead better, healthier lives than their parents, moving to the city to find jobs that better help them raise their families.

A year later, on Christmas Day 1983, I wrote an opinion piece, "Another

Christmas, Another World," that appeared in the New Jersey section of the *New York Times* which compared the simple Christmas I had spent in El Tablon with the lavish one I was about to experience in Princeton. I observed that:

> I felt I was closer [in El Tablon] than I had ever been in my life to the first Christmas morning in Bethlehem. I was among people with brown skin. I saw donkeys sleeping, heard oxen lowing. I caught a glimpse of a pregnant woman wearing a blue dress ... I was among the poorest people on earth. Yet, I was conscious of the sad irony of the situation: among the descendants of those for whom Jesus Christ was born—the poor and the meek of the earth—there was no sense of joyfulness.

I had come home from visiting Dwight with nothing but respect for Peace Corps volunteers. His future plans changed markedly after he served: he became a community organizer. His experiences in Honduras were reflected in what became his favorite expression: "Live simply, so others can simply live."

The trip that most excited Don was our three-week journey to Vietnam and Cambodia in February 1997 with our good neighbors Tom and Mary Lee Jamieson. Don wanted to return to Vietnam to see how it had fared since March 1954, when he covered the end of the French Indochina War. He had been present in Hanoi when three divisions of the People's Army of the Democratic Republic of Vietnam—or the "Communists," as Americans derisively called them—took control of the city as the remnants of the French army marched out of town. Don had left the city in a jeep that took him over the Pont Doumer Bridge to Haiphong, where he caught a plane to Saigon.

Our first stop was Hanoi and the Pont Doumer Bridge, where we recorded Don's return after 43 years. He turned his back to us and looked out at the bridge. Was he transported back to another time, when he was much younger and at the height of his career as a foreign correspondent? Was he thinking of the course that his life had taken since those days so long ago? He turned and faced Tom's camera and flashed his usual broad smile. Whatever his thoughts, he seemed satisfied at having closed the circle.

The trip helped me understand the dangers of Don's wartime experiences as a *Life* correspondent, which included identifying the body of his colleague, famed photographer Robert Capa, who was killed on assignment by a land mine. Don could have gone on that trip with him, possibly walking by his side, but he gave up his seat on the small plane to the *Time* correspondent. (Capa's body was flown back to Hanoi, where Don identified it at the military morgue and arranged the funeral service.) He always wondered what might have happened if he had been walking next to Capa.

Our trip's success was due partly to our superb guide, Tran Quoc Cong (or "Mr. Cong," as we respectfully called him), who decided to give each of us a nickname that best described our individual persona. He named Tom "the Scout," as he was never without a guidebook and studied the day's plans well in advance, and Mary Lee "the Scribe," because she always took notes to later prepare a superb account of our journey. The "Scout" and the "Scribe" were a well-matched pair. Mr. Cong insightfully designated Don "the Ambassador" because of his world travels as a journalist and his position in the Kennedy administration; Don did resemble a State Department official in many ways: tall, handsome, and always in command.

"What is it about me that makes you want to call me a nun?" I asked Mr. Cong after he announced his name for me.

"Dear Madame," he said, "because you want to give money to every single child who comes to you with his or her hand out."

He had a point: I found it hard especially in poor countries not to give a few pennies to the children clustered around us—children who saw with their own eyes the gulf that existed between them and the tourists in their countries. Of course, they were right: we had so much, and they so little, but I knew it didn't do much good to give a few pennies here and there. Mr. Cong had nailed me.

Our friendship with Cathie and Pitch Johnson over the years opened up a new pathway for our travels, and we attended many Olympic Games and world track-and-field championships with them. Cathie is my oldest friend, who I met in second grade at Brearley; my mother first brought us together by calling Cathie's nanny to set up a play date. We were also members of the class of 1951 at Vassar. Cathie and Pitch eventually settled in Palo Alto, where he became one of Silicon Valley's original brilliant and extraordinarily successful pioneers and they raised their four children.

Together we attended the summer Olympic Games—in Montreal, Los Angeles, and Barcelona—and four World Championship competitions—in Helsinki, Rome, Athens, and Paris. I admired the prowess of world-class athletes and loved listening and singing with the stadium crowd the national anthem of the gold medalist. We observed most nations competing peacefully with each other, and one could see the potential for these friendships to foster world peace. The athletes were proud, happy, and young—and I hoped they would become leaders in their countries and remember the harmony they had experienced together as international competitors. Sadly, the games now seem fraught with threats of terrorism and the need for added security for athletes and spectators.

Don and I traveled independently later in our lives; he often went to Eastern Europe to view the work of the Independent Journalism Foundation, a nonprofit he started with his friend Jim Greenfield that supported training for journalists in former Communist nations. I undertook trips that taught me about international issues, including the status of women in nations far different than the U.S.

My first such trip involved encouraging peaceful relationships between the U.S. and the Soviet Union, and the invitation had come from my son. In September 1988, I traveled to Central Asia, to the city of Tashkent in Uzbekistan, which was controlled by the Soviet Union. Dwight had invited me to participate in a sister-city partnership forged between Tashkent and Seattle, where he had been living since finishing his two-year service in the Peace Corps. His experience in Honduras had shaped his plan to try—in the words of Greek playwright Aeschylus—to "tame the savageness of man and make gentle the life of the world."

I thought it a novel idea to participate in finishing the last construction details and celebrating the completion of the world's first U.S.-U.S.S.R. Park of Peace and Friendship. I asked my friend Joyce Copleman, who lived in Lawrenceville, to join me, and we were soon on a plane for the first leg of our trip, from New York to Stockholm. It went smoothly, but we had to check our luggage again when we left for our next destination, Moscow. As we walked down a ramp in the Stockholm airport toward our plane, I noticed two signs: "Copenhagen" and "Moscow." The luggage attendant must have noticed the similarity of the names "Copleman" and "Copenhagen" when he saw Joyce's name on her bag, because he sent it on to Denmark.

We didn't realize the mistake until we arrived in Moscow late in the evening, several hours past our scheduled arrival. The situation only became worse the next day; our flight to Tashkent was scheduled for mid-morning, making it impossible for the Soviet national airline to retrieve Joyce's suitcase from Copenhagen and fly it to Moscow before our departure. We arrived at a giant Moscow airport, different from the one at which we had arrived the night before, only to find that our plane had been delayed until early evening. The woman who conveyed the news to us spoke only French, and I silently blessed all my French teachers when I convinced her to ask someone to fly the bag to Moscow before our plane took off that evening—and miracles of miracles, it arrived.

The flight to Tashkent took almost five hours, and Dwight had spent many hours asleep on the airport floor waiting for our plane's 3:30 a.m. arrival. The frustrations of our first day in the Soviet Union had caught up with me, and when I saw my dear son, I blurted out, "Dwight, this country does not need a peace park; it desperately needs computers," as I'd seen nothing but old typewriters and carbon paper while struggling to find Joyce's luggage. I soon calmed down and prepared to throw my heart into the peace-making adventure.

Seattle schoolchildren had made thousands of tiles to set into the wall encircling the park; previous groups had cemented the tiles into place. Our job was to clean off the excess grout from the tiles, and as I performed this rather dull task, I learned the meaning of the Russian word *mir*, which is "peace," since it appeared on many of the clever tiles. We had fun working with Dwight and his merry team in the brilliant sunshine and 100-degree heat. At the end of our ten days in Tashkent—after scrubbing tiles, spooning sand out of the "Pond of Life" fountain with teaspoons, working, laughing, crying, singing, and dancing with Uzbeks—Joyce and I agreed that international peace was possible!

I have to admit that I thought the park's fountain would never work without more sophisticated drainage equipment and few people would use the park, but I was wrong. I recently met a woman whose father served in the Tashkent Embassy, and she asked him about the peace park. "It is well attended, and everything is in good working order," he said. *Oh, you of little faith, why did you doubt?* I scolded myself. *Give peace a chance.*

In 2006, at 76, I joined a delegation of women from the Seven Sister colleges for a ten-day trip to the heart of the Middle East to forge connections between the colleges' American alumnae and prominent Jordanian women leaders. For company, I reached out to Mary Lee Jamieson, since I knew she needed a lift after her husband Tom lost a long, gallant struggle with esophageal cancer. She accepted my invitation, and together we joined 16 Americans and headed to Jordan to meet women leaders in government, education, business, media, and the arts.

In Amman, we talked with women leaders who owned small businesses and directed nonprofits aimed at improving women's and children's lives. The leaders discussed female genital mutilation and honor killings, and I learned that grounds for these killings included suspected adultery by a married woman or a clandestine relationship between young people not sanctioned by their parents. One speaker said that the problem of honor killings was overblown in the U.S., and there were no more than 20 per year in Jordan. One honor killing is one too many for me, but it is difficult to be a guest in a foreign country and debate a point as sensitive as this one.

Her Royal Highness Princess Wijdan Ali said that honor killings were introduced into Egypt in 1796 by Napoleon and were crimes "of passion, not

Islamic." She said that female genital mutilation is not Islamic either; rather, its roots are cultural, not religious. She added that the practice is more widespread in Africa than in the Middle East, prompting me to realize again that one has to be sensitive when talking about emotionally charged, cultural issues like these, particularly if one is American. A recent book, *however long the night* by Aimee Molloy, showed how women in Senegal and a few other West African countries took charge of ending female genital cutting in their villages in the last decades. The book confirmed a view I have come to witness and embrace: that lasting change *only* happens when it comes directly from the people most intimately involved with the problem rather than from outsiders who do not know the historical background, religion, or culture of those whose practices they want to change.

I learned that Jordan was concerned about child sexual abuse. We visited the Queen Rania Family and Child Center and observed small classes where a teacher used talk therapy to help children work through the abuse and violence they had suffered. We did not discuss the legal aspects of child sexual abuse prevention in Jordan, but any law in Jordan about this type of abuse would be difficult to pass.

On occasion, I would talk about my sexuality education work with one of the speakers, including Sa'eda Kilani, the head of the Arab Archives Institute who worked on press freedom and human rights. She said that the media did little reporting about honor crimes, and a journalist could not write about religion, sex, and politics. When I told her that I helped young people learn about sexual health, she looked me straight in the eye and said with sincerity, "That's beautiful." Moments like this, which validate my and others' sexuality education efforts, are rare and satisfying.

I haven't forgotten the lessons that I learned in Jordan: the importance of understanding the similarities between many problems affecting women and girls in different parts of the world; being open to new ideas about solving these problems; and developing a deeper grasp of cultural and religious customs. We didn't have time to make new friends on our journey, but I shall never forget the brave, intelligent Jordanian women who shared their ideas and hopes with us.

I came home with one lesson for my grandchildren: to learn all they can about the Middle East, since it will continue to play a role in their and their own children's lives. They might even consider studying Arabic, since the more we can converse with people in their own languages, the better we can understand each other. It is a sign of respect to learn another's language, and a foundation of peace is to show respect.

⁂

I care about causes the way bees are attracted to honey, and I continue to work as an activist and financially support organizations that work for reproductive rights and poverty-related issues. I also became an advocate for federal gun safety laws after the senseless killings of the Kennedy brothers and Martin Luther King, Jr., and my advocacy was only reinforced by the shootings of 20 little children and 6 adults at Sandy Hook Elementary School in Connecticut in December 2012, not to mention the countless other victims senselessly gunned down on our streets. Additionally, at Dwight's request, I have become more involved with climate change, which he feels is the number one issue facing humanity, and then, of course, there is the issue of peace.

My favorite form of advocacy is putting one foot in front of the other on a march, and I have participated in more than ten marches in the past two decades. A memorable one was the March for Women's Lives on April 25, 2004—which drew a reported 1.15 million people to Washington, D.C.—to protect and advance access to reproductive health care options, including abortion, birth control, and emergency contraception.

I love rising well before dawn to take a bus or train to Washington, D.C., for the marches, which always engender feelings of celebration and unity. Many people make homemade signs, and once when Dwight joined me at a March for Choice, he grabbed a piece of discarded cardboard and said, "Quick, Mom, give me your lipstick." I fished it out of my bag, and he scrawled, "East Germans for Choice," which made me laugh, since the Berlin Wall had come down just days earlier. He attracted approving smiles and confused looks as he held it high over his head, and I was happy to sacrifice my lipstick for the cause.

Every march offered a panoply of speakers who inspired us to work hard for the cause. At one, I looked down at the feet of my friend Barbara Boggs Sigmund, the marvelous first woman mayor of Princeton whose life was cut short at 51 by cancer, and was dumbfounded to see her marching in high heels. *Barbara's giving her all for democracy—right down to her heels*, I thought. So were we all.

The last march I attended was the 50th anniversary of Dr. Martin Luther King's monumental "I Have a Dream" speech, delivered during the March on Washington in 1963. It took place on August 24, 2013, and I cannot remember a prettier day in the Capitol. "Make some noise," implored Congressman John Lewis, who, as head of the Student Nonviolent Coordinating Committee, uttered the same words at the original march 50 years earlier. He was one of the civil rights marchers who were badly beaten when they attempted to cross the Edmund Pettus Bridge in Selma, Alabama, on Bloody Sunday, March 7, 1965. "Make some noise," he roared again. He meant that each of us in that huge crowd should make noise for the advancement of civil rights—not only at the rally, but when we returned home.

In May 2013, Dwight, my grandson Eli, and I visited some significant sites in the civil rights movement. Eli had just finished his freshman year at Rice University, and we met in Montgomery, Alabama, with the book *Weary Feet, Rested Souls: A Guided History of the Civil Rights Movement* as our historical guide and hotel reservations at different stops for the next week. There are almost too many highlights to mention: touching the pulpit in the Dexter Avenue Baptist Church in Montgomery, where Dr. King began his leadership of the movement; seeing the place where Rosa Parks boarded the bus, sat down in the section reserved for whites only, and refused to give up her seat; crossing the Edmund Pettus Bridge, where activists were tear-gassed and clubbed on Bloody Sunday; visiting the Sixteenth Street Baptist Church in Birmingham, where in 1963 four little girls attending Sunday school were killed by a bomb.

We stood on the balcony of the Lorraine Motel in Memphis, the site of Dr. King's assassination, looking toward the spot where James Earl Ray aimed his gun and shot him with a single bullet. We had lunch in Nashville with my friend John Seigenthaler, Bobby Kennedy's special assistant at the U.S. Department of Justice, who had been knocked unconscious while trying to aid two Freedom Riders during an attack at the Montgomery Greyhound Bus Station.

Travel—whether in my country or a foreign land, both with Don and, to my surprise, without him, or with my children, grandchildren, and friends—has provided worthwhile lessons for me. My travels have helped me to see myself as more of a world citizen now. The globe has shrunk immeasurably in my lifetime, and I want to set a good example for my grandchildren by showing them how much I care about it. With Don unable to tell our grandchildren about the importance of travel and the international side of life, I'm doing my best to keep abreast of world events and inspire in them the desire to immerse themselves in the world, which belongs to its citizens.

A Creative Marriage

Don published his memoir in 2004, and when copies of the book with its marvelous smiling cover photo of him as a young foreign correspondent arrived on our doorstep, we had a real cause for celebration: Don was the first author on both sides of the family and had spent two years writing his memoir, finishing it when he was 77.

Don's family history of Alzheimer's—from which his grandmother, mother, and sister suffered—may have prompted the intensity with which he undertook the memoir. He kept impressive notes for each chapter and drew on countless documents: sweet letters he wrote in his youth to his mother, older brother, and other family members; stories he wrote for *Life* magazine while covering the wars in Korea and Indochina; and letters he wrote to me during our months apart after our memorable "pre-honeymoon" in Asia. Don used his material wisely and gracefully.

To whom would Don dedicate his memoir? This may seem trivial in retrospect, but it was vitally important to me at the time. It may seem unlikely that I didn't feel secure enough in his love after 47 years of marriage to take it for granted that he would dedicate the book he cared so much about writing to me. Surprisingly, we didn't discuss the topic over dinner; I didn't even raise the subject in an offhand or jocular manner, and neither did he. We might have encountered a rough patch in our marriage as he was writing the book, and I steered away from discussing the subject, fearful that he had already made up his mind to dedicate the book to someone other than me. I was nervous as the time drew closer to its arrival. Since the book centered on his professional life, I thought that Don might logically choose someone he had worked with closely or a mentor from his years at *Life* or Time Inc. I thought he might dedicate the book to his four loyal golfing buddies, who brought so much pleasure into his life through endless rounds of golf. Other than one chapter, "Susan," in which he wrote about our courtship and wedding, Don did not write much about our marriage and family life in the memoir. He also made it clear that he had written it for our three children and five grandchildren.

Although I sensed that I was important in Don's life, he was not prone to telling me how much I meant to him and how much he counted on me to make his life move smoothly. Upon returning from his first meeting after he was appointed to the Vassar Board of Trustees, he exclaimed, "Was I ever surrounded by smart women!"—referring to his fellow board members who were Vassar alumnae. Stung a little by his comment, I wished he had added, "I live with one, so why should I be surprised."

During the early part of our life together in the late fifties and early sixties, men were expected to make all the decisions and not count on their wives for advice. Since Don and I had our differences on a range of issues, I wasn't sure that when he added up all my good and bad points, he would honor me with his book dedication.

I won the lottery. I was elated after Don handed me the first book he removed from the box, and I read: "To Susan and 46 years of a creative marriage."

I gave him a hug, more from relief than anything else; when the initial relief wore off, I thought, *a creative marriage? What in the world does that really mean?* I chided myself for being greedy and wanting more effusive praise from Don for my role in his life. I longed for him to have written some trite words like "to the love of my life," but he didn't use clichés. Every so often, though, I yearned for him to sweep me into his arms and tell me what a wonderful woman I was, how much he loved me, and how he couldn't live without me. One has to give as well as get to inspire such accolades, though, and I don't know how often I told Don how much I loved him (never enough would probably be the verdict).

After decades of marriage, I was insecure about the depth of Don's feelings for me, as he was possibly about mine. Today many couples say "I love you" with abandon, which is something my generation rarely, if ever, did. I believe constant repetition trivializes the phrase. We said it to each other more frequently in the last years of his life, which felt satisfying to me and I hope to him—if he was able to understand its meaning as Alzheimer's pulled down the shades.

Don made up for the paucity of words in his dedication with notes he wrote to me on two copies of the memoir that he gave to me. In one note, he used the word I so wanted to read, "love," and thanked me for "the love and the support you've always given me through the years." In his second tender note, he told me that his life had been enriched by me more than by any other person, and he loved and thanked me from the bottom of his heart. He added that I had always helped him make decisions about career and family, and that I was "always right."

I winced at the words "always right," because no one should be right all of the time; I'm sure there were plenty of times when my advice was simply wrong and Don rejected it, which is as it should be in a marriage of equals. Throughout my life, I've been prone to state my opinions in an authoritative way, which often crowds out other people's viewpoints. After all, my mother uttered her opinions fearlessly and emphatically, and although she often made me uncomfortable, I might have picked up some of her habits without realizing it. It wasn't until much later that I tried to temper how I made my points in conversation. My experience in sexuality education workshops and lessons I learned from the renowned sex educator Peggy Brick taught me to precede any opinion with the words "I think" or "I feel," because people respond much better when you do. As usual, one often learns about such annoying aspects of one's own behavior later rather than earlier in life.

Our marriage was indeed a long and loving one, free of any violence and abuse, which is more common than one thinks. Don was an easy man to live with: even-tempered and able to smooth out my varying moods. But couples change as the years go by, and Don once took me aback when he said, "You've changed." It was after we had left Washington, where I had been a traditional wife focused completely on being the perfect helpmate to my husband. I began to shift out of this role after we moved to New York and Princeton, when I started working on issues that interested me. I hadn't explained to Don why I was changing, though, and he probably felt that I was no longer attentive to him and his needs. He may even have thought I no longer loved him (we didn't discuss it enough), and I so wish we had talked about this and much, much more. But who has time in the daily onrush of life?

I was puzzled when Don told me I had changed, because I thought that change was a good thing, but he found it hard to suddenly be married to a woman with not one but several missions. At a certain point in our marriage, when we were living in Princeton, I decided that we should see a marriage counselor, and he agreed. I found a woman who ran a practice out of her home, and after three or four sessions of listening to our individual complaints about our relationship, including my feeling that it was sputtering a bit, she offered us some suggestions. She told me to allow Don to criticize me without taking the bait and responding, and she suggested that Don meet with her privately to work through some of his concerns about me.

"I'm not going back to her," Don said as we walked toward the car after one of our sessions. "I don't like her and her ideas, and if we want further counseling, we should find a male counselor."

He thought it was unfair that I had taken him to a female counselor, and he believed she favored me. Don was rarely that emphatic, and I knew I was on the wrong end of a losing battle—but we had already invested quite a few hours in the sessions, and I didn't want to repeat the process with a male, knowing that Don would feel he now had the upper hand. A friend had once shocked me by saying, "Don is a male chauvinist, don't you realize that?" after I had told her about some of his behavior. She did me a favor, though, and knowing that others saw him in this light made me better able to deal with his criticisms of me.

Our marriage counseling sessions came to an end, and I often wondered if our relationship would have improved had I been more flexible, found a male counselor, and continued our sessions. I've learned in life that talking about a difficult subject almost always defuses the pent-up emotions that surround it, which is why I urge parents to talk more often and openly with their children about sex, and why I think sex education programs are essential for young people who can't have these conversations with their parents.

Don and I walked away from couples counseling and lost our chance to take stock of our marriage, understand the reasons for its rough patches, and figure out how to love each other with a deeper understanding of who we were as people as we aged and, yes, changed.

I came away with one observation from the counselor that brought me comfort. She said that a marriage works best when two people are independent and pursue their own interests. She made me realize that being an independent woman was good for my marriage, and that I didn't have to squeeze back into the skin I had shed so long ago when I was the Washington wife.

When I look at the term "creative marriage" from the distance of years since Don's death, I see that it describes a union that gave us three loving children in whom we are inordinately proud, and the freedom to do what each of us wanted to do at different times over the years. The common bond was our desire to be of service to others and to ideas bigger than ourselves: Don through his service in the Kennedy administration, and I through my work in sexuality education and other health issues. The link of public service was bigger than both of us. It also protected us from the small, painful differences we experienced in our long marriage, which are now inconsequential. When I remember our years together, I have nothing but happy thoughts; the bumps have been smoothed away.

After we were married, the romantic letters became messages in greeting cards delivered unfailingly on holidays, birthdays, and anniversaries during our 54 years of marriage.

I have kept one Valentine among the hundreds of cards Don sent, because it brings back cherished memories. The front features a big red heart with these words in glitter: "Sex on the beach would be a nice way to celebrate Valentine's Day." Inside, an aging seagull with its beak open and a hard-shelled crab with huge eyeballs popping out of its head are staring at two pairs of flip-flops. Don wrote:

Susan,

In a few days we will be on the beach. You are a wonderful wife to put up with my crotchets. I look forward to our vacation with children and grandchildren, but No Cooking!!!

xoxox Don

A dotted line with a tiny pair of scissors at one end runs the length of the foldout. The words "Cut here. Place on bed" are printed next to it, along with pictures of a scallop shell, snail, and orange starfish to allude to the beach setting. I wonder if the card sparked in Don the same memories of our time on the beach in Hong Kong as it did in me: the playful fun we had swimming, I in my all-time favorite purple bathing suit, in the crystal clear waters of Repulse Bay. I remember the whitest of white sand on the beach that stretched sinuously along the island for miles, the clear azure-blue water, and how I had eyes only for Don.

In these cards, Don sometimes complimented my work, which made me particularly happy because I never knew if he was aware of what I did at Rutgers or in my home office over the garage. On my 72nd birthday card, he wrote:

> You have helped so many young women and men while catching bronchitis in your inadequate and tattered winter coat. So for your 72nd I am giving you a true winter coat that is both warm and chic. You can't say "no" anymore.

I certainly hope I had the good sense to accept his gift without protest. From a distance, I also see that Don's kind expressions of love should have been more than enough for me.

I have kept Don's final anniversary card, which he sent as the sticky plaques of Alzheimer's continued to obfuscate his thinking. The card shows the arms of two old folks like us: the man's arm is clad in a gray sweater, and the woman's arm in a pale-pink one. The man and woman sit in wooden chairs looking at the sunset with their hands intertwined. "I'm never letting go. Happy Anniversary," the text reads, and Don wrote in easy-to-read print:

> Susan–
>
> We have had our rocky times, but this card is correct. I'm never letting go because, underneath all—I love you.
>
> xoxox Don

I'm never letting go either.

Don, The Last Eight Years

As Don grew older, we often asked him if he was going to write a sequel to *The First 78 Years* about his life since its publication. He would smile back at us, but we could tell he was satisfied with the effort he had made writing the book and didn't crave doing a sequel. Don lived eight years longer, and the task has now fallen to me. I hope I can do justice to him and those years, with both their pleasures and their grief.

Our late-June birthday celebrations for Don continued unabated in his final years as we celebrated his 80th and 85th birthdays. His 86th, on June 27, 2011, would be his last, and it was a low-key celebration because of his Alzheimer's disease. None of us wanted to put him in an embarrassing situation where he might fumble with the names of people he knew well or make comments that were irrelevant or off the subject. He had his dignity, and we wanted him to keep it.

It was a remarkably different celebration than the one we hosted for his 70th birthday in 1995, which we held in our garden beneath a large white tent. The summer before the party, when we were on South Beach in Chilmark on the Vineyard, I had taken one of my all-time favorite pictures of Don. He is staring straight into the camera as he emerges soaking wet and smiling from the Atlantic Ocean, which he had loved since boyhood. He looks incredibly handsome, and his stomach as flat and taut as it was when I first met him 40 years earlier.

For the celebration, I had the photograph enlarged, slipped into a white mat, and set on an easel inside the front door. I placed pens and a sign nearby urging guests to write a note to Don on the mat. Nearly 50 friends signed it before proceeding into the garden, which was ablaze with lanterns buried in the bushes. The theme of many notes was that Don was the sexiest 70-year-old anyone had ever seen.

"Met you when you were almost 30—love you still, now that you're 70," I wrote. It still warms my heart to see Don so happy in the picture, because making him happy was important to me, and here he is, looking straight at me saying, "Don't worry, all is well."

We had a family celebration for Don's 80th birthday in June 2005, and I decided on a surprise weekend celebration at the Mohonk Mountain House, a Victorian castle resort in the Hudson Valley near New Paltz, New York. In my heart, I knew it wasn't Don's taste; he would have preferred a castle more like the one in *Downton Abbey* than a Victorian castle with its curlicues. He deserved the Ritz in Paris or a privately owned, remote island in the Caribbean.

I lied to him about our destination that weekend, telling him only that we were heading up the Hudson. I'm sure he thought we were going to Westchester Airport to prepare for a trip on a private jet—one that he hoped would carry us somewhere over the rainbow. It didn't happen, but he was a good sport from the moment we drove into the Mohonk driveway and he saw his grandchildren waiting at the gate, jumping for joy at his arrival. He participated in all the fun and games we had planned, including wearing a special T-shirt that I had designed. There was a different one for each of us: Don's tee showed his book cover, mine featured the two us smiling broadly in the limo minutes after we were married, and the children's and grandchildren's shirts each reflected a different aspect of his long, happy life. We had our picture taken as a group wearing our shirts, and it is a treasure.

We secured a private dining room for Don's actual birthday party, which was replete with toasts and speeches, and I wrote him a sonnet for the occasion. I had never written one to him before, and now of course I wish I had written him many. My one and only sonnet focused more on his professional accomplishments than on our relationship; I now wish I had told him more often in verse throughout our daily lives how deeply I loved and adored him.

To Don on His 80th Birthday
June 27, 2005

This day we mark, some 80 years ago,
The Gods of War were present at your birth,
They gave you special skills to help you grow
Into a journalist who toured the earth.
Reporting from the hot spots on the globe,
Two wars you covered filing stories fast,
The reasons for the conflicts yours to probe,
The future's news as well as histories past.
A clarion call came from the New Frontier,
A brave young leader summoned you to serve,
Our nation's voice and values to make clear,
The missile crisis showed the world our nerve.

And on this birthday night, we note your fame,
We honor you with love and with acclaim.

—*from Susan, with all my love*

For Don's 85th birthday on June 27, 2010, we celebrated with a party for our family and good friends in our condominium in Constitution Hill, to which we had moved in 2006 after selling our beloved house on Province Line Road. All the grandchildren wore white T-shirts emblazoned with the numeral 85 in bright blue (the colors of his alma mater, Yale). His grandson Sam presented him with a T-shirt that read, "Best Grandpa Ever!" and included the names of all five grandchildren on the back; Don seemed delighted by it. It was a happy occasion, although as we watched him tire easily and take longer naps we knew that the leaves were beginning to fall.

I framed as a memento of the day a picture of Don with Harry, Sam, Olivia, and Reed in their shirts and placed it on my living-room table. Kate and Penny didn't frame the copy that I sent to each of them, and when I asked Kate why, she said, "Dad has such a vacant look in his eyes." When I look at it, I can understand her observation, but I like it because the grandchildren are all smiling as they surround him.

Living with Don protected me from seeing the gradual physical changes in him that the children noticed when they came for visits, often months apart. They could see his problems with movement when we went for walks around Constitution Hill. Don always put on the best face possible in any situation, and I don't know if it was intentional or not, but he looked happy when he was with us. I believe he didn't want to burden us with his problems, which was gracious of him. He was a gentleman for as long as I knew him and treated his caregivers with the utmost kindness and respect.

As I observed Don, I wondered what it felt like to struggle every day with Alzheimer's. When he went to bed at night, did he think he would wake up the next morning and everything would be all right again with his mind? *That's much too logical,* I'd think. *Alzheimer's is the opposite of logical. You can't possibly know what he's thinking and feeling.* I will never know unless I, too, suffer from dementia, but even then, I don't think I could ever understand how anyone else feels in its grip.

Don was healthy throughout his life except for cardiac ventricular fibrillation in his late sixties, which was cured by a pacemaker, and prostate cancer, which was cured by radiation treatments. He enjoyed good health until his last years, when Alzheimer's invaded. He seemed so well, except for his mental restrictions, that our lives appeared almost normal. The worst part was when we decided that he shouldn't drive anymore and took away his keys. In our mobile society, a driving restriction is tantamount to a death sentence, and I hated every moment of the process of having his license revoked. It was hard for me to be the disciplinarian and say "no" to Don; nevertheless, I probably came off as too tough with him.

As the signs of Alzheimer's became more evident in him, I decided that we needed to move to a much smaller home. We were lucky that our good friend Anne Martindell, the former U.S. ambassador to New Zealand appointed by President Jimmy Carter, was about to put her condominium in Constitution Hill up for sale only two miles from our beloved home on Province Line Road. She invited me to see it a couple of times and even spend a night to see how I liked the nighttime free from traffic sounds. After a quick consultation with Don, we made an offer, Anne accepted it, and we moved.

I was determined for Don to see family members and close friends before he couldn't recall their names or connections to him. In May 2010, we had a reunion of his nieces and nephews—the children of his deceased brother, Jack Wilson, and his sister, Jane Wilson Rauch and their spouses.

I wanted to make sure that Don's side of the family felt that they were recognized as a significant part of his life and had a chance to see him when he still possessed some of his powers and could converse intelligibly with them. In the end, I probably derived more satisfaction from this family visit than Don did, because I wanted to give them the catharsis of farewell. I can only hope he was glad to see them, but I shall never know what the visit meant to him.

Don suffered from Alzheimer's for five years but remained the biggest presence in our lives until the very end, which was a gift to us all. I was determined that he not spend his final months in a hospital or nursing home, and I wanted to surround him with as much warmth and love as possible. His caregivers and friends deserve the lion's share of the credit for making his life palatable and happy.

Thanks to Bill Burks, a fine gentleman and surgeon who practiced for many years in Princeton, we were able to find outstanding caregivers for Don during the last six months of his life. Bill helped us find Monica Parsons, who led us to her son-in-law and model caregiver, Ken Talbert; he had the gentlest of touches and could always get a laugh out of Don. Ken led us to Karen Blades, a hip, fun-loving woman who did the late-afternoon shift and always evoked a smile from Don. Our housekeeper, Primina Evans, seemed to be everywhere—anticipating our needs, making nourishing food, and talking to Don with politeness and understanding, as if life were completely normal.

Don's golf friends Bill Augustine, Andy Anderson, Steve Paneyko, and Peter Lawson-Johnston—who should wear shirts with "L" for loyalty writ large—entertained Don for lunch at least once a week at the Bedens Brook Club. When golfing became impossible for Don, they drove him around the golf course in the cart, laughing all the way. Their kindnesses made it easier for me to live an almost-normal life doing errands, attending meetings, and even writing a blog about sexuality and public life.

I used to love to come home from my meetings, because Don would get up from his chair in the library, where he was watching TV, throw open his arms, and say with his big grin, "I love you." I always crossed the room so he could enfold me in an embrace. Physical contact can fill the void in a way that words, no matter how sweet, cannot, and in the years since his death, I have missed these wordless moments with his arms around me almost more than anything else.

When people offer condolences about Don's death, I find myself thanking them and saying, "Don died at 86. He struggled with the effects of Alzheimer's for five years, and now he is free from it. He had a happy and productive life and accomplished much …" I might amplify that and add, "… in which I shared."

The last summer of Don's illness, I took a two-week vacation on the Vineyard. Our three children divided up the time, tending to his needs and giving him his or her undivided attention. It was their final gift to him, and I know that being by his side helped them to accept his death when it happened, on November 29, 2011.

Five days before his death, we had a final Thanksgiving celebration as a family at our home; all 13 members of our immediate family gathered together around the dining-room table on November 24. Don sat at the head of the table, the center of our celebration (although I didn't have an inkling that it might be our last meal together). In lieu of a more formal blessing with religious overtones, which Don would not have appreciated, I had asked each family member to write why he or she was thankful for him and to read aloud each contribution to what I called, "Gratitudes." Before the meal started, we read what we had written as a form of grace, one at a time, standing alone while looking directly at Don. He responded to many of our comments with wit and insight. I was the last to read my Gratitude, and when I finished, Don looked at all of us and said, "My soul is rested."

Those words were printed in large letters on the spine of a book on the shelf maybe 15 feet from the table, but they had caught Don's eye and he was able to repeat them to us in a burst of mental energy. They couldn't have been a more perfect expression of what he was feeling; they signified his appreciation for the love and thankfulness that each of us had expressed to him. His words brought a measure of comfort to us when he suffered a serious stroke two days later and lost his power of speech. That Thanksgiving dinner was our final, private celebration, and we had communicated our love and appreciation to him as wife, children, and grandchildren, and he to us as husband, father, and grandfather.

I was blessed to share Don's final moments with him. He died quietly and peacefully a little after eight o'clock on the morning of November 29. For the last hour of his life, I was able to hold him in my arms as his breath became ever fainter. I arose to open the curtains on a rainy morning, and when I came back to his side, his breathing had stopped. He looked serene and completely at peace, as if death had finally found him and carried him to a more perfect place.

Some months later, I read a book in which after a woman died, one of her adult children opened the window in the room to allow her soul to fly away. I rather liked this idea, but I would not have done this for Don, as he would not have liked it. He believed that life ended with death; he was always the pragmatic journalist and clear-eyed realist who I married and admired throughout his life; I would not have wanted to dishonor his true nature.

Our family and I could not have asked for a more perfect ending for the man we had loved so much for so long. Don was 86 years old and set a new record of longevity in his immediate Wilson family. He had no fear of dying, which I believe sprung from his years covering wars and seeing many people die in them. He knew he had led an interesting life full of accomplishments and couldn't have asked for anything more. He had said it best himself: "My soul is rested."

Don's service of remembrance was held on a spring-like Saturday, January 28, 2012. Almost 600 people—possibly more—from as far away as Florida and as close as Princeton filled the Lawrenceville Presbyterian Church to say their final goodbyes to him. The white church stands on the village's main street and was founded by settlers in the seventeenth century. Revolutionary war heroes and a signer of the Declaration of Independence had come through the church's doors over the centuries. Although Don did not practice any religion and had never been inside the church, he certainly would have appreciated its history, because it was one of his greatest interests.

I designed the service as closely as I could to what Don's wishes might have been, since we had not had many conversations about our wishes for death and burial. I knew Don would have wanted me to highlight his service to the country as part of the Kennedy administration, as he considered these years to be the most important and gratifying ones of his life. On the program's cover, beneath Don's photograph and the dates of his life—June 27, 1925, to November 29, 2011—I placed the famous words from John F. Kennedy's inaugural address: "And so, my fellow Americans, ask not what your country can do for you; ask what you can do for your country."

I also included in the program a description of the Donald M. Wilson Fellowship, which funds a position at the Robert F. Kennedy Center for Justice and Human Rights enabling a recent graduate student to become more knowledgeable about its work worldwide in the struggle for social justice and human rights. It is our family's lasting legacy in Don's honor. Wade McMullen, the first Donald M. Wilson Fellow, attended the service and talked with many of Don's family members and friends.

We sang his favorite hymns—"America the Beautiful," "Amazing Grace," and "Battle Hymn of the Republic"—using the words printed in the elegant program, which was designed by Lara Andrea Taber. Lara is the daughter of George and Jean Taber, who together with Don co-founded the successful statewide newspaper *NJBiz* and ran it for many years. Deerfield Academy's "Evensong," beloved by graduates like Don, was played during the service's interlude. I tried to be sensitive to the different religions of our friends in my choice of prayers, which included, "A Prayer from Yom Kippur," "The Lord's Prayer," and "The Prayer of Saint Francis."

Three people spoke about Don's accomplishments at different stages of his life: Jim Greenfield reminisced about their time together in Tokyo as correspondents for *Time* and *Life*; Kathleen Kennedy Townsend, the eldest daughter of Bobby and Ethel, recalled his years in the Kennedy administration; and George Taber spoke about *NJBiz*. Their recollections were pitch perfect and included personal, delightful tidbits. Jim shared a story about the time that Don insisted on buying an electric blanket to counter the freezing temperatures in Tokyo without realizing that the city government turned the electricity off every night. And Kathleen brought down the house when she said that her mother always thought Don was "hot." (I was glad I didn't know about that until then!)

We had decided as a family to share with everyone at the service the "Gratitudes" we had spoken to Don at Thanksgiving. I had the pleasure of sitting in the front pew and hearing Dwight, Deb, Eli, Penny, Richard, Olivia, Reed, Kate, David, Harry, and Sam share the thoughtful, kind, funny, and endearing words each had written for him. I couldn't have been prouder of the two generations of family that Don and I had created and raised together. He would have glowed with pride to hear his children and grandchildren read their words, and I finally understood what he meant when he called ours a "creative" marriage.

After they had finished and returned to their seats, I climbed the stairs to the lower platform and read my "Gratitude." I was the last to speak on Thanksgiving when Don was still alive and the last to thank him at this final celebration of his life. I ended with the following words: "I am thankful most of all for hearing you say 'I love you,' every single morning when I wake you up and pull back the curtains on another day with you."

After I finished, the pastor read the final blessing, a Jane Kenyon poem, "Let Evening Come," which brings comfort to me every time I read it. The audience participated by saying "Let evening come" after each stanza. You can say those words now after this last verse:

> *Let it come, as it will, and don't*
> *be afraid. God does not leave us*
> *comfortless, so, let evening come.*

We held a reception in the church's Fellowship Center afterward and a much smaller dinner for family and close friends in the charming upstairs room of the D&R Greenway headquarters a couple of miles down the hill from our home. At dinner, we served excellent wine and other alcoholic beverages, which Don would have insisted upon, and both events brimmed with happiness about his full and complete life. The dinner was a joyful affair—no sad faces, but friends rising to their feet to recollect story after story about his accomplishments, generosity, and good humor. Michael Maruca, the third of the five Maruca children, regaled the guests with a description of living next to us on Province Line Road. (He did such a fine job that some of the guests who didn't know him thought I had hired a professional comedian.) A perceptive writer, he told his audience:

> Let's be clear here: going to the Wilsons' was a bit like going to summer camp, only it was all year round. The front green field was a veritable paradise. There was a pool and later a tennis court. There was the basketball hoop in the driveway and a beautiful back lawn. At times there was badminton and croquet. Inside and down the stairs past the boiler there was foosball and Ping-Pong. On the first floor past the dining room and to the right was the red-carpeted den with a big color television. There was pretty much all you could want and then some…
>
> Thank you, Don.

By the end of the evening, we felt we had done Don proud, and I suspect he felt the same way about us.

I enjoyed the entire day and didn't feel sad. We had honored Don to the best of our abilities, and I knew he would have felt we did a good job. He would have especially loved the dinner, because there was so much laughter and so much good wine. I was glad that he had died before me, so I could honor him and show him how deeply I cared for him at the end of his life and our 54-year-old creative—and loving—marriage.

God did not leave me comfortless.

Alone Together

A quilt made of T-shirts from key events in my life, including some of the races I've run, lies folded across the end of my bed. I have turned it back so only the first line of shirts is visible: a vivid ribbon of color softened by a blue-gray, polka-dot border. Not even a one-of-a-kind quilt can begin to describe the fullness of a person's life, but it can testify to some parts that make up the whole.

The idea for the quilt came from a fellow runner who had sewed a quilt for her husband from the T-shirts he had acquired at races. A picture of it appeared in my local paper, and I thought, *I have two plastic bags full of T-shirts, and I'm going to find someone who can turn them into a quilt for me.*

I've always been drawn to handmade objects and so-called "primitive" crafts, like paintings by the renowned folk artist Grandma Moses. The time had come for me to use those T-shirts creatively or throw them away.

I hired Sandy Merritt, a gifted quilter with the local Pennington Quilt Works store, to create the quilt, and when she came to my house one afternoon, I shared the history behind the shirts. She selected the ones she wanted to include and e-mailed me her design a few weeks later. The quilt's center features the shirt I wore when I ran the New York City Marathon. Its top row, which I see when I fold it back, contains six other shirts: an official one from Hillary Clinton's presidential campaign, one commemorating the 25th Chilmark Road Race (emblazoned with the words, "Who Says Women Can't Run the World?"), one from a 6.2-mile mini-marathon in New York City, the first *Sex, Etc.* shirt, a gray shirt with bright pink letters from Vassar College and a shirt made from a photo of Don and me in the limo on our wedding day, with broad smiles on our faces.

Life without Don

In the years since Don died, people have often asked the question: "How are you doing?" They want to know how I'm making my life work without him. As Don's Alzheimer's worsened and obstructed his fine mental powers, I had a dress rehearsal for life without him, so the transition wasn't as difficult as it might have been if I'd lost him suddenly. Writing this memoir has been a gift, as it has helped me relive the best moments of my fortunate life. The daily exercise of researching, writing, and rewriting has provided me a true compass and prevented me from feeling sad or sorry for myself. In the coming months, I will have to revisit the question of how I am doing, without the discipline, satisfaction, and warm coat of memories that writing has assured me.

One major decision I made was to share my home with relative strangers who would, in time, become friends. In the summer of 2012, I met Luke and Aubrey Yarbrough through my good friends Steffi and Bob Harris; the Yarbroughs had moved onto their organic farm in Hopewell for six weeks in the summer while the latter vacationed in Maine. At summer's end, they needed a short-term home, since Luke, who had recently received his Ph.D. in Near Eastern Studies from Princeton, wished to complete a three-month fellowship in Pennsylvania before starting a teaching position at Saint Louis University. I didn't hesitate to welcome them to 40 Constitution Hill.

Having people live with me was refreshing and a tonic, and Luke and Aubrey made my life easier in many ways. Luke was always eager to lend me a hand should I need to change the proverbial light bulb, and Aubrey, a sous chef, was always willing to share the delicious food she prepared. One of her favorite dishes was the famous crème brûlée, which only the best chefs can pull off (she never failed to do it perfectly). She seemed pleased to bake the custard in a set of white-and-gold porcelain ramekins that I had received as a wedding gift, and when before Christmas the time came for her and Luke to leave and drive to Missouri, I wrapped the ramekins and told them not to open the gift until after the clock struck twelve on Christmas Eve. They kept their promise, and Aubrey was surprised to discover that the little golden dishes had made the trip across the U.S. with her.

It didn't take me long to find another housemate: at a dinner party a few days after they left, a woman told me about the U.S. Rowing program's need for host families. She must have sensed my longing for company and relayed my interest to the program's director, because she called the next day to tell me about a rower in need of a host family. Emily Walsh was 24 and training for the 2016 U.S. Olympics in Rio de Janeiro. She moved in with me in January 2013 and departed eleven months later, and it was a pleasure to support her in her grueling effort to make the team. When she brought friends and fellow rowers to the house for impromptu parties, I felt as if a group of Amazons and goddesses had taken over the premises! Although they made me feel physically diminutive, I basked in the glow of their athleticism and determination to "go for the gold." On Halloween, Emily carved a pumpkin in the shape of a large "W": for "Wilson, Walsh, and Welcome," she said. After she returned to Pittsburgh to pursue goals beyond rowing, Kendall Schmidt from Milwaukee, WI, became my rower-in-residence, and I her "host Mom." She is a candidate for the position of coxswain in the 8+ boat for Rio and a delight to host in my home.

The first spring after Don's death, I went to Israel with my friend Isabella, members of her family, and our friend Barbara Coe to meet her eldest son, Cason, who was on a gap year between prep school and college. For three weeks, we visited Israel and Petra, an ancient historical site and archaeologically rich desert city in southern Jordan. The 19th-century poet John Burgon called Petra "a rose-red city half as old as time," because of the hue of its stone cliffs.

Climbing Masada, an ancient fortification near the Dead Sea atop a rock plateau with 1,300-foot-high cliffs, was almost as exciting as standing in the Garden of Gethsemane, in Jerusalem, or sailing on the Sea of Galilee, where Jesus is said to have walked on water. Young people climb Masada with relative ease, but most sensible people my age take a gondola over the rock face to the top. Isabella grabbed my hand at the base and said, "Come on, we're going to climb this together"—and we did. She carefully helped me as the route became steeper and narrower, and I absorbed her confidence that at 82 I was capable of climbing Masada. She stopped at certain points so we could drink water and I could look gingerly over my shoulder at the impressive view of the Dead Sea below.

I understood what climbers mean when they say they get a second wind. It seemed easier as Isabella and I climbed the stairs and approached the top, but I felt a fleeting sense of disbelief as we walked across the mesa's tabletop and I saw, once again, how far we had climbed. For the reverse trip, I decided to join Isabella's mother, her niece, and Barbara on the gondola; Isabella was free to climb down by herself. She skipped off, and I stepped onto the gondola after one last look at the shimmering sea and white sands of the surrounding desert, a world in miniature.

Ripples of Hope

Perpetual students like me benefit from living in a university town with its town-gown alliance, offering chances to learn from some of the country's most extraordinary professors. (My mother predicted this advantage years ago when she urged Don and me to settle here.) The university has an arrangement with the Princeton community that enables lay folk to audit a few courses each semester. Don tried to audit some courses, but I can see from the scant notes that he took, which pain me to look at, that it was hard for him to follow the lectures, and he couldn't tell me what he had learned.

So far, so good for me. Last semester I audited "Politics in Africa," a demanding, mid-level course on the history, economics, and politics of the continent. I wanted to learn more about Africa after joining the board of directors of the Fistula Foundation. This San Jose-based nonprofit works in the poorest parts of Africa and South Asia to provide lifesaving surgeries to repair obstetric fistulas, internal injuries that many teenage girls and women suffer during prolonged labor in childbirth. Its mission connects the issues I'm most passionate about: social justice for women and girls' reproductive health and the consequences of living and growing up in poverty.

Every Monday afternoon, I play the recorder with my friends Jeré and Ruth at Jeré's home in Princeton. Dorothy used to be part of the group we facetiously called The Second Winds, but she dropped out to write a memoir. We miss her and the delicious smells that wafted from the kitchen while her husband, Lloyd, cooked dinner. I joined the recorder group about 15 years ago when I decided that it might be nice to learn to play an instrument before I died, having flubbed my chance to do so as a child. I assumed that I would take piano lessons. "No, no, don't do that," a friend counseled. "The piano is much too hard an instrument to learn to play late in life. Try the recorder—that's what fourth graders play." I followed her advice and never looked back.

I play soprano, alto, tenor, and bass recorders. Ruth and Jeré, both innate musicians, suffer my inability to get the rhythms right and play smoothly—*do, do* instead of *tu, tu*. We aim to play in nursing homes, where the residents' hearing may not be all that sharp, but haven't done so yet. Even if we never perform, I'm pleased to play short pieces by great composers like Bach, Handel, Corelli, and Mozart. The recorder has given me a sense of continuity and led to solid friendships, and now that I'm alone, it is gratifying to hold old friends and traditions close. After Don's death, friends reached out to comfort me at first but then moved on with their lives. I must make more advances now to stay in touch and reward them for their friendship.

My political work continues: I still like knocking on doors, raising money, and urging people to vote as Election Day approaches. Recently, I worked enthusiastically for Democrat Cory Booker, who was elected to the U.S. Senate to fill the seat of the late Frank Lautenberg. Booker is only the second African-American in the Senate, and when I watched him take the oath of office on C-SPAN 2, I was pleased to have played a small role in his campaign. My activism for state Senator Barbara Buono, the only Democrat willing to take on Republican Governor Chris Christie in November 2013, didn't fare as well. She lost by 60 points, but I had no misgivings supporting her campaign.

I used the analogy of taking on sexuality education to grasping a snarling tiger by the tale. Although the tiger doesn't snarl now in the same way that it may for other leaders in the movement, I haven't been able to quite let go of its tail. Elizabeth Schroeder, who served as executive director at Answer (formerly the Network for Family Life Education) for almost six years and led the organization into the important world of social media, calls me "Johnny Applesex," for the way I promote *Sex, Etc.* and urge grandparents to talk more openly with their grandchildren about sexual subjects. Always gracious, Elizabeth asked me to serve as Senior Advisor to the organization, and she may have regretted the decision as I am not shy about offering suggestions.

Staying involved in sexuality education has given me the benefit of the long view: I have been able to see the progress that states and local communities have made over the last 30 years, and that is a necessary feeling for an advocate. Not all young people receive the high-quality school programs they deserve, but many more do than when I began my work in the 1980s. U.S. school districts now have a common core of national standards, the *National Sexuality Education Standards*, against which schools can measure their programs and attempt to improve them. The Friends of Sex Education (FoSE) developed these standards, and I am proud that Answer was one of the organizations involved in this process.

There is more good news: the teen pregnancy and birth rate in the U.S. has dropped sharply, fewer young people are having sex in their early teen years, and more young people are using reliable forms of contraception. As an advocate, these results reassure my belief that it takes many different approaches—not a single magic bullet—to solve complex social problems. I feel the work of Answer, its teacher training programs and *Sex Etc.*, made a difference in the progress of sexuality education.

For four years, I wrote a blog called "Sex Matters" for Newjerseynewsroom.com, which was started by former *Star Ledger* reporters. I published 111 posts on the intersection of sexuality and current events, and I never lacked for a subject. Writing a blog is like spitting into the wind or "shooting your face off," as my mother would say, but I enjoyed the freedom it offered me to speak out about my lifelong passions. I sometimes long to be more subtle and clever in making my points, so more people will take action—but as Bobby Kennedy counseled, "Each time a man stands up for an ideal, or acts to improve the lot of others … he sends forth a tiny ripple of hope." (I believe he meant these words for women, too.) Without Don to keep a check on me, I'm speaking out a lot more now, and I hope I'm sending out a few ripples.

Alone Together

I don't much care for the word "widow," and find I do not use it in conversations. It is how I'm classified now, but I prefer the word "alone," which isn't a category on any government form. My instinct is to attach the word "alone" to the word "together," because I feel I am never alone, even though I may not be with people all of the time. Some people I know simply can't stand being alone, but I've never had this problem. When I am alone, I am not lonely; I always have more to do than I have time for: books to read, e-mails to respond to, and dinner parties to plan to repay the hospitality of friends. I'm not alone even as I watch TV, since I'm inclined to talk back to the commentators, or "Top Talkers," particularly the egregious ones on *Morning Joe*.

It is interesting to observe how other women my age manage living alone. A friend of a friend joined Match.com after her husband died, because she wanted to meet a dancing partner. Her husband never liked to dance, and she wanted to get her feet moving again. My two closest neighbors from Province

Line Road are alone, too, but I don't think they're moving in this direction. Mary Lee's life focuses on her 12 grandchildren; she cheers them on at their athletic events, ferries them to and from airports for vacation, and tries to ensure that they have a successful experience at the Lawrenceville School. Sally has become more independent, confident, and politically outspoken—more the woman she always was but kept hidden, I felt, during her marriage. I first noticed a small change in her when she started using eye makeup, which she never did when her husband, Tony, was alive. When I asked her about the change, she said that Tony never wanted her to use it, so she acquiesced to his wishes. She's following her own drummer now.

Recently, I talked to another former neighbor, Mimi, who is long divorced and about to remarry at 75. She sounded absolutely elated when I congratulated her, telling me that her fiancé was designing their gold wedding rings. "Hurrah for late-life love," I said, and she agreed about its marvels.

I look at my friends and wonder if and how I've changed since Don's death. As usual, it is hard for me to see myself. Many years ago, some friends and I played a verbal game of choices. The leader asked each of us to answer questions about a walk through the woods, and when it was my turn, I had to describe a body of water I passed, a key I found, a bear along the path, and the structure I saw when I left the woods. I played along until it came to describing the key.

"I'm sorry, but I don't see a key," I said.

Other players had seen gold keys, small keys, keys to a city, a key to a summer house—but I saw none. The key turned out to be a symbol for how you see yourself, and I couldn't see myself. Over the years, I've wondered about the significance of not seeing a key. What is it that keeps me from finding the key to myself? My friend Lydia once described me, on a pink party bag that she handed me on my birthday, as "poetic, persevering, curious, and loving," and these qualities indeed feel natural to me. I should ask her to imagine a key that fits this profile.

If I were to play the game now, I would describe that key as my house key, the standard one with a hexagon-shaped top cut at my local hardware store. It's made of quite ordinary material, but there is a gleam to it. Best of all, it is dependable: I use it to open the door to my house, and when I walk inside, I feel safe and content.

When I come home, the first item I see on the little hallway table is a sign that reads, "I Am One of the 92% of Americans Who Support Universal Background Checks." If Don were here, there would be no such sign, but I'm more secure now advocating volubly for the issues that I care about than I was when he was alive. Others looked to him as the authority before, but now that I am alone, I speak out, and I like the feeling and hope it is respectful. Otherwise, I feel as if I am the same person since Don's death I've always been, for better or worse. Self-confidence comes and goes depending on the situation. As the saying goes, the more things change, the more they stay the same.

Death Is Nothing at All

Death is all around me, and I'm more aware of it every day. When I was younger, I hardly knew it existed, but it's omnipresent at my age. I feel its inevitability each week when I hear about the death of a friend or a distant acquaintance. It didn't help when a friend told me that at age 83, almost a third of the people you've known are dead. But I understand the truth of her comment when I walk up and down Princeton's main thoroughfare and realize that it is full of younger people, none of whom I know.

In my small adult community of Constitution Hill, I pass by the front doors of people who are dying of cancer or struggling with neurodegenerative diseases like Parkinson's and Alzheimer's. Don's wheelchair is still in the garage, and it catches my eye whenever I emerge from car. I know that these and other devices of aging are around the corner (I already need and wear hearing aids).

Reading the *New York Times* obituary pages is a wake-up call, and I recognize my good fortune in still being able to enjoy the desirable aspects of living alone, together. My friend Joyce, who is in her late sixties, spends a lot of time saying "not yet" and "so far" when people ask about her health.

"How are your knees?" they ask.

"So far, they're fine," she says.

"Are you taking any medications?"

"Not yet," is her standard reply.

I know what she means.

Sally talks openly about death and dying and helps me do the same. She also wears a silver "Do Not Resuscitate" bracelet on her left wrist in case she suffers a heart attack in her home and EMS arrives. (Her daughter, Nina, of the delightful wit, asked her if this was an invitation to murder.) I could wait to ask Santa Claus for one of those silver bracelets for a future Christmas, but it would make more sense to order one tomorrow. Since I don't believe in him any longer (and I hope I don't disappoint any grandchildren), I need to buy one myself.

If I were diagnosed with a terminal illness, I would not elect to receive treatment. I've watched too many older people struggle with surgery, chemotherapy, and radiation only to succumb to the disease. I would prefer to die with as much dignity as possible, having said my farewells. I have used up more than my share of the world's limited precious resources, especially food and water, and I do not wish to use too much more in a fruitless quest to extend my life by a few years. Young people deserve these resources far more than I do in my eighth decade. Eleanor Roosevelt said it best: "If you care for your own children, you must take an interest in all, for your children must go on living in the world made by all children." These words are taped to the bottom of my computer.

I've come to believe that people should have the right to end their own life with dignity and on their own terms. The national nonprofit organization Compassion & Choices has attracted my attention, because its mission is to enable everyone to have the best death possible. A few states permit residents with terminal diseases to end their lives with a physician's help rather than continue to suffer. I suspect this will grow as a reasonable alternative as the baby boomers enter their eighties and nineties. I hope that I will die with dignity, although Dr. Sherwin B. Nuland, the author of *How We Die,* which won the National Book Award for non-fiction in 1994, warned that death for most can be sudden and unexpected, messy, and anything but dignified. I always shudder when I hear of an airplane that blows up or falls from the sky, taking hundreds of people to their death in an instant. If I am luckier than most, then I would like to have my three children nearby, so I can love and comfort them and tell them how much I shall miss them.

Till Death Do Us Part

Sally and I talked about her search for a final resting place for her and her husband's ashes. Don had bought two plots in the Princeton cemetery across the street from the public library, where a small room bears a little plaque that reads the "Donald M. Wilson Reading Corner." Sally told me that after her death, her ashes will be mixed with Tony's, and I asked her if she might consider burying their urn in the plot next to ours.

"Oh," she said, "we shall be together for eternity."

When Sally and I would voice our opinions about something that her ever-wise husband, Tony, thought didn't make sense, he used to tease us and say, "You two feel deeply and think lightly." Our decision to stay together as neighbors and friends in death as we did in life arises from our feeling deeply.

The minister asked Don and me during our marriage vows if we would be faithful to each other "so long as ye both shall live." We promised one another that we would love each other "till death us do part." I do not feel that death has parted Don from me, at least not yet. Rather, I feel that he is nearby, and it is a feeling that I never expected to have. It reminds me of these words from Henry Scott Holland's sermon, "Death Is Nothing at All": "Why should I be out of mind, because I am out of sight? I am but waiting for you, for an interval, somewhere very near, just round the corner."

More amazing to me is that when I think of Don, he and I are not in our eighties, but in our twenties—our ages when we first met. We don't speak to each other in my thoughts, but I do speak to him when I visit the Princeton cemetery. Occasionally I lightly kiss one of his pictures by my bed or the cover of his book after I've reread the chapter entitled, "Susan," about our first meeting on the 33rd floor of the Time-Life Building. I never expected anything like these lingering feelings of youthful passion, and they comfort me. I suspect he'd be as surprised by them as I am.

A World Too Wonderful

Back in my acting days, I always wanted to play Emily, the ingénue lead in Thornton Wilder's *Our Town*. I tried out for the role a couple of times but was never cast in it (I was once cast as her mother). I wanted to play Emily because of her speech in the third act when she says goodbye to the world. The act starts in the town cemetery; Emily has died in childbirth, and her family and friends have brought her body there for burial. After they leave, Emily appears among the other dead, who are seated in chairs on their graves. She and the Stage Manager, who embodies someone with God-like wisdom, begin a conversation, and she begs him to allow her to return to her life as she knew it, although the other dead counsel against it. The Stage Manager permits her to return for one day, her 12th birthday, and she finds herself once more in her family kitchen. The experience turns out to be a hollow one, though, as she begins to observe the ordinariness of everyday life, people's shallow interactions, her mother's aloofness, and the pain that people cause each other. She asks to return to her grave.

Emily says goodbye to the world and what she loved most when she was alive: "Mama's sunflowers, food and coffee, newly ironed dresses, hot baths, sleeping, and waking up." She says with great feeling, "Oh, earth, you're too wonderful for anyone to realize you." She asks the Stage Manager, "Do human beings ever realize life while they live it—every, every minute?"

"No," he says. "The saints and poets, maybe—they do some."

I longed to say those words because I believed Emily's cry, "Oh, earth, you're too wonderful for anyone to realize you."

Do I still treasure Thornton Wilder's words because I believe in the innate goodness of human beings? Has my good fortune helped me to see possibilities and hope where others see only pain and ugliness? I don't know—but I do know that I will keep fighting for and loving that world too wonderful for any of us to realize.

Home

The quilt looks right at home in my bedroom among some of my treasured possessions: photos of Don; pictures of my sister in a pink suit, my kids, and my parents; a photo of Michelle Obama with me, Penny, Olivia, and Reed; a photo of sunrise over Chilmark Pond on the Vineyard; a postcard of one of my heroes, Florence Nightingale; a photo of the Network—now Answer—staff at a restaurant; and many greeting cards, including one from Sally that reads, "Life is slippery, take my hand." There is also a small urn containing Don's ashes and one of my all-time favorite children's books, *The Country Bunny and the Little Gold Shoes,* about a feminist bunny and her Easter triumph. On cold nights, among these beloved possessions, I pull the quilt up to my chin to keep me warm. This quilt wouldn't exist without the help of countless people who have touched my life. In their honor, I will wake up in the morning and go out for a good run.

Postscript

To my five grandchildren, Eli, Harry, Sam, Olivia, and Reed, I hope that after you have read this book, you will know that I have tried to be an activist for causes that make life a little better for people in my community, state, country, and even our world. I'm drawn to help those who've had the least advantages because I feel that I've had a multitude of them. I wonder how we, the privileged few, can make other people's lives better, so we can all thrive in a safer, more secure world. Nicholas Kristof, the respected *New York Times* columnist summed up my thinking well when he wrote, "Talent is universal, but opportunity is not."

I urge you above everything else to be kind, and also do your best in school and get the most out of your education—not so you can trumpet your marks, but so you can develop and implement ideas that help those who've had fewer opportunities in life than you've had. Advocates need to use their hearts and minds. They also need persistence, creativity, political knowledge, communication skills, and, lastly, moral courage.

"Moral courage is a rarer commodity than bravery in battle or great intelligence. Yet it is the one essential, vital quality for those who seek to change a world which yields most painfully to change," Robert Kennedy said. By moral courage, he meant standing up for your principles despite fierce opposition and taking the lonely, less-traveled path.

In my activist work, I have never had to demonstrate true moral courage and jeopardize my position, reputation, or life for a cause. But I admire people like Joan of Arc, Martin Luther King, Jr., Nelson Mandela, Florence Nightingale, and Susan B. Anthony, all of whom demonstrated true moral courage in their lives. I hope you will study their stories and learn from them how to overcome fear in order to speak out, take bold action, and hold fast to your cause despite opposition. I hope you will also treat all people as family and love others beyond the family circle.

I don't know if any of you will inherit the family gene of passion for public service from me and Grandpa Don and those who passed it on to us—in particular, your great-great-grandfather Benno Neuberger and your great-grandparents Harry and K. K. Neuberger. If you are truly brave, you might venture into politics, as it is fundamental to our democracy, and we need more honorable people like you to choose it as a profession. But I will love you whether or not you choose to enter politics or become activists for causes that will make the world more equal. I trust that at some point in your life, though, you will find yourself trying to make a difference, no matter how large or small, and I want to leave you with these words of comfort when the going gets tough. They come from the song, "You'll Never Walk Alone," from *Carousel*, which is my favorite of all the glorious Rodgers and Hammerstein musicals.

When you walk through a storm
Hold your head up high
And don't be afraid of the dark

At the end of the storm
Is a golden sky
And the sweet silver song of the lark

Walk on through the wind
Walk on through the rain
Though your dreams be tossed and blown

Walk on, walk on with hope in your heart
And you'll never walk alone
You'll never walk alone

My dear grandchildren, look at the sky and listen to the song to find the courage you need in your journey through life. Wherever you go or whatever you do, please know that Grandma Susie loves you without reservation. I always have, and I always will.

*Generations:
The Family Tree*

Love and Mystery on Valentine's Day

I spent Valentine's Day 2013 at two Jewish cemeteries in Brooklyn, New York. It was a pilgrimage to find the burial places of relatives who had died long before I was born, and the brainchild of genealogist Sue Hrabchak, of Princeton, who helped me learn more about them.

We had planned to see only the graves of my paternal grandparents, Benno and Stella Neuberger, in the first cemetery, Salem Fields, but Sue had learned that some members of my maternal grandmother's family—in particular, my great-grandparents, the Isaac Wallachs—were also buried in Salem Fields. She had also discovered that some members of my grandmother Stella's family were buried in Maimonides Cemetery nearby, so we decided to visit there too.

We traveled to Brooklyn as the morning mists turned into a clear blue sky, which I felt augured well for a day of learning. Cemeteries had played a significant role in my life: Arlington National Cemetery, in Washington, D.C., where I witnessed the sad and sudden burials of John and Robert Kennedy in the sixties; the military cemetery in Normandy, France, which I visited with Bobby and Ethel Kennedy on the 20th anniversary of the Normandy landing by Allied forces in World War II; and the Fairview Cemetery in Middletown, New Jersey, a small country cemetery where my mother and father are buried. Cemeteries held no fear for me.

About 80,000 prominent German-Jewish families from New York City spend eternity with each other at Salem Fields, and a cemetery employee instructed me in the history of my descendants. I gleaned my first lesson on this history in the tiny office where we stopped to get directions to the Neuberger and Wallach gravesites and pick up the key to Benno's mausoleum. The woman who gave us the key told us that the burials had begun there in the 1800s, and everyone buried in the cemetery then had been a member of the Temple Emanu-El in New York City. Back then, each mausoleum cost between $32,500 and $67,000—expensive real estate for the time—and property owners were allowed some leeway in designing their tombs and burial sites. The woman also related some distressing news: my grandfather's mausoleum had been vandalized.

※

I could never have imagined a place like Salem Fields: as far as my eye could see were hundreds of mausoleums designed like small Greek temples, reminding me of the Parthenon in Athens. Each grayish-white granite mausoleum had two columns in one of three traditional Greek styles—Doric, Ionic, or Corinthian. A family's name, carved in granite uppercase letters, was affixed to the pediment on the front of the columns.

It was an immaculate, tranquil site, and the graves and mausoleums seemed to gleam in the sunlight. As we walked around the oval area where the Wallach family was buried, we peered into the windows of the mausoleums' bronze doors. Many doors were intricately carved with vines and leaves reminiscent of the bronze Ghiberti doors in Florence. Almost every mausoleum interior contained a lovely stained glass window, some of them created by the famous artist and designer Louis Comfort Tiffany, and I looked forward to seeing the stained glass window in the Neuberger mausoleum. We soon found Isaac and Hannah Frank Wallach's elaborate gravesite, and I tucked on the ledge in front of its doors a few flowers from the bouquet I had brought.

My grandfather's mausoleum, with his name, Benno Neuberger, in the triangular pediment, stood on an outermost edge of a hilltop that formed the highest point of Salem Fields. Its exterior was so pristine that it looked as if it had been built the previous day. It had two Doric columns, the simplest Greek style, on either side of its bronze door. Beyond the tall pines, I caught sight of the Atlantic Ocean. Benno had spent many hours on the sea, sailing back and forth to Germany on business, and the view from his final resting place echoed his life.

As I turned to help Sue unlock the door, I noticed that one of its glass panes was broken. We pushed open the door and, to my dismay, I realized once inside that there was no Tiffany stained glass window. "Oh, thieves must have stolen Benno's window," I said, remembering what the woman at the office had told us about the many thefts over the years, "and the cemetery replaced it with an ordinary plate glass." I was disappointed.

"I was so looking forward to seeing what design he or Grandma Stella or even Daddy had chosen. The interior looks so sad," I said to Sue. "I wish I had known about this robbery long before now."

I saw the names and birth and death dates of my grandparents, Benno Neuberger (March 22, 1866-July 6, 1914) and Stella Mayer Neuberger (May 9, 1869-February 5, 1920) on the white marble wall near the entrance door. I assumed their coffins were placed directly behind the slab of marble. I ran my fingers over their names, and my first thoughts were sad ones: my father had lost his father when he was only 18 and his mother when he was 24. No wonder he had few stories about my grandparents' lives to share with my sister and me.

A black vase rested on the windowsill as if waiting for me to fill it, so I arranged my flowers in it with snow from outside and returned it to the sill. I ran my fingers along the incised letters of Benno's and Stella's names, kissed my fingers, and then touched their names again before leaving the little space. I would have liked to have actually kissed their names, since I was never able to kiss them in real life, but I would have needed a chair or a ladder to reach that high. I left, determined to restore dignity to the mausoleum by replacing the stained glass window inside and the lock and glass on the door. Not having known them in real life, I wanted to show my respect and thanks to my grandparents, Benno and Stella, for all they had done for me by raising my wonderful father.

Maimonides Cemetery was down the hill and up Jamaica Avenue from historic Salem Fields, but it was as different from its neighbor as night and day. It was rundown and overgrown, with vines climbing over the mausoleum walls and masses of untrimmed ivy covering the tombstones. One huge tree, obviously a victim of Hurricane Sandy, lay where it had fallen, crushing several gravestones beneath it.

Sue and I entered the office and asked where we might find the location of and key to the Mayer mausoleum. There was little furniture in the dingy room. One attendant talked on his cell phone while another hunted around for the key in a little closet containing haphazardly hung keys. It was clear that Sue and I were alone in our quest, so we left and began moving row by row through the cemetery. At one point, she ducked under some low-hanging branches; suddenly the Mayer mausoleum stood before us.

We wanted to find the grave of Max L. Mayer, my paternal great-grandfather and Stella Mayer Neuberger's father, who died young and unexpectedly, reportedly a suicide, in a New York City law office. Had he taken his own life, which is against Jewish religious law, he would have been barred from burial in a Jewish cemetery—yet here he was in Maimonides along with his wife, Fredericka Siesfeld, and several of their five children. (As I child, I had known two of them, my Aunt Anna and Uncle Edwin, who were Stella's siblings.)

The mystery of Max Mayer's death continues; we have no way of knowing if his reported suicide kept him from a burial in the more impressive Salem Fields.

We weren't able to enter the little vestibule of Max's final resting place, which contained a white chair and a rather soiled carpet, because the key the attendant finally found for it didn't fit. When we looked through the doorway glass, we could see two small, brightly-colored stained glass panels depicting an object that looked like the Olympic torch. Benno and Stella may rest in a more pristine cemetery, but their mausoleum was vandalized and their stained glass window stolen.

As we left the Mayers' mausoleum, Sue picked off a piece of ivy growing around the front door, handed it to me, and said, "See if you can root this in water and plant it in your garden, so you will have a touch of the Mayers in your life." (The rooting was successful, and the ivy grows in my small patio garden.)

As we drove home to Princeton, watching a lovely sunset turn the New York City skyline into a scene almost worthy of a Tiffany window, Sue and I talked about how I might replace the window in Benno and Stella's mausoleum. We agreed to make sure it was protected this time by a set of thief-proof iron bars. She told me that her brother, Tom Kellner, who is an artist, makes stained glass windows, and I got excited thinking about possible designs to fill the barren interior with beauty and light again. Sue recalled that Benno had once described young children as "rosebuds" waiting to be nurtured, so that they can bloom into roses in adulthood. One of Benno's philanthropic and volunteer interests was the Hebrew Infant Asylum in New York City that cared for Jewish orphans.

"I think the center of any design should contain a rosebud. It's the perfect symbol for Benno," I said.

I enjoyed making the mausoleum whole again as a gift of love to the grandparents I never knew. My feelings of sadness from not asking my father to tell me about them when I was growing up would fade, knowing that I had restored dignity and beauty to their final resting place.

I returned to Salem Fields with Sue and Tom early in the spring. Again the sun shone brightly. Tom spent some time looking at the stained glass windows in other mausoleums to get a better feel for their designs. Sue, ever the genealogist, kept pointing out more graves of my distant ancestors. When we arrived at the Neuberger mausoleum, I found that the cemetery staff had replaced the broken glass pane and removed the ugly padlock holding the door in place. We entered, and this time I felt more comfortable standing in the little interior.

Tom studied the space and then asked Sue to cup her hands and give him a lift up to the ledge below where the purloined stained glass window had been. He began to take careful measurements for a replacement. After he jumped down, he discovered some pieces of the original window's brass frame and decided that he could reuse them, forging a nice connection between past and present. He seemed genuinely excited for the opportunity to create a new stained glass window, and we chatted briefly about whether its centerpiece should be a rosebud or a rose in full bloom. He asked which one I preferred, but I didn't have a strong preference.

Tom said that he would draw up some designs, and when he returned to put in the new stained glass window, he would bring a marble cleanser to wash down the walls and grime that had accumulated over the decades. I liked that idea.

We prepared to leave. Again I had brought flowers and a jug of water. I arranged them in the vase and placed it on the ledge. I then turned and blew a kiss to my grandparents, pulled the door closed behind me, and joined Tom and Sue in the sunlight.

My Paternal Grandfather: Benno Neuberger

I didn't know my paternal grandfather, Benno Neuberger, who was born in Arnstein, Bavaria, Germany, on March 22, 1866. His parents, Heinrich and Lena Rosenwald Neuberger, gave birth to another son, Moritz, six years later. My grandfather and my great-uncle both emigrated from Germany to New York City and became United States citizens.

I didn't know even these facts until a genealogist helped me uncover the history of my maternal and paternal grandparents. My father didn't speak often about his father, but he did share one story that illustrated how much he adored him when he was a boy ("more than anything in the world," he said).

He would tell me the story whenever the subject turned to who I loved more: Mummy or Daddy, which, depending on my mood at the moment, could be one or the other or both. My father liked to tell me stories to prove a point, and he told many of them over meals. He'd sit at the foot of the polished cherry table in the dining room of our 1760 farmhouse, with its original, hand-hewn wooden beams in the low ceiling—the low ceiling made in Colonial times when people were shorter. The beams made the room darker, which heightened his storytelling. I'd sit to his right on the orange cushion on a copy of an antique Hitchcock chair.

"One day," he'd tell me, "when I was about four years old, my father and I had a disagreement. My mother came into the living room in time to hear me sob, 'All right. Now I don't love you more than anyone else in the world.' My mother—hoping to get some of my love for herself—immediately asked me, 'Do you love *me* now more than anyone else in the world?' I stopped my sobbing and moaned, 'No, I don't love you or anyone else if I can't love Daddy anymore.'"

Daddy had the only photograph of his father that I ever saw, which he kept on the bureau in his dressing room at our farmhouse. I remember catching a glimpse of it whenever I went into his room, which, because it was private and in a distant wing of the house, was seldom. In the photo, Benno looked straight at me with his large dark eyes. He wore an exceptionally bushy, long mustache, and I used to wonder what it would be like having so much hair resting above one's upper lip.

I never picked up the photograph or asked my father about it, and today I wish I had asked him to tell me more about my grandfather. I wish I knew what Daddy remembered and loved so much about him, but I never asked and he rarely spoke of him.

I never heard, for instance, that Grandpa Benno had come from a small, wealthy group of German-Jews and had come to America to escape anti-Semitism. Arriving in New York City on September 10, 1881, on the *SS Elbe,* when he was 15 years old, he immediately began a promising career as a tobacco merchant for E. Rosenwald & Bros. on 145 Water Street, later becoming a key figure in the company. On March 22, 1887, his 21st birthday, he became a naturalized U.S. citizen. He never left his German roots far behind, traveling extensively across the Atlantic to Europe on tobacco-related business matters.

⁂

Grandpa Benno had a successful business career, as indicated by the spaciousness of his private home at 55 East 74th Street in Manhattan. He married Stella Mayer at the Hotel Brunswick on April 21, 1891, and, according to the *New York Sun*'s account of the wedding, the bride wore a white satin gown trimmed with duchesse lace and a tulle veil caught up with flowers. Benno and Stella became parents when their daughter, Florence Edna, was born on July 18, 1893. Three years later, on July 4, 1896, my father, Harry Hobson, arrived in Far Rockaway, Queens.

If writing almost daily to one's son while he is away at boarding school is any indication of love, then my grandfather adored his only son. While cleaning out my mother's attic after her death, my sister, niece, and I found more than 100 letters that Benno and Stella had written to their beloved Harry while he attended Phillips Exeter Academy, in New Hampshire. My grandfather wrote to my father almost daily, even when he was traveling abroad a great deal.

My only sorrow when reading the letters was knowing that my grandparents would die at such young ages. This knowledge often made my eyes smart with tears as I would think, "Daddy, read this letter carefully; your father is going to die in a year's time."

Benno wrote many letters in gorgeous flowing script on his company's official stationery; indeed, he and Stella wrote with such frequency that I wondered why they had sent my father away to school. My grandfather visited my father on numerous occasions, often writing that he was headed to Boston and would stop by to bring him a box of "edibles." ("Mother packed up a fine chicken for you," he notes in one letter.) He wanted to see his son so much that he would settle for visiting with him for only a few minutes between his train's arrival and departure. He wanted to show my father how much he cared for him, even if it was only to give him a hug and kiss.

My grandfather's letters reveal anxiety about my father' progress at school.

"Your marks show improvement over last year," he wrote in October 1912. "Do your best to keep it up, for the more thorough you go into things now the easier you will have it as time goes on." Benno shows concern about my father's social life in another letter. "I don't want you to go out with the boy you mentioned, and I have firmly made up my mind to that, so you might as well make the best of it. I didn't think he was nice, and his companionship can't do you any good," he wrote.

Grandpa Benno's letters were generally upbeat except for one written on June 1, 1913. Obviously deeply concerned, he wrote, "I have never heard you speak so disgustingly of Exeter. What happened? You liked it so much. I will come up to see you get your diploma."

My grandfather's concerns about my father at Exeter affected me, so I called the archivist at the prep school and had her check the records of the 1913 graduating class. She assured me that my father did indeed graduate, and on time, in June 1913. She couldn't find a record of his grades, because those from that time period had been lost. My grandfather might have been pleased to know that his son established at Exeter in 1928 the Benno and Stella Neuberger scholarship in his parents' names. Many students have benefited from this gift, which demonstrates that my father was pleased with the education he received there.

My father was a conscientious correspondent, and he wrote to me faithfully wherever I was—at camp, theater school, or college. I always looked forward to receiving his letters written in his flowing script. Benno had been a good role model.

Grandpa Benno's other passion in life besides his family was the Hebrew Infant Asylum. He spent a long time on its board of directors and served as president for several terms. He was a great believer in what today would be called early childhood education. In his yearly "President's Letter" for the Asylum's 1904 annual report, he wrote that if orphans were given "almost constant care and supervision as they are reared, so they succeed." He used a lovely analogy to describe the importance of providing the best services to these little children: "The early years, though forgotten, cannot be erased no more than we can admire the full-grown rose and then overlook the fact that it developed from a healthy bud."

Grandpa Benno noted in his 1906 letter that the Asylum needed to increase its accommodations for Jewish infants from Russia, whose parents were "our poor brethren … helpless inoffensive Jews [who] were fleeing persecution, murder and torture" in their homeland.

My father was a legendary fundraiser in our community, and I can only assume that Grandpa Benno had passed these abilities down to him. Benno gave generously and raised large sums from his friends and the larger Jewish community. New York Governor John Alden Dix noted his achievements by attending the 1912 dedication of a new Asylum building in the Bronx.

Benno was a passenger on the *SS Rotterdam* on April 15, 1912, when the *Titanic* sank on its maiden voyage, taking 1,502 people, including many Americans, to their deaths. The tragedy affected him deeply, since 36 donors to the Asylum had died, and in 1913, a year after the catastrophe, he wrote the following in his presidential letter:

> As always, the harvest of death has been the one inevitable grief in our otherwise happy year of association. With the tragic grimness which is not given to us to understand, God took unto Himself many of our best friends, among them were some whose passing, because of their extraordinary interest in the Hebrew Infant Asylum, left in our hearts a sense of pain and loneliness … I refer [in particular to] Mr. and Mrs. Isidor Straus and Henry B. Harris.

To show his appreciation for Harris, Grandpa Benno went beyond just writing about his friend. On April 15, 1913, the first anniversary of the tragedy, he stood at the rail of the Cunard liner *Mauretania,* which had slowed down when it reached the latitude the *Titanic* was at when it sank, and dropped two large wreaths into the swirling Atlantic waters in memory of Harris. My grandfather would die 15 months after performing this act of friendship.

My grandfather died of a sudden heart attack at age 48 on July 6, 1914, in Königstein, Saxony, Germany, a small town on the Elbe River. My father was only 18 when he went with his mother and sister, Florence, to bring his father's body back to the United States for burial in Brooklyn, New York. His funeral was held at Temple Emanu-El, and the *New York Herald* ran his obituary on July 31, 1914. "A real leader in thought and action in his field of charitable work, munificent in his support of its cause, lavish in the use of his time in its behalf, this truly good man was justly beloved by the tiny inmates of the Infant Asylum, followed by the members of its directorate and respected by its working force," the obituary read.

In 1915, some months after my grandfather's untimely death, the Honorable N. Taylor Phillips, one of the Asylum's board of directors, eulogized him at its annual meeting. He included this sweet story about his visit to the organization, where he found his friend Benno in the middle of a group of children: "I heard one little boy say, 'This is my father,' and another little boy said, 'He is my father,' and in a few minutes they were all claiming him for their father. Can you imagine anything more beautiful than this? His whole life was an inspiration, and his ardent endeavors in the cause of infantile humanity have won for this institution many friends."

Grandpa Benno was an exemplary philanthropist, and though the bequests he made may seem paltry when compared with sums given by the wealthy a century later, they were considerable at the time. His $1.3 million-dollar estate included bequests of $80,000 to Jewish charitable institutions. At the top of the list was his beloved Asylum, to which he gave the largest amount, $10,000. He also left smaller bequests to two hospitals and the Young Men's Hebrew Association.

I was pleased to see that he left money to the Hebrew Technical School for Girls, because perhaps he realized that girls needed skills to hold jobs, live independently, and contribute to their family's welfare. I always considered my father a feminist in his encouraging me to go to work after college, and I can only assume that Grandpa Benno had helped shape his thinking.

The Hebrew Infant Asylum lives to this day as part of the Jewish Child Care Association of New York, and the merits of early childhood education, in which my grandfather saw such promise, are now widely accepted. President Obama, among other political and education leaders, is promoting universal pre-kindergarten programs for all four-year-olds with a mix of federal and state funding.

The grandfather I never knew left a proud legacy that I hope will inspire my heirs. The same lovely words used to describe Grandpa Benno's philanthropic nature and community contributions could be used to describe my father's as well. Daddy chose to support some of the same causes as his father, and now I comprehend the source of the family fundraising gene.

My father taught my sister and me that with wealth comes responsibilities to those who have not been blessed with similar good fortune. He never saw wealth as simply a means to accumulating more wealth, but as a way to help others in need. I believe that my father's wise values about money were inherited directly from Benno, a man of fine character. These values regarding wealth that he passed along to my father, who passed them along to me, are the same values that I hope I have passed along to my children, who in turn will pass them on to theirs.

My Paternal Grandmother:
Stella Mayer Neuberger

Although I never met my paternal grandmother, Stella Mayer Neuberger, I felt close to her because we shared the same initials: SMN. It is Jewish custom to name a child after or link a child's name to the closest deceased relative of the same gender. My parents never explained the religious connection to me, but although it was a bit scary knowing that my name was connected to a dead person, I liked the idea that my grandmother and I were associated in this familial way.

I have only one tangible possession that belonged to my grandmother Stella: a silver buttonhook engraved in pretty script with her initials, which rests on my bureau beside a dresser set of two brushes, a mirror, a shoe horn, a nail file, and a comb that I received on my eleventh birthday. I used to look at the buttonhook when I was young and imagine my grandmother using it on her high-button shoes or coats and dresses; and I used to worry that I would lose it—and with it, an important connection I had to her. I will give it to my only granddaughter, and Grandma Stella's only great-granddaughter, Olivia, with the hope that she will continue to keep it in the family and pass it along through the female line.

◦◦◦

Stella Mayer was born on May 9, 1869, in Jonesboro, Tennessee. Her father, Max L. Mayer, who was born in 1838 in Wurttemberg, Germany, came to America as a teen and became a naturalized citizen around 1859. He lived in Lynchburg, Virginia, and after he married Fredericka Siesfeld, the couple moved to Jonesboro, where Stella was born.

My great-grandfather Max had an interesting political life and something of a mysterious death. He began his political career after a rather short stint as a confederate soldier in the Lynchburg militia in 1861, at the beginning of the Civil War. He quickly discovered that military life didn't suit him and found a substitute soldier to take his place in the ranks (a common practice of both sides in the war). After the war ended, Max served as an Assistant United States District Attorney. He also served as a delegate to the Republican political conventions of 1868 and 1872 and as an elector of the victorious Republican presidential ticket in 1868, when Ulysses S. Grant defeated Horatio Seymour.

The family left Tennessee for New York City after a cholera outbreak struck Jonesboro. Max joined the law office of Edward Lauterbach and built an extensive practice in the city. My great-grandfather died suddenly on April 16, 1878, his death surrounded by mystery and confusion. An article in *The Tribune* reported the cause as a sudden heart attack, yet in a subsequent article the assistant coroner attributed his death to "suicide from hydrocyanic acid, a deadly poison." Max did not leave a note though, and there was no bottle of poison found in the office. Along with a puzzling mystery, he left behind his wife and five young children, including my grandmother, Stella.

My great-grandmother Fredericka lived longer than her husband. She was born in 1843 in Bavaria, Germany, and immigrated to the U.S. with her parents in 1865. In ten years, she gave birth to five children—Edwin, Stella, Florence, Anna, and Lothair—and lost not only her husband at an early age but also two of her children, Florence and Lothair. She died from diabetes in New York City on January 4, 1911, but lived to see the weddings of some of her children, including Stella, and the births of at least eight grandchildren, including my father, Harry, and his sister, Florence.

My grandmother Stella always looked glamorous in family photographs. Dark haired with large brown eyes, she was perfectly coiffed in elegant clothes made of fine materials: brocades, satin, and tulle.

There is little information about her life in the city other than what she shared in dozens of letters to her son, Harry, at boarding school. She absolutely adored her only son and would usually open her letters with, "My own dearest Harry!" "My darling Harry!" or "My own darling Harry!" She had no problem expressing her love for him, often ending her letters with "an extra fond embrace and hug and kiss" or "many fond hugs, kisses & hearty embraces," and then always, "Lovingly, your mother."

Her letters always included details of her life as the wife of a wealthy, international businessman. On the surface, her days seemed repetitive, superficial, and even a bit dull, but her life reflected the expectations for women of her social class at the time. Stella lived in the present, describing plays and operas, luncheons and dinner parties, bridge games, and plans for the family's yearly move from their winter townhouse at 55 East 74th Street to a summer rental in Elberon or Long Branch, New Jersey, and, eventually, to their own summer home on Long Island.

She never mentions books or current political events or asks about her son's academic work or his opinion of Exeter. She does mention his clothes, including supporting his decision to buy an expensive suit from a New Haven tailor. She writes that she has sent him "4 sets of underwear, $5 for the set—$20 for the 4," and expresses happiness that a local woman is "taking care of your laundry." She tells him that their chauffeur, Wilhelm, a family fixture, is ferrying her about town from one social engagement to another. The weather—good, bad, rainy or sunny—is also a favored topic.

My grandmother's devotion to my father extended beyond his school days and into his service in the Army during World War I. She lovingly created a scrapbook of articles and photographs about his military service and included snapshots of mother and son at a training camp, a copy of a General Order from the Fourth Army Corps headquarters, and postcards and telegrams my father sent to her and his sister from France. One telegram from Paris—written after the armistice that ended the war—reads, "Feeling splendid. Hope all well. Love kisses." I'm sure my grandmother was thrilled to receive such good news from her beloved son.

My grandmother Stella died at age 51 on February 5, 1920. Rabbi Joseph Silverman of Temple Emanu-El, who had officiated at her wedding, delivered her eulogy. It extolled her inner beauty and exemplary qualities as a wife and mother. I never knew precisely why she died at such a young age: the whispers of family members attributed her death to ovarian or uterine cancer. Rabbi Silverman chose as his text for "In Memoriam Stella Neuberger" verses 25-28 from Proverbs XXXI:

> *Strength and dignity are her clothing.*
> *And she smileth at the time to come.*
> *She openeth her mouth with wisdom.*
> *And the law of kindness is on her tongue.*
> *She looketh well to the ways of her household.*
> *And eateth not the bread of idleness.*
> *Her children rise up and call her blessed …*

The eulogist portrayed my grandmother as the ideal woman, extolling her "qualities of spiritual strength, dignity, optimism, wisdom, kindliness, industry and motherhood." He said that she possessed "a rare and charming personality, an innate graciousness of manner and charm of deportment and a fine mind—pure yet searching, a kind heart—indulgent, yet firm and an optimism which did not blind her to the bitter realities of life." My father, often called "Happy Harry," didn't fall far from the tree, as these same qualities, especially "optimism," applied to him.

I knew two of Grandma Stella's siblings: her older brother, Edwin Mayer, who married Lillian Phillips, and her younger sister, Anna Mayer, who married Theodore Werner. They were my great-aunts and great-uncles, and as a child, I would occasionally see them at Uncle Edwin's apartment on 72nd Street in New York City. They were kind to my sister and me, fussing over us and patting our heads.

I also knew briefly another great-aunt, a grand old lady whom I called Aunt Fanny, who was my great-grandmother Fredericka's sister. She lived a long life and died at 90 in March of 1934. When she turned 85, on December 12, 1929, her family threw an elegant dinner party for her at the Ritz Tower Hotel. The menu used family names to describe the courses, starting with "Le Caviar Neuberger" and ending with "Le Gateau Anniversaire Tante Fan." A guest composed an original song to celebrate the lady who looked exactly like Queen Victoria when the latter was old, but without her tiara. The chorus catches the spirit:

> *Three cheers for dear Aunt Fanny*
> *Three cheers for her I say*
> *Altho she's old as Granny*
> *She gets younger every day.*

I took pleasure in the notion that my father's family liked to hold celebrations, and I saw that in Daddy. He would have had a party every Saturday night at our house if he could, but socializing on such a scale was anathema to my mother. Daddy had to wait to kick up his heels, make merry, and—from time to time—sing a song at other people's parties.

My initials became SNW when I married Don, but every so often over the years I think back to when they were SMN and remember the lovely photograph of my grandmother on the piano in our different homes. (I'm pleased that it now rests on my daughter Penny's piano in her house in the Bronx.) Beyond this bond forged at my birth, I most admire my grandmother's love for and constant devotion to my father. My father was the beneficiary of a loving home, as was I.

My Maternal Grandmother: Elsie Frank Wallach Kridel

My mother never talked much about her parents or her comfortable upbringing in New York City, and so I didn't know much about my maternal grandmother, Elsie Frank Wallach Kridel. I knew more about my maternal grandfather, Samuel Kridel, because he lived until I was a young adult. In retrospect, I feel I should have known them both better, because their apartment at 1075 Park Avenue was only two short blocks from ours at 1100 Park Avenue; I walked under their building's awning on daily excursions for many years.

Elsie (or Elsa, as her name sometimes appears in documents and letters) was born on February 20, 1881, into a large German-Jewish family with at least one distinguished member: her father, Isaac. There is a bronze bust of him on the marble staircase landing in the Administration building entrance of Mount Sinai Hospital in New York City, one of the most well-known hospitals in the world. The bust commemorates his 30 years of service as the hospital's director, vice president, and president. During his tenure, he emphasized the three themes of the hospital's mission: research, education, and social responsibility.

After Isaac died, the *New York Times* ran an article about his funeral on March 18, 1907. His service was held at Temple Emanu-El, and in his eulogy, the Rev. Dr. Joseph Silverman related Isaac's success as a businessman, philanthropist, and community leader.

It's like looking at a black-and-white rather than a color photograph when comparing my grandmother Elsie's muted life to her father's accomplished one. There is little information about her. I do have a short letter she wrote to her father on September 8, 1892, when she was 11 years old. In neat, cursive script, she writes to her "Dear Papa," who had been in quarantine on a ship for some reason: "I'm working a cravat case for you with forget-me-nots. … With lots of love and lots of kisses, I remain your devoted daughter."

I most associate Elsie with needlework, and the walls of Sunnyside Farm showed off her fine creations. My mother hung one of her charming petit-point bell pulls on our living-room wall at the farm, and after her death, I put it on my dining-room wall so that I could admire my grandmother's artistry. The bell pull still reminds me of her when I see it, and I often stop and touch the tiny stitches she used to create her work of art.

After my mother died, my sister, niece, and I cleaned out her attic, and I found a large piece of needlework depicting orange and red flowers on a gray background. I assumed that my grandmother had made it and my mother hadn't had time to frame it or have it made into a footstool. I decided to honor Elsie's striking piece by turning the needlework into a substantial, handsome bench for my living room, where I enjoy seeing people sit on it during visits.

In photographs, my grandmother Elsie appears tall and thin with deep-set eyes. My mother would occasionally tell my sister and me that Elsie was intelligent and spoke seven languages, which surprised me since I had never heard her speak anything but English. Although Grandma Elsie never went to college, she possessed an ear and a tongue that could easily learn many different languages. She and my grandfather Sam must have had a fine time using her linguistic facility on their honeymoon trip to Europe.

I used to marvel that anyone could learn seven foreign languages, especially after I spent years trying to master one. I'm convinced that my grandmother didn't have the opportunity to use her significant brainpower in a satisfying way, given the expectations of women to dedicate their lives to housekeeping and raising children.

My mother said that my grandmother had many fears: fear of strangers, fear of travel—although she undertook an extended automobile tour of Europe for her honeymoon—and fear of her family dying in a house fire. Somehow she transferred this last fear to my mother, who left small, flexible metal ladders in boxes beneath each of our bedroom windows at the farm, so we could climb down to safety in case of fire.

When my mother was eight years old, her baby brother, Billy, arrived, and he became the apple of her mother's eye. She said that her mother "ceased to love" her after his birth. In 1937, my grandmother wrote a little poem with prose at the end in honor of Billy's 21st birthday. The prose bears repeating because it reveals the intensity of her feelings for my Uncle Billy:

> With blessings and wishes for the fulfillment of all life's richest gifts, robust health, contentment, culture and happy associations. My love is deep and true and will be with you forever. You have brought me much happiness. Continue to do so. By your success and your love for me, I shall continue to feel that life holds much for me now and in the future.

My mother said that her mother never spoke such loving words to her.

My final memory of my grandmother Elsie occurred in our New York apartment early in the morning of Sunday, January 27, 1940. I was looking forward to the day because my sister and I were giving a costume party for our friends at our apartment. In the middle of the night, I heard a commotion in the hallway, ran to my bedroom door, and saw my parents rushing out the front door.

The next morning, they told me that my grandmother had died earlier that morning and our party would be canceled. I remember for the first time in my life seeing my mother shaking with sobs. It was upsetting, but I behaved selfishly in that sad moment. Instead of trying to console my mother, I looked at the white satin dress with red hearts that I had planned to wear to the party. *Now I won't be able to wear it,* I thought, feeling anger rise against my grandmother for dying before our party.

I was only ten years old at the time, and perhaps it was normal to be self-centered, but I wish I had risen to the occasion, embraced my mother, and told her how much I knew she would miss my grandmother, because, "Mummy, if anything happened to you, I would miss you terribly." In life, wishing doesn't make it so.

My grandmother is the only one in my immediate family who is not buried in a Brooklyn cemetery with family members. She wanted to be cremated and have her remains scattered where the Atlantic Ocean and Hudson River merge in New York Harbor. I always considered it a daring request, but it made sense: in life and in death, my grandmother was different.

My Uncle Billy kept her ashes in an urn in his New York apartment almost up to the moment of his death, because he wasn't comfortable releasing them to the swirling waters. I went to visit my uncle when he was close to death, and he told me that he had given his mother's ashes to someone who had released them into the harbor. He seemed relieved that 40 years after her death, he had acceded to her wishes.

"Uncle Billy, " I said, "you've done what your mother asked you to do."

I leave my grandmother—or the shadow of the woman she really was—with melancholy feelings, because I missed my chance to know her. I wish someone had said something warm and kind about her to me, so I could keep those thoughts close to my heart. Nevertheless, she did raise my mother and perhaps instill in her the drive to be different, pursue her ambitions, and make a real contribution to society, which she herself had been unable to do.

Of all my ancestors, I feel I am more physically like my grandmother Elsie, because I am tall and thin. Whenever anyone mentions my slenderness, I always say, "I inherited my figure from my grandmother and for that I am grateful; I've never had to struggle with my weight as many people do." I am also grateful to my grandmother Elsie for giving me a mother who encouraged me to attain my goals of being an independent woman and serving others.

My Maternal Grandfather: Samuel Kridel

My maternal grandfather, Samuel Kridel, was born in New York City on January 20, 1868, the youngest of the three sons of Jacob and Augustina Rubenstein Kridel. Jacob was born in Krakow, Austria, and Augustina in Germany, and both immigrated to the United States. She died at age 43 in New York City from typhoid fever, and he died in Germany at age 65.

My grandfather was educated in the New York City public schools and attended City College. He and his brother Abraham wed two sisters from the Wallach family; he married Elsie, and Abraham married Martha, her oldest sister.

Samuel and Elsie were married on February 5, 1906, at her family's home at 12 East 62nd Street. The *New York Times*'s account of their wedding noted that they left a few days after for "a trip through Southern California by way of Florida." The newlyweds then spent the summer on an automobile tour of Italy, Austria, and Hungary and arrived back in New York City by November. (Honeymoons at the turn of the century clearly were much longer than the ones couples take today.)

My grandfather was one of the country's leading silk manufacturers and importers until his retirement at 80. As a young college graduate, he studied silk manufacturing in France, then the center of the world's silk trade. He resided there for a considerable number of years to study its manufacture.

Grandpa Sam promoted Franco-American trade throughout his business life and later received the National Order of the Legion of Honour (*Ordre national de la Légion d'honneur*), a prestigious award from the French government, for advancing this relationship. The award came with the right to wear in his lapel a small red rosette, which resembled a tiny button of shirred material. He sported the rosette on his lapel with much pride whenever I was with him.

Upon his return from France, my grandfather worked for the Bethlehem Silk Company, which had a factory in Bethlehem, Pennsylvania. He worked in the silk industry along with his brother, Alexander, for 50 years. The business suffered some reversals when other materials like nylon came on the market. I remember dinner table conversations about my grandfather's company losing money, which made me sad and anxious for him.

Although I never exchanged a single word of French with my grandfather, he was obviously bilingual. He would have been pleased that his great-granddaughter Penelope spent her junior year of high school in Rennes, France, soaking up the culture and language. My grandfather and I might have had a good conversation in French had he lived another ten years after his death in 1952. When Don worked for the Kennedy administration from 1961-63, one of my few "perks" as a government wife was being able to attend the Foreign Service Institute (FSI) to intensively study a foreign language, and I chose French. For three months, five days a week, I rose early at our home on Lowell Lane and drove to FSI in Virginia, and spoke or listened to nothing but French for three solid hours. By the end of the course, something must have clicked in my brain. I found myself counting the sheets in my linen closet in French. I would have liked to have demonstrated to my grandfather my competence in the language he loved had he still been alive.

❧

Shortly after my grandmother Elsie's death, my grandfather moved to an apartment in the Ritz Tower Hotel on the corner of 57th Street and Park Avenue, where he lived alone until his death. Sometimes our governess took my sister and me for Sunday lunch with him at either his apartment or a popular restaurant like Longchamps. I had never eaten in a hotel apartment before we went to visit him, and I still remember the waiters bending over Grandpa to offer him tempting food on silvered dishes.

My grandfather was a gourmet and might have appreciated the fact that I became a devotee of Julia Childs. Her marvelous cookbook, *Mastering the Art of French Cooking,* became near biblical in its importance to me. I always said that if I were trapped in the wilderness, I would know how to prepare a delectable meal because of what she had taught me. I believe my grandfather Sam would have been pleased to know I could make "poulet roti" and "boeuf à la Bourguinonne" (prior to becoming a vegetarian).

Grandpa dressed impeccably and often wore spats over his shoes and a cravat with a pearl-topped stickpin. He exhibited his sense of style at the Harmonie Club, a private men's club established in 1852 whose members played bridge and other card games and dined together.

He was a gentle, caring person. He demonstrated our family's interest in the welfare of hospitals, perhaps triggered by the passionate concern for Mount Sinai Hospital of his father-in-law, Isaac Wallach. My grandfather was a trustee of Montefiore Hospital in the Bronx for most of his life and a director of Monmouth Memorial Hospital, in Long Branch, New Jersey, for many years.

My grandfather lived a long life and died in August 1952 at age 84. I don't know why I did not attend his funeral, as I was working nearby at

Time Inc., and I don't understand why my mother wouldn't have considered it essential that I attend. Grandpa Sam is buried in Beth Olom Fields Cemetery in Brooklyn, near the cemeteries of other family members. His wife's ashes were scattered in the ocean waters of New York Harbor, but he spends eternity with other members of his family. I am glad he is not alone.

Author's Thanks

"Don't thank people by name," a foundation director once told me. "You'll surely leave someone out, and that person will be disappointed, maybe even resentful. No one likes to hear a long list of names of people they don't know. Keep your thanks general."

I'm going to bend this rule and thank a handful of people by name, because this book would not exist without them.

Ellen Papazian has served as the memoir's editor and my writing coach for more than a year. I shall always be in her debt for her contributions to content, editing, and sound and gentle but often profound advice on an infinite number of topics. If this book is interesting, it is primarily because of Ellen's knowledge of writing and the workings of the human heart. She was always one step ahead of my thinking and helped me shape my thoughts and feelings into chapters. I might have changed the title to *Go Deeper*, because Ellen made this suggestion many times, and when I did, the outcome was better. She signed her e-mails, "All best," and that is what I shall always wish for her. I always signed mine, "All thanks."

Sue Hrabchak is a world-class, ultra-endurance athlete and the genealogist who led me back to my Jewish ancestors. We went to Salem Fields and other cemeteries in Brooklyn to visit the graves of most of my grandparents and some of my great-grandparents. Sue made our field trips happy experiences and her brother, Tom, created a stained-glass window to replace the one stolen 90 years ago from the Salem Fields mausoleum of my Neuberger grandparents.

I have written my memoir for our children, Dwight, Kate, and Penny Wilson; their spouses, Deborah Davis, David Breault, and Richard Falkenrath; their families, Betty Lou Davis, Patty and Roger Breault, Maggie O'Rourke, and Dick and Dee Falkenrath; and my grandchildren, Eli, Harry, Sam, Olivia, and Reed. I am writing it for the Neuberger/Kridel side of the family, which includes my sister, Joanie, her husband, Mac Woodhouse, and their children, Hope, Amy, and Henry, as well as their spouses, Richard, Tobey, and Meg, and their children. I have also written it for my cousin Linda Kridel Smith and her husband, Vic Ferrell, and her family. She is the daughter of William J. Kridel, my mother's younger brother.

My younger sister, Joanie, whose memories about many events are often sharper than mine, never failed to answer a question or amplify a recollection, and we had a wonderful time reliving memories and exchanging views. When we spoke, our beloved parents always seemed close by. I hope she will forgive me for any mistakes I have made in our family history.

The Aiguier-Havemeyer family has played a pivotal role in my life. Genie Aiguier Havemeyer was my roommate (along with Shirley Oakes and Keren Ellington) for two years at Vassar. We served as bridesmaids in each other's weddings, godmothers to each other's children, and friends for more than 60 years. Genie and Harry's youngest daughter, Catherine D. Havemeyer, of New York City, designed and produced this memoir, and I am grateful to her for her remarkable contribution.

Janet Stern copyedited the memoir with her considerable professional expertise. Emily Tseng and Joan Stevens provided additional editorial assistance. At age 97, Eleanor Ellis, my parents' faithful secretary, clarified many details about Sunnyside Farm. In an attempt to control my overflowing personal files and computer's desktop Rebecca Lustgarten helped me in innumerable ways.

And then there is Google....

My thanks go to each and every member of my memoir team.

"The secret is that in our extended family we are united not by what makes us all obviously different—black, white, American, European—but by the essence of what we all have in common: members of the same human family with a deep awareness of our common responsibility for our fellow human beings .... Together we dare to hope, to love, and to care. And together we are all, along with you, creating a better world for tomorrow."

>Molly Melching
>founder and executive director of Tostan,
>a nongovernmental organization
>in Dakar, Senegal